State and Society in Contemporary Britain

A Critical Introduction

Edited by
Gregor McLennan, David Held
and Stuart Hall

Polity Press

First published 1984 by
Polity Press, Cambridge, in association with Basil Blackwell, Oxford. Reprinted 1985.

Editorial Office
Polity Press, Dales Brewery, Gwydir Street, Cambridge, CB1 2LJ, UK

Basil Blackwell Ltd
108, Cowley Road Oxford, OX4 1JF, UK

Basil Blackwell Inc.
432 Park Avenue South, Suite 1505 New York, NY 10016 USA

British Library Cataloguing in Publication Data

McLennan, Gregor
State and society in contemporary Britain.
1. Great Britain—Social conditions—1945-
I. Title II. Held, David
III. Hall, Stuart
941.085'8 HN385.5

ISBN 0-7456-0008-5
ISBN 0-7456-0009-3 Pbk

Library of Congress Cataloging in Publication Data

State and society in contemporary Britain.

Contents: The representative/interventionist state/
Stuart Hall—State and economy in Second World War/
Laurence Harris—Economic intervention/Grahame Thompson—[etc.]
Includes index.
1. Great Britain—Politics and government—
1945- —Addresses, essays, lectures. 2. Great
Britain—Economic policy—1945- —Addresses, essays,
lectures. 3. Great Britain—Social policy—Addresses,
essays, lectures. I. McLennan, Gregor. II. Held, David.
III. Hall, Stuart.
JN324.S7 1984 361.6'1'0941 84—17684
ISBN 0-7456-0008-5
ISBN 0-7456-0009-3 (pbk.)

Typeset by Pioneer, Perthshire
Printed in Great Britain by T. J. Press Ltd., Padstow

Contents

List of Contributors

Stuart Hall is Professor of Sociology at the Open University, formerly director of the Centre for Contemporary Cultural Studies at the University of Birmingham, course team chairperson of the Open University's *State and Society* (D209), co-author of *Policing the Crisis* (1979) and co-editor of *The Politics of Thatcherism* (1983).

Laurence Harris is Professor of Economics at the Open University. He is author of *Monetary Theory* (1981), *Re-reading Capital* (1979), with Ben Fine and *The City of Capital* (1983) with Jerry Coakley.

Grahame Thompson is senior lecturer in economics at the Open University. He is the author of a book on the Conservative government's economic policy and is a member of the editorial board of *Economy and Society.* His current research interests lie in the monetary and financial aspects of economic calculation.

Christopher Pollitt is senior lecturer in government at the Open University. In 1980–1 he was Visiting Professor at the Georgia State University. His main research interests lie in the fields of health policy and administrative structures.

Paddy Scannell is senior lecturer in the school of communication at the Polytechnic of Central London. He has published widely on broadcasting history and with David Cardiff is preparing a major social history of British broadcasting.

Fred Steward is lecturer in the technological policy unit of the University of Aston in Birmingham. His published work concerns the role of the state in promoting and regulating technology and the role of organized interest groups in this process.

David Wield is lecturer in the technology faculty of the Open University. He has written in the areas of technology policy and in development studies.

Mary McIntosh is senior lecturer in sociology at the University of Essex. She has written extensively on social policy and feminist politics and is the author, with Michele Barrett, of *The Anti-Social Family* (1982).

Gregor McLennan is social sciences tutor at the Open University Edinburgh. He is the author of *Marxism and the Methodologies of History* and co-editor of *On Ideology* (1977), *Making Histories* (1982), *Crime and Society* (1982) and *The Idea of the Modern State* (1984).

David Held is lecturer in social sciences at the Open University. His publications include: *Introduction to Critical Theory: Horkheimer to Habermas* (1980); *Habermas: Critical Debates,* edited with John B. Thompson (1982); and *Classes, Power and Conflict: Classical and Contemporary Debates,* edited with Anthony Giddens (1982).

Acknowledgements

This book is based upon the Open University Social Sciences course *D209, State and Society* first presented in 1984. Material is reproduced by permission of the Open University. The editors, contributors and publisher are also grateful to the following for permission to reprint previously published material in this book:

The American Enterprise Institute for Public Policy Research for table 8.3, originally from Finer, S. E. (1980) *The Changing British Party System.*

The American Political Science Association for figure 10.1, originally from Hibbs, D. (1976) 'Industrial conflict in advanced industrial societies', *American Political Science Review,* Vol. LXX, No. 4.

Basil Blackwell Publisher Limited and John Redwood for table 9.2, originally from Redwood, J. and Hatch, J. (1982) *Controlling Public Industries.*

The Controller of Her Majesty's Stationery Office:
Extract on pp. 59–60, originally from Inman, P. (1957) *Labour in the Munitions Industries.*
Figure 3.7, originally from the *Treasury Economic Progress Report,* May 1976.
Table 4.2, originally from *Hansard*, 15 March 1983.

Croom Helm Ltd:
Table 8.2, originally from Waller, R. (1983) *The Almanac of British Politics.*
Table illustrating chapter 10, note 5, originally from Jessop, B. (1980) 'The transformation of the state in post-war Britain' in Scase, R. (ed.) (1980) *The State in Western Europe.*

The International Labour Organisation for table 10.1, originally from the *Yearbook of Labour Statistics* (1977). © International Labour Organisation, 1977.

Lexington Books for table 4.1, originally from Maxwell, R. J. (1981) *Health and Wealth: An International Study of Health Care Spending,* Lexington, Mass.: Lexington Books, D. C. Heath and Company. © D. C. Heath and Company, 1981.

Richard Pryke, MacGibbon and Kee Ltd. and Granada Publishing for figure 3.6, originally from R. Pryke (1971) *Public Enterprise in Practice.*

The Organization for Economic Co-operation and Development for figure 3.2, originally from OECD *Economic Outlook*, No. 32, December 1982, Paris.

Oxford University Press for figure illustrating chapter 10, note 5, originally from Halsey, A. H. (1981) *Change in British Society.* © A. H. Halsey, 1981.

Sunday Times 9 October 1983, for table 9.1 © Times Newspapers Ltd.

Victor Gollancz Ltd, Will Lawthor and Margot Heinemann for extracts in chapter 2, originally from Heinemann, M. (1944) *Britain's Coal.*

Editors' Introduction

Debates about 'the state' or the 'apparatus of government' are considerably more diverse today than they were 10 or 20 years ago. This is partly to do with the welcome tendency in the work of some 'political scientists' to break away from a narrow focus on the institutional spheres of government and government alone in their search for an account of the state. Similar developments in history, sociology, political economy, among other disciplines, have helped create a new and vast range of empirical and theoretical literature on the nature of the state. It is one of the aims of this book to introduce this literature. The book is written in the belief that the conventional boundaries between disciplines actively hamper the proper study of the state. This is because an understanding of the state must grasp the complex *relations* between polity, economy, social structure and the international world of states.

A second aim of the book is to evaluate critically the ideas and theories that have conventionally informed writings about government and political life in Britain. In so doing we hope to supersede the partial and one-sided accounts often found in single discipline approaches to the state. But the chapters in the book are also 'critical' works in a second sense; that is, they acknowledge that there can be no simple 'value free' accounts of political or social phenomena because we have no access to a descriptive language of political and social phenomena about which we could all readily agree. For facts do not simply 'speak for themselves'; they are, and they have to be, interpreted; and the framework we bring to the process of interpretation determines what we 'see', what we notice and register as important. In charting a way through theoretical debates the authors are aware that their accounts have practical implications for positions taken in political life itself.

A third objective for trying to produce a 'textbook', or at least a critical introduction, is that the state is seldom in itself the subject of one text. There are countless expositions – some good, some not – on the workings of British government, on electoral history, on the 'strange death of liberal England', on the state in relation to the media, or the family, or the economy. But there are very few texts that take account of the way in which the British *state*, as a distinct formation, has been shaped by and in turn has reshaped, the sectors and institutions of the wider civil society.

Thematically, then, the book seeks a degree of coherence that is sometimes lacking in single-discipline and even interdisciplinary studies. The coherence derives not from a monolithic approach but from the unitary focus on the state as such. It comes also from the concern shown in each essay to connect a review of relevant empirical material to central theoretical questions about the state and thus to the main traditions of political theory. The determined way in which the pieces try to integrate empirical and conceptual analysis is, we think, rather rare; as is the degree to which each chapter develops a *historical* treatment of its topic. No one theoretical position unites all the authors, but we do share the belief that a theoretically informed assessment of the state is politically as well as intellectually important. Our focus is on Britain, but we hope to illuminate many of the general issues about the state/society relationship. How are 'the people' 'represented' in and by the state? What are the main mechanisms by which the state 'intervenes' in civil life? How does the state mediate class and gender relations? Can the state restructure an economy? Is the modern state in crisis?

It is by trying to weld together an interdisciplinary approach, theoretical awareness, historical texture, and particular empirical materials, that the study of the state – indeed social science as a whole – can best advance. We certainly make no claims to have achieved this completely. Too many obvious and important aspects of the state's activity (law, education, defence) have been left out for that claim to comprehensiveness to be realized in a book of this type. (We have, though, brought in some previously understressed areas: science and health care, for example.)

Another reason for due caution is that for all our sense of the importance of theory, there is no exact correspondence between the perspectives from which each chapter is conducted. This 'pluralism' is in fact quite useful when the main task – like ours – is to be introductory and informative as well as critical. Nonetheless, crucial issues are raised and tackled in the assembled chapters. By the end, we hope that readers – students, teachers and laypersons – should be able to link together some key empirical events and movements in Britain to some basic theoretical preoccupations about the state generally. If these discussions are then taken further as a result, the book will have served its purpose.

Before introducing the themes of the book it might be helpful if we defined the notion of the state a little more fully. At a very abstract level we can talk about something called 'the state' and juxtapose it with other forms of social and economic power. Thus we can say that the state is a set of agencies claiming supreme authority for the co-ordination and continuity of a population within a particular territory, backed by a virtual monopoly of force. However, this conception of the state should not lead one to the view that the state is simply a unified entity or abstract power: the state forms a set of relations and processes. Moreover it is a conglomeration of agencies, departments, tiers and levels, each with their own rules and resources and often with varying purposes and objectives. Abstract statements about the state are always a shorthand for this 'conglomeration' and must be consistent with an exploration of its dynamics. In order to understand the relations and processes of the state and their place in shaping civil society, we must grasp both the way the state is embedded in a particular socio-economic system (with a distinctive structure and set of institutions) together with its nature as a site of political negotiation and conflict.

Chapter 1 deals with a period in which, arguably, the essential elements of the modern state in Britain became sedimented. More than simply a 'period', the 1880s—1920s was a turning point in the formation of the typical modern relations between the British state and social forces. The chapter attempts to connect this turbulent interaction of politics 'from above' and 'from below' to the ways in which state, economy, and ideology can be conceptualized. In chapter 2, another major formative influence on today's political world is examined: the Second World War. The immense collective effort mobilized in the war resulted in a significant turn to collectivism in the state itself, particularly in its economic dimension. The interesting – and still resonant – issue considered is whether or not these visible changes towards centralization took Britain in the direction of socialism, as some argue. Chapter 3 charts the most important phases of economic policy since the war and discusses three main variants of the state/economy relation: Keynesianism, nationalization and economic corporatism. Though differing in scope and emphasis, these three chapters together provide essential background for the rather more specific concerns of the rest of the collection.

Chapter 4 deals with the institutional consequences of the

emergence of the post-war welfare state. In particular, the National Health Service is examined. As the chapter shows, the facts about health care in Britain reveal not so much an embodiment of a 'collectivist' or, as has been argued, a socialist project, but a tangled web of ideals and pragmatic interest group politics. The simple dichotomy of private and public interests is shown to break down in key respects. Chapter 5 continues the mixture of historical perception and current controversy, as the role of the state in the formation of public opinion and in the regulation of the new means of communication is assessed through an analysis of the organization and symbolic codes of the British Broadcasting Corporation. In the next essay, the fundamental but often neglected part which science plays in a state's economic and political profile is illustrated by a series of detailed examples. This analysis again raises the issue of whether *without* the active sponsorship of the state, a free market economy is capable of resolving the problems it brings into existence.

Chapter 7 addresses the principal form in which the state, ideologically and materially, conditions the social life of women and men in society: the family. This essay frames our approach to family policy by discussing four major conceptions of the family in modern industrial society. Then two concrete issues – responsibility for children and community care – are briefly exemplified in order to highlight some of the dislocations between theory and practice in this controversial area. Chapter 8 returns to a pervasive and general theme of British politics: the relation between electoral democracy and social class. The essay presents some basic facts about British elections in the post-war period but tries to give these a theoretical as well as empirical context. Thus the central relationships between class, democracy and representation are shown to be problematic. The chapter also considers the actual extent of class polarities in this country and focuses on the specific problems of the Labour Party in its uncertain identity as 'the' party of the British working class.

In chapter 9, the economic focus of chapters 2 and 3 is picked up again, this time looking at attempts to reorder the British economy so as to 'roll back the state' as a social presence. Here the important differences between monetarism, supply-side economics and the 'economics of politics' approach are identified. The chapter presents some grounds for thinking that the actual problems of growth and decline in the contemporary economy cannot straightforwardly be connected to ruling intellectual paradigms. Thus, the 'monetarist' recipe cannot be expected to sweep all before it. The book ends with an extended examination of the extent and character of the popular *legitimacy* of the British state. Taking a broad post-war canvas, the adequacy of a variety of theoretical notions – from 'civic culture' to 'legitimation crisis' – are critically assessed. The argument of the chapter is that while the British system enjoys a degree of popular support, it has come to depend more and more in the post-war years on administrative and coercive means to ensure stability.

We hope the book will be sufficiently novel to interest specialists. However, the main aim is to address the many courses which are being developed in the area and to provide a critical and introductory resource. The essays originated in work presented for the popular Open University second level course, *State and Society*. They have been revised and edited (in some cases very extensively) in this book. We would like to express our thanks for the cooperation of the course team (in particular Bram Gieben) and secretaries (especially Michelle Kent).

April 1984

1

The rise of the representative/ interventionist state 1880s—1920s

STUART HALL

Introduction: 1880s—1920s — a formative moment

The period from the 1880s—1920s was a *formative* one for British society. Many of the dominant patterns and relationships which defined the character of British society and the role of the state in the earlier decades of the nineteenth century were eroded or transformed. New social forces emerged on to the political stage, struggling for and to a significant degree winning wider representation in the state. In fact, the whole field of political and industrial representation was reconstructed during these decades; the balance of social forces was significantly redressed. The character of the state did not change overnight; but old *laissez-faire* conceptions began to be challenged, new 'philosophies' of state action took shape, the scale of state activity enlarged and the state did begin to pioneer new modes of action of a more interventionist kind.

A key factor in the relations between state and civil society in this period is the shift in the character of representation. By 'representation', here, I mean very broadly all the ways in which classes or other social forces in society win power in or influence over the state, so as to make it conform more closely to their interests. Formally, the most advanced point in this process was the move towards universal adult suffrage — a process only completed in Britain at the end of this period. By 'intervention', I mean all the ways in which the state intervenes in society so as to lead it in a particular direction, secure particular policies or maintain a particular structure of social relations. This process enlarges the state's scope of action and redefines civil society. The

British state made significant advances in this direction during these four decades.

We have chosen to examine a period in the history of the British state which proved critical on both these scores. Between the Reform Act of 1867 and the Representation of the People Act of 1928, Britain became for the first time a fully-fledged, formal, mass democracy. In the same period, British society abandoned its commitment to *laissez-faire* and relations of a more interventionist kind developed between the state and social forces in society. The term 'interventionist state' is probably best reserved for the 1960s and 1970s, when 'interventionism' became for a time the normal and regular mode of operation for the British state. But it is commonly agreed that the critical move in this direction began in the period between the 1880s and the 1920s. It is therefore appropriate to consider this period as a 'formative' one in relation to both modern democracy *and* the interventionist state.

Since these changes took place in the same period, it is appropriate to ask whether or not the two processes are connected. Is the 'rise of democracy', which culminates in the later decades of the nineteenth century and the early decades of the twentieth century, linked to the 'growth of interventionism' and more 'collectivist' conceptions of the state, which characterize the same period? Does the state, for example, become more interventionist *because* it has now become more representative? And how was this apparent contradiction resolved? What happened to class relations in society when the state became 'democratized'? If the popular-democratic basis of the state was widened, did this legitimate an increase in its interventionist powers?

The chapter aims not only to show how these transitions actually occurred, historically, but also to test out and offer tentative answers to some broader theoretical questions. How, theoretically, do we define or characterize the relationship between 'society' and 'the state'? What sort of theoretical perspective offers us the most satisfactory way of explaining why these relationships between society and the state shifted so significantly, at particular historical moments?

The most common characterization of these transitions is grounded on a liberal-democratic and reformist perspective. It could be summarized as 'the triumph of democracy and reform'. British society, it is argued – not without strong resistance, but yielding ground at the eleventh hour – was able to absorb the challenge of mass democracy and reform itself without precipitating a breakdown or overthrow of the whole system. This shows that there is no fixed, determining relationship between the form of the state and society – or to put it more accurately, between the state and its determining 'base', the economy. After all, British society and economy remained capitalist, in the very period when the state was becoming democratic. Those who owned and controlled capitalist industry continued to accumulate capital, amass wealth and dominate economic life. The economy continues today to be organized and function along capitalist lines. Now, if the economic base really determined the form of the state, then the economically dominant class would rule and dominate society politically, too. It would use its economic power to colonize the state, politically, preventing even the formal democratization of political power. The minority class, which controlled the economy, would prevent political power passing to the majority classes of society. The fact that 'democracy' *did* come is therefore read as a sign that the system *can* be reformed. Economic wealth and power *can* be separated from political power. The economy does *not* entirely determine the nature of the state. Those who lack political or social rights can be 'enfranchised', without toppling the whole class system. Or, as T. H. Marshall, one of the foremost exponents of this reformist, liberal-democratic perspective would say, the capitalist class system can be 'abated' without destroying capitalism as such (Marshall, 1950). The period 1880 to 1920 thus saw the great reconciliation between Capitalism and Democracy.

Now, reformism or liberal-democracy explains developments in this way because of a particular way of theorizing how society is linked with the state. Basically, the perspective rests on a pluralist theory of state-society relationships. Pluralism, in all its variants, does *not* see the class system as dominant. It does not see 'the ruling class' as homogeneous or so unified across all the different domains of social life (economy, politics, culture, etc.) as to prevent reform from having important effects. For pluralists in the liberal-democratic tradition, the economic base does *not* have an absolutely determining effect on politics or on the form of the state (what Marx called the political superstructure). So, one principle of articulation – e.g. capitalist competition and concentration – can, for the pluralist, prevail in one sector of society (e.g. the economy) while another principle – democracy – prevails in the political realm. Further still, the state does not have any singular social or class character. It is largely an administrative entity which regulates the competition between different interest groups, and negotiates compromises which are not in the interest of any one particular class but the best compromise in the interest of every section – the general interest. For pluralists, there are no over-arching class interests which dominate the state, either in the immediate or in the long-term sense.

The main contrast I want to draw is between this reformist-liberal perspective and the Marxist tradition. Economic power, Marxists would argue, remains basically intact during this period, in the hands of the dominant capitalist classes. The needs of capital or the interests of the capitalist class therefore provided the main imperatives for society, which the state had somehow to meet. To introduce 'democracy' – the sovereign will of the people – into this system did not displace those fundamental dispositions of wealth and power. Therefore, democracy must have been a way of incorporating and containing working-class pressures for greater power and participation in political life. Hence, the classical Marxist contention: formal democracy inserts the dominated classes into the power equation in a permanently secondary or subordinate position. It may give 'the people' the illusion of increased political power: but this is more formal than real. Democratic concessions fragment the working class into individual voters, weakening its collective power *vis-à-vis* capital, but constructing the misleading idea that the vote means real power. The 'march of democracy', then, was really the form in which popular consent of the governed was won to the continuing power of the governing classes over them.

There are two broad ways in which this determination of state by the economy is seen to work among marxist writers (cf. Jessop, 1982). The first derives the state, so to speak, from the 'laws of motion' or needs of a capitalist economy (capital-theoretical). Thus, in our period, it might be argued that a more developed, corporate type of capitalist economy needed a more collectivist type of state – and got it! The second explains the form of the state in terms of class relations and the logic of the struggle between social classes (class-theoretical). From this viewpoint, in our period, the collectivist and democratic state can only be explained as a product of class struggle.

In recent times, doubts have grown amongst some marxists about the highly logical, rationalist character of the 'capital' approach to state-society relations, and the instrumentalist character of explanations of the state which treat it as simply a 'tool' of the capitalist class. A problem with both approaches is that they basically reduce the state *to* the economy – whether in the form of capital as such or in the shape of a unified ruling class. The economic base determines shifts in the state; the needs of capital *will* be fulfilled by the state; the state is only an instrument for realizing the interests of the economically dominant class . . .

These approaches, especially in their simpler forms seem over-reductionist.

There is, however, a more subtle, less reductionist way of analysing the relations between society and the state stemming from the writings of the Italian Marxist Antonio Gramsci (1971). Gramsci was sufficiently a marxist to believe that one must give considerable weight to the relationship between the economy and the state, and between the fundamental classes of capitalist society and struggles around the state. But, Gramsci argues, we must not reduce the latter to the former. We must see the state as having the specific role of creating the political and ideological conditions in which the whole society can be conformed to or brought into line with fundamental trends or tendencies in the social formation. The conditions in which this 'reconstruction' can come about are, however, conditional on the effective mastery of the political and ideological, as well as the economic, terrain; also, on the formation of a social bloc, comprising sections of different classes, which forms the necessary underpinning for the state; and on the winning over to this bloc of a significant section of the popular classes. This perspective not only gives the state a more significant and relatively independent role. It also gives much greater weight to the real effects which the coming of democracy has had on the conduct and outcome of political struggles around the British state. If and when conditions of political leadership in the state have been created (for there is, for Gramsci, no determining necessity about it), this represents a moment of what he calls 'hegemony'.

We have contrasted principally a liberal-democratic, reformist and pluralist perspective with a variety of Marxist perspectives (logical, instrumental, 'Gramscian'). Each contains certain key ways of characterizing the period. Each relies on certain theoretical assumptions. Each rests on a particular way of conceiving society-state relationships. I want now to explore these explanations further, not by conducting further theoretical argument, but by turning instead to some of the actual historical processes and events of the period.

Crisis? Which Crisis?

So far, we have been assuming not only that there was a transition in this period from one form of state to another, but also that this occurred as a result of a crisis in the old order which helped to create the conditions for the emergence of a new set of relations between society and state.

The term 'crisis' is itself a bone of contention between analysts and among historians. Some object to its use because it seems to assume there *was* one major historical turning-point and that it *was* bound to be followed by something qualitatively different. Others are fundamentally sceptical about *any* general concept which tries to sum up a set of complex historical trends with the use of a single generalization of this kind. They would restrict its use to massive historical seizures, like the English Civil War, the French or Russian Revolutions. My own view is that the term 'crisis' is quite properly used to refer to a period when a significant rupture, break or breakdown occurs in the processes and institutions which are fundamental to the working of a society. A crisis is a break in the social relations and institutions which bind society together; or which enable it to maintain and reproduce itself on the same basis as before. This is how the term 'crisis' is used here.

Historians of different viewpoints all seem to agree that, by the 1880s, the old system *was* entering such a period of considerable difficulties. They agree that, in the years immediately before and after the First World War, the term 'crisis' was no longer an exaggeration. They all suggest that, by the 1920s, Britain had effected, during the crisis, a transition to a new stage of economic and political development.

Hobsbawm, the Marxist economic historian, observed in *Industry and Empire* that 'This sudden transformation of the leading and most dynamic industrialized economy into the most sluggish and conservative in the short space of thirty or forty years (1860/90–1900) is the crucial question of British economic history' (Hobsbawm, 1969, p. 178). I would say that there are four main threads to the economic dimension of crisis.

(1) A sharp decline in Britain's economic performance: downward pressure on prices, after a long plateau; a fall in profitability; a dramatic fall-off in domestic investment in manufacturing; a steep decline in the staple export industries which had underpinned growth. Britain's average rate of growth fell from 3.6 in the 1860s to 2.1 in the 1870s to 1.6 in the 1880s.

(2) Britain's loss of world leadership in manufacturing and trade. She was rapidly surpassed in this period by her industrializing rivals. By 1913 both Germany and the US outstripped Britain in the production and export of the new chemical based industries, in electro-technics, machine tools, iron and steel.

(3) The slow and sluggish pace at which Britain transferred, in terms of economic organization, to the more modern basis (large-scale production, new technology, etc.) on which her rivals were industrializing. In these countries, industry was increasingly concentrated and centralized into large combines or joint stock firms; mergers and amalgamations were created: out of the many small, family enterprises emerged larger corporate economic units. Production was increasingly organized on the basis of modern 'flow' and assembly-line processes, with an advanced division of labour, a much higher scientific and technical component per head of worker, more standardization and intensified forms of 'scientific management'. Britain moved in this direction slowly, fitfully, unevenly and incompletely.

(4) Capital formation flowed increasingly away from domestic manufacture into foreign investments and the financing of trade. Overseas investment grew from £1,200 million in 1870 (when it overtook domestic investment) to £4,000 million in 1914, with an annual yield of £200 million. One effect of this was to strengthen the 'imperialist' connection, the City and the financial and insurance institutions as against manufacturing: 'making money' in stocks and shares was the ambition of the new 'plutocracy', as opposed to the enterprise to which the earlier, industrial bourgeoisie had devoted itself – making *things*. Britain became the financial hub, rather than the workshop, of the world.

In his seminal study of the period 1910–14, Dangerfield picked out the more *political* dimension of the crisis of society, indicated by the title of his study: *The Strange Death of Liberal England:*

> I realize, of course, that the word 'Liberal' will always have meaning so long as there is one democracy left in the world or any remnant of a middle class: but the true pre-war Liberalism – supported, as it still was in 1910, by Free Trade, a majority in Parliament, the ten commandments and the illusion of Progress – can never return. It was killed or it killed itself, in 1913. And a very good thing, too. (Dangerfield, 1961, p. viii)

Dangerfield identified the 'break' with two related factors: the collapse of the Liberal Party – the political formation which stabilized the political scene right through the period of early industrialization and Britain's ascendancy to world leadership on the basis of free trade. But he also refers to the disintegration of the whole ideological complex of Liberalism. This refers to the current of ideas with which the vast majority of people 'thought' their way through the first three-quarters of the century. Liberalism was the pool from which the dominant conceptions of the historical process were drawn.

Dicey, the apologist of Victorian *laissez-faire* and an eminent professor of jurisprudence, in a book published at the time, *Law and Public Opinion in England,* drew attention to what he regarded as the great shift in ideological conceptions of the state and legislation away from classical liberalism:

> The current of opinion [has] for between thirty and forty years been gradually running with more and more force in the direction of collectivism, with the natural consequence that by 1900 the doctrine of laissez-faire, in spite of the large element of truth which it contains, had more or less lost its hold upon the English people. (Dicey, 1963, p. xxxi)

For Dicey, 'collectivism' was only a polite name for 'socialism'. He identified the end of *laissez-faire*, with the rise of the working class to political power, the loss of leadership by the liberal middle classes and the growing influence of an alien creed — socialism.

Another central aspect of the period is what has been termed 'the crisis of imperialism' (Shannon, 1974). A. F. Thornton, one of imperialism's many historians (Thornton, 1966), has observed that 'It was an idea that moved, an idea that expanded, an idea that had to continue to move and to expand in order to retain its vitality and virtue'. It became the dream of a ruling class; the jewel in the crown of a monarch (Queen Victoria — the 'Great White Queen'); the saving grace of a national party (the basis of Disraeli's bid for a popular conservatism). In the form of 'jingoism', it captured for a time the popular imagination. We normally think of 'imperialism' as referring primarily to Britain's destiny as a colonial and imperial nation abroad. And indeed this was a period which saw the intensification of the rivalry between European nations for the final carve-up of colonial territories and markets sometimes politely referred to as the 'scramble for Africa'. However, 'imperialism' in this period always referred *both* to the international *and* domestic scenes. Its political significance arose precisely from the fact that it spanned both. It tied together the dream of a great imperial world formation, and the promise of a protected trade zone for British products, with the idea of a trade-off of benefits from the empire against 'social reform' of a non-socialist kind for the working classes at home. Paradoxically, in this period the Imperial Idea rose to its zenith, but it is *also* the beginning of the crisis of imperialism.

Finally, there are the more directly *social* repercussions of economic change:

> The years between 1880 and the First World War transformed Britain more swiftly and more profoundly than any other comparable era. British society became more urbanized and sub-urbanized, secularized, democratized; general assumptions about social relationships and politically legitimate behaviour shifted from the basis of vertical and hierarchical community groups to stratified classes; in a word, it became 'modern'. (Shannon, 1974, p. 11)

There is something novel and challenging about Shannon's idea that a social formation can be modernized through crisis. The proposition is that crises can be formative and productive, as well as destructive. Yet while Britain may have become 'modernized' in the process of the crisis of imperialism, it was also structurally weakened in comparison with its international rivals – and for good. Britain entered 'the crisis' as the leading manufacturing nation, and 'workshop of the world'. It emerged from the 'transition' in the 1920s and 1930s (and continued, many argue, into the 1970s and 1980s) as one of the weakest links in the chain of imperialist nations, with an economy 'modern' in form, but sluggish and declining.

We still have to show, however, how these various dimensions of crisis can be related together, and what the actual historical processes were by means of which they helped to transform the state. In the next section we look more in detail at new pressures and social forces arising in society – 'from below' – which challenged the old relations of representation and helped precipitate a major shift in the character of the state.

The challenge of democracy

Between 1880 and 1920, Britain became a 'mass democracy'. The backbone of this process was the successive, contested extensions to the suffrage which took place across the period. This process totally changed the basis of representation on which the state rested. Until this period,

> Victorians did not claim that their system was democratic, a term that smacked of continental abstraction . . . rather, it produced

> effective government, it guaranteed 'liberty' and it was representative. What it represented directly was those considered fit by reason of their independence, their material stake in society, their education and political knowledge to exercise the parliamentary franchise with beneficial effects upon political life. Men wholly absorbed in the daily struggle for existence were unlikely to develop the capacity for political judgement . . . (Pugh, 1982, p. 3)

What changed was not simply that the 'lower orders' and women won the formal franchise – the rise of 'The Democracy'. The entry of these new social forces into the political nation changed the whole dynamics of political life – and thus the state. The mobilization, organization and control of 'popular opinion' became the central factor in mass democratic electoral politics. This fractured the mid-Victorian basis of political relationships in British politics.

The 'challenge of democracy' had its roots in the economic and social dimensions of 'the crisis' we have just broadly sketched. Economic historians no longer speak of the period as having the 'unified character' of a 'Great Depression'. But even those most active in dismantling that 'myth' agree that 'the last quarter of the nineteenth century was a watershed for Britain, as competition developed overseas and the rate of growth markedly slackened' (Saul, 1969, p. 54). Its main characteristics were falling prices and falling profits. Unemployment became once again a persistent feature – especially in the 1880s and 1890s. Real wages improved slowly overall, though after 1900 they were stagnant or declined. Surveys and investigations revealed the depth of urban poverty, especially among the unskilled and casual trades. Gradually and unevenly, new technological processes were brought in, introducing new internal divisions within the labour force. There was a renewed drive to defend profits, in part intensifying the exploitation of labour and the introduction of new labour disciplines.

The social impact of all this on the popular classes was complex. At first, it highlighted and accentuated the gap between the minority of skilled, unionized, better-paid workers – the 'labour aristocrats' – and the unskilled, unorganized and lower-paid majority. Enfranchised by the 1867 Reform Act, the former remained wedded, by and large, to the radical tail of the Liberal Party. The latter were semi-skilled or unskilled, unprotected by trade unions, exposed to the severe fluctuations in Britain's economic fortunes and largely the bearers of casualized labour and urban poverty. Booth and Rowntree, in their studies of London and York estimated that, at the top end, 15 per cent of labour lived in relatively modest comfort whereas, at the other end, 40 per cent lived in abject poverty; two-thirds of them – the residuum – would end up paupers. It was part of this second group which spearheaded the new forms of industrial representation and the accompanying labour unrest of the 1880s; and it was in that soil that the revival of socialism took root.

Later, as mechanization and large-scale production were unevenly introduced, and labour more intensely exploited, the whole basis of the old craft unionism began to be eroded. New sectors began to arise. In the long run, the line between skilled and unskilled was blurred, creating a more homogeneous and class-conscious class. The political alliances developing out of this greater class cohesion spearheaded the drive to independent political representation in the 1900s, precipitated the final separation of the mass of labour from Liberalism, and led to the formation of a new political force – the Labour Party. This process altered radically the ways in which the working classes were politically and industrially represented, reconstructed the whole political face of the nation and altered permanently the balance of political forces.

The revolt of labour

The conditions of urban poverty were studied afresh with the new techniques of investigative journalism and social sciences. They revealed the depths of 'ingrained and obstinate poverty' in which the residuum subsisted. Charles Booth, in *London Life and Labour*, set out to prove that the estimate that 25 per cent of wage earners fell below subsistence level, which Hyndman, the marxist leader of the Social Democratic Federation had made, was a wild over-estimate. Instead, he discovered that Hyndman's estimate was too modest (Shannon, 1974, p. 120). As part of a spate of studies which explored the 'condition of England' question, a series of Royal Commissions investigated social conditions on behalf of the state: the Royal Commissions on the Housing of the Working Classes (1885), on Labour (1891–4), on the Aged Poor (1895), the Inter-Departmental Committee on Physical Deterioration (1904) and the review of the Poor Law (whose famous Minority Report, written by the Webbs, became a founding document of the modern welfare state), were only some of the more relevant ones. Chronic unemployment made all these problems worse.

But even as the lower orders were becoming the object of study, investigation and Liberal conscience, they took matters into their own hands and struck out an independent path. The new unskilled ranks began to form their own, more general, industrial unions: the National Labour Federation in 1886, the Dockers' Union in 1887, the Miners' Federation in 1888, and the Gas Workers' Union in 1889. At the head of this movement was a new, more militant kind of leadership, of which Tom Mann, Will Thorne, Ben Tillett and John Burns were representative. They were opposed to the old guard of the TUC and much influenced by socialist sects such as the Socialist League and Social Democratic Federation, whose arguments began at last to permeate some sections of the industrial working class. The 'new unionism' was soon involved in a wide, class-based agitation for recognition and the eight hour day which the London gas workers won. The match-girls at Bryant and May, urged on by the socialist Annie Besant, also won their strike for better conditions in 1887. The dockers, among whose members the scourge of casual labour ran deep, won a notable victory for the new forms of industrial representation in the historic dock strike of 1889. There was an insurrectionary climate when Trafalgar Square was forcibly cleared by police on 'Bloody Sunday', November 1887. By 1890, the London East End 'was a key centre of socialist co-operation and agitation' (Adelman, 1972). But the new unionism declined somewhat in the 1890s. There was a continuing tussle between 'old' and 'new' unionists, socialist and non-socialist elements, in the TUC. What is more, the frontier between 'old' and 'new' unionism began to blur with the onset of depression after 1891, a sharp counter-attack from the employers' organizations, and a series of negative legal judgements in the courts. Several powerful anti-union employers' associations were formed: anti-socialist organizations like the Liberty and Property Defence League and the Anti-Socialist Union were set up, and non-union, free labour 'unions' were created. Lock-outs (in the coal and cotton industries, following wage cuts, in 1893, in engineering in 1897–8) became the order of the day.

This offensive was followed by an attack, via the state, on trade union immunities and the use of the strike weapon. Union immunities from legal action while in pursuit of a trade dispute, established by legislation in the 1870s, began to be eroded by a series of judgements in court which construed strikes as 'malicious'. The successful suit for damages brought against the railway union by the Taff Vale Railway Company in 1901 confirmed union vulnerability. In fact, this dispute stimulated a rapid growth in union membership, and accelerated the drive for more independent political representation. As part of their bid to retain the leadership of this block, the Liberals eventually rescinded Taff Vale by the Trade Disputes Act of 1906. But in 1908 the employers tried another tack to block the path of labour. A Mr Osborne, with heavy employers' backing, took action against the railway union for the right to withhold that part of the levy from his union subscription going to the fund for political objectives. He was successful – in the now famous 'Osborne judgement'. This legal struggle over trade union rights indicated the depth of the resistance to more democratic forms of industrial representation and to the transfer of legitimate industrial power to the very classes which the reform of the suffrage in 1867 and 1884 had enfranchised.

The unintended consequence of this class struggle was to constitute 'that close alliance in thought and purpose between the Trade Union movement and the Socialist movement,' as Ben Tillett put it, 'which produced in due time the Labour Party' (Tillett, quoted in Adelman, 1972, p. 16). The Independent Labour Party was founded in 1893 and in 1900, the Labour Representation Committee (LRC) was formed, with the ILP the leading political group. The TUC voted to affiliate – a decision which 'revealed a real change in the attitude of the unions to political action' (Pelling, 1965, p. 206). A secret electoral pact was concluded between the Liberals and Ramsey MacDonald for the LRC – the Social Democratic Federation withdrawing in disgust at this evidence of a 'sell-out' to the Liberals. (The ILP finally withdrew in the 1930s.) The LRC thus entered the 1906 election on a substantially Liberal platform (including, for example, the reaffirmation of a commitment to 'free trade'), except for the issues of trade union legislation and a rather vague but firm commitment to greater social reform. Yet 29 LRC candidates were voted in on the tide of the Liberal landslide. And when they resolved to sit separately in the House of Commons, a new independent parliamentary Labour Party had, in effect, been formed.

Labour and Liberal reformism

It is often claimed that it was the threat of industrial unrest, confrontation between labour and employers and the steady development towards labour's political independency – all of them a challenge to Liberal hegemony – which stimulated the reforming social zeal of the Liberal government of 1906, and led to legislation on Workmen's Compensation, the alleviation of 'sweated labour', school meals, the medical inspection of school children, pension and national insurance schemes – a programme often hailed as the 'origins of the modern welfare state'.

Was this, then, the first fruits of a successful, popular, working-class struggle to change the basis and forms of social representation and thus to widen and deepen the democratic basis of the state? Did the massive agitation of the 1880s and 1890s precipitate the radical, reformist and democratic programme of the new Liberal administration and thereby initiate the early moves which ultimately transformed the state in the direction of a *welfare* state? To answer these questions, we have to know something, not only about who was being represented, but also about those who were doing the representing.

At this time, Lloyd George was the leading figure on the radical wing of the Liberal Party – those still committed to free trade, anti-imperialism, a programme of social improvement, and the links between Liberalism and working-class trade unionism. Radical Liberals were outraged by the Boer War, very suspicious of figures who floated through Liberalism in its dying days without being 'Liberals' in spirit (like Joseph Chamberlain), deeply disquieted by the resurgence of 'imperialist jingoism' at home, and what they regarded as its corrupting influence. They wanted to retain the old Liberal connection with working-class reformism, and were impressed by the investigations into poverty and unemployment. J. A. Hobson was one of this group of 'new Liberals', who attempted to develop a more modern, ethical, reformism (cf. Clarke 1978).

The new Liberals knew that due to Britain's economic decline the old recipe of self help and *laissez-faire* was finished. They were genuinely sympathetic to the cause of working-class reform. At the same time, they refused the *class* implications of working-class politics and the radical thrust of working-class socialism. They wanted to subsume reform into something which would benefit the whole of society: to substitute, for a class politics, the vision of a growing social harmony between different interests, within a general programme to advance the Common Good. They believed that state could and should genuinely represent the Common Good by expanding the rights of social citizenship, giving all classes a genuine stake in society; and especially, discharging the ethical responsibility to support and redistribute benefits to those who could not survive under unregulated competition.

The new Liberals thus helped to construct a new political formation through which to represent the new forces. They helped to create an ideological fusion between the old Liberalism and the new Social Democracy. This has turned out to be an extremely important political formation, which – in a number of different actual forms – has sustained reformist political programmes in Britain ever since. It has been an influential force in the Labour

Party; in the revived Liberal Party after the Second World War, and most recently in the SDP-Liberal alliance. In the 1930s it was identified with Keynesian economic policies. More significantly, it is the body of ideas which helped effectively to underpin that great surge of state intervention and social reform which subsequently bore fruit, after 1945, in the welfare state. What exactly to call this new ideological formation greatly preoccupied the new liberals at the time. Hobson defined it as 'Socialism' in 1908; but later renamed it 'the New Liberalism'. Its closest modern equivalent is 'Social Democracy'.

The reform programme of the new Liberals, and the Liberal administration of 1906–11, was however driven by deeply contradictory impulses. 'What was reform, after all,' Dangerfield once asked, 'but the skilful balancing of incompatibles, the ingenious expression of that middle class philosophy which believes in resisting at once the aggressions of the rich and the pretensions of the poor?' (Dangerfield, 1961, p. 226). Among these contradictory impulses were:

(1) the pressure exerted by the rise of a more independent and militant 'labour interest';
(2) the requirements for greater 'national efficiency' and economic regeneration;
(3) the desire to maintain the liberal-labour alliance and, within that, the hegemony of Liberalism over socialism;
(4) the moral imperative to meet the distresses of the poorer classes;
(5) the pressure to supplant older Liberal conceptions of the state with a new philosophy of the state, organized around notions of the Common Good and universal citizenship.

This was a complex set of imperatives: and, as they worked out in practice over the succeeding years of our period, they led to highly contradictory and unexpected conclusions.

Educating Labour

Labour's attitude to all this was itself contradictory. First, many of the new leaders of the Labour Party had been formed in and by the Lib-Lab alliance. So Liberalism's influence remained, even when the commitment to a formal alliance declined. Second, the ambiguous relationship to Liberalism reflected the mixed internal political character of Labour. The Labour Party, after all, even then was a coalition embracing both committed socialists and more practical reformists and trade unionists. Third, the new Labour Party was committed to improved social reform and better social conditions. But it had no detailed social programme worked out. Further, working-class attitudes to a state-orientated or 'collectivist' type of state provision were ambiguous. Some people were – with justification – suspicious of the state, regarding it as fundamentally 'on the other side'. They feared that state-run benefits would simply provide an excuse for the state to interfere in and run or 'police' the lives of ordinary working people (cf. evidence of some labour movement sympathy, for Hillaire Belloc's rather reactionary anti-statist tract, *The Servile State*, 1912).

In general, however, the broad case for increased state intervention to advance reforms was widely accepted within the labour movement, and led intellectually by the Fabians. In parliament, Labour tried to deepen the democratic content of many of the Liberal welfare measures, but after 1908 the initiative was lost. The Liberals made little impact on unemployment or on wages and living standards, which began to decline. Whilst genuinely suspicious of the new health insurance and pensions schemes, trade boards and labour exchanges – the Liberals' collectivist answer to unemployment – Labour found it impossible to resist them outright. In short, the momentum of reform passed decisively to the Liberals, brilliantly led by Lloyd George and Churchill. Even for Beatrice Webb, the 'plain fact' was that they had 'out-trumped the Labour Party' (Adelman, 1972, p. 41).

Against the background of Labour accommodation, a certain disillusionment and revolt set in amongst the newly-formed ranks of Labour itself. In 1911, the British Socialist Party – forerunner of the British Communist Party – split off from Labour. Much more threatening to the state and the forces wielding political power was the onset of the most sustained period of industrial insurgency which the country had seen since the early years of the previous century. A new and different brand of socialism had begun to seize hold of some of the leading elements in the workers' rebellion. *Syndicalism* (Holton, 1975) was rooted in industrial unionism and in the self-activity of the working class. Its emphasis was on direct action, spontaneous mass insurgency, leading to an overthrow of the state in a general strike. It rooted itself directly in the struggle for control in factory or workshop, in the independent shop stewards' movement, and in the politics of 'class war' (Hinton, 1973). Its emphasis on working-class self-activity meant that it fell outside the control and influence of the more reasonable trade union leaders with whom people such as the Webbs and Lloyd

George were anxious to deal. Syndicalism had penetrated into the ranks of the transport, dock, and railway unions, among the engineers of the Clyde and the miners of South Wales, and spearheaded the formation of the Triple Alliance (transport, miners and railway unions) in 1914 on the brink of war. The first outbreak was among the dockers and seamen in 1909, much influenced by Tom Mann and Ben Tillett, who had embraced syndicalism. In 1911, it spread to the railways, with the threat of a general strike. In 1912 there was serious industrial unrest across the country. A general strike seemed imminent. To this was added the spectre of the linking of forces with the newly-established Transport Workers' Union set up by Jim Larkin in Dublin — threatening to bring together industrial unrest and the Irish Question.

In addition, from 1908 onwards, the movement for female suffrage rapidly began to gather pace. Angered by the endless delays, postponements and prevarications of the Liberals and their leader, Asquith, some of the suffragette campaigners transferred their allegiance to Labour (many of whom, with honourable exceptions, were rather embarrassed by it). But the majority, under the leadership of Emmeline and Sylvia Pankhurst and the new Women's Social and Political Union, turned to the fiercest campaign of direct action. They burned churches, destroyed letter boxes, defaced pictures, chained themselves to the railings, refused to be force-fed in prison, and returned after release at once to the fray in an open running battle with the police and the state. The advance of labour had occurred in close tandem with the struggle to extend the franchise; now women, increasingly advanced in society, and adopting a far-reaching independent attitude towards their place in it, were determined to have equal political rights, too — a difficult demand to deny in a state which could hardly claim to be 'universally representative' when half the population remained disenfranchised.

On the eve of the 1914—18 War, then, the country was in ferment: the claims of the unrepresented, of 'the democracy', and the radical forms in which these were advanced, had raised the level of the popular-democratic challenge to an extremely high pitch. How did the state respond? Was it shifted principally by popular democratic pressures from below?

The most important figure in orchestrating the strategic response of the state to this popular agitation was in fact Lloyd George. He conjured up a series of radical-populist causes — land reform, an attack on the House of Lords and the insurance and health schemes. Important too was the work which he and Churchill had done to adapt the machinery of the state to deal with the growing challenge of industrial relations. The Labour Department of the Board of Trade became in this period an extremely important, strategic department, under the able leadership of one of the new breed of civil servants, Llewellyn-Smith. As the 'labour question' developed, so the size, role and functions of the department extended. When the spate of legislation dealing with social reforms and benefits was introduced, the Board of Trade was made responsible for implementing and regulating it. It was through this Department that the plan to introduce Labour Exchanges was implemented. Also significant was the establishment of Conciliation Boards and the appointment of George Askwith as official arbitrator. This process of collaboration and conciliation, sponsored through an expanding department of state, and basing itself in the 'neutral' territory of state administration, developed *alongside* the industrial unrest and syndicalist revolt. By 1913, 325 such Conciliation Boards had been set up (Halèvy, 1926, p. 477). The state was increasingly active in the role of 'negotiator and compromiser', as referee, in search of a 'national settlement'. And this work required an enlarged state machine. Halèvy noted that 'England was becoming bureaucratic' (p. 262). 'We are driven to the paradoxical conclusion,' he added later, 'that during those very years in which revolutionary syndicalism was so vocal, co-operation between the trade unions and the Government became closer than ever before' (p. 479).

A parallel strategy was the search for a national political settlement. This was a strategy to overreach, enclose and contain the challenge by raising politics 'above politics' to a national level. This, too, could only be pursued in and on the terrain of the state. Lloyd George in fact made several separate bids — unknown to his Liberal colleagues — to do a deal with the Conservatives and form a *national*-coalition government (sacrificing his leader, Asquith, into the bargain). He called a constitutional conference along these lines to circumvent the stalemate over the budget. He put out an ambiguous Memorandum to try to get cross-party support on National Insurance: 'joint action' in the cause of 'national reorganization' — a 'national programme' against the 'extreme partisans' of the political party factions; a 'larger settlement' to meet the emergency of the times. 'These are times,' Lloyd George said after the failure of this initiative, 'when the Party system stands seriously in the way of the highest national interests . . .' (Scally, 1975, p. 210; from Lloyd George's *War Memoirs*, vol. 1, p. 23). The assault on the party system had opened in earnest — and from a base *inside* the state.

He made a third attempt at a 'grand coalition' in 1912: this time with the danger looming of a breakaway to the right in the Irish Unionist ranks over Irish Home Rule, and again, on the very edge of war, he proposed another coalition of moderates 'to make a national settlement of some of the great issues of the day'. By that time Unionist Ulstermen and Tory backwoodsmen were drilling in secret; the army at Curragh was refusing to march north to prevent Ulster going independent and senior Conservative MPs were seriously contemplating an Ulster rising against Westminster. The 'Bonapartist' thrust of Lloyd George's trajectory at this time is clearly evident – the search for a national solution of containment. ('Bonapartist', on the model of the appearance of Napoleon Bonaparte, the strong man, at a moment of crisis and stalemate, offering to impose order in the 'national interest'.) His ambitions failed to materialize then. But the war gave him his chance, as we shall see; and in 1916, he ditched Asquith and assumed the leadership of the wartime coalition government. And, when the war was over, he preserved his political base through a new coalition, made his peace with the Conservatives, deserted the Liberal cause, and assumed direction of the process – from a base deep within the national state – by which labour and women were finally allowed to become part of 'the nation'.

Did democracy triumph?

It is time to pause and draw some interim implications of the story we have been telling. We have been looking at a period of crisis and transition from the vantage point of the 'challenge of democracy'. What has concerned us is the way in which the crisis unleashed a whole range of pressures which were brought to bear, *from below*, on the late-Victorian socio-economic and political system. These new social forces and movements engaged in a series of struggles on different fronts, designed to challenge the existing dispositions of power, to advance the claims, expand the power and enlarge the influence exercised by them over the character of the state and the direction of state action and policy.

Some of these new social forces are best characterized in class terms – the different sectors of the industrial working classes: though, as we saw, these did not have a wholly homogeneous class character. Some of the new forces had no clear-cut class character and are better defined as 'social movements': the suffragettes were perhaps the best example of the latter. We have considered them all part of the democratic forces because their ultimate effect was to expand the power and influence of the popular classes and other unrepresented social strata. The aim of their struggles was to deepen the democratic content of political and social life generally and to make the state – formally, at least – more widely representative.

We say 'struggle*s*' rather than 'struggle' because they assumed a variety of actual forms and arose from a number of different currents, rather than from a single source or social contradiction. They included the formal extension of the franchise (male and female); also, new forms of industrial and political representation; the mobilization of a variety of campaigns and other forms of popular protest or agitation; the generation of new political organizations; the germination of new political ideologies. These all implied the widening of democratic forms of representation.

This advance of 'The Democracy' met with some success. It helped to transform the character of the mid-nineteenth century state. It forced the state on to a new basis – universal adult suffrage. It helped to establish a new kind of 'citizenship'. It was one of the factors leading the state to assume a new responsibility for representing the social interests of *all* – not just those of the already-enfranchised political classes. In short, it transformed Britain into a mass democracy. It obliged the state greatly to expand its machinery to take on its new responsibilities (for example, state welfare benefits) and to meet new challenges. It stirred the state, in general, into a more interventionist role. And the more the state attempted to derive its legitimacy from the *whole* of society, the more the state itself became the base from which alone *national* strategies, compromises and settlements could be devised and implemented.

Did 'the challenge of democracy', then, wholly democratize the state? Not in the far-reaching ways this suggests – though Britain after this period *is* clearly more of a democracy than it was before. The powerful classes were obliged to take more notice of the demands raised by the new social forces. Indeed, for a time, the former were transfixed by the popular challenge – they could think of no problem which did not ultimately turn on the question of how to respond to, deal with or contain the 'challenge of democracy'. From this point onwards – in formal, but also in other terms – the masses simply could not be ignored. They had to be organized *into* the political strategies, calculated about, mobilized. They became *the* factor without which mass democratic politics could not operate.

As to explanations: did the economy dictate or determine the ultimate form which the state, in response, was forced to assume? My answer to that is to say *yes* – *if* we mean that the economic dimensions of the crisis set trends in motion, made active certain forces, with consequences in the popular mobilizations and shifts in state policy which occurred. But from the account I have offered it does not seem possible to 'read off' the character of the political and industrial struggles or predict the ultimate form of the state simply from an analysis of economic tendencies. 'Economy' and 'state' do not seem to be related in this direct, unmediated way. It is more appropriate to see the crisis as a crisis of the social formation *as a whole*. Those forces which can be traced to economic factors determine the character of society and the state only *in, through* and *by way of* the variety of political movements, social and ideological formations which emerge in the conjuncture. The political and ideological frameworks and forces positively mediate the connections between economy and state.

The rise of the interventionist state

We turn now to view the impact of the crisis, and subsequent transformations in the state, from the vantage point of the dominant classes. Did new social forces, new political movements and new ideological formations arise here, *too*? What role did struggles *within* the dominant sector play in the slow and uneven shift of the state towards interventionism? Did different sections within the power bloc enter into struggle over the form of the state, in addition to the struggle to defeat or incorporate the popular-democratic forces?

Much of this part of the discussion will be focused around the concept of collectivism. One popular way of describing the transition through which the advanced capitalist state is said to have passed in this period is 'the transition to collectivism'. Dicey saw this, retrospectively, as an unstoppable drift. In fact, a number of different 'collectivisms' were constructed by different political forces and discourses in the period. The collectivisms were the principal political-ideological programme through which a variety of social forces attempted to transform the state.

Crudely, collectivism signifies the opposite of 'individualism'. Collectivists no longer believe, as supporters of *laissez-faire* did, that things work best when individuals are free to maximize their self-interests, and the state intervenes as little as possible. Collectivism assumes that society consists, not of 'bare individuals' but of corporate classes, groups and interests. The state should therefore plan and act on behalf of society conceived as an organic whole – a 'collectivity'. The rise of collectivism was therefore connected with the incorporation of all adults into the political nation and entailed a novel conception of citizenship.

The break-up of the Liberal bloc

The political impact of the crisis on the ruling bloc was immense, even though this was not felt all at once. First, it precipitated the fragmentation and break-up of Liberalism. With its economic and political individualism, its non-conformist and sober moral tone, its commitment to slow, evolutionary reform and adjustment, its steadfast sense that the 'classes' must lead, but must be mindful of their duties to the enlightenment of the unenfranchised 'masses', its fervent belief in order, liberty and conscience, retrenchment and reform, Liberalism had been a powerful integrating ideological force for most of the century. Liberalism claimed to represent at least three distinct social elements. It claimed the allegiance of the Whig gentry and great landowners – those who had identified with the 'Glorious Revolution' and the Protestant ascendancy, established their independence of the aristocracy in the early stages of agrarian capitalism, then used their landed wealth and property as the basis of an entry into the capitalist business of rents and profitable farming, supplying the new markets, through trade and commerce. They formed a great family oligarchy with its basis in landed property: the landed interest, excluding the old Tory aristocratic connections. Gradually, this Whig element came to ally itself with and to represent, within the state, the second element: the new manufacturing bourgeoisie, the industrial and commercial classes, who made the economic and industrial revolutions of the eighteenth and nineteenth centuries, and were beginning to lay their final claim to political power and social influence. Third, beneath the shadow of the radical wing of Liberalism could still be found clustered the unenfranchised working classes, especially the skilled craftsmen of the Victorian trade unions.

This political bloc slowly began to fall apart, disturbing the delicate political equilibrium of the state. The doctrines of individualism, enlightened reform and political economy, associated with the *laissez-faire* conception of the state, were criticized first by Liberal philosophers and political theorists, such as T. H. Green and Ritchie (Richter, 1964), then by the new Liberal intellectuals such as Hobson, Hobhouse, Wallas and the Hammonds.

Another symbol of the break-up of the Liberal bloc was the dominating figure of Joseph Chamberlain. Chamberlain's career began, among the manufacturing classes of industrial Birmingham, with an attempt to resuscitate grassroots Liberalism. He campaigned for universal, compulsory and free education, led the non-conformist and dissenting Liberal families via the new 'civic gospel' into an active 'caucus' in Liberal city politics and set up the National Liberal Federation. And yet Chamberlain's career marked, not the revitalization of Liberalism but its cross-over into other things. In Birmingham, he initiated a far-reaching programme of municipal reform of a distinctively 'socialistic' or 'statist' character: public buildings, street planning, slum clearance, the new university, gas and water supply taken into municipal ownership, the establishment of parks, libraries and swimming baths and more. It was commonly known as 'gas and water socialism' but it could also be thought of as the creation of the 'local state'. In fact Chamberlain was also a very authoritarian figure, adept at populist agitation but free of any impulse to submit to democratic direction. He was a state reformer 'from above'. In spirit, he was not a liberal. His career is only understandable as the product of the transition out of an old political formation. He later led many radicals out of the Liberal Party on the Unionist issue (i.e. for maintaining the unity of nation and empire and therefore opposing Irish Home Rule), formed an alliance with the Conservatives and ended his life as the leading imperialist figure, the main architect and inspiration for tariff reform and the protectionist doctrine in trade.

In some ways, the most dramatic break-up of the Liberal alliance occurred with the emergence of the skilled trade unions and the 'labour aristocrats' of the late Victorian period from under the shadow of the Liberal Party, and the slow advance which the working class in general made towards political independence.

This fracturing of the political balance set in motion all manner of new forces, strange doctrines, bizarre cross-alliances. It also reshaped the power bloc. Though never the dominant political class, the great dynamic force within the Liberal bloc was, of course, the industrial and commercial bourgeoisie. They did not yet govern but they managed increasingly to *rule* (i.e. to dictate the direction of legislation) through their alliance with the Whig landed cousinhood. When the decline in Britain's staple export industries set in, and its leadership in world trade began to fall behind that of its rivals, what happened was *not* a collapse of the ruling class so much as a recomposition of the ruling power bloc; a new fraction emerged in a leading position within the bloc.

This concept of a power bloc is an important one for our analysis. It means the fractions of different classes, organized into a bloc and providing the social underpinning of the state. Its use allows us to replace the highly simplified concept of a more or less homogeneous or unified ruling class with the alternative, and historically much more accurate concept, of a ruling bloc or alliance of social forces, organized around the state and composed of different fractions. Political changes often appear first through the opening up of internal differences *within* the power bloc; by a change in the balance between the different elements within the alliance of forces; or through a shift from one section to another in terms of its leading element.

What seems to have happened in the 1880s and 1890s is that, as prices fell with cheap imports from new sources of supply, and rents reduced, the great landowners began to look for non-agricultural sources of income. They turned, increasingly, to revenue from urban property, mineral rights, fees from company directorships. As profits fell after the commercial crisis of 1873, a similar process occurred within the industrial bourgeoisie. They, too, turned to investment in urban property, government issues, stocks and shares, overseas investment, the finance and insuring of trade and revenue from 'invisible exports' (i.e. on the movement of trade, rather than on producing things to trade). The big landowners and the big bourgeoisie entered a process of coalescence, forming what, in the period, came to be known as the 'new plutocracy'. This was the super-rich: drawn together by increasing ties of marriage and family, common interest and life-styles; and separated from the struggling smaller and middle sectors of each group. The gap between the well-off and the poor became more exaggerated.

One of the main consequences of this internal recomposition was a change in the whole balance of the power bloc. The influence of the manufacturing classes began to decline, and with it the entrepreneurial drive which had sustained Britain's earlier growth. The financial, imperialist and investment sectors, always strong, now became the leading ones. This was increasingly a financial and *rentier* bourgeoisie, rather than a manufacturing one: a new plutocratic business class.

National efficiency

In addition to the recomposition of the power bloc, the crisis also manifested itself in terms of generating new doctrines and movements within the leading echelons of society, struggling to formulate new historic tasks for the state. One of the triggers, which set this process in operation, was the impact of the Boer

War. Britain's involvement in a war against the Boer settlers in South Africa arose as a result of the growth of imperialism as a strategy designed to restore Britain's prosperity at home and commercial fortunes abroad. The Boer War reflected the growing importance within the power bloc of the 'imperialist connections' (those whose economic and trading interests were tied up with foreign investment, colonial expansion and British dominance in world markets and mineral raw materials). British interests in Southern Africa had gradually been moving towards the policy of a grand unification of its vast lands and mineral resources under British rule. A leading capitalist adventurer in the new mining enterprises and convinced imperialist, Cecil Rhodes, ensnared Britain in a plot to oust the Boer settlers and unite Southern Africa under British sovereignty – with Chamberlain's tactical knowledge if not encouragement. The conduct of the war does not concern us here, but its consequences do. First, it exposed the dangers implicit in the new policy of imperialism as the solution to Britain's problems. Second, it shocked traditional Liberals, many of whom had long subscribed to the theory that the maintenance of free trade was incompatible with an imperial destiny. Third, it led to military disasters. The Boers proved an extremely tenacious enemy. The British army suffered several serious reversals; it resorted to questionable military tactics which brought its high-minded generals into public disrepute. The main result, however, was to precipitate the most searching re-examination of the consequences of the crisis at home, and the plight into which declining economic fortunes had pushed Britain.

It is out of this ferment that the cause of 'national efficiency' arose. The verdict on the war was that the whole system was radically inefficient, and that Britain's fortunes could only be restored, and her imperial interests safeguarded, by the most far-reaching programme of national reconstruction – spearheaded by a more active state. This was the logic by means of which substantial sectors of the ruling bloc were detached from *laissez-faire* and harnessed to collectivism. It became increasingly clear that the 'free market' and the 'minimal state', left to their own, could *not* achieve the national dynamic and far-reaching reforms required. The immense programme of social reconstruction required the impetus of a collectivist state, acting as a political powerhouse, to drive the whole programme forward. However, the state had to be *converted* to this new historical programme. 'National efficiency' as a doctrine thus implied at every turn the transformation of the state into an instrument of social intervention on a very broad front.

G. R. Searle (1971) has observed that '"National Efficiency" was not a homogeneous political ideology. It served as a convenient label under which a complex set of beliefs, assumptions and demands could be grouped.' A variety of different political forces, alliances and organizations sought, through struggle, to realize a roughly similar programme. One prominent current subscribed to the belief that the low level of efficiency of the army reflected the threatened degeneration of the 'race'. The British were a chosen race, destined for historic achievement; therefore, positive ways must be taken to 'improve the race', if necessary by controlling the rights of the more 'degenerate' sections of the population to breed, and engineering a stimulus to the birth rate, especially amongst the well-off sections of society. National efficiency thus provided a powerful stimulus to the 'social Darwinism' of people such as Benjamin Kidd and Karl Pearson, who advocated theories of the 'degeneration of certain national types' (for example the Jews and the Irish), and advanced threats of the 'race suicide' which would follow continued breeding by the 'less abler' classes. They favoured biological engineering, to plan and control the rate of reproduction of the 'abler' classes – an emphasis which led to the Eugenics movement.

Paradoxically, Professor Pearson continued to call himself a 'socialist'; and Sidney Webb, the founder of the Fabian Society, advanced *his* schemes for the 'endowment of motherhood' as one solution to Pearson's problem. So collectivism belonged simultaneously to both left and right. Webb (1907) argued that 'once the production of healthy, moral and intelligent citizens is revered as a social service and made the subject of deliberate praise and encouragement on the part of the government, it will . . . attract the best and most patriotic of citizens'. (For an account of these movements, see Semmel, 1960.) We should particularly note the significance of the Eugenics movement – because it bore down in its consequences and programme directly on mothers and influenced debate on the contentious issues of birth control. It thus had a formative impact within feminist circles.

The social imperialisms

In practice, national efficiency and social imperialism were difficult to differentiate. Both movements contained the same ideological elements, but inflected in a different way. In the former, the task of raising national efficiency and making the society and state more efficient took pride of place over, though it did not replace, the imperialist theme. In social imperialist circles, imperialism was seen as the means by which efficiency could be achieved as well as the end towards which efficiency should be directed. In their different ways, these were attempts, ideologically, to define what the causes of the crisis were and how to remedy them. They were also programmes for the reform of society around which new political alliances began to form, and about which the political struggle for the state was increasingly conducted.

The term 'social imperialism' was first applied to Bismarck's Germany, where a policy, under heavy state sponsorship, had been inaugurated to introduce social reforms designed to 'ditch the socialists' and win the working classes 'for the national interest', together with tariff protection for agriculture and industry and an expansionist foreign policy (Semmel, 1960, p. 23). Chamberlain and the Tariff Reform League represented the dominant form of British social imperialism in the period. They looked out over a 'Greater Britain', with 11 self-governing colonies, covering 11 million square miles, a white population of 11 million, apart from its native populations, and vast territorial, mineral and market potential – and saw the answer to Britain's crisis. Undoubtedly, powerful ideas of 'mission', imperial destiny and national glory infused their minds. But whereas Britain's commercial command of world markets in the earlier phase of industrialization had been accomplished with the protection of the navy, but primarily under the drive of free market forces and *laissez-faire* principles, the new imperium would have to be positively organized. It would have to develop the policies of imperial preferences within, and protective tariffs around, the expanded trading area. It would need a new system of imperial alliances. None of this could happen without the state becoming, in effect, an imperialist/collectivist state.

However, the political and social aspects must not be forgotten. Chamberlain's municipal reforms had been designed to win the working classes away from radical schemes by reform 'from above'. This strategy was now transferred to the national scene. The fruits of imperialism, Chamberlain argued, would finance the needed social reforms at home: workmen's compensation, old age and health insurance schemes, etc. In this way, imperialism would 'buy off' domestic social discontent: a trade-off which came to be known as Chamberlain's 'squalid argument'. But he had correctly observed the national arousal which the Boer War had stimulated amongst the populace at home. Popular feeling and sentiment could – he believed – be mobilized by the 'jingoism' which accompanied imperialist adventure and perhaps diverted from class resentment into nationalist channels. 'Social imperialism was designed to draw all classes together in defence of the nation and empire and aimed to prove to the least well-to-do classes that its interests were inseparable from those of the nation' (Semmel, 1960, p. 24).

Imperialism was thus in part a substitution for the dangerous alternative of socialism. The imperialist strategy was to win over and insert the popular classes into a new kind of political bloc. In a subordinate position, to be sure, as they had been within Gladstonian Liberalism: but positively incorporated into the nation by a new mechanism – reform. 'The democracy,' Chamberlain observed, 'wants two things: imperialism and social reforms.' By giving it both the social imperialists pioneered a new basis for national consensus and integration around the state. Their project was to contain and absorb independent popular movements within the disciplines of a greater national project: to construct in effect, a national-populist politics under mass democratic conditions. That is why Scally calls social imperialism 'a socialism of the Right' (Scally, 1975).

There rapidly developed a struggle for ascendancy within the power bloc. The first phase can be identified with Chamberlain's entry, as a powerful, populist, ex-Liberal-Radical figure, into the Conservative Party, and the effort, from his base within the state (the Colonial Office), to win the Conservative Party from within. Then he made his bid for popular support, appealing over the head of the party to the populace outside the power bloc, on a well-defined programme linking imperial preference with social reform (at a famous speech in Birmingham), countering the charge that tariffs would mean dearer bread for the working classes because of high duties on imports of corn. Balfour, the Conservative leader, wished politically to hold together the alliance within his party of pro-protectionist and anti-protectionist elements. In 1902, Salisbury, the Prime Minister, resigned; the King sent for Balfour, not Chamberlain; and in 1903 Chamberlain resigned. This was the signal, not for Chamberlain's retirement but for a shift to a different type of political struggle: a populist extra-parliamentary agitation. The main instrument of this tariff reform campaign, initiated through a whistle-stop tour by Chamberlain, was the founding of an agitational organization, the Tariff Reform League. The League then launched a popular mobilization, seeking this time to make an assault on the state from outside, uniting a sector of the leading classes with the masses in a populist upheaval against *both* the established parties of the state. These are the classic steps in one type of political struggle 'from above'.

After Chamberlain's untimely stroke, the League's leadership passed to even tougher campaigners: Garvin, his great disciple and editor of *The Observer*, and Viscount Milner, a powerful, if distant, figure of authority in the social imperialist camp, with an active group of supporters whom he had trained in the service of empire ('Milner's Kindergarten'). Milner regarded himself as a collectivist and openly subscribed to what he called 'a nobler socialism', by which he meant avoiding class antagonism, and integrating the working man into an organic, patriotic imperialism. This attempt to capture the representation of the working classes and to represent them in ways strikingly opposed to that of the socialist sects and the new Independent Labour Party, was a running theme in tariff reform propaganda.

The tariff reform agitation did not succeed in its own terms. It led to the Conservative-Unionist defeat and the landslide to the Liberals in 1905. The initiative in defining the crisis and promoting a strategy of reconstruction passed to the opposing side. Then came the First World War. By the time the Tariff League strategy was adopted, its political impact had been dissipated. And yet, in other respects, its mission was accomplished. It helped to destroy the doctrines of free trade and *laissez-faire.* It fractured the old alliances and forged new ones. It popularized the notion that the old parties and party politics were dead, played out. Viscount Ridley, a League supporter, said that there were really only 'two parties in the state which knew their own mind'. Not the Liberals and the Tories but the 'Tariff Reform Party and the Independent Labour Party'! Indeed, powerful cross-party impulses became characteristic of the period, challenging the parties which had previously ensured the smooth passage of power and legitimacy within the state. Even more powerful was the influence of those advocating the transcendance of the political party system itself, and the establishment of a leadership grounded directly in the state.

Fabian collectivism and the 'Limps'

Social imperialism of the Chamberlain-Tariff Reform variety was by no means the only form in which imperialism and collectivism were linked together. There was also a powerful group of social imperialists within the Liberal Party. They were committed to imperialism, national efficiency and the collectivist state; but distinguished from the tariff reformers by their support for free trade and opposition to protectionism. They were 'Liberal imperialists' — or the 'Limps'. They found a political figurehead through whom to advance their cause in the former Liberal Prime Minister, Lord Rosebery who, in his famous 'Chesterfield Speech' in 1901, announced his candidacy. 'Briefly,' commended the *Daily Mail*, 'Lord Rosebery threw over both the Liberal and Tory Parties and offered himself to a new party whose watchword will be Efficiency . . .'

Rosebery despised the parties and was impatient with representative democracy. He wanted to bypass *both*. This ambition he shared with Chamberlain, the Webbs, Milner and, as we shall see, secretly, with Lloyd George. There was an ominously 'Prussian' or 'Bonapartist' ring to Rosebery's proclamations, and indeed the scene was suddenly full of 'little Caesars' who know better than the fickle mob. At the right moment they would resolve the stalemate and end the crisis by – reluctantly – agreeing to take the emperor's crown in order to save the nation.

Rosebery's supporters included Milner and Haldane, one of the most indefatigable 'go-betweens' and 'inside fixers' in British politics. Outside the Liberal ranks, his most formidable support came from the Fabian Society, led by Sidney and Beatrice Webb. Initially, the Fabian Society aimed to bring together a group of experts and intellectuals in support of a non-marxist evolutionary socialism. But the Fabians were always suspicious of the more popular democratic aims of the labour movement, and after the imperialism issue split its ranks, the Society increasingly turned towards the implementation of a collectivist programme, not through mass politics but by *influencing* one or other of the potential popular political leaders, capturing one or other wing of the established parties or generally spreading their ideas and plans through the process they called 'permeation'. Sidney and Beatrice Webb formed one of the most formidable political partnerships in British politics and stamped their mark on the science of government administration, the subsequent character of the British welfare state and the 'Labourist' philosophy of the Labour Party and the British labour movement. Haldane saw it as his express mission to bring these two forces – the Liberal imperialists within the Liberal Party, and the Fabian collectivists – together; though the marriage eventually collapsed.

Haldane and the Webbs had first made contact on the key collectivist issue of education reform. In this area, the most significant pieces of legislation were the 1870 Act which made elementary schooling a state responsibility; and the 1902 Act, the work of Balfour, very substantially under the inspired guidance and skilful political manoeuvering of another of the collectivist civil servants – Robert Morant, of the Education Department.

Morant, however, in turn was powerfully influenced by Sidney Webb through his key position in the London County Council. The character of the 1902 Act, accordingly, bore the visible imprint and signature of national efficiency and collectivist thinking. Compulsory education was seen essentially as part of the drive for national efficiency. The state must set educational standards for the whole society. 'Bad education was like bad health, bad housing, unemployment, bad hygiene' (Shannon, 1974, p. 304). State education must weld the nation together in a common regenerative purpose.

When Rosebery announced his conversion to the cause of national efficiency, Sidney Webb hastened to welcome him ('Lord Rosebery's Escape from Houndsditch', 1901). In a series of Fabian tracts Webb worked out a full collectivist programme: reform of slum housing, the poor law, sanitation and the sweated trades; efficiency and 'virility' in government; a 'national minimum' standard of life, to be set and maintained by the state, to help gird industry for trade competition; education reform, since 'It is in the classrooms . . . that the future battles of the Empire for commercial prosperity are being already lost.' Steps, in short, 'to insure the rearing of an Imperial race' (quoted in Semmel, 1960, p. 73). This brings out well the conflicting strains of bureaucratic coercion and impatient reformism in Fabianism, in the Webbs themselves and in collectivism as a whole in this period.

The Webbs applied a scientific, social Darwinist, attitude to social problems. Though themselves socialists, they regarded problems as administrative rather than political questions. They approached them in a spirit of rational diagnosis. The facts spoke for themselves: all one had to do was produce a mountain of them, and people with commonsense would see the remedy at once. Rational political figures would give their political support, whatever the cast of their politics; and, having created the political environment for a programme of national efficiency, would then sensibly stand aside and let 'the experts' design ways of reconstructing British social institutions. They hurled themselves into a series of campaigns throughout their life in the firm conviction that these would attract support from trade unionists, civil servants, and enlightened capitalists alike, and that 'all rational people would eventually come round to their view' (Harris, 1982). They exhibited a commitment to socialism, a deeply statist and anti-democratic instinct, and a passionate faith in administrative functionalism and professionalism. The collectivism of the Webbs was 'socialistic' *and* statist at one and the same time.

The Webbs were thus unashamedly elitist, despite their close connections with the labour movement and trade union leaders. Sidney Webb regarded collectivism as 'the economic obverse of democracy' (Hay, 1978, p. 25). The elitism of intelligence and expertise must, they thought, be preserved. Their vision was the replacement of unregulated individualism and *laissez-faire* by organic collectivism; and the substitution of politics by administration. They identified themselves with and helped to define the emergent 'philosophy' or ideology more perfectly adapted to the operations of the collectivist state which was beginning to emerge. For the state which aimed to administer 'rationally' and 'efficiently', rather than serve privilege and interest, *had* to evolve a working philosophy (for civil service and welfare bureaucracy alike) which centred on the surpassing of politics and the emergence of the neutral, disinterested state. In the new Liberalism and social imperialism, national efficiency and Fabianism we see the many different forms in which key sections of the power bloc were converted to the contradictory cause of collectivism, and led to a series of intense struggles against *laissez-faire* and the whole conception of liberal policies and the liberal state.

Lloyd George and the exceptional circumstances of war

The state was not, however, immediately converted to 'interventionism' in its policies and practices. For example, with respect to the modernization and restructuring of the British economy – the issue at the centre of the crisis, as Hobsbawm, Pollard and others have shown – it was not until the 1930s that Britain 'turned from one of the least into one of the most trustified or controlled economies, largely through direct government action' (Hobsbawm, 1969, p. 242; also Pollard, 1969).

The one significant area where the state did have a direct impact on the economy before the First World War was in those sectors connected with armaments (by 1913, 35 per cent of the national budget), where state contracting created the momentum 'for a staggering series of corporate organizations to grow . . . in a breath-taking succession of mergers, take-over bids and informal trade and cartel agreements' (Schwarz, 1985, p. 7).

And yet, when the war did finally arrive, state/economy relations *were* dramatically transformed.

> By 1919, the government had taken over the running of several industries, controlled others by requisition or licensing, organized its own bulk purchases abroad, restricted capital expenditure and foreign trade, fixed prices and controlled the distribution of consumer goods. Fiscal policy was used – clumsily – to shift more resources to the war effort than the people were willing to forego. (Hobsbawm, 1969, p. 240)

At first, the assumption was that it would be preferable 'to rely on private enterprise and the laws of supply and demand . . . for the successful prosecution of the War' (Lloyd, 1924, p. 261).

It was only as these highly traditional mechanisms failed to deliver the goods that the country was driven down the road to a massively augmented state intervention in the economy. Lloyd George had emerged as the strong man of the war effort with his assumption to the newly formed Ministry of Munitions in 1915, and his leadership of the coalition in 1916. Under these auspicies, the state assumed direct control over production in several areas, extended state control progressively over the railways, collieries, flour milling and, by the end of the war, shipping. It commanded the supply of war equipment and munitions by direct production, and an extensive system of contracting.

Even more dramatic was the extent and depth of control over labour through the state-sponsored manpower policy. Early in 1915, a succession of orders making strikes on government work illegal and proscribing restrictive practices were incorporated into the Treasury Agreements, signed with the consent of the leading trade unionists involved. This was followed by the Munitions of War Acts, which set up committees to settle wage questions, but which in return secured union agreement to permit 'dilution' of labour (the substitution of unskilled men and especially women for skilled jobs for the duration only) and to renounce the right of workers in 'controlled' munitions firms to leave employment without permission, to strike or to refuse to go to industrial arbitration. The Treasury Agreements and Munitions of War Acts, described by Lloyd George as 'a great charter of labour', represented in fact 'the most far-reaching control of the labour market by the state, short of outright "industrial conscription"' (Burgess, 1980, p. 162).

In the exceptional circumstances of war, the state apparatus itself was extensively reshaped. A number of powerful new ministries were established (Llewelyn-Smith, from the Board of Trade, went to Munitions, the new powerhouse of state intervention). Businessmen were drawn directly into the work of the state machinery. Civil servants and other intellectuals (like Beveridge, drafter of the Munitions Bill and later the 'architect' of the post-1945 welfare state) who identified with the new collectivist spirit, seized the opportunity of the war to articulate it more fully and to realize it in state practices. They had become identified with an organic current of thinking in the power bloc. They were – to use Gramsci's suggestive term – the new 'organic state intellectuals' of collectivism.

The new regime only went so far. Requisitioning was accompanied by compensation or a 'fair price'; the original boards of management were retained; patterns of ownership and managerial control were not replaced. Fixed prices cushioned often uncompetitive industries. High freight rates yielded record profits, large capital gains – and the well-substantiated charge of 'war profiteering'. State intervention guaranteed dividends to the coal owners. And, as soon as the war ended, the interventionist 'advances' were almost entirely abandoned. 'Dismantled with unseemly haste' is how Hobsbawm puts it. Many were shocked by 'the vast expansion of Government control . . . without parallel in the history of the world' (Pigou, 1918, p. 53).

'Back to 1914' became a common cry, according to Tawney (1943). 'Industrialists, despite the considerable protection from the cold winds of competition which the war economy had afforded them, were impelled by the false promise of new opportunities for British industry to wind controls up as rapidly as possible and get back to "the good old days"' [sic]. 'By the middle of 1922,' Pollard observes, 'virtually the whole machinery of government control was disbanded.'

Interventionism, therefore, did not sweep the board. Indeed, in Britain, it has had an extremely uneven (and unfinished?) history. There was therefore no automatic and permanent conversion of the state to collectivism, following a fundamental shift in the underlying economic organization of society. Yet the war proved to be a formative period. During its short-term and exceptional circumstances, interventionism was pioneered, for the first time, as a real and exemplary set of national practices for the state. The post-war return to 'business as usual' was swift; but the war period planted ineradicable traces of an alternative to the *laissez-faire* state. It laid the basis of the state machinery through which the welfare state was implemented after 1945, and set many precedents for the fuller operation of 'the interventionist state', from the Second World War to the 1960s and 1970s.

In addition, though the post-war state returned to a more restricted brief in relation to the economy, its conciliatory industrial role continued to be developed through the inter-war period (cf. Middlemas, 1979), and it never again abandoned its stake in economic policy. Moreover, its *political* role became, if anything, more pivotal. For the war did not stem the rising tide of industrial and political unrest. The period between 1918 and 1921 saw perhaps the most serious direct challenge posed to the state by labour in this century, notably in Glasgow. In 1919 red flags and tanks were in evidence in Glasgow; a battle for George Square ensued, and the last surge of syndicalism was only defeated when the Clyde leaders were arrested, and the full force of the state exhibited.

With the end of the post-war boom in 1920 and the rise in unemployment, the threat escalated to crisis proportions – stimulating public panic and alarm, rumours of revolution and alarmist reponses from the state (Mowat, 1968, p. 123). The panic was not confined to Britain. There were revolutionary uprisings across Germany in the major cities; a Soviet republic was declared in Hungary; factories were occupied throughout northern Italy; there was a wave of strikes in France – all in the wake of the success of the Bolshevik Revolution in Russia in 1917. Events in Britain began to be seen in this context. Only last minute negotiations postponed the strike which the miners called in January 1919. Following a police strike, the Triple Alliance of unions was regenerated, and the coalition's refusal to accept the Sankey Commission's recommendation to nationalize the coal industry precipitated the threat of a general strike. The coalition took emergency powers. Leave among the armed services was cancelled, reservists called up, the parks converted into food and ammunition depots, and 75,000 'volunteers' recruited (Middlemas, 1979). It was only at the eleventh hour that a deal between Lloyd George and Hodges for the Miners' Union was struck and the strike called off. This, rather than the general strike of 1926, was the turning-point in the post-war period. It has come to be known in the Labour movement as 'Black Friday'. Mowat, the standard reference work for the period has said that 'Black Friday' was regarded in the Labour movement as the day of a great betrayal, when 'not only was a general strike abandoned, the Triple Alliance ruined and the miners sacrificed but the whole structure of a united working-class resistance to an expected attack on wage and living standards was demolished at a blow' (Mowat, 1968, p. 123). The recession then settled in and the unemployed dole queues of the inter-war years were born. Labour never looked afterwards like a social force capable of taking over leadership of society or of reconstructing the state. The coalition had done its work. It had educated, negotiated and confronted labour into place, and constitutionalized the Labour Party, making it an acceptable part of the state. The fall of the coalition and Lloyd George restored the Conservatives to a position of electoral supremacy they were to hold for 20 years. When minority Labour governments succeeded to power in the state in 1924 and 1929, they were to preside over the slump, were governed by circumstances rather than governing them, applied exceedingly conservative fiscal and economic remedies and fell — through the formation of yet another national government by Macdonald in 1931 — into a trough from which Labour was rescued only by the Second World War and the 1945 victory (Skidelsky, 1967).

A 'historic compromise'

This containment was accomplished by a twofold strategy. First, there was the 'tough' response — the state mobilized against what had been constructed as the threat of Bolshevik revolution. The state bore down on the Clyde Workers' Committee and the Triple Alliance. Geddes, the main wielder of the axe on spending, took over the Emergency Committee, which co-ordinated intelligence about the industrial-political scene and the securing of vital supplies. Later the Supply and Transport Committee co-ordinated state anti-strike activity, spending, unofficially, £100,000 per week on the propaganda effort.

Second, there was the struggle to organize and win public opinion, by constructing a public definition of the unrest which would mobilize popular consent against it. 'The party that secures on its side either general opinion or the opinion of the working class of the kingdom, must win' Balfour declared. Lloyd George had been advised that 'the great mass of working men are against violent revolution, but at the moment they are very sore about a number of minor [sic] points . . .' But his response was the private observation that 'Bolshevism is almost a safeguard to society, for it infects all classes with a horror of what may happen if the present organization of society is overthrown' (Middlemas, 1979, pp. 152—3). 'It is essential,' he added, 'that the press should be on the side of the government' — a loyalty he ruthlessly pursued. He was one of the first politicians to understand and deploy the role of 'public opinion' and the manufacture of consent in the era of mass democratic politics.

The focal point of the strategy was to split 'moderates' from 'extremists'. The syndicalist, rank-and-file insurgency of the Triple

Alliance had to be separated from 'moderate and responsible trade unionism'. The trump card was the recognition that, in this enterprise, the TUC and the Labour Party were actually the state's strongest allies. As Balfour observed, 'Trade Union organization was the only thing between us and anarchy.' Thus it was necessary, not only to defeat the exceptional, extra-constitutional challenge, but to incorporate and win over the moderates and the constitutionalists. Lloyd George pursued this 'divide and rule' operation with great finesse – deploying the full resources of the state. To achieve incorporation meant making concessions to the moderates, even as the rest were isolated and defeated. The expansion of the formalized machinery of industrial bargaining, conciliation and negotiation through the state was one key element. Here, in faint outline, we can detect the origin of that corporatist triangle – the incorporation of the organized representatives of capital (the employers' organizations), labour (the TUC) with the state – which later became the centrepiece of the interventionist state strategy in the 1960s and 1970s.

In short, the containment of the more extreme and challenging forms of 'the democracy' could only be achieved, not by excluding the masses from power, but by ensuring that they were properly and moderately represented within the councils of the state. Lloyd George and Baldwin both recognized that the incorporation of the proper vehicle for working-class representation – the Labour Party – within the state was necessary to the stability of the state and the new forms of national popular politics. First, 'the disappearance of the Liberal Party . . . The next step must be the elimination of the Communists by Labour. Then we shall have two parties, the Party of the Right and the Party of the Left' (Ramsden, 1978, p. 265). Thus, and for those reasons, was the essential shape of twentieth century British politics determined (Cowling, 1971, p. 1). This was how a national settlement was constructed, which set the terms on which 'the democracy' was to be represented. Not only did the state provide the basis for the bargains, negotiation and confrontations through which this compromise was reached. The state was itself the site on which the 'bargain' between interventionism and democracy was sealed and struck. Central to this process of compromise were the transformations wrought around the new conception of the state itself – the ambiguous forms of modern collectivism. Collectivism represented *both* the form in which the popular forces defined their interests *and* the form in which the ruling bloc tried to lead society and the state to confront a new set of historical tasks. Its importance in reconciling apparently contradictory forces lay precisely in its Janus-faced character. Its political complexion – left or right – was ultimately less important than its common element – its powerful statist emphasis. The outcome was therefore neither the total defeat of the popular forces nor the triumph of democracy but rather a 'historic compromise' – a sort of unwritten settlement between 'the democracy' and the power bloc. The question is – on whose terms was this settlement made? Overall, in whose favour did the balance of forces point? A profound historical judgement about the British state is entailed here and any answer must be couched carefully and with qualifications. My own view is that democracy was contained by the very process which ultimately allowed it to be represented. To put it another way, the popular forces *did* get wider representation in the state: but at the price of remaining a subordinate, rather than the leading or hegemonic element. The power bloc was therefore modified and reshaped: it had to pay greater attention to the winning of popular consent. But it was not radically democratized.

Conclusion – crisis of society, transformation of the state?

In this chapter I have been examining one formative moment in the emergence in Britain of the democratically-representative and the interventionist state. Our first concern was to describe the process in something of its real historical complexity as a *process* of change. But a second aim has been to reflect on this case study as an approach to questions relating more widely to relationships between 'society' and 'state'. It is time now to draw together the threads of these investigations and to provide some tentative conclusions.

One common way of thinking how a crisis in society is connected with a transformation of the state was outlined at the beginning: that is, that the economy is the principal connecting thread. Using this perspective in relation to our particular case, the proposition would run: it was the crisis of the British economy at the end of the nineteenth century which pushed the state towards a new stage of development, and determined its political character, its increased interventionism, its new modes of operation.

In the light of the historical materials we considered, two rather contradictory factors seem to emerge: (1) the economy/state connection *is* a powerful link. This link carries considerable explanatory power in accounting for major historical crises or periods of transition; (2) on the other hand, 'determination by the economic' is not, *in itself*, an adequate explanation of what actually occurred historically. The correspondence between corporate economy and interventionist state do not unfold in anything like the predictable, necessary or logical way this theory, in its more doctrinal form, would lead us to believe.

In the different industrial capitalist societies in this period, for example, no such irreversible process inevitably and automatically brings the state 'into line' with the functional needs of the economy. Rather, the process happens, in different social formations, at a different pace: by significantly different routes: with more or less degrees of completeness: and with strikingly different results. As to pace, the Prussian state made a very late start compared with Britain in the state-stimulation of industrialization: nevertheless, it moved much more swiftly and decisively to collectivist state policies, under Bismarck, than the British state did. As to routes, again, one has to contrast the 'authoritarian' or 'Prussian' route, taken by the German and Japanese cases with the 'democratic' one which was characteristic of the American and British examples. As to completeness, Britain is a good case of a never wholly or successfully completed movement, from a first to a second, more advanced, stage of capitalist social and economic organization. Finally, in terms of results, one need only note the very wide variations through which the economies and the states of the advanced capitalist societies are in fact combined in the twentieth century.

So, if correspondences are working in this period, it is in a much looser, less predictable way than the capital-theoretical version of the marxist approach suggested. This alters how we think about 'economic determination' in general in relation to the state. The economy may 'determine' in the sense of favouring certain lines of development in the state over others (tendencies). Or economic development may set certain limits to the type of state development. Or economic crises may set tasks for the state which any state – whatever its particular form or shape – will have to confront. But this is a much looser conception. Advanced capitalist economies – with many significant variations – did *tend* to move towards the 'monopoly' form. And all the relevant states – even the United States – did *tend* to expand their activities and become more interventionist. But, in any more historically concrete sense, the economy cannot predict or determine more precisely than 'tendentially'.

Our example certainly pushes us towards seeing the historical process of crisis in society and change in the state as resulting from the social formation as a whole. Transformations of the state do *not* appear to be explained outside of the social, political and ideological, as well as the economic, processes specific to a particular social formation.

The main alternative to this whole line of thinking was that provided by the liberal-democratic/pluralist perspective. Now, much that we have been discussing could be said to resemble the interest-group conflict characteristic of pluralistic competition. We have given this form of political struggle more significance than in classic Marxist perspectives. But we have not characterized it as 'pluralist'. Though whole classes are rarely 'on stage' politically, the fact that we identify them as 'fractions' or sectors of fundamental classes enables us to relate immediate political struggles to the maintenance of long-term, structural class interests and divisions in society. These *do* seem to be at work in a long-term sense behind the play of political struggles and are affected by how the latter work out or are resolved. So though the state is not just the instrument of a ruling class or the pawn of 'the economy', the compromises, negotiations and settlements imposed through the state on society *do* have structural consequences for the maintenance of capitalist social formations as a whole.

What, then, of the role of crisis in precipitating transformations of the state? It seems that crises, when the normal functioning of society is interrupted or things break down, are likely to provide particularly propitious or favourable circumstances for change. They bring on to the stage new social forces which may have long been developing. For a new conception of the state to win through, or for a specific crisis to be resolved through the state, it is necessary to break up the existing political formations and parties which stabilized the previous phase. The reigning ideological conceptions of the state must be displaced. This led, in our period, to the destruction of the particular constellation of political and social forces which underpinned mid-Victorian stability, and the opening of a period of intense political and ideological contestation and struggle for leadership. This involved the struggle to define ideologically a new role for the state; to build a coalition of political forces – a social bloc – capable of taking a leading role in the state; to transform the state and state machine itself; finally, to achieve social leadership and authority in society (hegemony – in Gramsci's terms).

Does this emphasis on different sites and degrees of conflict also imply a sort of 'pluralist' reading? Different conflicts, different struggles, different resolutions – but no overall shape to the settlement arrived at, no general structure of dominant power assured? On the whole, no. The dominance of particular social forces was, in the end, 'settled' in a certain way. This settlement helped to maintain a particular disposition of power and wealth in the social formation, through a particular compromise. The compromise was therefore not 'neutral' in its effect, so far as the balance between different classes was concerned. To be sure, it was not the result of a class using the state as a pure instrument of its will. Yet British society remained essentially capitalist and the dominant power bloc emerged embattled but ascendant.

My use of the term 'bloc' here is nevertheless pivotal for our theoretical summing up, for it suggests that whole classes, as such, rarely if ever rule politically. Within the dominant classes, one sector or fraction is usually in the leading political position — as the financial sector, with strong imperial connections, became the leading element in the new power bloc in our period, displacing the manufacturing interest. This leading sector is likely to give a distinct political colouration to the policies of the state in the period of its dominance — as we saw with the increasing dominance of imperialist interests and policies within the British state from the period of the Boer Wars onwards. This leading section so to speak 'represents' the general interest of the dominant class as a whole, within the political arena. But it alone does not directly drive the state, nor colonize it as its instrument. It must form, together with groupings and fractions of other social forces, a bloc of social forces, which supports and underpins the state. Indeed it seems crucial that sectors of the popular classes, in a democratic political system, must also be won to support the bloc — albeit in a subordinate role. Again, the state has a key role to play in the formation of such 'blocs', and often in forcing on the leading fraction those concessions (e.g. reforms, welfare measures, etc.) which are necessary if the bloc is to attract enough popular support to keep the whole operation stable. Representation and intervention are therefore linked: the extension of the state's democratic base provided the necessary legitimation for its expanded powers of intervention. In sum, then, one result of our study of the 1880—1920 period is to lead us to reformulate the terms in which we understand the relationships between 'class struggles' in society, and political conflicts and their resolution in the state. It also modifies considerably our understanding of the role of the state itself in these political struggles. If the historic task for the ruling bloc was to restore the conditions of successful accumulation in the economy, that task was an exceedingly complex one. And the 'instrument' for its achievement — the state — is also the site of contradictions — both within its own structures, and in relation to external social forces.

References

Adelman, P. (1972) *The Rise of the Labour Party,* London: Longman.
Burgess, K. (1980) *The Challenge of Labour,* London: Croom Helm.
Clarke, P. (1978) *Liberals and Social Democrats,* Cambridge: Cambridge University Press.
Cowling, M. (1971) *The Impact of Labour,* Cambridge: Cambridge University Press.
Dangerfield, G. (1961) *The Strange Death of Liberal England,* New York: Capricorn.
Dicey, A. V. (1963) *Law and Public Opinion in England,* London: Macmillan.
Gramsci, A. (1971) *Selections from the Prison Notebooks,* London: Lawrence and Wishart.
Halévy, E. (1926 on) *The History of the English People in the Nineteenth Century:* Vol. 5, *Imperialism and the Rise of Labour;* Vol. 6, *The Rise of Democracy*, London: Benn and Co.
Harris, J. (1982) 'The partnership of the Webbs', *New Society,* 25, November.
Hay, J. (1978) *The Development of the British Welfare State,* London: Arnold.
Hinton, J. (1973) *The First Shop Stewards' Movement,* London: Allen and Unwin.
Hobsbawm, E. J. (1969) *Industry and Empire*, Harmondsworth: Penguin.
Holton, B. (1975) *Syndicalism,* London: Pluto.
Jessop, B. (1982) *The Capitalist State,* Oxford: Martin Robertson.
Lloyd, E. (1924) *Experiments in State Control,* Oxford: Oxford University Press.
Marshall, T. H. (1950) *Citizenship and Social Class and other Essays,* Cambridge: Cambridge University Press.
Middlemas, K. (1979) *Politics in Industrial Society: The Experience of the British System since 1911,* London: André Deutsch.
Mowat, C. L. (1968) *Britain Between the Wars,* London: Methuen.
Pelling, H. (1965) *Origins of the Labour Party,* Oxford: Oxford University Press.
Pigou, E. (1918) 'Government control in war and peace', *The Economic Journal.*
Pollard, S. (1969) *Development of the British Economy,* London: Arnold.
Pugh, M. (1982) *The Making of Modern British History,* Oxford: Basil Blackwell.
Ramsden, J. (1978) *The Age of Balfour and Baldwin,* London: Longman.
Richter, M. (1964) *The Politics of Conscience: T. H. Green and His Age,* London: Macmillan.
Saul, S. B. (1969) *The Myth of the Great Depression,* London: Macmillan.
Scally, R. J. (1975) *The Origins of the Lloyd George Coalition,* New Jersey: Princeton University Press.

Schwarz, B. (1985) 'The corporate economy 1895–1929' in M. Langan and B. Schwarz (eds), *Crises of the British State, 1880–1930*, London: Hutchinson.
Searle, G. R. (1971) *The Quest for National Efficiency*, Oxford: Basil Blackwell.
Semmel, B. (1960) *Imperialism and Social Reform*, London: Allen and Unwin.
Shannon, R. (1974) *The Crisis of Imperialism*, London: Paladin.
Skidelsky, K. (1967) *Politicians and the Slump*, Harmondsworth: Penguin.
Tawney, R. H. (1943) 'The abolition of economic controls 1918–21', *Economic History Review*.
Thornton, A. F. (1966) *The Imperial Idea and its Enemies*, London: Macmillan.
Webb, S. (1907) *The Decline in the Birth Rate*, Fabian Tract 131, London.

2

State and economy in the Second World War

LAURENCE HARRIS

The Second World War was 'total war' in which Britain's economy and social life were enmeshed as much as the military. Indeed, Britain's sound industrial base which in the last years of peace had begun to show signs of regeneration from the inter-war depression, was a condition for victory. Without it (and other economic strengths such as the raw materials obtained on virtually forced credit from the colonies and Sterling Area) the supplies to sustain both large forces and the civilian population would not have been produced and the production of high technology military equipment (aeroplanes, radios, radar, modern artillery, tanks and arms) would have been problematic. In a 1983 report on the links between military technology and civil industry Sir Ieuan Maddocks wrote: 'Of the many reasons why Britain responded so well to the technological challenge of the European War (1939—45) the most important was the fact that there existed a very healthy civil industrial base.'

But the economy's underpinning for Britan's war did not 'just happen' and succeed because of an underlying strength. It was organized and given direction by the state, although it was not until mid-1940 that Britain's ruling class let go its belief that the war could be won with 'business as usual' and the state assumed the powers and purpose to give it a fully directive role. The state's direction of the economy has led many to comment, in retrospect, that the Second World War was a model of socialist planning in action, although there is no unity on whether it was a 'democratic' or centralized 'bureaucratic' socialism.

Michael Foot, having become leader of the Labour Party, said in 1982:

> The best example that I've seen of Democratic Socialism operating in this country was during the Second World War. Then we ran Britain highly efficiently, got everybody into a job . . . We also produced, I would have thought, probably more than any other country including Germany. We mobilised better. The conscription of labour was only a very small element of it. We also did what I think we ought to do on a far greater scale now, looking after the people who are worst hit. . . . It was a democratic society with a common aim in which many of the class barriers were being broken down. (*Guardian,* 6 December 1982, p. 13)

For Foot this was not just socialism but democratic socialism. He does not mention state direction, controls and coercion except to minimize it ('conscription of labour was only a very small element of it'), possibly believing that such forceful measures are the antithesis of democratic organization. Others, however, have remarked that state direction was very extensive and this is often taken to be an integral part of socialism. As Arthur Marwick put it: 'direction and control of life and labour were probably more total (and more efficient) than in any other country, save for Russia' (Marwick, 1974, p. 151).

One *Guardian* reader wrote to the paper, taking issue with Michael Foot over the relative absence of state control and also over the cohesiveness of British society during the war. For him there was a highly bureaucratic form of socialism during the war, and it was clearly unpleasant for him, bearing 'a strong resemblance to George Orwell's 1984, and the socialist regimes of Eastern Europe and the Soviet Union'. He wrote:

> There were other features of Mr Foot's wartime socialist Britain besides the direction of labour, which may have been 'a small element' to a middle-class journalist employed on Lord Beaverbrook's Evening Standard, but which placed a genuine strain on working-class families.
>
> It should also be remembered that almost everything was subject to rationing (food, clothing, furniture) and that such items as were not (cigarettes, matches, spirits and the like) were invariably handled in under-the-counter transactions. If you had the money, almost everything could be bought on the black market, from eggs and bacon to a length of suiting.
>
> The phenomenon of the black market and the corruption of the trading classes introduced a new word into the English language:

> the spiv, defined in the dictionary as 'a man or boy who makes a living by underhand dealing or swindling; black marketeer' (Collins).
> Meanwhile, a new class of privileged bureaucrat was emerging, entitled to car and petrol ration. Mr Foot believes that 'class barriers were being broken down' and so they were – the old ones, that is, while new ones were forming: the distinction was between the working man and woman, and the bureaucrat who would never have to fire a shot in anger.
> Substantial numbers of these new class were employed in the Ministry of Information, our genteelism for ministry of propaganda. It was their business to persuade the population that everyone was getting fair shares; but just in case anyone stepped out of line, they risked being pounced on by the thought police for spreading alarm and despondency. (*Guardian*, 10 December 1982)

In that letter, socialism is characterized by state direction and coercion and by the existence of new kinds of social division, cleavages different from those between capitalists and workers but nonetheless divisive. They were Britain's wartime socialism.

For Angus Calder, the historian of 'The People's War' the broad picture was one where there were great changes. Whether or not they were socialist in character they were brought about by the classic engine envisaged by socialist orators, the mass strength of ordinary people. The people, having temporarily wrested power from their unresisting rulers got on with prosecuting the war under the leadership of 'their' state:

> 'Morale' – that word which haunted the politicians, the civil servants and the generals. What the people demanded, they must now be given. Had they taken the tubes as deep shelters? Oh well, they must keep them. Did they demand fairer shares in food? Tinned salmon must be rationed 'on points'. Were they puzzled by set-backs in production? Let them elect representatives to joint production committees. Were they depressed by their conviction that victory would be the prelude to a new slump? Then plans must be made to ensure that life really would be better for them after the war.
> So the people surged forward to fight their own war, forcing their masters into retreat, rejecting their nominal leaders and representatives and paying homage to leaders almost of their own imagination – to Churchill, to Cripps, to Beveridge, to Archbishop Temple and to Uncle Joe Stalin. The war was fought with the willing brains and hearts of the most vigorous elements in the community, the educated, the skilled, the bold, the active, the young, who worked more and more consciously towards a transformed post-war world. (Calder, 1969, p. 18)

Calder's broad sweep takes us too far afield. Considering just economic policy the important questions about whether the state's role was socialist during the war hinge upon the characteristics of socialism that have already been picked out, the degree of state control and the existence of divisions between classes or other groups in the economy. The chapter examines these two aspects of the war economy:

(1) *State control.* Was the economy under central direction with the state intervening in market forces and even replacing them with direct controls in significant areas of the economy?
(2) *Class divisions.* Did the war economy continue to be marked by class divisions between workers on one hand and the owners and managers of private industry on the other? Or were they replaced by new social divisions, more characteristic of socialist, centrally planned economies?

Keynesian planning

The relationship between the state and civil society is, in normal times, two-way. In terms of this economy the state in capitalist societies (and others) depends upon the private sector for the taxes and loans to pay its employees and buy resources, but the private sector itself depends upon the state for many of the conditions that enable it to operate: for laws defining and protecting property, for guaranteeing the stability of money, and for regulating competition at the very least. In modern capitalism the state's interventions are much wider than that.

However, many economists at the start of the Second World War saw only one role for the British state – to mobilize and direct the nation to win the war; they judged economic policy (almost) wholly in the light of that objective. Introducing his official history of one part of economic policy Richard Sayers wrote:

> The central task in a war economy, the mobilization of resources for the war effort and the maintenance of that effort, calls for help from the financial system internally both in promoting the transfer of resources from one use to another and in raising to the utmost the productivity of the mobilized resources. Externally the task of financial policy is to ensure that the goods and services that are needed and are available from abroad – or to be denied to the enemy – can be bought. (Sayers, 1956, p. 1.)

In this view the relationship between the wartime economy and the wartime state was one-way: the state's function was to win the war and the economy was to serve that externally-oriented state. It contrasts strongly with the concept of the capitalist state that is now well established, for that state is seen to have an orientation toward domestic society; whilst drawing from the economy it also has the function of reproducing its capitalist structure.

But the implication of the perspective expressed by Sayers, that the normal relation between state and economy was suspended while the state pursued the single aim of winning the war, gives only a partial view. Political choices had to be made between different methods for controlling and directing the economy. On the one hand were the policies John Maynard Keynes advocated, aiming to shift resources to the war effort with a minimum of state intervention; on the other were policies for state direction and controls to replace the normal mechanisms ('market forces') of the capitalist economy. The British state's economic policies were not as non-interventionist as Keynes wished, but nor did they go all the way to the latter extreme. The basic features of a capitalist economy remained intact. The wartime economy was one where most factories and commercial enterprises were owned by private capital, where profit was their yardstick, and where wages played a central role in the labour market. Thus, although the state did have to harness these forces toward providing the resources for winning the war, the relationship was not one way. The normal relationship between the state and civil society, in which the state maintains the conditions under which capital can generate and accumulate profits, remained.

Before examining the actual character of the war economy, let us set out the policy advocated by Keynes, in 1939, for redirecting resources with minimal intervention. Subsequently I shall argue that Keynes's hopes were not realized; there was much greater intervention and abrogation of 'market forces' than he wished, but not enough to undermine the basic character of the capitalist economy.

In a series of articles in *The Times*, in correspondence and memoranda arising from them, and in a pamphlet based on them, *How To Pay for The War*, Keynes posed a stark problem. War would require a vast shift of resources from, say, producing cars, bicycles and fairground contraptions for private buyers to producing tanks, aircraft and guns for the armed forces of the state. How could the state obtain the necessary resources?

That question breaks into two, Where would the state obtain the money to pay for this spending? And where would the real resources, the goods and people, the state spent money on come from? Keynes's solutions were simple and linked.

To obtain the money for the swollen armed forces and civil service the state would have to raise taxes. An alternative would be to force people to save and lend their savings to the state to be repaid after the war. The latter was a novel plan which Keynes pursued with great energy. He thought it preferable to taxation because people would not be having money confiscated but would be lending it and regaining its use when peace returned.

The real resources for the state's war spending would be released from other uses as a result of this taxation and compulsory saving. The main source would come from the reduction of private consumers' demand induced by these policies. But that does not guarantee that the released resources would be switched toward the output needed by the state for the war. One way to achieve the switch would be by direct controls and requisitioning, but Keynes argued that 'market forces' themselves should be relied upon instead.

The plan for compulsory savings was not a purely technical, economic plan but a highly political strategy. Keynes was very conscious of the need for legitimation of the state; even the great upsurge of wartime patriotism and defence of democracy might not guarantee it if the state's economic policies were divisive. Thus, although the plan was for compulsory savings, Keynes attempted to makes its acceptance voluntary, devoting much effort to persuading all sections, but particularly the trade union leaders of the working class, that his scheme was equitable. In this respect it is noteworthy that he was conscious of the disruption class divisions could cause. It was inescapable that the switch of resources to war production would leave less for consumers and, in aggregate, a reduced standard of living which would harm the working class and could lead to a legitimation crisis for the state. Keynes thought that compulsory savings which postpone rather than merely deny consumption could achieve working-class support in a way that high taxes might not. He speculated that this saving would enable workers to accumulate wealth and thus blur class divisions.

Although the reliance on taxation and, particularly, compulsory savings was intended to achieve support for the reduction in living standards, Keynes argued against policies which, irrespective of the support the working class might have given them, would have interfered with capitalism's ways of working. He was opposed to raising high taxes on profits (believing that profits taxes had already almost destroyed entrepreneurs' 'incentive to effort') and he was opposed to 'the complex tyranny of all-round rationing', believing that free markets were essential to permit the 'choice and initiative' that was one of capitalism's greatest benefits.

In Chancellor of the Exchequer Kingsley-Wood's budget of April 1941 Keynes's positive ideas were put into effect. Taxes were raised and a scheme of compulsory saving (Post-War Credits) was put into effect. But Keynes's negative principles against state intervention in the markets had fared less well, for in May 1940 the state had taken extensive powers to intervene.

Planning and the labour market

Keynes's writings on 'How To Pay for the War' date from the months before the war became real, the phoney war before the débâcle of Dunkirk. His view that free markets not only should but could remain more or less free, that they could ensure an appropriate allocation of resources and manpower and woman-power was in sympathy with the sluggishness with which state economic policy moved at the beginning of the war. However, as the British Expeditionary Force was defeated in May 1940 the state's powers to direct the economy were increased dramatically, particularly with respect to the supply and use of labour. On 22 May 1940 the House of Commons passed, in three hours, a more powerful Emergency Powers Act justified on the argument that 'It is necessary that the Government should be given complete control over persons and property, not just some persons of some particular class of the community, but of all persons, rich and poor, employer and workman, man or woman, and all property.' Under it a Defence Regulation was made which enabled the Minister of Labour

(1) *to direct* (through the Ministry's National Service officers) any person in the United Kingdom to work anywhere or perform any service required in any place;
(2) *to prescribe* the pay, conditions and hours of work of such services;
(3) and to *require* people to register details of themselves with the authorities so that the state would have details of the available pool of labour to match to needs.

In the words of W. K. Hancock and M. Gowing in the official history, *British War Economy* (1949), 'this Regulation armed the Minister of Labour with powers undreamed of in the philosophy of any previous British Minister . . . Into his hands had been given the unrestricted powers of industrial conscription.'

The Minister of Labour acquired these powers at the start of a great intensification of the war effort and thereafter there was a massive transfer of labour towards the war industries and the services. Between June 1940 and June 1943 the net increase in workers employed in the highest priority industries (the Group 1 industries such as iron and steel, engineering, aircraft manufacture) was 1,674,000, a rise in those industries' labour force of 47 per cent, and a further 400,000 were sucked into the next highest priority industries. At the same time the net increase in the armed forces was two and a half million over that period so that even more people were drafted into industry to replace the men and women who entered the services. These transfers of labour were enormous by any standards and, occurring as they did after the government took the power to conscript labour into industries, it is at first sight easy to attribute the shifts to government direction. Instead of high wages pulling women and other new workers into the labour force or high relative wages pulling workers into the industries that particularly needed labour, the transfer appears to have been achieved by government direction. To reach such a conclusion so quickly, however, is dangerous for it rests on the false assumption of *post hoc ergo propter hoc*, after it therefore because of it. To see if the conclusion is justified we have to examine what happened in more detail. What we find is that the direction of labour was not wholly responsible for the transfer of industry to the war industries, it was combined with a variety of pulls and pushes including higher wages. Michael Foot's view that 'conscription of labour was only a very small element of it' may be an exaggeration, but it contains some truth.

From spring 1941 two of the most important of the Ministry of Labour's instruments in directing men and women were available, the Registration of Employment Order and the Essential Work Order. The former compelled all men and women to register and, if their particulars appeared to make them suitable for war work, they were interviewed with a view to directing them to war work. Registration was essential to the system of manpower budgeting by which the state decided upon the allocations of labour to the priority industries, but it was only one end of the process; at the other end was the drawing up of the manpower budgets themselves and the allocations to industries which were ultimately the responsibility of the War Cabinet, and in between was a complex administrative structure of Labour Exchanges, National Service officers, the zoning of the country into areas according to the degree of labour shortage (scarlet areas being those with the greatest deficiency), and priority industries. The direction of labour was very extensive but its most famous, if untypical, example was the Bevin Boys.

In 1943 the shortage of manpower in coal mining took on crisis proportions and appeals for volunteers failed. The previous year's report of the government-appointed Forster Committee had blamed low recruitment upon four factors:

(1) workers' memory of the industry's susceptibility to shocks causing unemployment;
(2) low wages compared to other industries;
(3) uncongenial working conditions;
(4) boys being deterred by parents and teachers partly because of the high accident rate.

Wages had been raised in the industry (although not without industrial strife) after the 1942 report by Lord Greene's Board of Investigation but even this failed to ease recruitment. The Bevin Boys solution attempted by Minister of Labour, Ernest Bevin was not, despite the name, to send his sons down the pit, it was to select by ballot young men from throughout the country to go into the mines instead of the services. The scheme was highly unpopular and probably a failure in terms of production because of the Bevin Boys' resentment and unsuitability for the work.

The direction of labour for which the 1941 Registration for Employment Order was the foundation was oriented to allocating supplies of labour to different industries. But market forces could induce workers to move from one job to another in search of higher wages. In the early years of the war the 'poaching' of labour, especially skilled labour which was in short supply even before a general labour shortage developed, was believed to be common. Preventing this competitive bidding for labour was the prime function of the Essential Works Orders which were applied to industry after industry from March 1941. It tied workers in scheduled factories to their employers and tied their employers to them. No employee of a scheduled undertaking could leave, be discharged, or transferred without the permission of a National Service officer (except for serious misconduct). By the end of 1941 about 29,000 undertakings employing almost six million workers were covered by the Orders.

Now, this daunting machinery for allocating, directing, and controlling labour suggests that Keynes's views did not materialize in their entirety. Free markets in labour were abolished; instead of a growing industry's demand for labour causing it to offer high wages and thereby attract workers, workers were directed into it. The individual freedom, at least freedom of choice, that Keynes associated with market forces gave way to a bureaucracy that Keynes had attempted to avoid, writing: 'There is a fatal family resemblance between bureaucracies in Moscow, Berlin and Whitehall; and we must be careful.'

But the replacement of the labour market by state direction is only part of the story: first, the state was not wholly effective in preventing competitive bidding for labour, and second, it attempted to reproduce the forces of the market in its own mechanism for wage setting. The official historian of labour in the munitions industries explains both these phenomena:

> Thus the existing voluntary machinery for wage negotiation was never set aside. On the other hand there were certain means by which the Government could influence the rates of wages paid and the earnings of workers in the munitions industries. The contracts department of the supply Ministries through fixing of prices possessed a certain measure of control over wages; but it will be shown below that this was potentially greater in theory than in practice it proved to be.
>
> The contracts departments were, for example, unable to prevent employers from offering high earnings to attract labour. In 1939–40 this practice was a potent factor in forcing up earnings in the munitions industries. In theory the Essential Work Orders made in 1941 should have put a stop to it, for under the Orders workers could only leave their employment with the consent of the national service officer, who would not normally accept low earnings as a reason for their doing so. In practice, however, if low wages were paid in a particular establishment, the workers, assisted by their trade union officials, used many and devious methods to transfer to better paid work, though the real reason for leaving their employment would never be mentioned to the national service officer or to the Appeal Board. Workers thrown on the labour market were, of course, equally attracted by highly paid work and, as has been said, the Ministry of Labour was very hesitant to direct them to lower paid work against their will.
>
> The making of the Essential Work Order did not therefore put a complete stop to the raising of wages in order to attract labour. On the other hand, of course, such freedom of movement as remained to workers protected them from being forced to enter or remain in badly paid employment. The Order, however, contained specific safeguards on this point; for it gave the Minister of Labour power to satisfy himself that conditions of work reached a certain standard before scheduling an establishment under the Order. This gave him a sanction to secure increases in wage rates in badly paid industries.

> In fact even outside the terms of reference provided by the Essential Work Order the Government did intervene in wage negotiations by putting pressure on one or both sides of industry, especially where wages questions appeared to influence very strongly the supply and productivity of labour. For example, in June 1940 the Minister of Labour intervened to secure an important agreement in the engineering industry ensuring that skilled toolroom workers on time rates did not earn less than productive workers on piece rates. Later in the year he tried unsuccessfully to persuade the engineering industry to equalise district rates in order to make labour transfers easier.
>
> On the whole these interventions had at least a measure of success when the Government tried to raise the earnings of the indubitably underpaid categories of workers, as when the Ministry of Labour and the Ministry of Supply made efforts to raise the minimum wages in the lower paid heavy industries; or when the Ministry of Labour and the M.A.P. did the same for the wages of women and girls in the radio valve industry. Similarly the Ministry of Labour and the Admiralty had some success in securing an extension of payment by results in the shipbuilding industry. Employers, with an eye to post-war conditions, were naturally reluctant to raise wage rates; but they wanted labour, and in wartime in any case the Government paid the bill. (Inman, 1957, pp. 318–19)

It seems, then, that one principal element of capitalist economies was partly suspended, the allocation of labour by market forces was replaced by administrative allocation according to a plan, the manpower budgets. But it was not a wholesale repudiation of the market; market forces continued to work and to some extent the state was obliged to emulate them, to set wages in order to attract labour to those industries which were short.

Class conflict in the coal industry

Those changes in the labour market bear upon the question of whether wartime Keynesian policies were accompanied by a great extension of administrative direction of the economy, one of the considerations that, as we showed in the first section of this chapter, seemed to enter people's minds when judging whether the system was becoming socialist. At the same time, they were concerned with the question of society's divisions. Michael Foot said that it was both a socialist and a democratic society because 'many of the class barriers were being broken down'. Were they?

No one would expect the class conflicts of the inter-war years to be magically conjured away by the war and the change in the state's role. But two areas where conflicts between workers and their employers are inescapable in peacetime are wage bargaining and the control of production, and both these areas were considerably changed during the war. To what extent did this change the terms on which conflicts occurred, or change their nature? Ideally, to answer the question we would have to examine a whole number of industries, incidents of strikes, arbitrations, prosecutions and expressions of attitudes. To make it manageable, however, I shall concentrate mainly on one industry, coal.

The previous paragraphs on manpower budgeting and the direction of labour easily give the impression that the state was running the factories to which the labour was directed. I gained that impression while reading the historical material, and I had to force myself to remember that it was not so. Industrial production in Britain took place almost wholly in factories, plants and mines that were privately owned. When labour was directed toward aircraft production it was to the factories of A. V. Roe, Hawkers, and a few other privately owned aircraft plants. When the Bevin Boys were sent to the mines they were working for the private mine owners. The economy continued to be founded upon the private ownership of capital, and although the private ownership of mines had been a hotly contended political issue since the First World War, they remained in the hands of the mine owners.

The declaration from Westminster that accompanied the 1940 Emergency Powers Act, which I quoted above (p. 56) ran: 'It is necessary that the Government should be given complete control over persons and property, not just some persons of some particular class of the community but of all persons, rich and poor, employer and workman, man or woman, and all property.'

The union leader, Will Lawthor, writing four years later on the miners' demands, argued that the miners 'have seen that principle applied only to the workers required for the mines, never to the owners' with the result that now as the offensive against Germany was being mounted 'there has never been a time when there was such unrest and dissatisfaction in the nation's coalfields' (Lawthor, 1944, pp. 6–9). Now Lawthor, President of the Mineworkers' Federation of Great Britain, was less than accurate in claiming that the owners of capital were not subject to controls for there were controls over what could be sold where, there were government policies regarding the prices at which they could sell, and there were controls over a crucial element of capitalism, a firm's ability to raise money on the stock market. Nevertheless, he does present the miners' view of the issues over which class conflict persisted in the mines during the war.

> It has taken World War Number Two to bring home to the public the importance of coal and of the miners. Only in recent months has the miner been guaranteed a national minimum wage. We have had the Lord Greene award, the Lord Porter award, we have had almost two years of the Ministry of Fuel and Power and the Control Scheme it introduced. We have seen the Prime Minister bring two thousand miners and managers to London to explain the importance of the coal industry. We have had, as an industry, advances in wages larger than those gained by any other section of the working class (though in relation to these one must remember the appallingly low level we were on when the war commenced). We are now promised a stabilisation of wages until June 1948, and yet the coalfields are seething with unrest.
>
> In fact, there has never been a time when there was such unrest and dissatisfaction in the nation's coalfields.
>
> There are a variety of factors to account for this, such as the attempts of the owners to avoid paying the full amounts that Tribunals have decided on, the bungling and blunders of the Government in applying their part of the awards, the reluctance of other workers to enter the coal industry. Now a point has been reached where the miners are determined that an end shall be made for all time to the root cause of all their troubles and difficulties – namely, the private ownership of the mining industry.
>
> The miners see the owners working through a variety of ways to discredit any form of Government control and to oppose nationalisation. They have got the bit between their teeth, and are determined that the mines shall be publicly owned. This is the outstanding feature of the position in the mining industry that both the Government and the public must make up their minds to face.
>
> The miners do not forget how in one of the gravest hours of this nation's history (May 22nd, 1940), Mr. Attlee stated in the House of Commons:
>
> > 'It is necessary that the Government should be given complete control over persons and property, not just some persons of some particular class of the community, but of all persons, rich and poor, employer and workman, man or woman, and all property.'
>
> They have seen that principle applied only to the workers required for the mines, never to the owners. They have also seen that when such workers have been conscripted for the mines fierce resistance is offered. As I write these lines there is a strike of young apprentices within sight of Durham and Northumberland pits, against being conscripted for the mines. Is this not the measure of the shame and degradation to which we have allowed Britain's greatest industry to fall?

> Now we face a crisis in coal which, because we are in sight of victory, is more urgent than it was in the days of retreat. There is only one way in which this crisis can be solved, that is by the nationalisation of mines.
>
> What is our case based on? You will find a thousand arguments in the present book, but I will try to give here a simple and popular presentation of our case, and it will be for you not only to judge, but to act.
>
> It is half a century since the miners and the Labour Movement first launched the demand for public ownership of the mines, but in the present emergency of war, when coal is so vital for victory, we have seen an enormous extension in the support for our demand from all sections of the community.
>
> Why? Because although we have some of the richest coalfields in the world, the most skilled miners in the world, we have seen the inability of the coal industry under private ownership to respond to the nation's need.
>
> The miners' one desire is that Britain's rich coal resources shall be utilised to the full. This will only be possible if two things are recognised. First, that never again are the miners and their families going to be the Cinderellas of British industry; and secondly, that under private ownership it is impossible for any permanent solution of the problems connected with the industry to be secured.
>
> If proof of this latter point were needed, it is to be found in the fact that there have been more Government Commissions and enquiries, more debates in Parliament, more deputations to Cabinet Ministers, more strikes and lock-outs and more criticism of the ownership and inefficient management of the coal industry than any other in Britain. A point has now been reached where I frankly declare that the miners are in a mood of sullen resentment and anger in relation to their industry, a mood so deep that no matter what proposals are made in regard to wages and working conditions, their confidence in the industry will never be restored until it has been taken over by the State. (Lawthor, 1944, pp. 8–9)

Lawthor's views were clearly strong and bitter, and definitely framed in terms of class conflict. He picked out three main issues as foci for conflict:

(1) *Wages.* The classic trade union concern remained an object of conflict despite the relatively high wage awards that were given to attract labour. He accused mine owners and government of failing to pay up smoothly and saw this as an object of great discontent.

(2) *Ownership and control.* In Lawthor's view the wartime crisis of the coal industry had greatly strengthened the merits of

the workers' long-held objective, nationalization of the mines.

(3) *Needs of the nation.* Higher wages and nationalization were not demanded for their own sake, or only for the benefits they could bring to the miners, however important these benefits were seen to be. A third element was workers' patriotism, willing the industry 'to respond to the nation's need' and facing 'a crisis in coal which, because we are in sight of victory, is more urgent than it was in the days of retreat'.

The conflicts over wages and over ownership and control directly involved the state. They illustrate well the contradictions in the state's position attempting to run a war while sustaining an economy based on private capital. In wages the state initially sought to encourage market forces but was increasingly forced to intervene, while on ownership and control the machinery established by the state to achieve co-operation between labour and capital did not disrupt the employers' power over production.

Wages

Early in the war the government decided that wages throughout the economy should be set by negotiation between employers and employees and, where these failed, by the machinery of arbitration. These were the two normal methods of wage-fixing familiar in peacetime, but a third method equally familiar in Britain, strikes and lockouts, was effectively declared illegal by Order 1305 under the Emergency Powers Act. According to the Order the parties to a dispute could refer it to the Minister of Labour who would pass it to the industry's existing joint negotiating machinery for settlement between the sides. If that failed the Minister was to refer the issue to be compulsorily decided by the National Arbitration Tribunal. Only in cases where this procedure was not followed were strikes or lockouts legal: effectively the right to strike legally was withdrawn.

Negotiations between the two sides in coal mining made their mark quickly; in October 1939 they were the first wages issue to face the war cabinet. The miners' trade union strength had been considerably eroded in the inter-war years, particularly after the failure of the 1926 general strike. On a list of earnings in about 100 industries miners' earnings were eighty-first in 1938. By 1942 various wage settlements had brought them up to about fifty-ninth but there was great unrest in the coalfields, 685,000 working days being lost in disputes, in the first half of that year. The most significant dispute, significant because of its effect on the state's involvement in labour troubles, was at Betteshanger colliery in Kent, a colliery opened in the 1920s with miners from Wales. One thousand and fifty miners struck in pursuit of a wage claim against local mine owners; the government (against the advice of Ernest Bevin, the Minister of Labour who had been the powerful leader of the Transport and General Workers' Union) decided to prosecute, three local officials were temporarily imprisoned and all the strikers were fined. However three months later only nine had paid their fines and, recognizing the practical and political impossibility of imprisoning the rest, the authorities let the legal action die. The experience reinforced the cabinet's unwillingness actually to use legal remedies in wage disputes; during the war there were only 71 prosecutions under Order 1305 in Scotland and 38 in England and Wales.

In the absence of national negotiating or arbitration machinery a specially created Board of Investigation under Lord Greene recommended a major upward revision of wages in 1942. The award was seen as a victory for the miners who had struck at Betteshanger and elsewhere in the first half of 1942. By 1943 national conciliation machinery had been established but disputes accelerated; a National Tribunal award of January 1944 was so unsatisfactory that a wave of strikes ensued in the coalfields. According to Angus Calder 'About a hundred thousand men came out in South Wales, and more than that number in the Yorkshire field.' These strikes forced the state into a change of position with respect to wage negotiations in the coal industry. The government's 1942 White Paper on the industry set out a wartime structure in which not only would mining remain privately owned but also the state would keep out of wage fixing. Initially the policy was to avoid interfering in price fixing, too, and all aspects of finance. But in 1942 the state had to take over pricing arrangements and their financing (through a Coal Charges Account); it did so in order to ensure that pits that were unprofitable and which in peacetime would have been eliminated by competition on the market, were kept alive. But once the state was involved in pricing policy it could not avoid determining wages; whether the owners could meet the miners' demands in 1944 for more than the Tribunal offered, indeed for a revamping of the whole structure of wages, depended on whether the government would agree to price rises to cover it. With preparations for D-Day intensifying, the Ministry of Fuel and Power took responsibility, devised a new wages structure which was approved by the war cabinet and six weeks later accepted by the two sides in the industry.

By the end of the war miners' earnings had risen considerably so that instead of being thirty-eighth they were near the top of the earnings league; and, since coal was not subsidized, the mine owners' profits were maintained by increases in its price. These changes occurred as a result of strikes, absenteeism and unrest in the coalfields; conflict between the workers and the owners over wages did, therefore, continue during the war. It was a continuation of the very sharp forms of class conflict that had marked the industry since the start of the First World War; in fact the new war had produced an upsurge in militancy on the part of the workers (and a weakening of the employers' resistance) as a result of full employment, of the Essential Works Order that weakened the owners' rights to hire and fire, and of the desperate need for coal at crucial points in the war effort.

Ownership and control

The state became involved in pricing and wage determination although at the beginning the policy had been to leave these matters to the owners and union and to leave ownership in private hands. The Mineworkers' Federation had, for years, fought for implementation of the 1919 Sankey Commission's recommendations 'that the principle of State ownership of the coal mines be accepted . . . and that Parliament be invited to pass legislation acquiring the coal mines for the State . . .' and the owners had opposed the recommendation with equal determination. One of the arguments that Lord Sankey had brought in support of his recommendation, and that he repeated in a 1943 House of Lords debate on the industry's wartime position, was that the merits of state ownership from the workers' point of view were not only a better climate for wage negotiation but also a role for the workers in running things: 'Half a century of education has produced in the workers in the coalfields far more than a desire for the material advantages of higher wages and shorter hours. They have now, in many cases, and to an ever-increasing extent, a higher ambition of taking their due share and interest in the direction of the industry to the success of which they, too are contributing.' Although the war did not bring nationalization, the control scheme announced in the 1942 White Paper did establish Pit Production Committees where the miners, formally at least, shared control over operations with the owners.

I have explained under the heading of wages that the intention in 1942 was for the state to leave wages, prices and financing to the industry itself, but a system of 'dual control' was set up under which state bodies took control of production. These bodies at national and regional levels had both owners' and workers' representatives on them; Pit Production Committees at each pit were the link between this state machinery and each pit's workers and management. The Pit Production Committee was intended to make suggestions for improvements in work organization and report on such things as poor equipment and shortage of supplies. The Committees were supposed to consider the things that were the responsibility, respectively, of the two sides in the industry, workers' co-operation and discipline on one hand and management's intentions on techniques of production. In principle they were a radically new element in the conflict between miners and owners over the control of production: they were on the surface an instrument for co-operation instead of conflict.

However, the Pit Production Committees and the machinery above them that implemented the 'dual control' system under which the state was responsible for organizing production did not eliminate conflict but, instead, were vehicles for it. Margot Heinemann, an economist sympathetic to the mine workers wrote in 1944:

> Thus the final set-up of the machinery was very far from 'full control' and 'a basis of national service' in any sense in which those words are either popularly or legally understood. The Government's control was not 'full', but partial; it was nominally operational control without financial control, but in practice it left control with the coal-owners. Nor were the workers and technicians placed 'on a basis of national service'; they were not working for the Government, but for the owners, and their Pit Production Committees had no statutory or executive powers.
>
> The composition of the National and Regional Coal Boards revealed the same weaknesses. The Controller-General, appointed after the scheme had been approved by Parliament, was Lord Hyndley, till that time director of Powell Duffryn Associated Collieries, the biggest amalgamation in the country, and also of Guest, Keen and Nettlefolds (iron, steel and coal) and the Bank of England. The Production Director was Mr. Charles Reid, formerly director of the Fife Coal Co., the biggest Scottish combine; the Labour director Mr. J. Armstrong, formerly of the Scottish Mineworkers. This type of organisation, with miners and coal-owners represented as the two sides among the full-time officials, is paralleled in the regions; the production directors are coal-owners,

> the Labour directors miners' officials. The fight that had gone on outside the State machine continues within it. (Heinemann, 1944, pp. 141–2)

She was writing of the National and Regional Coal Boards within the context of which the Ministry of Fuel and Power's officials exercised their control but she thought the conflict over Pit Production Committees (and in them where they worked) was more significant. Workers complained that the Committees were obstructed by management and management complained that workers were not competent to pronounce on the organization of improved production. The workers' complaints described by Heinemann included the powerlessness of the committees:

> Many good suggestions are accepted by a local manager, referred back to the agent (the company's financial controller) and there quashed. To quote one lodge secretary:
>
> 'Whatever we suggest is never tried. The reason for same is unknown. The local manager is very helpful but is just one of the big machine'.
>
> . . . And here are . . . opinions expressed from [other] collieries . . . :
>
> (a) 'Within the limited scope allowed, the Committee has done well, in spite of the management's wholesale condemnation of our suggestions. We feel that much more could be done if the present Dual Control was abolished and National Control by the Government substituted'.
>
> (b) 'Progress has been made in many small issues, but anything of principle is generally resisted very strongly by the management side. Further progress could be made if the manager had a free hand. We realise the value of the Pit Production Committee with all its shortcomings, but still believe that more power is necessary for the complete functioning of such a body'.
>
> (Heinemann, 1944, pp. 149–50)

The managers' complaints reflected partly the threat to their own position and partly the interests of the owners. Heinemann reports one

> cry from the soul, taken from a feature article by 'Special Investigator' in the South-Wales coal-owners' organ, the *Western Mail* (October 11, 1943): 'Managers feel that while they are still being held responsible, all authority is taken away from their position. They are at the bidding of pit production committees and

of National Service Officers, and thus at the mercy of the men whose activities they are supposed to govern'.

And their complaint was not only that they as managers had lost the right to manage, but that they had lost it to workers who were not competent to manage. One colliery agent gave a speech in 1942 in which the complaint was put very clearly:

> For reasons which, he feared, were more political than practical, great stress was laid on the services of Pit Production Committees in connection with output. He considered that they were expected to achieve results quite beyond their ability. The management side of the Pit Production Committee has spent the whole of its working life on the question of production. Was it feasible to expect that men with no special training could acquire such experience simply by sitting once a week on the committee? . . . In no well-managed pit would they find much to suggest, and it was vain to hope that they could turn the scales or even go a long way towards turning the scales between a deficiency and a surplus of output. . . . The alarming thing about these recent developments was the way in which the colliery manager, who in practice was the keystone of the whole mining edifice, was almost completely ignored. (Heinemann, 1944, p. 151)

Conflict did occur within the Pit Production Committees, but it also occurred over them so that many became ineffective: in 1943 parliament was told that one out of every four Committees was 'almost ineffective for the purposes for which it was set up'. Later in that year a manager wrote to *The Times* identifying the fundamental conflict of class interests as the source of unavoidable weakness in the Committees:

> The miners have put forward suggestions to improve output, but they appear to do no more than improve the position of the men . . . Why should it be assumed the men's side of the Pit Production Committees should be able to improve output in any way? Their training, inclinations and very jobs depend on their obtaining the best for the electors rather than for production. (quoted in Heinemann, 1944, p. 157)

The conflicts over wages and the control of production in the coal industry are one example of a more general phenomenon. Whatever the validity of the idea that class divisions were breaking down in the upheavals of the Second World War, it cannot mean that they actually disappeared. In several respects they actually intensified, and socialist ideas gained a great hold on mass consciousness during the war. It was fuelled by the determination not to return to the unemployment of the 1920s and 1930s, which socialists associated with the inevitability of economic crises under capitalism; by the militancy that full-employment strengthened; by the changed international alignment of Britain, now in alliance with the Soviet Union; and by the fact that the state's role seemed to prove that state direction was technically feasible.

In the introduction to his book *Engineers at War, 1939–1945* Richard Croucher argues that the trade unionists in engineering were fighting a war on two fronts, against their employers and against the Axis powers. He sets out his assessment in this way:

> When reading books on the Second World War years, it is very often difficult to resist being enticed into the atmosphere of nostalgic patriotism which they evoke. Today the nation may be divided, but then things were different: everyone knew the job that had to be done. All agreed that Nazism was a terrible nightmare and that the Axis simply had to be defeated. Almost nobody, therefore, had any reservations about pulling together to win the war . . .
>
> The traditional view is not, of course, entirely mistaken: the war years *were* in many respects years of unprecedented national unity. But this is a partial one-dimensional truth which does not capture the ambiguity of working-class attitudes of the time. Just as working people were determined to defeat Nazism in the war with the Axis, they were equally determined to root it out wherever it appeared, albeit in diluted form, in the factories. Foremen and managers who were seen as 'little Hitlers' were given just as short shrift as the foreign enemy. Engineering workers, along with many others, shared an historical experience which prompted them to suspect their employers' motives in every sphere. This experience and the consciousness which was its result could not be spirited away by a declaration of war. As some contemporary commentators pointed out (generally in private), the engineers were fighting a war of their own which had begun long before September 1939. (Croucher, 1982, pp. iii–iv)

But although socialist ideas were given a great impetus during the war, the state's intervention in the labour market, and its policy towards the coal industry were far from marking the socialist system that Michael Foot and others discerned in the running of the war economy.

Direct controls on trade and finance

If the state did have extensive powers in the labour market and used them in conjunction with market forces in that respect, its relationship with the economy was neither the extreme of state direction nor the minimal form of intervention envisaged by Keynes. For many people, however, their direct experience of the state in wartime concerned not its role in the labour market, but its intervention in exchange. Direct controls over what people could buy and sell, and over their prices were extensive (although they did not completely replace free markets).

Lionel Robbins in his 1947 Marshall Lecture *The Economic Problem in Peace and War* saw extensive direct controls as the inevitable result of Keynesian policies. Keynes' hope of relying on budgetary policy was bound to break down, the government would be forced into some detailed interventions and intervention is cumulative:

> For all these reasons, the necessities of supply, the abnormal conditions of risk, the unreliability of market price as an allocation mechanism . . . and the development of severe shortage on the consumption front, it is surely clear that in a major war the fiscal theory of war economy must break down . . . The development of severe shortage takes time; some parts of the economy are more vulnerable than others. But there is a kind of snowball logic about this kind of intervention. You intervene here to fix prices, or to sustain supply, and automatically you are drawn on to prevent developments elsewhere from frustrating your original intentions. Once you are committed anywhere to this kind of policy on a large scale, it is almost inevitable that you will find yourself committed nearly everywhere else. (Robbins, 1947, p. 42)

Direct controls during the war had a twofold purpose: to hold back consumers' and firms' demand for scarce commodities, and to ensure that scarce resources were channelled into the production of items that were considered essential in one degree or another.

Spending on consumer goods, especially food, clothing, fuel was restrained and controlled through the system of rationing, under which certain items could only be bought if both money and a 'coupon' with a certain number of points were tendered. Not every item was rationed, but many staple foods, clothes, furniture and fuel were. Bread was not (until after the war) nor were fish, fresh fruit or most vegetables. At the same time spending on investment goods, plant and machinery was controlled by the necessity to obtain a licence for obtaining machinery and for all but the smallest building works. Imports were strictly controlled by the government, especially after 1940. In fact the majority of imported goods, especially food and raw materials, was bought by the government rather than private traders and 90 per cent of the latter's business was subject to licensing.

The importance of free markets for the economy's operation was severely curtailed by these controls. The forces of demand and supply could not work freely because purchasers' choices were constrained and restrained by these controls and licensing schemes. Moreover, prices, which are the key to the operation of a free market system, were also controlled in many cases. Free markets affect the allocation of resources in society through prices: if there is too much demand for a particular commodity its price rises and calls forth a greater supply. But during the war the prices of a wide range of consumer goods and food were controlled by the government. Food prices were controlled under the 1939 Emergency Powers (Defence) Act and other prices under the 1939 Prices of Goods Act and 1941 Goods and Services (Price Control) Act; by the end of the war price control covered about half of total consumers' expenditure. In the case of much food and some other items price control was linked to rationing. If excess demand was not allowed to push up prices and thereby be choked off, it had to be contained by rationing.

The state, therefore, intervened considerably in the detailed processes of exchange – buying and selling – during the war. This, combined with the state's power to direct labour was the basis for Arthur Marwick's statement quoted earlier, 'direction and control of life and labour were probably more total (and more efficient) than in any other country, save for Russia'. But the adoption of planning with direct controls was not completely at the expense of the price system. For example, we saw above that the level of wages continued to be a very important influence on the allocation of labour.

These moves in the direction of centralized planning were not adopted as a result of administrators and politicians making an abstract choice for socialism, deciding in principle that planning was superior to the market system for a wartime economy. It was brought in, bit by bit, in response to the force of events and socialism was not the result. Robbins's view of what inevitably happens with intervention policies, that they spread cumulatively, was based on what did happen during the war. It is true that Winston Churchill's coalition government that came to power in the panic of 1940 included the Labour Party's leading figures and that it was only thereafter that planning became significant. But it was not the fact that Labour was in government that produced wartime planning: rather, both were the result of the sudden realization in mid-1940 that defeat was possible, even likely, and that the war was total war embracing the whole of economic and social life.

Indeed, as Middlemas notes, Labour's leaders in government were in a relatively weak position apart from Ernest Bevin. And Bevin's strength stemmed from the force of real circumstances, the overriding importance of the shortage of labour, rather than from a swelling of the tide in favour of socialism:

> In the first stage of the Coalition, the Labour Party drew response appropriate to the context: a measure of equality in the War Cabinet (Attlee, Deputy Leader and Lord Privy Seal, and Greenwood, Minister without Portfolio, to match Chamberlain and Halifax, under Churchill) and outside, with Bevin (Minister of Labour), Morrison (Supply), Dalton (Economic Warfare) and A. V. Alexander (Admiralty); but, lower in the ranks, only sixteen junior ministers to fifty-two. Moreover, among the leaders themselves, Attlee made little impact, Morrison became enmeshed in problems of detail, and Greenwood increasingly incapacitated himself through drink. During the first stage, until Chamberlain's physical collapse in the autumn, only Bevin — a trade unionist not even yet an MP — influenced the management of the war itself.
>
> Appropriately revealing the importance of personality in political life, photographs taken of the Cabinet on VE Day in 1945 show the King flanked by Churchill and Bevin — with Sir John Anderson in attendance, and the party politicians, with the Chiefs of Staff, standing discreetly at the rear. Practically as well as symbolically, Bevin made himself the personal and political match of the Prime Minister, as no one else in wartime. According to Lord Beaverbrook, Churchill instructed the setting up of a Committee of Public Safety, if the Germans invaded in 1940, composed simply of Churchill, Bevin and himself. But Bevin's career in the War Cabinet, uninterrupted after November 1940, signifies much more: not only his capacity as Minister of Labour, but the culminating importance of Labour in wartime and its recognition by the war directorate — something which Arthur Henderson had urged, unavailingly, on Lloyd George. In the crucially important period 1940—2, before the Beveridge Report and planning for reconstruction, when defeat always seemed imminent and necessity drove Conservative ministers to decisions almost free of party ideology, Bevin was able to demand control over manpower (and fight for it against Beaverbrook's Ministry of Production), and then utilise the system of manpower budgeting, which was instituted in December 1942, to elevate his

> Ministry into the principal department of government.
> The war emergency made labour the ultimate resource. Manpower finally ranked above both finance and production, so that Bevin stood where no Cabinet Minister had previously done, rival to the Chancellor of the Exchequer himself. (Middlemas, 1979, p. 270)

Middlemas's epithet, 'manpower finally ranked above both finance and production' is suggestive in relegating finance to a subordinate position. For Keynes it was dominant. For him real demand in the economy could be constrained by the policies used to raise finance for government, taxation and compulsory saving, and, for the rest, the free operation of the economy's markets could be relied on to deliver the goods. The reality turned out to be different. Great shortages, the need to shift production on a large scale toward the satisfaction of priority needs – needs whose priority was largely agreed in a social consensus – meant that intervention had to be quite direct and extensive. The government's fiscal policy alone could not be adequate and both manpower and production (not just the former) became of more concern than finance.

Conclusion: war socialism?

The British state's direction of the economy 'for the duration' did mark a great change from its pre-war role. 'Market forces' were subordinated to administrative decrees over wide areas. However, this change was not enough to warrant the view that it was socialism in practice – either 'democratic' or 'bureaucratic' socialism.

The state's involvement in the economy, although extensive, was largely confined to the regulation of exchange and production itself remained in the hands of private capital. 'Market forces' under 'pure' capitalism generate prices which determine the amounts bought and sold, and in the labour market they generate wage rates which determine the volume of employment in each sector. During the war some prices were controlled, for many goods the amounts bought were regulated by rationing and (for raw materials and imports) licensing, wages in some industries were state determined and the volume of employment in different sectors was regulated by the manpower budget. Thus, although as we have seen, market forces were not completely superseded, the buying and selling (i.e. exchange) of many goods and of labour power was tightly constrained. But production itself was not, on the whole, in the hands of the state. Private ownership ruled throughout most of the economy and even industries whose output was most vital to the war effort – the coal mines, aircraft manufacturing and shipbuilding – were privately owned and run for profit.

The war, and the great upheaval it imposed on the lives of masses of people engendered great social mobility, or, at least, an appearance of movement. But the private ownership of capital meant that the economic basis of the old class structure was unchanged. In consequence, although patriotism amd hostility to fascism were powerfully unifying ideologies (the former helping to overcome the pre-fascist tendencies that, during the 1930s, had threatened to grow) wartime Britain's significant social divisions were class divisions. Looking at these within the economy alone we have seen their significance both in wage determination and the control of production in coal mining. The class conflicts within the engineering industry during the war are also well chronicled, and in this respect the essential character of the capitalist economy was reproduced during the war. Although state intervention in the economy during the war was exceptional in character, it was not the installation of socialism.

References

Calder, A. (1969) *The People's War*, London: Cape.

Croucher, R. (1982) *Engineers at War, 1939–1945*, London: Merlin.

Dow, J. C. R. (1964) *The Management of the British Economy*, Cambridge: Cambridge University Press.

Hancock, W. K. and Gowing, M. M. (1949) *British War Economy*, History of the Second World War, UK Civil Series, London: HMSO.

Heinemann, M. (1944) *Britain's Coal*, London: Gollancz.

Inman, P. (1957) *Labour in the Munitions Industries*, London: HMSO.

Keynes, J. M. (1936) *The General Theory of Employment, Interest and Money*, London: Macmillan.

Keynes, J. M. (1978a) *Collected Writings*, Vol. XXII, The Royal Economic Society, London: Macmillan.

Keynes, J. M. (1978b) 'How to pay for the war', in *Collected Writings*, Vol. IX, The Royal Economic Society, London: Macmillan.

Lawthor, W. (1944) 'Foreword' to M. Heinemann, *Britain's Coal*.

Marwick, A. (1974) *War and Social Change in the Twentieth Century*, London: Macmillan.

Middlemas, K. (1979) *Politics in Industrial Society: The Experience of the British System since 1911,* London: André Deutsch.
Robbins, L. (1947) *The Economic Problem in Peace and War: Some Reflections on Objectives and Mechanisms* (Marshall Lecture), London: Macmillan.
Sayers, R. S. (1956) *Financial Policy,* London: HMSO.

3

Economic intervention in the post-war economy

GRAHAME THOMPSON

Introduction

This chapter looks at the role of the state and governmental bodies in the organization of the economy over the post-Second World War period up to the mid-1970s. The discussion will mainly refer to Britain but a number of contrasts to other advanced capitalist economies are also made. The chronology of events ends with what is seen by many as a watershed in the state's involvement with the economy – the mid-1970s period. At this time a serious recession in the world economy (some would say a 'crisis') disrupted established practices and mechanisms of economic organization. In turn this interrupted and produced a reaction against what was seen as something of a secular feature of the post-Second World War period, namely growing state and governmental intervention in and regulation of domestic economies. The recession was accompanied by a fairly widespread political and ideological reaction against state involvement with economic mechanisms. This characteristic of the 'rolling back of the state' is examined more closely in chapter 9.

The chapter here concentrates upon *three* main aspects of economic intervention that have typified the post-war period, nationalization, macroeconomic management and economic corporatism. It explores their character and implications with respect to the economy and the state. In addition the chapter serves to introduce some of the factual evidence associated with the level and size of state involvement in the economy. This is the task of the following section.

The extent of state economic activity

The statistical indices most widely employed to measure government involvement in an economy are the percentage of Gross Domestic Produce (GDP), or alternatively of Gross National Product (GNP), that is attributable to the activity of governmental or state apparatuses. These product indices are measures of 'output' produced by an economy; domestic product, being that output produced by domestic residents in an economy, whether they be nationals or foreign residents, and national product, being that output attributable only to the nationals of an economy, some of which may actually be produced abroad. These two measures are not necessarily equivalent. I have defined them both here because figures 3.1, 3.2 and 3.3 express measures of the government's share of GNP and GDP respectively over various time periods and for a range of countries.

Figure 3.1 shows the trend levels of governmental activity in relationship to GNP for Britain, West Germany and the USA over the long term. The period of rapid growth has been during the twentieth century for Britain, and this growth is paralleled in West Germany and the USA. Nor are these three countries untypical of what has happened in other western capitalist economies. In figure 3.2 a more detailed picture is given of the growth of government expenditure in the three countries since 1960 — this time expressed

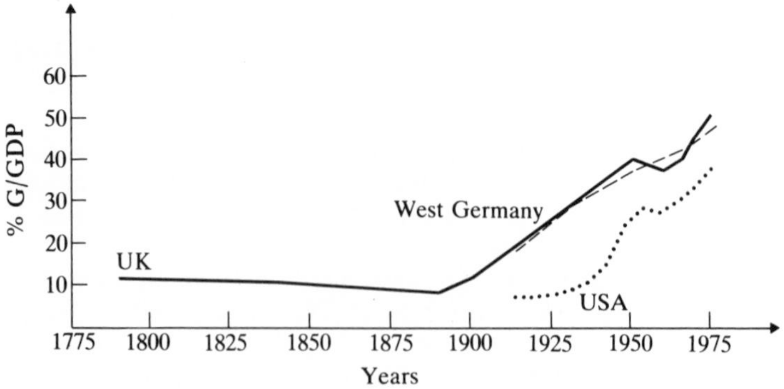

Figure 3.1 Growth of government expenditure as a percentage of GNP for UK, West Germany and USA
Source: From *Open University D323*, Figure 1, p. 9, Open University, 1979.

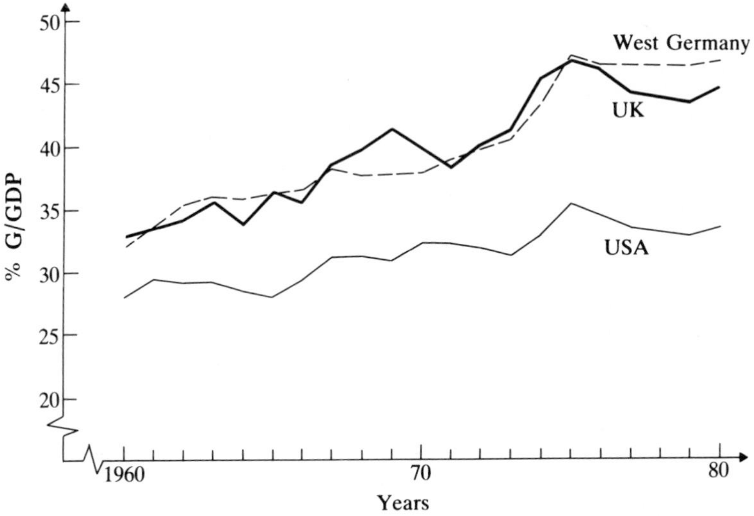

Figure 3.2 Public expenditure as a percentage of GDP for UK, West Germany and USA 1960–80
Source: OECD *Economic Outlook*, No. 32, December 1982, Paris.

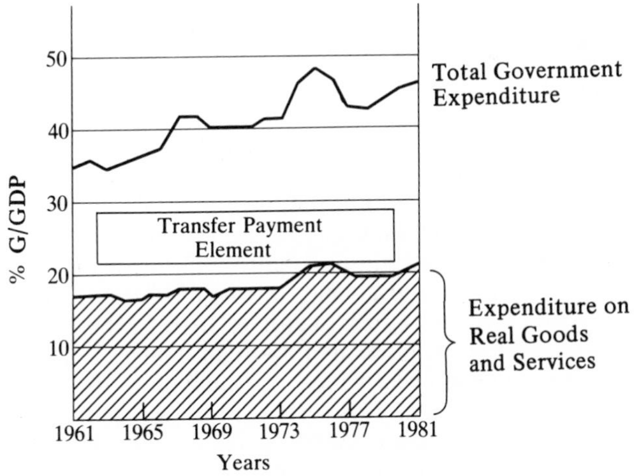

Figure 3.3 Growth of government expenditure as a percentage of GDP in UK (1961–81)
Source: *Social Trends 1982,* Chart 6.7, p. 88.

as a percentage of GDP. The peak for this was in 1975 when it reached some 47 per cent for Britain. The general trend over the whole of the period is upwards in all three economies.

An important distinction within the category of 'government expenditure' is introduced into figure 3.3 Expenditure on 'real goods and services' is differentiated from the 'transfer payment element' and you can see that the former is less than half of the total in 1981 (22 per cent as opposed to 46 per cent). In addition, it has been the transfer payment element that has grown at a faster pace over the period shown than expenditure on the real goods and services element (both in terms of their share of GDP). Transfer payments comprise items such as social security payments, unemployment benefits etc., which are transferred between different sections of the community. Economists argue that it is only the expenditure on the real goods and services element that represents the state's actual claim on economic resources. The transfer element simply represents a redistribution of income between different sections of the community, although this is carried out in the main via state interventions involving taxation and subsidies. To claim, then, that the state was usurping nearly 50 per cent of economic resources in 1981 is a mistake and an exaggeration, it is argued. The real cost of the state's economic activity was only 22 per cent of GDP, or thereabouts in 1981. Clearly these figures should be borne in mind when assessing the ideological debate about the growth of government expenditure and its supposed consequences in later chapters.

Figures 3.1, 3.2 and 3.3 show 'output' measures of state activity. We can now switch to looking at some 'input' measures. One such input is capital formation. Figure 3.4 shows the share of Gross Domestic Fixed Capital Formation for 1951 to 1982 (GDFCF) for the public sector overall and for the two sub-components of general government (local and central government less any transfers between them) and the nationalized industries ('public corporations' in figure 3.4). Of course, this figure does not show the net capital stock of the public sector relative to the private sector. It only shows that proportion of the additional gross capital formation undertaken each year which was secured by the public sector and its components. This proportion has been on a downward trend over the period shown. It seems to have peaked at well over 50 per cent in the early 1950s mainly due to general government capital formation and then slumped through to the early 1960s. The share picked up again during the 1960s and early 1970s, again mainly because of the general government activity, but since the mid-1970s it has slumped dramatically. This reflects first the Labour government's and subsequently the Tory government's determination to cut public expenditure; capital expenditure being very much easier to cut than current expenditure. What is perhaps surprising about the figures shown in the graph is the relative stability of the public corporations' investment as a percentage of total investment. This was very steady throughout the 1950s and 1960s, slumped slightly during the early 1970s but regained its position by the mid-1970s, and only began to fade away in the late 1970s and early 1980s.

A different input measure is shown in figure 3.5. This looks at the percentage of the total working population which was employed in the public sector over the period 1961–1981. The share of the public sector in total employment has risen by some 9 per cent over the period, with central government and particularly local

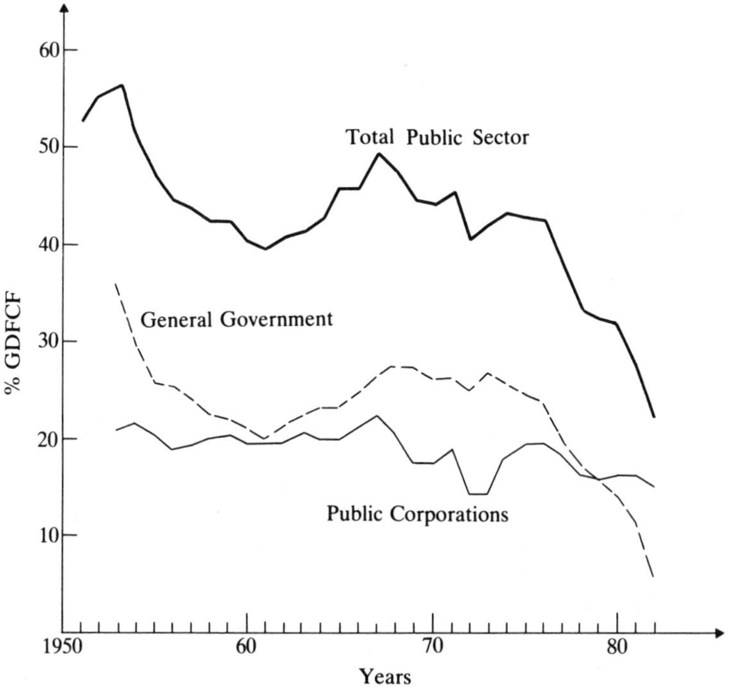

Figure 3.4 Percentage gross domestic fixed capital formation in the public sector 1951–82

Calculated from: *National Income and Expenditure*, 1962, 1972; *Economic Trends*, March 1983.

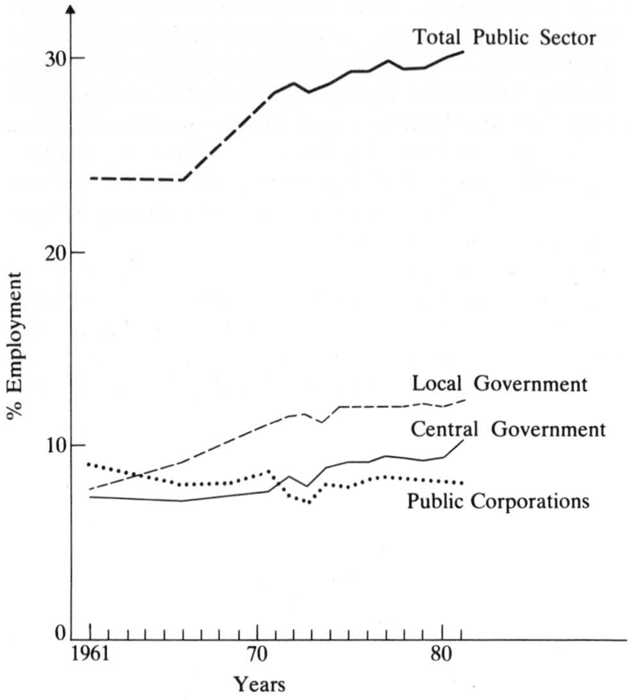

Figure 3.5 Percentage of the working population employed in the public sector 1961–81
Calculated from: *Social Trends 1983*, Table 4.7, p. 55.

government employment growth contributing to this. The percentage of the working population employed in the public corporations declined slightly over the period.

These figures have been presented and discussed here because they play an important role in debates about the appropriate levels of state involvement in the economy, about the trends over the post-war period, and because they also provide the background to arguments about the so-called 'dangers' of growing state involvement in economic relations. There can be little doubt that the state sector has increased its involvement in the economy over the periods detailed in these graphs, although this has to be said with some qualification. Whilst the state's share in investment has fallen after the high immediate post-war 'reconstruction' levels, the trend in employment share has been upwards. In addition, the share of the state sector's overall expenditure with respect to various measures of national output, or income, has been growing over this century. However, most of this growth in more recent years can probably be attributed to 'transfer payment' expenditure rather than to the state's appropriation of real economic resources. Some of the reasons for those trends and their possible consequence will be taken up in the rest of this chapter.

Nationalization

The first of our three aspects of economic intervention is the widespread nationalization in the 1945–51 period of what were termed the 'basic industries' such as coal and steel, those industries involved with energy production and distribution, and those associated with transport. This group of industries formed the 'core' to which other sectors were added in later years. (Steel, first nationalized in 1951 was denationalized in 1953 and subsequently renationalized in 1967. British Aerospace and British Shipbuilders were also added during the 1964–70 Labour administration.)

Nationalization has been very much a feature of the twentieth century in Britain and in other capitalist economies. Significant sections of heavy industry, energy provision and transport have been taken over directly by the state, creating a new set of property relations somewhat akin to those of the centrally planned economies of eastern Europe. This process formed the bedrock for the creation of a 'mixed economy' with publicly owned and operated economic activity existing alongside privately owned and operated activity. These activities, however, have not always existed in an easy relationship, the boundaries between the public and private spheres being the subject of fairly sustained and sometimes intense political and particularly ideological debate during the post-Second World War period; the struggle over steel nationalization is a case in point. However, successive Conservative governments seem to have accepted the basic framework, as laid down just after the war by the Labour administration. It was only after the traumatic events for the British economy that came to a head in the early 1970s that this seemingly stable consensus was upset. Since then the precise character and position of the nationalized industries has come under increasing public and political scrutiny, a theme returned to in chapter 9. The question posed by the rather sudden increase in the scope of public ownership is whether it marks a qualitative change in the character of the state under capitalist regimes. Does the quantitative increase in the scope of its ownership of economic resources secure a radical change in its character as a state? Whilst there was a definite transformation of the scope of property ownership during this period, its *significance* in terms of wider social and economic implications is open to dispute. It is towards a number of the features of nationalization's wider implications that the rest of this section is devoted.

Why nationalization?

In general, the motives for nationalization have been a mixture of the economic and the political, and they have varied between different nationalized industries. It will be useful to enumerate a number of these motives in terms of the arguments used to justify nationalization.

(1) A number of nationalized industries were already in municipal ownership well before they were organized under a central control body. Examples are gas and electricity supply. These were drawn into municipal regulation largely because they were 'natural monopolies' and required a high standard of public service. Their reorganization into a national framework was predicated on a perceived need for rationalization and the existence of 'economies of scale' in production and supply (declining average cost per unit as output increased).

(2) Some industries were nationalized for what were thought to be strategic reasons. This was the case with the 'communications' industries. Air transport was thought vital to the global strategic interests of the UK, mainly in relation to the 'Empire' and later the 'Commonwealth', as were cable and wireless communications. Later in the 1970s these kind of arguments were used to justify the renationalization of steel and the takeover of the aerospace industry.

(3) Under private ownership a number of industries were in a state of severe economic distress. For a variety of reasons they had become somewhat 'run down' (e.g. the railways) or in some cases were suffering badly from foreign competition (e.g. coal). Structural reorganization was thought to be necessary for post-war reconstruction, which would involve large injections of capital. It was thought that this would not, or could not, be provided by the private owners. In these cases, while there was a general ideological opposition to 'nationalization', the private owners themselves did not

resist nationalization very vigorously (other than steel in the 1950s). They were, in fact, generously compensated for what was a run-down and economically inefficient capital stock and thus actually benefited directly from nationalization. The 'capitalists' benefited in this case, which somewhat undermined their opposition.

(4) 'Commanding heights' arguments were used to justify a need to take over certain sectors of the economy or provide planners with direct instruments of control of the economy. 'Planning' as an ideology in a rather technocratic form had developed in the inter-war period and was strongly advocated during the war (chapter 2). In the post-Second World War period this was strongly represented in a somewhat elitist form — something on to which arguments about nationalization of the 'commanding heights', as well as Keynesian planning, could be quite easily grafted. This motive for nationalization raises the more political arguments that were (and still are) made to justify nationalization.

(5) Motives (1)–(3) concern the economic rationale for the public ownership of certain parts of industry involving arguments about monopoly, economies of scale, structural reorganization and rationalization of investment deficient, but strategically placed, industries. But in addition to this set of reasons, there was the general political view of nationalization as a means of fundamentally altering the system of ownership of the means of production and through that the distribution of wealth and power in the economy. This, then, constitutes a fifth motive for nationalization. It was written into the Labour Party's constitution (the famous 'Clause 4', which still exists to haunt the Labour Party). In addition, this motive has from time to time been allied closely with a view about the benefits of nationalization in terms of industrial relations. There were strong pressures on this score from some trade unions in the inter-war period, and these were consolidated during the war itself, with the growing trade union involvement in managing production decisions and the like. Ironically, perhaps, it was in the coal industry that this movement for nationalization as a means for ending 'exploitation' of the workforce and securing improvements in labour relations was most strongly felt.

Motives (1)–(5) form a complex of reasons for enacting legislation for nationalization. Some predominated for one particular industry at a particular time, while others were used in relation to other industries at different times. It is difficult to pin down any 'key' and universal motive. Roughly speaking, however, they can be grouped into two main types. On the one hand are the 'economic' reasons. Motives (1)–(3) fall strongly into this category. By and large these were associated with 'rationalistic' arguments about the need to reconstruct the industries to cope with the problems facing, or likely to face, the British economy in the context of a reorganized and growing world economy. The depression of the 1930s had thrown into sharp relief the relative decline of Britain's trading position in the world economy. A whole series of commissions and parliamentary committees had been organized during this period, and these continued during the later years of the war itself, to attempt to find solutions to the relative decline of the international competitiveness of British industry. In a sense 'nationalization' can be seen as just another attempt to provide the conditions for such a restructuring and reorganization to take place. Other pre-war attempts at the administrative reform of industrial organization had failed to halt this relative decline, and nationalization was simply a different tactic in this longer-term strategy of state involvement in the economy. Judged on this basis, then, widespread nationalization was the peculiar British response to a long-standing and fairly intractable problem of structural reorganization of a declining economy. It was something that economic liberals could grudgingly support as well as socialists. Far from providing a strategy of more widespread socialization and transformation of the economy, it fitted into a strategy of moderately radical reform under conditions of support for the existing social structure and economic and political relations. While it did alter these, in various ways and with various consequences, it did not mark a fundamental break with the previous set of state economic practices.

This type of argument obviously connects with the other main aspect of the motives referred to above. This refers to the more overtly 'political' reasons for nationalization (motives (4) and (5)). No doubt many socialists did see nationalization as a political means to the radical transformation of the social structure. For some socialists 'nationalization' was, and indeed still is, the key economic policy in the pursuit of a planned and socialistically organized society. This is in some senses a peculiarly British (and perhaps also French) notion of 'socialist transformation', at least in the context of advanced capitalist states. Nationalization, for instance, has never figured very strongly in socialist strategy or debate in the Scandinavian countries or in West Germany. However, any further assessment of this capacity of nationalization to effect a 'socialist transformation' in the context of capitalist economies requires a look at exactly how those industries that *were* nationalized were run in such economies. This is pursued in the following section.

Running the nationalized industries

The central problem that has faced the state and successive governments in their relationships with the nationalized industries is the methods of control to be implemented. Any state-run economic enterprise requires an administrative apparatus to control and organize it, whether this be in the context of a socialist or a capitalist economy. With respect to nationalization in capitalist economies, there have been two basic forms of administrative control that have developed. The industries have either been run as departments of government, or in the form of relatively autonomous public corporations in which the property rights associated with economic activity have been invested. The Post Office was run until 1976 as a department of government. It was then reconstituted into a public corporation. The public corporation has been the predominant mode of nationalized industry organization in Britain since the 1940s. Such public corporations involved some form of 'arm's length' control, whereas departments of government are subsumed under the general administrative apparatus of government. Their day-to-day running is under the direct administrative control of the government.

With the public corporation, however, a ministry of government is only a sponsoring department, which in the British context was supposed to have left the day-to-day running of the industry to a designated autonomous board and its chairman. The sponsoring department, in the guise of a minister, is only supposed to give broad and long-term objectives to the board. The board then conducts its day-to-day operations as it sees fit, in the light of these general constraints. Nationalization statutes have always been of a very broad and general character in their construction and do not provide clear statements of aims and objectives. Although the intention was that ministerial control would provide such clear and unambiguous aims and objectives, these have not always been forthcoming and have anyway been subject to fairly rapid and sometimes drastic change in the light of changing governmental complexion or economic climate. The result has been that the 'Morrisonian guidelines' approach (named after the Labour minister in the 1945–50 government who originated this mode of control) has, for the most part, been replaced by a much more 'interventionist' stance. Ministers and departments have developed systems of control based on direct intervention in the planning and decision-taking process. 'Decentralized' decision-making has progressively given way to more 'centralized' forms of control and organization. In this context it is ministerial/chairman relationships that have been crucial. The influence over, and amendment of, specific decisions with respect to nationalized industries on a more day-to-day basis has become the norm rather than the exception. Of course one might argue that in fact this is quite correct: the nationalized industries should be run in the light of close political control. They should be directly and clearly accountable to parliament and should be seen to be run in the public interest.

This kind of argument clearly raises a number of very important, though problematic issues. To start with, the nationalized industries have never been clearly accountable to parliament. They have been accountable, in one way or another to a minister, which is quite a different matter. Secondly, while it was the case that *one* of the main reasons for nationalization involved the political aspect of potential socialist advance set within a broader framework of the 'public interest' and 'democratic accountability', it is interesting to note that socialists have seldom seriously considered in detail what that public interest might involve, or exactly how any democratic accountability might be organized. In fact this raises one of the more fascinating features of the process of nationalization in the British context. Although this policy measure resounds with socialist rhetoric, in the eyes of both the left and the right of the political spectrum, socialists themselves have had very little to say about exactly how the nationalized industries should work. The precise organizational structure to be associated with, and the functioning of, an ostensibly, and to some extent overtly, socialist measure, has by and large been left to the practitioners of social administration, to civil servants and to academic economists working within the context of neo-classical economics. It is these that have designed the 'decision rules' and characteristic modes of intervention associated with the control of the nationalized industries. In this sense, then, nationalization has had little to do with 'socialism'.

One consequence of the relative lack of interest in the operational detail of how the nationalized industries might be organized is that they have by and large been integrated back into the 'market mechanism' despite their changed status in terms of property rights. It has been argued that the structural position of the nationalized industries within the context of the economy overall is that of provider of cheap and basic products and services, both to privately operated manufacturing activity and to consumers. In the case of manufacturing output, the decision rules for the nationalized industries of 'pricing equal to marginal costs' for instance (i.e. setting price equal to the net additional cost of one more unit of output rather than, say, equal to average cost of all units of output) have had the effect of providing cheap energy inputs for private industry, thereby enabling capitalist enterprises to keep their costs lower than might have otherwise been the case. In addition, the nationalized industries have been politically constrained at various times to keep their prices low because of various anti-inflation drives conducted by governments. One of the consequences of all this has been that the nationalized industries have had to be heavily subsidized from general taxation because they have been making financial losses (at least up until the late 1970s). Similarly, the argument goes, consumers have been receiving cheaper fuel, communications and transport services than would have been the case if the 'true costs' of supply had been presented to them. This again has benefited private manufacturing and service interests in that they have as a result been able to provide lower wages than might otherwise have been the case. In both cases, then, the 'state' has in effect worked the nationalized industries to the benefit of commercial and business interests. More generally, it has presided over the total reintegration of these industries into the market structure of a capitalist economy.

How are we to assess this kind of argument? Of course, a lot of it must be speculative, as there is little hard evidence on which to base some of these generalizations. Quite a complex and subtle calculation of the income redistributions occasioned by subsidies to the nationalized industries would have to be undertaken to ascertain which group benefited and which lost overall. In fact I would guess that it would be impossible to conduct such an analysis thoroughly as just too many factors would be involved. In addition, *some* of the nationalized industries have managed to make quite reasonable surpluses at various times since the war. Thus, there is no overriding reason to suppose that the benefits have gone to any particular interests.

What *is* clear, however, is that most of the nationalized industries are in a relatively vulnerable and weak position within the structure of the economy. They tend to be labour-intensive while at the same time requiring huge amounts of capital inputs. These capital inputs have not necessarily been forthcoming either in quantity or at the correct time. In addition the industries tend to be located in markets facing either fierce domestic or international competition (some of the transport industries) or with very erratic or declining demand (some of the energy industries, shipbuilding, steel production). This has meant that significant productivity increases have been difficult to achieve (something that has typified the government sector more generally). In fact, the productivity differential between the nationalized industries and privately owned manufacturing industry seems to have been growing. This is shown clearly in figure 3.6 for the period 1948 to 1968. The 1948 index number of production for the manufacturing industries, was below that of the nationalized industries, but overtook them in the late 1950s by growing at a faster rate. Given that the composition of the two groups stayed approximately the same over the period, the implication is that productivity gains, produced by one means or another in the private sector, have outstripped those of the nationalized industries.

But there has been some legitimate dispute about whether these kinds of results reflect the true comparison between the private and public sectors. Millward (1982), in an extensive international comparison, has found little difference between the managerial efficiency of the public manufacturing or service sector and the private sector, when proper account has been taken of political interventions of where like with like comparisons are made. Despite this, however, arguments to the contrary have caught the political imagination and been propelled into the public limelight.

This kind of result has led some commentators (e.g. Pryke, 1981 and 1982) to call for a radical shake-out in the nationalized industries and to make them really 'accountable to the market'. As the position stood up to the 1980s, whatever the structural characteristics of the nationalized industries, they had not been completely integrated into the capitalist market system because they could never be legally declared bankrupt. Public subsidies have prevented this. Clearly there may be very good reasons for these structural difficulties. The term 'structural' is used here to emphasize that some of the key problems are not really of the nationalized industries' own making, as many of the more conservative commentators and politicians would imply, but arise rather because of the structural characteristics that tend to typify these industries and the government intervention that has accompanied them. The problems would continue to exist to some extent even if they were privately owned. This is one of the reasons why private interests have shown a reluctance to 'take over' what might for them constitute something of a liability, when some of these industries have been offered for sale during the post-1980s 'privatization' period for nationalized industries.

But while what is termed the 'ultimate sanction of the market', i.e. bankruptcy, had not formally been a feature associated with the publicly owned industries, these had in effect been progressively

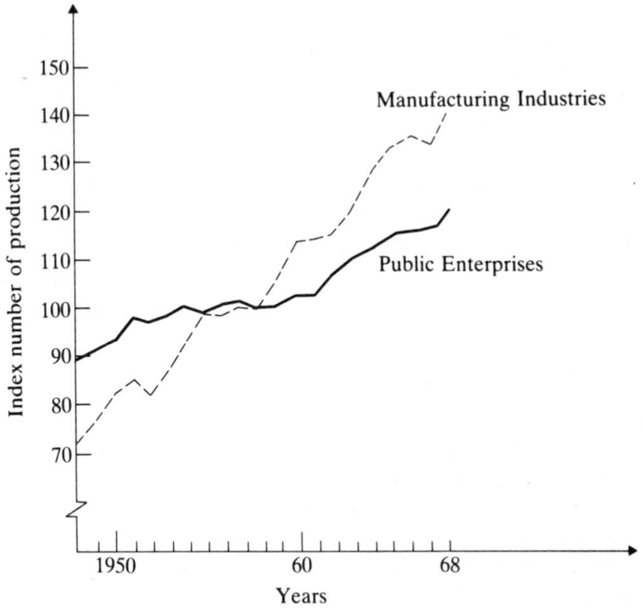

Figure 3.6 Index numbers of production (1958 = 100) *1948–68*
Source: Taken from Pryke, R. (1971) *Public Enterprise in Practice*. London: MacGibbon & Kee Table 3, p. 16.

integrated back into the market economy long before the question of their 'privatization' came onto the political agenda. Until 1967 the industries were generally required to try to 'break even' financially over a period of five years or so, although many were not in a position to meet even this minimal objective. From 1967 onwards, however, much stronger financial objectives were set up for the industries in terms of investment decision rules and rates of return to be earned on their assets. These by and large mirrored private sector practice. Profit targets were progressively introduced, borrowing objectives set, and in 1981 strict cash limits on expenditures instituted. For all intents and purposes the *attempt* has been to turn these industries into commercial businesses despite some residual social obligations that they seemed reluctantly to have to cope with.

Economic management

The second aspect of state involvement concerns what might be termed the attempt by government to regulate the general position of the economy at an 'aggregative' level. This is known as macroeconomic management of the economy, which until recently has been most closely associated with the 'Keynesian revolution' of the late 1930s. The general idea here is that the post-war period has been typified by a *new* commitment on the part of successive governments to employ state apparatuses (including the 'nationalized industries'), and organize other state economic activity, to regulate the level of aggregate demand in the economy. This would thereby prevent or restrain any tendency for cyclical behaviour of the economy to engender serious economic booms and slumps. In particular, the argument goes that post-war governments, by adopting Keynesian demand management policies, could simultaneously achieve acceptable levels of economic growth and low levels of unemployment, control inflationary pressures, and satisfactorily regulate the balance of payments. These four objectives became the *sine qua non* of the economic policy typifying the period; what is more, successive governments demonstrated a capacity to deliver these objectives, although at times with difficulty. Perhaps the centrepiece of this consensus with respect to economic regulation was the commitment to full employment in the economy. The instruments available to governments in their armoury of economic management weapons were exchange-rate policy, and budgetary, monetary and fiscal controls. These were to be set at levels and under appropriate conditions to achieve a judicious *mix* of the objectives mentioned above and, particularly, to secure a high, relatively stable level of employment.

Such a policy regime seems to have been successful during the 1950s and 1960s. Between 1952 and 1964 average unemployment stood at only 380,000. But between 1965 and 1973 it rose to 590,000; and between 1981 and 1983 it had sharply increased to reach 3.3 million. Does this seemingly spectacular growth of unemployment signal the successive abandonment of Keynesian policies, a central tenet of which has been that mass unemployment was a thing of the past? Before we confront this question it will be useful to elaborate the structure of Keynesian economic policy advice in a little more detail.

Keynesian counter-cyclical policies

The idea here is that the growth course of the economy can be managed and stabilized by 'fine tuning' the broad economic aggregates of the economy and particularly by adjusting the stance of government revenues and expenditures. If, for instance, the economy looked as though it were getting 'overheated' – i.e. that production was increasing very rapidly, inflation rates increasing, balance of payments difficulties emerging, labour markets tight, credit lines over-extended, etc. – then the role of government would be to 'dampen down' the economy by increasing taxation levels (fiscal policy) and to run up a budget surplus. This would withdraw spending power from the economy and so restrain economic activity. In addition the government might try to engender an increase in interest rates (monetary policy) so that credit were restricted; investment would then become more expensive to undertake, monetary growth would be restrained, the balance of payments might improve as higher interest rates would encourage capital inflows into the economy, inflationary pressures would ease. This policy package would help to dampen down excessive domestic economic activity.

On the other hand, if the economy were on the downward part of the business cycle the government would step in to try to stimulate economic activity. It would reverse the policy measures mentioned above by decreasing taxation levels to leave more money in the economy and increase its own expenditures autonomously by borrowing, thereby running up a budget deficit. In addition it would try to reduce interest rates to stimulate investment and consumer credit and expenditures. In extreme circumstances the government would even devalue the national currency to try to stimulate internal demand. Devaluation makes imports more expensive in terms of the national currency while it makes exports cheaper in terms of overseas currencies. This could stimulate an 'export led recovery'.

Such a menu of Keynesian policy objectives and instruments of control arose out of Keynes's own theoretical reflections of the causes and consequences of the great depression of the inter-war years, and out of his experiences of trying to organize war finance during both the First and Second World Wars (chapter 2). Keynes became convinced that the economic system did not automatically adjust itself to the best possible outcome (something assumed by 'pre-Keynesian' economists and policy-makers). Rather, it might get into a position of severe and continual depression, where there are no 'natural' economic forces that could shift it into a growing trajectory. Such a position was characterized as an underemployment equilibrium, manifesting a lack of aggregate demand. It would then be up to the government of the day to act to stimulate and increase demand in the manner suggested above. In particular this would mean a budget deficit for the state. During and after the Second World War, it is argued, this became established as a fully fledged economic policy for controlling capitalist mixed economies.

The Keynesian revolution in economic theory and practice: an assessment

In this section I raise a number of points about the role of Keynesianism as both a set of 'ideas' about the economy and as a certain 'policy regime' with respect to state management of the economy. To my mind these are two different aspects to 'Keynesianism', and they need to be analytically separated if we are properly to appreciate the exact characteristics of post-Second World War government economic policy-making and explore its limitations and consequences.

There are four broad areas of debate here.

(1) First, I look at the question as to whether a change in theoretical ideas, i.e., the Keynesian revolution, was the *main* cause of the changes in economic policy adopted by post-war governments.

(2) The second issue arises as a consequence of the first and revolves around the important changes in the constraints on the economy which allowed a Keynesian budgetary policy to emerge during the 1930s and 1940s. As we shall see this did not simply mean deficit financing of an unbalanced budget, as is often implied.

(3) The third issue concerns what the legitimate province of Keynesian policy might be. To my mind this has to be quite closely demarcated rather than interpreted as a very broad general stance towards the totality of state economic involvement.

(4) Finally, I look at the role of the changed *political* conditions during and just after the Second World War which may have contributed to the rise of Keynesianism.

Keynesian ideas and Keynesian policy

The way this issue is generally discussed is to collapse those two aspects into one. Put very simply, the argument goes that the first problem for Keynes was to convince policy makers of his *ideas* about the economy and how it worked. Once this was done policy makers then went about conducting economic policy in a different manner, and this happened to implicate the state much more actively in regulating the economy. Thus the direction of causality goes more or less directly from the battle of 'ideas' into the change in economic policy and role of the state. I want to argue for a much more complex relationship between the two aspects. Emphasis is placed on the conditions in the economy which 'encouraged' or 'allowed' Keynesian ideas, in a modified and highly contingent form, to establish themselves as the seemingly directive force of state economic management.

Thus one problem with ideas of the Keynesian revolution is that state economic policy formation is seen to be *primarily* constrained by particular economic theories of the 'ideology of policy-makers'. But to reformulate this issue, we might suggest that it is less one of what people would like to do but more one of what can be done. This is not to dismiss the role of theory altogether but it is to give theoretical ideas a rather more secondary position. It is to see that these ideas are mobilized on a quite specific terrain of already objectively constrained possibilities rather than as being *the* overarching influence on policy. If one holds to the conventional view of the 'battle of ideas' and the winning of this battle by Keynesian theory, a misconception of the character of economic policy formation arises and with it a misconception of the character of the state. The state, then, is not 'rolled forward' or 'rolled back' for that matter primarily as a result of the adoption of a particular ideology or a particular economic theory but rather by a complex of always constrained 'partial' and problematic sets of 'objective' possibilities for action and negotiation. Thus it would be more appropriate to argue that it was not the commitment or will on the part of policy-makers or the 'state' to maintain employment at historically low levels after the war that led to the *fact* of this but rather the reverse. The possibility of the fact led to the commitment or will to maintain such high levels of employment. The centrepiece of Keynesian policy was determined by conditions in the economy rather than by the commitment to a set of ideas (Tomlinson, 1981).

A very good example of this over-reliance on 'theoretical ideas' in the conduct of economic policy is the debate during the 1920s and 1930s. Here the so-called 'Treasury view' is attributed with preventing the earlier adoption of Keynesian ideas on demand management. The Treasury view was one that stressed the impossibility of adopting the proposals for relieving unemployment as detailed in the Liberal Party's pamphlet 'We Can Conquer Unemployment', with which Keynes was associated. The Treasury view is usually attributed to a theoretical commitment to 'sound finance' and to balanced budgets on the part of the Treasury. It is argued that they did not understand the necessity to 'unbalance the budget' and stimulate aggregate demand in true Keynesian fashion. But the actual arguments about this conducted at the time seemed to be of a very practical nature rather than relying upon an overtly theoretical objection (Peden, 1983).

The Keynesian/Liberal view was defeated more because (1) the Liberal proposals presumed a dramatic change in administrative apparatuses of the state to supervise the generation and implementation of projects. This would have involved a radical centralization of decision-making and administrative mechanisms of implementation. This apparatus was just not in existence at the time – the relief of unemployment being largely decentralized and dependent upon local authority initiative. The Treasury argued that this necessary centralization was not administratively or *legally* possible within the time period suggested in the proposals. Whilst this might have been exaggerated it points to the more practical and 'non-theoretical' character of the arguments at the time they were being advanced; (2) the second set of arguments made against the Liberal proposals involved questions of government expenditure. This would have had to have increased at a time when the Treasury was severely constrained in terms of government debt. The First World War was financed in Britain, not by printing money as in Germany, but by borrowing on credit from the private financial markets and institutions. This meant that there was a great deal of credit or money in the economy after the war which governments were at pains to manage without increasing inflationary pressures. To have increased government debt, which was implied as a consequence of 'unbalancing the budget' to finance any increased government expenditure, would have meant increasing interest rates and adding to inflationary pressures. The Treasury acted like a debtor – which indeed it was. In addition the fact that the world monetary system was on the Gold Standard, or fighting to get it back on to it, severely limited the autonomous conduct of a national economic policy with respect to domestic demand management.

All in all, then, the argument is that any state involvement of a Keynesian character implying *additional* government expenditure, was severely constrained in this period not so much by the wrong ideas but more by the objective conditions of the economy and of the social structure.

The emergence of a Keynesian budgetary policy

We can now look a little more closely at the changing economic conditions that enabled a Keynesian budgetary policy to emerge after the Second World War. Three of these conditions can be highlighted.

The first is the fact that Britain was no longer on the Gold Standard. This meant that a nationally orientated monetary and fiscal policy was at least possible. Thus it was feasible to think seriously for the first time about policies specifically for the 'national economy' as a whole. In fact it is probably true to say that this heralded a new conception of the 'national economy', something that involved the other conditions discussed immediately below. It also had quite profound effects on the centre of gravity with respect to the conduct of the state's economic policies. It is important to remember that the Bank of England was a private company until it was nationalized in 1947. The existence of the Gold Standard, the consequences of which were that domestic economic activity was heavily dependent on international flows of gold and reserve currencies into and out of the economy, meant that the Bank of England was in a very powerful position, since it conducted these relationships on behalf of the government. The Bank embodied the ideology of sound finance and calculated like any private financial institution in these matters. Its nationalization and the advent of a domestically orientated monetary policy put the Treasury unambiguously in charge of the conduct of economic policy generally and relegated the Bank to a secondary, though still powerful, position.

The second point concerns the *size* of the government budget. If the government is going to use its budget, i.e. run up a budget surplus or budget deficit to dampen or stimulate the economy in a Keynesian fashion, this budget must be sufficiently large for it to be manipulated in the interests of such aggregate demand management. As we have seen above state expenditures (its budget) were increasing rapidly after the First World War and, by 1945, were quite large. In addition government expenditure and finance must be under the control of the central authorities if they are to be used effectively to regulate the economy so that they are not totally offset by local or regional state fiscal policies. The reorganization of the local/central axis of administration and fiscal control immediately prior to and after the Second World War was thus an important and novel feature of state relations. This is something not confined to Britain. The USA is a case where the federal budget has grown in importance relative to state budgets and has contributed to the immense power lodged in Congress and the President, again providing one of the conditions for the conduct of a viable budgetary policy.

The final point under this heading concerns the amenability of budgetary policy to quick changes if it is to be successful. The PAYE system of income tax collection, instituted in 1946, allowed this condition to be met. This enabled variation in taxation policy to affect consumer demand quickly or enable the government to raise taxes to increase its expenditures rapidly.

The final point here concerns the construction of an elaborate system of integrated national accounts, including a balance of payments account. Before one can chart a managed course for an economy, information about its character must be available. Far from these accounts being the creation of Keynesian theory they were being developed *before* the Keynesian revolution, essentially by American economists. Their economic basis and conception is in fact pre-Keynesian in character, being predicated more upon the neo-classical approach which stresses 'factor rewards'.

When all of these conditions were combined with Keynesian economic theory during and after the Second World War a complex matrix of diversely constructed and determined conditions was generated that provided the contours in which a new approach towards budgetary policy could be thought about and made to work. But this budgetary approach was of a limited character – something I think best referred to as a 'modified Keynesian budgetary approach'.

So the argument is not that there was no change in budgetary policy during the 1950s and 1960s. There is no doubt that such a policy began to be used during this period to affect levels of employment and other economic variables in ways not heard of a decade and a half earlier. But this budgetary policy was in no way *unconditionally* subordinated to the issues of the levels of unemployment. Its specific effectiveness was contingent and circumscribed by, the underlying character and strength of the economy. When this strength began to deteriorate, so did the possibility of conducting that kind of budgetary policy.

In the first place, with the demise of the Gold Standard and the construction of an integrated set of income and expenditure accounts the balance of payments became an object of policy for the state. But when severe difficulties with the balance of payments arose, policies were pursued which resulted in decreasing employment so 'full employment' was sacrificed in the interests of the balance of payments. Indeed, preserving the dominant role of the City of London as a financial centre and with it the perceived centrality of a stable sterling currency rate has been stressed by some as the overriding objective of government policy during the post-war period (Coakley and Harris, 1983).

Secondly, the use of budgetary policy to regulate unemployment was conditional upon a generally buoyant world economy. During the 1950s and 1960s the world economy was booming. Trade was increasing and the British economy was experiencing unprecedented levels of private investment. Mathews (1968) argues that this meant the regulation of employment – 'full-employment' – could be undertaken within very narrow parameters conditioned by the buoyant nature of the economy. In a sense here there was no problem of the long-term unemployed as there had been in the 1930s. Those workers laid off during the 'stop' phase of the 'stop-go' cycle of business activity would have prospects of re-employment during the 'go' phase which were realizable. The fiscal stance of the state in this period was generally deflationary. Throughout the 1950s and 1960s there was a large current account surplus on the state's budget not a deficit. This position began to deteriorate rapidly in 1974, and such a surplus position had virtually disappeared by 1976 though the first current account deficit did not appear until 1978. Until this period of the mid-1970s budgetary policy was largely a matter of varying the level of the current account surplus rather than there being any need for serious deficit financing of a Keynesian character. There had been, however, a positive but small public sector borrowing requirement (PSBR – the difference between government receipts and expenditures which must be financed by borrowing) during this period since the public sector overall had a deficit on its investment account. But the PSBR only began to become a problem, indeed *the* problem of the economy for a while, in the mid-1970s when the surplus on the current account began to slip away rapidly.

Thirdly, the commitment to 'full employment' was also temporarily sacrificed in the interests of maintaining price stability. The 1947 inflationary upsurge led to early post-war measures to curb internal demand (Booth, 1983). Subsequent inflationary periods called forth a range of policy responses such as incomes policies and price controls (discussed in chapter 9) but by and large sustained and dramatic inflationary pressures did not emerge until well into the 1970s. Under these conditions a Keynesianism modified budgetary policy was severely tested and, it would seem, largely failed.

The limits of Keynesianism

In an interesting article on the post-war rise of demand management policy Kerry Schott argues that 'Keynesianism' should not be viewed as a single homogeneous entity (Schott, 1982). She suggests there were two (and probably three) different variants. In the first place there was what is termed the 'neo-classical synthesis', or narrow version, which restricts intervention to the level of the manipulation of aggregate demand characteristics only of the economy, much as was discussed in the opening remarks in this section of the chapter. In this the state's role consists in 'ironing out' fluctuations in the economy by alternatively trying to stimulate demand in the economy and trying to dampen it down. Sometimes, Schott argues, this also includes attempts at managing an incomes policy particularly when the Phillips curve mechanism of trade-offs between inflation and unemployment was shown to be breaking down in the latter 1960s. Generally with this variant, the state's role is one of 'intervention at a distance', trying to encourage the private sector to adapt its behaviour to the state's favoured position by altering the broad conditions under which the private sector works in the economy, and by setting the state's own stance on expenditures and the like to fit with this favoured position.

The second variant is what she terms the 'wide' version or 'socialist Keynesianism'. Such a socialist Keynesianism combines the traditional mechanisms with a much more active stance in respect of intervening directly in the private economy. This would involve active and direct financial support and assistance to industry. It might involve widespread price and income controls, the thorough planning of a greater proportion of economic activity, an active nationalization or socialization policy, etc. The longer-term objective of such a Keynesianism would presumably be to use this active role in managing the economy to promote a socialist transformation. The political form of this, it would seem, is something akin to left social democracy.

The final version is not very well developed in the article and may be a variant of the second. However it is worth isolating it since it further widens the range of policy instruments that can become attached to Keynesianism. This variant can be termed 'war Keynesianism'. Schott is concerned to argue that Keynesianism won the battle over policy changes very rapidly and was installed as a budgetary mechanism as early as 1941. This was combined with a manpower policy and an industrial policy that was geared up to wartime conditions. Laurence Harris has dealt with this wartime period in chapter 2 which gives a clear idea of what these involved. Kerry Schott argues that during this period significant advances were made by the working class in terms of living standards (admittedly under the constraint of restrictive wartime conditions) and, perhaps more important, in terms of levels of consultation and planning of production. These advances were successively whittled away after the war, she suggests.

The problem with this attempt to argue that Keynesianism comprised more or less the total package of economic policy undertaken throughout the period from 1941 to the late 1960s, and more if its socialist variant had been pursued, is that it includes just too much under what she terms the 'broad church of Keynesianism'. If Keynesianism is *everything* about economic policy then it is also *nothing* about it! What Keynesianism is must be limited to a fairly narrowly demarcated field of legitimate interventions – legitimated by Keynesian theory in this instance. It comprises a limited set of possible practices of state intervention associated in the most part with budgetary policy. It arose in a period when the *main* economic problem was unemployment, and was directed, in its 'modified form', mainly at manipulating broad economic aggregates and stances to regulate employment levels. Clearly it also had implications for the other objectives of government, particularly questions of inflation and the balance of payments (it was thought that these provided the conditions under which the fourth objective, economic growth, could take place). These other objectives were however not incompatible with this main one while the underlying conditions in the economy were favourable to economic growth. When they did become partially or temporarily incompatible during this period the main objective was generally sacrificed for the other two. But this only involved a temporary reorganization of the priority of objectives because the dynamic of the economy provided the conditions for their subsequent reordering. To expand the definition of Keynesianism much further than this seems to me to make it more or less synonymous with the welfarism of a Beveridge kind or with social democracy in general. Both of these ideas provide *other* fields of possible state intervention in the economy which should not be conflated with Keynesianism (though they *may* be combined with it at times). Under certain circumstances it is possible to install or find a 'modified Keynesianism' in areas where these other two forms are completely absent, e.g. in much of the post-war history of the USA.

The political conditions during and after the Second World War

The political and ideological conditions prevailing during and after the war were obviously crucial to the development of economic policy during the period. Schott highlights the importance of the USA in post-war reconstruction. She argues that it uses its financial power and influence to impose a particular solution on the international monetary system that was beneficial to US interests at the expense of European and other interests. In particular with respect to Britain, she argues that the USA forced sterling to become convertible too early, and that this led to a run on sterling which depleted much of the reserves of sterling built up via US loans for British reconstruction. Schott suggests that this was a deliberate policy on the part of the USA to try to weaken the British economy's ability to recover its former position in the world economy. But perhaps it is slightly too Machiavellian to suggest that the USA as a whole somehow calculated to prevent British post-war reconstruction on as sound a basis as was possible. Clearly there were a number of policies being pursued during this period probably *all* of which were designed to restabilize the international economy in one way or another. However, as with all policy combinations, quite contradictory effects result from such good intentions, some of which are quite uncalculated. It would seem an exaggeration to pit the USA *against* the rest of Europe, and Britain in particular, in this period, though no doubt with respect to specific policies those in charge of US agencies did calculate on a rather narrower brief. However, it is generally agreed that Marshall Aid, which is the name given to US assistance to Britain and Europe during this period, was primarily intended quickly and effectively to reconstruct the economies of Europe so that they could act as a bulwark against eastern European influence.

In addition to this international dimension of the post-war political conditions, the domestic situation is obviously important. In this context how did the objective of full employment become the centrepiece of government economic policy in this period?

This is an important though not uncontroversial issue. (It is extensively discussed in Tomlinson, 1983; Booth, 1983; Peden, 1983; and Glynn and Booth, 1983.) One element involved the feeling that an extension of wartime planning of manpower and the like could be pursued uncontroversially in peacetime. In particular Beveridge's position on post-war social redevelopment assumed this (Harris, 1977). But he was just one of a number of technocratic wartime administrators and scientists who saw in planning a kind of 'neutral' and essentially non-political way of pursuing socially desirable goals. Keynes was also one of these as mentioned earlier. 'Disinterested' experts were the ones to formulate policy independently of political argument. 'Problems' were constructed in very rationalist terms and were to be solved by 'technique'. Clearly something of this did get into post-war management ideology precisely through the Keynesian revolution idea. It also accompanies a certain 'foot-looseness' in politics, something that, as we have seen, does not escape the Keynesian revolution idea either if it can be extended all the way from Liberal-Conservative to socialist variants.

There is also the argument concerning the way in which popular sentiment shifted during the war from its earlier 'self-interest' stage to a more radical concern with the kind of social and economic arrangements that would ensue after the war. It is suggested that full employment was seen by the population at large as a price that would have to be paid for by an all-out effort by them during the war. Here it is likely that the sentiment was capitalized upon as an election strategy by socialist political elements. It was thus a 'constructed' political strategy which subsequently found its adequate representation via the Labour Party. Combined with the idea of planning in its technocratic form, this proved an unstoppable, but temporary, winner for the Labour Party in the 1945 election. Of course, this strategy was also one seized on by other parties. It became *the* most widely accepted economic objective of the post-war era – supported by all parties – until its demise in the late 1970s. It was when such 'technocratic planning' seemed to become unnecessary – when it was rendered unnecessary by the objective boom in the economy – that the Labour Party's hold on the strategy of full employment was undermined and became an easily accommodated objective within the political strategies of other parties. In a sense it cost little in political terms to hold to this objective, particularly when it was a 'modified budgetary policy' that seemed to be delivering the required growth and stability.

An alternative account of this period with its establishment of a fully-fledged Keynesian regime would see this as essentially a defeat for the radicalized wartime working class. Thus although there had been, and was, widespread support for radical social and economic reconstruction, the apparatuses developed during the war which could have formed the basis for this began to be dismantled more or less as soon as the war was over. This was aided by two features: (1) the way the 'capitalist class' reasserted its control over the state machinery and calculated its interests as a class; and (2) the way the Labour movement acquiesced to this largely because of its reformist leadership who lacked the will to fight for the more radical socialist form of Keynesianism or for an even more comprehensive socialist planning regime.

Economic corporatism

The third aspect of state intervention is linked to the second, but takes a slightly different focus. It concerns the issue of one particular form that the reorganized post-war state might have taken. This reorganized form is known as corporatism.

In this section of the chapter two aspects of corporatism will be developed. One concerns the more general political and social characterization of corporatism as a possible state form, and the other concerns the particular economic inflection given to it by writers of the mid-1970s. In the main the discussion will focus on the way the concept has been employed to discuss specifically economic forms of organization and intervention. The focus is on corporatism as a rather narrow representational and organizational form under which economic activity in particular is co-ordinated. Something of this can be summed up by the definition given by Panitch where he suggests corporatism is a '. . . political structure within advanced capitalism which integrates organized socio-economic producer groups through a system of representation and co-operative mutual interaction at the leadership level and mobilization and social control at the mass level' (Panitch, 1979a, p. 123). So we have here an idea of a 'political' mechanism which largely co-ordinates the various economic interest groups in the economy, but which does this more at the level of leadership and bureaucracy in an attempt 'socially' to control the mass membership of those groups. In this way the corporate mechanism is seen to deny serious democratic attempts to organize initiative and debate at the base, and to some extent to outmanoeuvre existing democratic institutions by developing parallel and largely informal means of reaching agreements. These are then more or less imposed upon the constituencies of those groups involved (Martin, 1983; Crouch, 1983).

With respect to economic activity the concept has come to play something of a central role in debates about the ways in which the trade unions in particular in Britain may have been compromised and incorporated as something akin to state agencies. They are thus seen to act in a manner of state agencies involved with social control rather than with representing the true interests of their members. Such a corporatist strategy is particularly focused around incomes policies and with respect to other mechanisms of economic negotiation and regulation such as the National Economic Development Council, 'The National Plan', The National Enterprise Board, etc. which have been supported by Labour governments in the main but also, though to a lesser extent, by Conservative governments up until the return of Margaret Thatcher's government in 1979.

This is sometimes referred to as 'tripartitism' — the two sides of industry getting together with the elected government of the day and under the umbrella of the state to work out arrangements for compromise and consensus on pressing matters of the conduct of economic activity. Potential and actual conflicts are thereby defused. This is either in the best interest of all concerned *or* to the real disadvantage of one or other of the parties involved, depending upon one's theoretical and ideological point of view.

The discussion of corporatism in these terms developed very rapidly during the late 1960s and early 1970s. In the British context the reference points for the discussion were events associated with the economy over the period roughly between 1960 to 1975. These events are summarized in box 3.1 and explanations of the functions and role of a number of organizations referred to in the subsequent discussion given.

To some extent much of the corporatism debate has now been eclipsed, as the situation of the economy has changed and the ideological attitude towards economic intervention undergone its own transformations. This is certainly so in the British context, though in many other countries where social democratic regimes are still in power, or where socialist parties are strongly represented in the national political arena, the issue is still a hotly debated one. Even in the British situation it could be argued that corporatist tendencies are still strongly represented in the policy stances of the centre and left-wing parties.

BOX 3.1	*Calendar of events pertinent to the discussion of corporatism*
Dates	*Events*
1951–64	*Conservative governments*
1962	*National Economic Development Office* (NEDO) set up – a forum for economic discussion. Its task is to gather information and make recommendations over a wide range of national economic planning matters. Attached to this are a series of *Economic Development Committees* (NEDDYs) which involve extensive consultation between ministers, trade union representatives and industrialists.
1964–70	*Labour government* under Mr Wilson.
1964	*Department of Economic Affairs* (DEA) set up under Mr George Brown with the task of developing an 'indicative' plan for economic growth. Partly a rival to the Treasury, it published its *National Plan* in October 1965. The Department was disbanded in 1970.
1965	*National Board for Prices and Incomes* (NBPI) set up to supervise prices and incomes policies. This was abolished in 1970 but replaced by the *Pay Board* and the *Price Commission* of the Conservatives in 1972 which fulfilled much the same tasks.
1966	*Industrial Reorganization Commission* (IRC) set up with the task of encouraging and later scrutinizing industrial reorganization in Britain. Reorganized in 1972 and disbanded in 1980 under Margaret Thatcher's government.
1970–4	*Conservative government* under Mr Heath.
1974–9	*Labour governments* under Mr Wilson and Mr Callaghan.

Dates	*Events*
1974–7	Social Contract period.
1974	*Advisory Conciliation and Arbitration Services* (ACAS) set up to deal with industrial disputes.
	Manpower Services Commission (MSC) set up to help develop a plan for the labour market.
	Health and Safety Regulation Act set up Health and Safety Commission. Introduced compulsory health and safety regulations in firms with wide trade union involvement.
1975	*Industry Act* set up the *National Enterprise Board* (NEB) and initiated *Planning Agreement* mechanisms.
	Employment Protection Act established rights of workers over questions of dismissal and redundancy payments whilst contract of employment was still in force.
	Sex Discrimination Act designed to reduce sexual discrimination with respect to work and other employment practices.

The 'new corporate system'

This section outlines in more precise terms what economic corporatism was argued to be in the debates of the 1970s. In doing this I draw heavily on the work of Winkler (1975 and 1976), of Panitch (1979a, 1980 and 1981) and particularly of Pahl and Winkler (1974). The summary below highlights corporatism as a political system as well as a specific approach to the management of state economic interventions in the 1960s and 1970s.

Economic corporatism is thought to be an economic system combining private ownership with state control. This differentiates it from capitalism proper in that there is a tendency away from private control. Similarly it is not straightforward socialism either, since there is a tendency away from state ownership as such. Nationalization is not on the agenda as a desired objective, only as a reluctant necessity. In fact for Pahl and Winkler in particular, this kind of corporatism marks a new stage in society's development which is different from socialism, capitalism, pluralism or syndicalism. Their approach also embraces the idea of the lack of explicit legal codification of many new economic control mechanisms that emerged in the 1960s in Britain. These were lodged in administrative edicts, enabling enactments and the like rather than being written in terms of firm legal statutes and contracts. Finally the definition involves the idea of the end of a *laissez-faire* economic order. Competition in markets gives way to regulation and 'co-operative' efforts to administer economic interaction 'politically'. Exemplar institutional instances of this kind of activity are thought to be the NEDC, or those mechanisms set up by the 1975 Industry Act, namely the NEB and 'Planning Agreements'. It is argued that these latter in effect compulsorily commit firms and enterprises to invest at the behest of the state.

This new corporatism also highlights a set of 'goals' set for society. These are organized around order, unity, nationalism and success. Let us take these one by one.

Order

This relates mainly to the 'market' which is seen (in rather classical and orthodox terms) as being 'anarchic' — liable to fluctuation and disruption. Stability must be positively created by state regulation and individual self-restraint. The workers and trade unions thus have a *duty* to exercise such self-restraint in their own bargaining situations. Co-operation and collaboration, and where necessary compulsory arbitration, are the order of the day. This duty of self-restraint also applies to commercial interests as well and their activity is hedged with price and profit constraints administered by the state.

Unity

Economic goals are best achieved through co-operative effort rather than through competition. Society itself is seen as an organic unity (hence *corpus* and corporatism). There is an underlying shared or functional interest in collective existence which unifies social interdependencies into one social body. Thus industrial conflict must be, and can be, negotiated out of the system via incomes policies, arbitration councils and the like. But industrialists also must subsume their own sectional interest in profit to this unitary interest as well.

Nationalism

This involves the elevation of the 'general national will' over and above sectional advantage and self-interest. Economic policy must be pursued to the advantage of the national economic interest. This is typified by the 'National Plan' of 1964 and by hostility to multinational corporations. It is fostered by 'Buy British' campaigns, 'Putting the nation first' and so on. 'Holding the nation to ransom' is profoundly unacceptable whether this be by industry or by labour.

Success

Corporatism is more concerned with effectiveness than with efficiency. The state sets unambiguous national goals and provides the framework for the allocation of resources. Targets and priorities are set for the privately owned economic agents and their rationale is to meet these by the best means possible. The *ends* are important and provide the criteria of success not so much the means or the relative efficiency of getting to those ends. The system is pragmatic in this sense.

The main reasons for the transformation to the corporatist economy are changes wrought in capitalism itself. The principal reason here is the 'crisis' in the economy brought about by a markedly falling aggregative economic performance. As a result of this businessmen demand a different form of intervention as does organized labour. This goes along with a growing industrial concentration, which alters market structure so much that the state can allow no 'failure' on the part of the new dominant corporations, but at the same time it can allow them no 'success' to exploit their growing monopoly position. The state must direct them for stability reasons. This stability had been undermined by the undoubted decline in profitability of corporations over the period between 1955 to 1975 (see figure 3.7). Some mechanism for compulsory investment must be found which by-passes the lack of liquidity of privately owned firms, hence the creation of such institutions as the NEB. In addition there must be assistance to

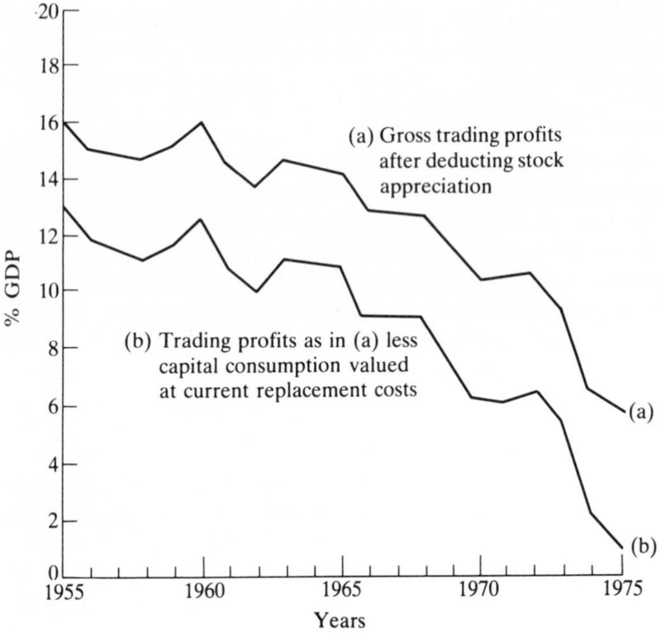

Figure 3.7 The decline in profitability
Chart 1: Company Profits as a Proportion of Gross Domestic Product.
Source: *Treasury Economic Progress Report,* May 1976.

reorganize production on lines which are more likely to lead to corporate success. This paves the way for institutions such as the IRC which can also assist with technologically advanced processes of production (See Young and Lowe, 1974, on the role of the IRC). Rapid technological development which requires significant 'pump-priming' investment is also better financed by the state than by individual private firms. Risks can then be shared. Finally all this becomes more pressing in the face of increasing international competition and stimulates attempts at a nationally organized response which would sacrifice 'free trade' ideology if necessary and introduce various forms of protectionism. All these provide reasons for the transformation of capitalism into corporatism in Pahl and Winkler's view.

This clearly has a profound impact on the state. Whilst under capitalism the state is thought to play a supportive or facilitative role in relation to the economy it now takes on a directive role. There is not only a quantitative change in its functions but also a qualitative change in these. This new directive role is not confined to situations of emergency but characterizes the normal day to day activity of the state in its capacity as leading a goal and success orientated economic system.

Still a capitalist state?

It is perhaps this last issue of the character of the new corporatist state that has occupied most of the discussion in the literature responding to the arguments of those supporting the idea of a new corporatist system. From the point of view of marxism the stress on the state's role is immediately familiar but the main proponents of this corporate state idea, Pahl and Winkler, are not marxists. They see corporatism as a system in contradistinction to the marxist insistence of capitalism *or* socialism in the modern era. A useful and interesting defence of the marxist position with respect to corporatism and its analysis of the state was provided by John Westergaard (1977).

The state, argues Westergaard, is peculiarly disembodied in the Pahl-Winkler analysis. It seems to exist 'above' or 'outside' the competing social interests that would inevitably accompany any social system. Westergaard wants to reinstall the state's class character in a familiar marxist fashion. As it stands, though, the 'corporatist state' is very much of its own making. It directs the 'collective interest' where there seems to be little scope for that collective interest to be discerned or articulated. It exists as a faceless administrative bureaucracy in the mould of a technocratic machine – autonomous in generating its own will and interests. In addition if the corporatist state is a novel form of state which represents a novel set of economic relationships, then it should be accompanied by a new and different set of mechanisms for the allocation of economic resources. Westergaard argues that the elaboration of such a set of economic mechanisms is not forthcoming from those who support the 'new corporate state' idea. As a result, he suggests that it is the traditional capitalist criterion of the 'maximization of profit' which still typifies the system. The way of allocating resources has not changed fundamentally and so neither has the character of the capitalist mode of production as an organizing set of relationships. The state is still a capitalist state, although one that has had to readjust to a changed post-war economic and social environment.

Corporatism as a means of restoring profitability

Rather than rejecting corporatism outright, however, might it not be possible to reinterpret and extend Westergaard's approach? To suggest that in fact the essential feature of economic corporatism is just this aspect of the attempt by the state to restore profitability and profit maximization as the criteria of economic decision-making? This is fundamentally the line that Leo Panitch has argued in a number of articles (Panitch, 1979a, 1980, 1981 amongst others). Panitch sees corporatism as a political strategy at the level of the capitalist economy which integrates the classes into a collaborative system in an attempt to suppress working-class industrial militancy. This form of corporatism, then, is not even-handed between the classes as it is in Pahl and Winkler's version, but involves the intention and result of undermining working-class opposition to its exploitation within capitalism. The object is to restore profitability by reducing the capacity of the working class to fight for higher wages. Panitch gives prominence, as a result of this, to incomes policies. The object of these, particularly in their more coercive forms, is to define, codify and back by state sanctions the obligations of unions to employers and the state in a way consistent with securing a stable corporatism. He writes:

> The reason that incomes policy generally lies at the heart of corporatist developments is that, far more than is the case in other fields of state intervention in the economy, it requires the direct cooperation of the trade unions. Unions might be induced to legitimate other policies, such as taxation policy, automation, manpower policy, and so on, but the administrative arm remains the state or the corporation. The union is the direct object of an incomes policy, however, for it is its behaviour the policy is designed to affect, and it must be the vehicle for administering the policy to the rank and file. And because business groups must in turn agree to at least nominal state supervision of prices, profits, and dividends, the stage is set for that cooperative behaviour between the groups themselves in the framing and administering of public policy that is the 'distinguishing trait' of liberal corporatism. Moreover, the establishment of a wage norm inevitably involves the unions in discussions of what fiscal, monetary, and even private and public investment policies are consistent with the norm. With a social democratic party in office, the prospect of union influence on decision-making and of state control over profits and prices and

thus the distribution of incomes becomes a tempting inducement to union cooperation in wage restraint. (Panitch, 1979b, pp. 135–6)

The central position accorded to incomes policies in this account, and the marginal role afforded to employers and their organizations stems from Panitch's basic Marxist position on the character of the state. The 'capital class' has control of the state so it will act in their interests when necessary. The unions, as representatives of the dominated working class will always be outmanoeuvred in this framework. The fundamental problem for the system is to rekindle the fires of accumulation and restore the conditions for profitability. Business and industrial interests will be the beneficiaries if the state can secure the co-operation of the trade unions and if the leaders of those unions can sell the 'compromise' (read 'defeat') to their members. In a way, the employers do not have to be centrally involved in this process of 'negotiation' (read 'outmanoeuvring'). The state does this on their behalf and they can hover in the wings making suitably conciliatory noises.

The corporatist debate. A summing up and an assessment

In making this assessment let us take the period of the 'Social Contract' (1974–7) which Panitch (1979b), in particular, suggests is something that clearly confirms his thesis. This Social Contract was a period of concordat between the trade unions and the Labour government. It was a bargain, struck between these two elements in the main, in which, for a series of non-statutory agreements on wage increases, the Labour government would offer a package of social and employment legislation as well as some commitments on the way the government would try to direct its macroeconomic stance towards the economy. In fact, this macro-stance was under severe constraints at the time, a point raised in relation to the discussion of Keynesianism earlier. Any agreement the government made to raise expenditure, for instance, happened at a time when such a commitment was becoming increasingly difficult to fulfil. Inflation was rising rapidly and in 1975 it reached its highest post-war peak of 24 per cent. The economy was heading for a recessionary period. Oil prices had quadrupled in 1973 and doubled again a few years later. There was a severe run on sterling in 1976 largely because of persistent balance of payments deficits during the previous three years. The PSBR reached an unprecedented £11 million in 1975. All in all, then, there is a question of whether *any* government would have been in a position to have delivered significant increases in public expenditures during this period.

What the government did deliver, however, was a series of legislative changes on social and employment conditions (detailed in box 3.1). These were clearly easier for the government to effect as they did not come up against severe 'external' constraints. It may well be the case that more could have been done in this area and that these acts were not as bold and clear-cut as it might first seem. But on a certain type of calculation it could be said that the trade unions and rank and file unionists obtained some significant political and economic advantages and concessions. ACAS was set up, and health and safety legislation enacted. The Employment Protection Act gave considerable additional protection to employees, something which they have found most useful as the recession deepened. The Sex Discrimination Act has had some effects upon women's social and employment conditions in particular (although not as much as many would like). These, along with the NEB and the *commitment* to Planning Agreements did not necessarily constitute a defeat for the trade unions or a victory for the 'state'. They opened up significant new fields of trade union and political struggle. Whether or not these were fully capitalized upon by the trade unions is another issue. In addition, the commitment by rank and file trade unionists to the wage restraint of the period was not unconnected to a widespread and genuine fear of the consequences of rapid inflation. This reached 30 per cent over some months in 1975.

This general assessment undermines the rather simplistic dual class model adopted by Panitch. It is interesting to note, for instance, that from the point of view of the intellectual right the Social Contract was also something of a disaster, but for very different reasons. Samuel Brittan argues that incomes policies of this sort are to be avoided because they give too much power to the trade unions, not that they undermine that power (Brittan, 1981). His argument is that they bring trade union leaders close to the centre of decision-making where they can have a genuine and sometimes decisive impact on economic policy. He wants to push back such 'political' decision-making in favour of straightforward 'market' mechanisms, where presumably he feels trade unionists are weaker, and where union leaders do not have *political* power.

Here we can take up another familiar argument advanced in the above discussion. This concerns a certain apprehension about the generation of new and different state institutional forms, outside the narrow confines of party and parliamentary forms. The period witnessed an innovative series of these, connected with problems of economic management. Clearly, not everything about these forms was necessarily desirable, but they did open up a range of new representational mechanisms – in some cases paralleling or overlaying existing ones. It is only when one takes an overtly legalistic conception of society, where there is a single legitimate hierarchical channel of representation leading towards the sovereign state, that these parallel and sometimes conflicting channels of representation become problematical. Again, these opened up a 'field' of representational institutions that were the site of fairly diverse and at times contradictory political and economic struggles within the state itself.

It could be argued, then, that the state is not a monolithic and homogeneous entity that represents one class interest at the expense of another, however 'sophisticated' its juggling of their interests to maintain social harmony. If we conceive the state and society more generally in this manner then the idea of 'corporatism' itself becomes highly problematical. What is it that people are being incorporated into? One implication is that there is no single and unambiguous objective or reason for state activity in the economy. To suggest that it is simply to renew the conditions for profitability or to re-establish 'profit maximization' as the criteria for economic management is surely to underestimate and misunderstand the range and complexity of economic and political calculative mechanisms that operate in any society? Furthermore it is probable that such a complex series of mechanisms leads to quite unforeseen and contradictory effects, thereby undermining the notion of any single representational channel of 'interest' or an all-pervasive objective of profit maximization associated with it. If this were the case, economic regulation of an economy would be a great deal easier than it actually is.

While it is necessary at least to question this argument about corporatism as just another form of class domination at the level of the state, it is also useful to question the argument about the supposed displacement of capitalism and the 'disembodied' character of the state. On this limited score it seems that the marxist argument is more convincing. Capitalist social relations have not been displaced by increased state intervention in the economy; they have probably been strengthened, if in an altered form. Economic corporatism as a 'system' of economic organization and regulation lacks any coherent and *distinct* criteria of resources allocation which it can claim as unique to itself as a system. There have been a number of innovations in economic management involving the state, but these hardly form an integrated system. They have operated on quite diverse criteria.

To sum up, we can say that capitalism has changed during this period, that this has involved existing state apparatuses in new ways, and that a range of novel state institutions have come into existence (and some subsequently gone out of existence — see box 3.1). What is unlikely is that this can be said to constitute a different 'corporatist system' of economic management, *or* that is simply reinforces capitalist domination over subordinate classes in the interest of renewed profitability and accumulation. Detailed arguments about the economic effects of particular state institutional and legislative changes need to be conducted to specify their diverse and ambiguous impact on a range of economic mechanisms. General theorizing about systemic state/economy relations of the 'corporatist' variety are rather a substitute for this more detailed work.

Conclusions

Do the three major forms of state economic intervention discussed in this chapter mark a radical and fundamental change in the character of capitalism and of the state which seems to have organized these? Clearly we have seen that a new and different range of economic mechanisms have been put into play during the post-war period, and initially this must have altered somewhat the characteristics of capitalism. A consolidated 'mixed economy' emerged, with a large part of it owned or directly controlled by a series of new state apparatuses. It was 'managed' in various novel ways to achieve the objectives of full employment, growth, low levels of inflation and a reasonable balance of payments position. At least, this is the conventional story. But as we have seen, two major qualifications should be made.

In the first place a number of changes are perhaps not as radical as might at first seem. There was a certain continuity in the set of problems facing the economy, and 'nationalization' and the other forms of specific legislative intervention after the war probably represented changed tactical stances towards dealing with these rather than a fundamental transformation in social objectives or relations. Secondly, it needs to be stressed that Keynesian demand management policies formed a rather more restricted set of management tools than is often argued. They were highly conditional upon changes wrought in the circumstances of the economy during the inter-war period *and* were highly contingent on the characteristics of its growth in the immediate post-Second World War period.

But what about the role of the war itself and the supposed heightened working-class consciousness that seemed to have developed during the war, and the reactions to this? The Second World War is often given a somewhat exalted status in this respect by a wide range of writers. But I have argued that this is again less clear-cut than it might at first seem. In terms of its determinations and consequences, the whole thing was something of a modest affair by any international standards. It seems to have posed no real threat to existing social arrangements, and by and large it was effectively accommodated within a moderately reforming strategy that both celebrated and exhibited continuity rather than fundamental change. By and large, this was a *shared* strategy of all those political forces involved. We should not exaggerate this, but neither should we forget that all those changes took place in the context of a capitalist domestic economy. It was capitalistic before, during, and after the war.

References

Booth, A. (1983) 'The "Keynesian Revolution" in economic policy-making', *Economic History Review,* Second Series, Vol. XXXVI, No. 1.

Brittan, S. (1981) 'Why British incomes policies have failed', in R. E. J. Chater *et al.* (eds) *Incomes Policy,* Oxford: Clarendon Press.

Coakley, J. and Harris, L. (1983) *The City of Capital*, Oxford: Basil Blackwell.

Crouch, C. (1983) 'Pluralism and the new corporatism: a rejoinder' *Political Studies,* Vol. XXXI, pp. 452–60.

Glynn, S. and Booth, A. (1983) 'Unemployment in interwar Britain: a case for re-learning the lessons of the 1930s?', *Economic History Review,* Vol. XXXVI, No. 3, August, pp. 329–48.

Harris, J. (1977) *William Beveridge – A Biography*, Oxford: Clarendon Press.

Martin, R. M. (1983) 'Pluralism and the new corporatism', *Political Studies,* Vol. XXXI, p. 86–102.

Mathews, R. C. O. (1968) 'Why has Britain had full employment since the war?' *Economic Journal*, Vol. LXXVIII, September, pp. 555–69.

Millward, R. (1982) 'Comparative performance of public and private ownership', in E. Roll (ed.) *The Mixed Economy,* London: Macmillan.

Open University (1979) D323 *Political Economy and Taxation*, Unit 3, 'The growth of the government sector', Milton Keynes: Open University Press.
Pahl, R. E. and Winkler, J. T. (1974) 'The coming corporatism', *New Society*, October.
Panitch, L. (1979a) 'The development of corporatism in liberal democracies', in P. C. Schmitter and G. Lehmbruch (eds) *Trends Towards Corporatist Intermediation*, London: Sage.
Panitch, L. (1979b) 'Socialists and the Labour Party: a reappraisal', in R. Miliband and J. Saville (eds) *The Socialist Register 1979*, London: Merlin.
Panitch, L. (1980) 'Recent theorization of corporatism: reflections on a growth industry', *British Journal of Sociology*, Vol. 31, No. 2, June, pp. 159–87.
Panitch, L. (1981) 'Trade unions and the capitalist state', *New Left Review*, No. 125, January/February, pp. 21–43.
Peden, G. C. (1983) 'Sir Richard Hopkins and the "Keynesian Revolution" in employment policy, 1929–45', *Economic History Review*, Second Series, Vol. XXXVI, No. 2, pp. 281–96.
Pryke, R. (1981) *The Nationalized Industries: Policies and Performance since 1968*, Oxford: Martin Robertson.
Pryke, R. (1982) 'The comparative performance of public and private enterprise', *Fiscal Studies*, Vol. 3, No. 2, July, pp. 68–81.
Schott, K. (1982) 'The rise of Keynesian economics: Britain 1940–1969', *Economy and Society*, Vol. 11, No. 3, August, pp. 292–316.
Tomlinson, J. (1981) 'Why was there never a "Keynesian Revolution" in economic policy?', *Economy and Society*, Vol. 10, No. 1, February, pp. 72–87.
Tomlinson, J. (1983) 'Where do economic objectives come from? The case of full-employment', *Economy and Society*, Vol. 12, No. 1, February, pp. 48–65.
Westergaard, J. (1977) 'Class inequality and "corporatism"', in A. Hunt (ed.) *Class and Class Structure*, London: Lawrence and Wishart.
Winkler, J. T. (1975) 'Law, state and economy: the Industry Act of 1975', *British Journal of Law and Society*, Winter, pp. 103–28.
Winkler, J. T. (1976) 'Corporatism', *European Journal of Sociology*, Vol. 17, No. 1, pp. 100–36.
Young, S. and Lowe, A. V. (1974) *Intervention in the Mixed Economy*, London: Croom Helm.

4

The state and health care

CHRISTOPHER POLLITT

Aspects of health care

In Britain in the 1980s, the link between 'the state' and 'health care' may seem obvious. If I were to conduct a word association experiment, asking people to say what other words the phrase 'health care' brought to mind, I would expect many people to reply 'doctors', 'hospitals' or 'nurses'. Since most doctors and nurses are employed, and most hospitals owned, by the state, the link may seem both strong and quite 'natural'. Of course, most professional medical care in Britain *is* (at the time of writing) provided by the National Health Service – a state organization. But before plunging into the details of what the state does, I want to draw attention to some of the limitations of any approach to health care which takes the NHS as its exclusive focus.

The first and most obvious point is that most health care is *not* provided by the NHS and never has been. In fact it is not provided by professional doctors and nurses at all. Many studies confirm that only a minute proportion of illness ever gets taken to a doctor. Most illnesses are treated by self-care (including self-medication), or by informal care provided by relatives and friends. It is perhaps not surprising, therefore, that most surveys show the use of non-prescription ('over the counter') drugs exceeding that of prescribed items. (Two examples of the literature here are Dunnell and Cartwright, 1972 and Wadsworth, Butterfield and Blaney, 1971).

The third point is historical. It is that, while the NHS may absorb many resources and much public attention *now*, the system only dates from 1948. British central government did not begin to provide state health insurance until Lloyd George's bill in 1911 (though central and local authorities had been active in the public health field – provision of proper sewers and clean water supplies, and so on – since the 1840s). So the role of the state has changed, and is still changing.

Fourth, there is the comparative point that the state looms larger in British health care than in most other 'advanced' countries. Whatever forces may have combined to create the NHS, they have not dominated professionally provided care to the same extent elsewhere. Table 4.1 shows for the mid-1970s the percentage of all health care spending that was paid for out of the public purse. In

TABLE 4.1 % OF TOTAL HEALTH-CARE EXPENDITURE THAT IS PUBLICLY FINANCED (1975)

United Kingdom	92.6
Sweden	91.6
Italy	91.3
West Germany	77.1
France	76.0
Canada	75.4
Netherlands	71.1
Switzerland	66.5
Australia	64.4
USA	42.7

Source: Maxwell, 1981, pp. 60–1.

what follows, therefore, you should bear in mind that in all countries most health care is still provided by self, family and friends; that everywhere there are still private doctors and hospitals (though in different countries these represent very different fractions of total professionally provided care); and that much of the role states play in direct provision is of recent historical growth.

Before proceeding further I would also ask you to consider what one might term the emotive content of health care. That is, for most people the phrase 'health care' has a positive charge. It conjures up thoughts of doing good, helping the sick, being helped oneself: health care is a 'good thing' – humanitarian, symptomatic of a caring, altruistic disposition. I want to point out that, without in any way denying that much health care *is* in practice associated with these noble emotions, there are other important aspects to the concrete activities behind the title. Thus health care is also, for various people at various times, a career, a business, an investment and a powerful means of exerting control over other individuals and groups. Let me quickly illustrate each of these for each is important to the achievement of a rounded understanding of the role of the state in this field.

Health care is clearly a *career* for many of the 61,000 doctors and 370,000 nurses who work in the NHS (1982 figures). For them it provides not only a means of 'doing good', 'healing the sick', and so on, but also an income and status. This can create significant tension: for example, when health ministries try to put more emphasis on preventive, community health measures, while most doctors regard these branches of medicine as having low status and continue to favour acute hospital-based specialisms (for example, surgery and pathology) as being better for their careers. This is actually a very common problem indeed: in Britain, despite the Department of Health and Social Security's long-standing policies in favour of community health services and the significantly nicknamed 'Cinderella services' (geriatrics, mental illness and mental handicap), the bulk of the NHS's resources continued (in the early 1980s) to go into acute hospital services. Similar problems arise in even more marked form in the less tightly government-controlled US system.

Even in a centrally planned communist state, doctors can resist being pushed down the community based educative and preventive path. Here is a description of part of the Polish health service: 'Linked to the over-emphasis on specialist, hospital medicine is the problem of over-emphasis on clinical curative medicine; prevention ("prophylaxis") is supposed to be one of the chief defining characteristics of Eastern European health systems, but in practice this counts for nothing. Clearly, doctors find clinical medicine more stimulating than routine preventative work' (Hodgson, 1982, p. 188).

Notice that, in the Polish and British cases, this is not so much a conflict between the state and the 'private sector' as one that takes place *within* the apparatus of the state, between politicians and health planners on the one hand, and a powerful professional group on the other.

Health care is also a *business*, even in a state-run system such as the NHS. Health is one of the largest central government spending programmes and is therefore constantly vulnerable to being used to some extent as an instrument in macroeconomic management. Furthermore, though 92.6 per cent of the expenditure may originate from the state (see table 4.1), much of it finds its way into the accounts of private sector companies. The NHS's annual pharmaceutical bill for England alone is about £1,000 million (1982), and the pricing agreements between the Department of Health and Social Security and the (mainly multinational) pharmaceutical companies have been sources of allegation and counter-allegation since the 1950s. To take another example, hospitals and other health facilities are usually built by private sector construction firms, for whom a big hospital contract may be of vital commercial importance. More recently, since the early 1980s, there have been the Conservative government policies in favour of the 'privatization' of hospital cleaning and laundry services. The air is thick with accusations that private contractors fail to provide an effective or efficient service or (on the other side) that when the NHS provides these services for itself they are often poorly organized and needlessly expensive.

Finally, there is the idea of health care as a medium for attempts at *social control.* To put it more directly, health care services may be provided not only (or even primarily) to offer cure, and care, but to enforce what those controlling the services see as 'good behaviour'. Barrett and Roberts illustrate this in respect of presumed gender differences:

> Working with GPs over some time it became clear to us that our respondents made certain unspoken assumptions about the 'nature' of men and women. Men, it was clear, had a primary, natural 'drive' to work to support their wife and family. Women had a similar drive to nourish and cherish their husband and family . . . Numerous cases were found, for example, of a woman performing two jobs (one inside the home and one in paid employment) and suffering from symptoms of stress, anxiety and tiredness. . . . The common response was to advise the woman to give up her job. Not only might this advice come from the GP, we also found it advocated by the psychiatrists to whom the women had been referred. Many of the women patients we interviewed had been given, and followed such advice. (Barrett and Roberts, 1978, p. 44)

Similarly, the fact that at least until 1982 one had to obtain a 'sick note' from a doctor before being 'legitimately' absent from work put the GP into a role which had 'controlling' as well as 'caring' aspects to it. To be sick was a legitimate reason for failing to discharge one's normal responsibilities to one's employer, but sickness was a matter defined by the doctor, not the sufferer. This is not to say that the medical profession necessarily sought this element of social control (indeed, many GPs have found the business of sick notes a tiresome administrative chore), but it does provide an example of the state vesting doctors with powers to determine whether or not individuals were entitled to certain non-medical benefits and privileges.

Theories of state 'intervention'

How may these various aspects of health care be organized into a coherent view of the relationship between the state and health care? Different theorists approach this task in very different ways. So here I shall examine how three major schools of political theory characterize the relationship. Then in the next section I will take a necessary, if brief, look at the history of state intervention in Britain. Thus it should at least be possible to make a start at comparing what kind of sense each body of theory makes of recent history.

Of course, this procedure will not yield final and definitive answers about which theory is 'best' (or generates most meaning). There are several reasons why theories cannot be measured simply for 'good fit' against a solid and unchanging bedrock of historical facts. For example, the theories themselves tend to 'privilege' certain kinds of 'fact' over other kinds. They partly pre-select from the infinity of possible facts by saying, in effect: 'look over here, not over there, if you want to find the most valuable/important/significant facts'. And each theory encourages its adherents to look in rather different, if often overlapping locations. So the 'facts' turn out to be 'theory impregnated', not solid bedrock at all. Nevertheless each of the three theories outlined below does proclaim the need to pay *some* attention to empirical evidence ('the facts'), and world developments certainly 'act back' on to the theorists, obliging them, from time to time, to modify, elaborate, or even surrender aspects of their ideas.

Marxist theories

Being a more over-arching, 'holistic' theory than the others, Marxism has the virtue and vulnerability of making more explicit statements about the *general* relationship between the state and the health of the community. Here is one exponent:

> A major factor in the development of modern medicine has been the tremendous expansion in the role of the state in organizing health care in most advanced capitalist countries. In Britain this process of intervention culminated in the creation of the National Health Service (NHS) which came into operation in 1948. The introduction of 'socialized medicine' is often defined simply as a gain achieved through working-class struggle. Clearly it was a gain, and its progressive elements must be defended. However, we must also recognize the implications of sickness and health for the wider functioning of the capitalist system. The labour power which the worker sells is an essential input into the capitalist production process, and hence it becomes a matter for concern for capital as a whole to maintain the physical health of the labour force at a satisfactory level. As a consequence, it is workers and potential workers who receive rather better standards of health care than do, for example, the old or the chronically sick. However, as well as being maintained at a reasonable level of physical efficiency, it is also important that the current labour force should reproduce itself by providing the next generation of workers (but not too many of them!). To the extent, therefore, that medicine has now developed areas of effective reproductive technology (obstetrics, contraception, abortion), it has become an increasingly important agent in the effective physical reproduction of labour. Finally, and probably most important, it is vital for capitalism that the labour force should be reproduced not just at the level of physical fitness and in adequate numbers, but also at an ideological level. This involves, on the one hand, socialization processes whereby individuals are prepared in a variety of ways for the part they will play in the social division of labour, and for the rewards they will receive for so doing. On the other hand, it involves the legitimation of the existing mode of social and economic organization, so that it appears in general terms to be the only right and possible way in which society could be organized. In the context of monopoly capitalism, one of the most important of these agencies of legitimation and socialization is the 'welfare state' which, of course, includes the provision of socialized medicine. (Doyal, 1979, pp. 239–40; other useful examples of Marxist, or at least Marxian, texts include Navarro, 1978, and Thunhurst, 1982).

The expectation generated by this approach, therefore, is that the state will intervene to provide socialized medicine:

(1) when forced to do so by pressure from the organized working class; and/or

(2) to maintain the labour force at a reasonable level of physical efficiency, and to enable it to reproduce itself into the next generation, so that capitalists can continue to profit from the labours of the workers; and/or
(3) as part of a range of measures designed to convince the subordinate classes that the state has their interests at heart and is therefore deserving of their allegiance, or at least acquiescence (i.e. that the state is *legitimate*).

Notice that (2) and (3) stress what I earlier termed the *social control* aspect of health care. Marxists, with their view of capitalist society as irredeemably conflictual, concentrate on this aspect, as well as on health care as a *business*. Consequently, they tend to minimize the importance of the 'humanitarian', 'caring' aspect. Those who believe that state interventions arise or are maintained by altruistic caring motives are regarded as perhaps a little naive, not 'seeing through' the surface of things to the underlying patterns.

Liberal-democratic theories

From this vantage point society is powered by the aspirations of individuals, 'competitively pursuing their own interests', and armed with the rights of the vote, free speech, free association, and so on. The state is conceptualized as relatively neutral, intervening in civil society only when a sufficient weight of individuals, acting through the channels of political representation, express the wish for the public regulation of some activity or provision of some service. Usually such interventions would only be sought when a 'harm' needed to be contained or eradicated, and where this could not be done effectively by the voluntary, 'private' effort of individuals, either singly or in free associations. Steps by a municipality to improve the general system of water supply and sewerage, and thereby diminish the probability of epidemic, would be an example of such an intervention. Other kinds of health care would not, however, require state intervention. Thus, individuals could prudently take out private health insurance and other individuals could work as 'private' doctors and nurses to provide cure and care tailored to what private individuals, or associations of such individuals (for example, in Friendly Societies) decided they were prepared to pay for. Normatively, the liberal democrat would be loath to prohibit or limit the freedom for private initiatives of this kind.

The 'New Right' are one contemporary variety of liberal democrat. In effect, they take just one limited aspect of John Stuart Mill's liberalism (anxiety about large state bureaucracies oppressing individuals' freedom) and place it at the centre of their programme. (They tend to ignore or understate other aspects of Mill's philosophy: for example, his support for feminism and for the 'developmental' advantages of extensive public participation in government). Here is one example of the New Right's view of health care:

> Not only double but multiple standards are the only way to raise standards for all – especially the poorest. The search for an equal-service NHS is vain as long as people differ, as long as they put their loved ones before abstract political dogmas, as long as incomes differ, and as long as incomes rise. The whole issue of equality has been confused with that of poverty, and both have obscured the overriding objective of liberty.
>
> Inequality in access to medical care arises from two causes. The first, emphasized by the obsessive egalitarians, is that of inequality of incomes, 'poverty', inability to pay. But that is an obstacle that can be increasingly surmounted, by methods constantly explored in Britain and other countries from the British Family Incomes Supplement, through the Australian topping-up of low incomes (to enable the poor to have a choice of health insurance and doctor or hospital), to the American idea of the voucher recommended to the Department of Health most recently by the Ambassador in Britain.
>
> The second cause of unequal access to medicine, ignored by the egalitarians, is the readiness to pay more for better medicine. Many in Britain would pay more, but the NHS stops them. Yet this is the great hope for the future; that more and more people will voluntarily spend more than the state now allows them to do. And that will be the source of the additional funds for medicine. The method of the NHS is compulsion – taxation. (Seldon, 1980, p. 145)

To summarize (and to return from the normative to the descriptive), a general reading of liberal-democratic theory would lead to expectations that state intervention in health care would have the following characteristics:

(1) they would follow manifest pressure by a broad constituency of citizens, expressed *inter alia* through the ballot box and in public debate;

(2) they would supplement, not supplant private initiatives;
(3) they would be found only, or mainly, in areas where there was some special technical difficulty in meeting individuals' wishes through their own 'voluntary' efforts, and/or where obvious harms required the application of the public and visible authority of the state. The 'emotional tone' of state intervention would therefore be that of meeting individuals' rational and legitimate interests in good health, *not* of social control.

Pluralist theories

Pluralist analysts of the state/society relation typically lay less emphasis on individuals acting as individuals than do their liberal-democratic counterparts. Pluralists put more weight on the processes resulting from many individuals combining their efforts in groups and institutions. These groups and institutions compete for power, and the apparatuses and authority of the state are extremely useful instruments in this competition. Institutions – both 'pressure groups' and state agencies – develop their own rewards for loyalty and successful service and their own sanctions against those of their members who do not conform. They may acquire a 'life of their own', in which they progressively lose touch with their original 'mission' and/or their 'rank and file' membership. Institutional policies should not, therefore, be accorded unquestioned the status of a manifestation of the majority wishes of their membership. There are dangers of bureaucratic elitism and bureaucratic ossification within both the state and private sector. Thus, modern pluralists would *not* assume that the actions of state officials are necessarily 'neutral' or even necessarily that they are responses to representations by some significant body of citizens. They would want to analyse 'who gets what, when and how', that is, the interests of the various groups and institutions involved in an issue, and the power resources they could bring to bear. But they would not assume, as Marxists frequently do, that social class was bound to be the crucial 'dividing line' underlying most issues. While acknowledging the importance of class, pluralists would recognize other bases of status and power as important: in some circumstances dominantly so. Thus, while a Marxist might attempt to link the evident power of the medical profession with the fact that top doctors are members of, or are closely associated with, the 'ruling class', pluralists would be more willing to regard professionalism as a new species of power relationship, not necessarily linked with any one class position. Pluralists would be interested in examining health care as a career, *as well as* a business, an investment and a means of social control.

What, then, are the expectations for state intervention in health care generated by contemporary pluralist theory? This is actually a very difficult question to answer. On this point pluralism is even more diversified (and less clear) than Marxism. 'It all depends on the balance of power' might be one fairly typical response, but if one then moves up one level of abstraction and asks 'And what, in general, does *that* depend on?', there is no big, single pluralist answer corresponding to the Marxists' 'balance of class forces' or 'relations of production'. In some ways it is easier to say what contemporary pluralists would *not* expect. Thus, they would:

(1) not expect to find the wishes of individual citizens determining policy. Rather they would expect the best organized, best resourced groups to be most successful at gaining the ear of 'authoritative state actors';
(2) not expect a neutral or passive 'referee-type' state. As modern states have developed large organizations concerned with regulation and the delivery of services, so pluralists would expect these bureaucracies to acquire interests and a momentum – even a 'subculture' – of their own.

More positively, one might predict, following Weber, that:

(3) there would be an element of 'copying' and 'one-upmanship' *between* states, so that, in health care as elsewhere, a state would be anxious to represent *its* interventions as at least 'up to par' with those of neighbouring states, if not 'better' than theirs.

Finally, if I were to follow the more critical wing of pluralism represented by Lindblom's writings (1977), I would add:

(4) the state provision and regulation of health care must not significantly undermine the ability of business corporations to grow and make profits (for example, the taxes necessary to finance public health must not be such as seriously to threaten the process of private capital accumulation, at least not for any extended period).

The development of state intervention

In all western states, state intervention in health care has grown enormously in the last 100 years. This is true whether one uses the criterion of ownership or that of financing or the vaguer, broader one of education and exhortation. In every country there are more officials taking (or refraining from) more actions than 100, 50 or even 25 years ago. Even the cuts of the Reagan and Thatcher administrations in the USA and Britain have not yet 'rolled back' state health care services to the point reached 30 years ago; indeed, it seems unlikely that they will.

Yet this growth of state activity has definitely not proceeded on some universal smooth upward curve of progress. Extensions of state intervention have come in bursts, at different times and taking very different forms in different countries. From time to time academics have speculated about whether there is 'convergence' among western health care systems (i.e. whether they are becoming more and more like one another), but neither in expansion nor now, when there are widespread economic pressures to contain or reduce health spending, does the similarity seem to hold except at a very general level. There are certainly problems which are common to most systems (such as the reluctance of many doctors to develop preventive and environmental health services mentioned earlier) but, in so far as the state tackles them, it does so in one way in one country and by quite a different approach in the next.

Large-scale intervention by the British state stretches back at least as far as Victorian public health legislation directed particularly at improving sanitation and thereby reducing the incidence of disease. Within the compass of this chapter, however, only a most truncated and highly selective history is possible. There are many more detailed histories available, but readers who are looking for a specifically political treatment of at least the last 50 years can be recommended to begin with Rudolf Klein's admirable introduction, *The Politics of the National Health Service.*

1911 National Insurance Act

In Germany Bismarck introduced compulsory sickness insurance in 1881 (the law came into operation in 1884). The legislation took place despite strong opposition from private insurance companies, liberal political groups (who objected to the collective compulsion) and, initially at least, large sections of industry. Britain had industrialized earlier than Germany, but had to wait another 30 years before Part 1 of the 1911 Act established compulsory health insurance for most employed manual workers between the ages of 16 and 70. Why were British governments, though prepared to act on sanitation and water supplies, slow to address the provision of medical services to individual workers?

> The first reason may have been the enduring strength of the individualist ideology in Britain: the leading political economists from Adam Smith to Ricardo continued to exert an almost decisive influence on political and economic thought throughout the nineteenth century. Secondly, and as a counterpoint to this, collectivist political movements were slower to develop in Britain than in Continental Europe. As some compensation for this theme was, thirdly, the rapid expansion of private and voluntary collective welfare (through the friendly societies, for example) which, because of their widespread coverage of the affluent workers, may have blunted the sharpness of the demand for centralized and universal schemes. Fourthly the voluntary, decentralized form of social welfare was strengthened by a legal system, which continued to accord primacy to property and reciprocity as manifested in contract law. The fifth reason combines the other four: the notion of the supremacy of the state's responsibility, the collective good, and of a bureaucracy ready to impose it on the population at large was alien to the British liberal and democratic tradition. (Ogus, 1982, p. 165).

The 1911 Act therefore represented a significant shift in both philosophy and practice. The force of 'national efficiency' and allied arguments finally broke through the tradition of individualist liberalism. Lloyd George was concerned about illness-induced poverty. Some employers were worried about the fitness of their workers. The armed forces were anxious over the health of potential conscripts. The medical profession, though habitually resistant to 'state intervention', was concerned about its economic situation. Competition among doctors contracted to Friendly Societies was pushing fee rates down. A 1905 British Medical Association report proposed a public medical service for those just above Poor Law level: from the doctors' point of view this held out the attraction of a steady income not tied to the Friendly Societies. As for the hospitals, many of them too were very short of income.

Then, in 1909, an influential minority report from the Royal Commission on the Poor Laws put forward an ambitious scheme for a unified, salaried medical service to be provided by local authorities. This would have covered both domiciliary and hospital care. The Liberal government shied away from such extensive state encroachment, particularly in the view of its likely cost to the public purse. So in 1911 Lloyd George went for a limited bill, aimed at relieving poverty among waged manual workers during sickness. The medical services provided only extended to care from GPs and the supply of a few appliances. The existing Friendly Societies became 'approved societies', to one of which an eligible worker had to belong, and which actually paid the benefits.

The debates over the social reform during the 1906–14 Liberal government included many of the ingredients that have characterized arguments over the state and health ever since. The responsibility for military defence requires the state to take an interest in the physical fitness of the general population. Furthermore, employers need a strong and reliable workforce, and have frequently been prepared to see the cost of ensuring this *socialized*, that is, transferred from their own private pockets to become a financial and organizational responsibility of the state. Equally important, in so far as the government is seen as responsible for the general social order, it comes under pressure to ensure that the benefits of modern medicine are made available to a broad spectrum of groups and classes. The fairness of the social order is called into question if only a small elite of wealthy patients have access to competent medical care, and the perceived legitimacy of government as a guarantor of social justice declines. One reason why Lloyd George had to do something in 1911 was to defend his government against the intellectual and electoral challenge of the emerging Labour Party, and – beyond parliament – the discontent of organized labour generally. Two of the most influential voices among the Royal Commission minority had been the Fabians Beatrice Webb and George Lansbury. And trade unions had put forward suggestions for model systems of social insurance. Meanwhile, 'on the streets', an unprecedented wave of major – and bitterly fought – strikes had begun, a period of unrest that was to last for more than two years and highlight the threat that unrelieved poverty posed to the social order.

It would be quite misleading, however, to characterize the Edwardian debate as being simply between mildly interventionist Liberals and more radically interventionist Fabians and socialists. There were also powerful forces opposing further state intervention. The Tories portrayed the insurance provisions of the 1911 Act as plundering the wages of working men by state-enforced deductions. Behind this overt political opposition other, arguably more formidable, opponents constrained the reforming impulses of the more interventionist wing of the Liberal government. Although some sections of the (already powerful) medical profession were prepared to accept various forms of state finance they were adamant in resisting any corresponding state *control* of medical practice.

Thus, in the end, Lloyd George pushed through a scheme which, while 'collective' and compulsory for most manual workers, still retained strong traces of liberal individualism. It was aimed at the 'dignified' working class, not the pauper (who was still left to the stringencies of the Poor Law). It was financed through individual contributions, not from general taxation. It provided for the workers themselves but not their dependents. It was administered largely by the Friendly Societies and insurance companies, not directly by a state bureaucracy.

1911–1946

During this period medical care was provided by a mixture of public (state) and private sources. The public sources (district nurse, welfare centre, panel or public assistance doctor, local authority hospitals) were financed out of general taxation and National Health Insurance contributions. But most advanced or high quality medicine was still provided by private doctors and private ('voluntary') hospitals. Many people simply could not afford these services. Others avoided the expense as long as they could – with consequent deterioration in their health – but when forced to seek help paid by drawing on personal savings or through their premium-paying membership of hospital savings schemes. A 1938 Ministry of Health Survey showed the following national picture:

Voluntary hospitals (private: supported by charitable donations and patient payments)	78,000 beds
Local authority hospitals (including public assistance – 'Poor Law' – institutions)	320,000 beds

A historian and ex-senior Ministry of Health official describes the situation in the late 1930s in these words:

> . . . no one could regard the general position as satisfactory. The voluntary side continued to look down on the local authority

> hospitals with their poor law associations, and to develop independently (they did not have to consult the local authorities before doing so); the local authorities regarded themselves as providing most of the hospital services . . . including all the long-stay care. They disliked having chronically sick patients transferred from the voluntary hospitals, and objected strongly to the lack of reciprocity over consultation about development. They also greatly resented the fact that voluntary hospitals could pick and choose whom to admit, while they as public authorities were obliged to admit anyone in need of care. (Pater, 1981, p. 16)

Note particularly Pater's last point. 'Public' institutions were obliged to admit anyone in demonstrable need (though actually this is a slight exaggeration). 'Private' ones were able to restrict their services to those who could pay and/or exhibit interesting and unusual – to the medical profession – symptoms. Thus a two-class medical system existed in which the public sector, despite its excellence in certain institutions and localities, was obliged to act as a sink for the indigent and those whose chronic ailments were of a type that defied quick curative interventions. The public sector was obliged to consult the private, but the private was free to act without returning the favour.

Thus, during the 'interlude' between 1911 and 1946 much was in fact happening. The very poor continued to suffer from limited access to health services which, even when they reached them, were often of suspect quality. Waged workers were insured for GP treatment but their dependents were not. Hospital treatment was often beyond them, or something which quickly exhausted their savings. The hospital system was poorly co-ordinated and split between the voluntary and local authority institutions. Even the middle classes found it difficult to afford care, and the financial basis of many hospitals was crumbling. Gradually the expectation was growing – even in the medical profession – that the government would have to 'do something'.

The National Health Service Act, 1946

As the Second World War progressed it became clear that, for the health services as in many other spheres of activity, there could be no post-war return to 1939. Many hospitals had been desperately under-financed during the 1930s and there had been little time or energy to spare for maintenance during the war. The wartime experience had also been positive in the sense that the government-imposed Emergency Medical Service had shown the scope and practicability of state co-ordination of the entire hospital system. Doctors could no longer claim that such co-ordination would threaten effective medical care. Furthermore there were firm proposals for a new system in circulation. Churchill's government, initially cool towards the Beveridge Report (1942), eventually responded to heavy parliamentary and popular pressure by adopting a more welcoming stance.

The final pieces to fall into place were electoral and tactical. The 1945 general election returned a Labour government with a huge parliamentary majority. It was clearly a vote for social reform, giving the cabinet high legitimacy in its purpose of implementing Beveridge and other reforms. The foundations of the welfare state were laid in a series of major statutes. The wartime coalition had produced the 1944 Education Act and the 1945 Family Allowances Act. Now the new Labour administration carried through the 1946 National Insurance Act, the 1946 National Health Service Act, and the 1948 National Assistance Act. Tactically, the Minister of Health, Aneurin Bevan, managed to divide the medical profession, getting the Royal Colleges (broadly representing the hospital doctors) largely on his side. Relations with the British Medical Association (representing GPs) became bitter, but eventually Bevan was able — though not without considerable concessions — to defuse their threats of non-participation. By the time the NHS became operational in 1948 a majority of doctors had registered to participate.

So came to pass a massive — and very expensive — extension of state intervention. It is instructive to examine the reasons government spokespersons gave for the legislation. Two main arguments were used. One was to emphasize the benefits of *effectiveness* and *efficiency* which a better co-ordinated, more reliably financed service would bring. Overall state control would ensure rationalization of a fragmented and often under-funded system (and many groups including most doctors' representative organizations, agreed that a strong dose of rationalization was needed). Thus Bevan, in the Commons second reading debate on what became the 1946 Act, stressed how the current distribution of hospital facilities had little logic to it; how many individual hospitals were too small for efficiency, and how dental, eye and hearing services were grossly inadequate. The government's case for appointed Regional Hospital Boards rather than lodging the responsibility with democratically elected local authority rested on a 'rationalization' argument. Winding up the debate for the

Labour government Charles Key pointed out that local authority areas were in many cases too small for rational hospital planning. (It seems highly probable that another important reason why local authority control was not favoured was that the medical profession had repeatedly made it clear to government that it was strongly against it.)

The other main concern of government was to *reduce inequality*. This was a more controversial aim, more strongly pursued by Aneurin Bevan than most of his successors. Bevan believed that, particularly in relation to health, 'poverty should not be a disability' and 'wealth not an advantage'. He wrote that: 'A free health service is a triumphant example of the superiority of collective action and public initiative applied to a segment of society where commercial principles are seen at their worst' (Bevan, quoted in Widgery, 1979, p. 25). Indeed, as a socialist, Bevan believed that public intervention, efficiency and equality were closely intertwined. In his biography of Bevan, Michael Foot records a conversation between the Minister of Health and Lord Moran, President of the Royal College of Physicians.

> Bevan: 'I find the efficiency of the hospitals varies enormously. How can that be put right?'
> Moran: 'You will only get one standard of excellence when every hospital has a first-class consultant staff. At present the consultants are all crowded together in the large centres of population. You've got to decentralize them.'
> Bevan: 'That's all very well, but how are you going to get a man to leave his teaching hospital and go into the periphery?' (He grinned) 'You wouldn't like it if I began to direct labour.'
> Moran: 'Oh, they'll go along if they get an interesting job and if their financial future is secured by a proper salary.'
> Bevan: (after a long pause) 'Only the State could pay those salaries. This would mean the nationalization of hospitals.'
> (Quoted in Foot, 1973, p. 132)

1946–83

There are many books describing what has happened to the NHS since its creation, but in a number of ways what has *not* happened is more striking than what has. For example:

(1) The social context of medical practice remains very much the same. The doctor is still the figure of authority to whom

patients, nurses and administrators ultimately defer. And the hospital consultant is still the top of the professional tree. 'Socialized medicine' (as Americans term our nationalized system) may have improved access for those on low incomes, but it has not noticeably spawned much 'democratic control' of the individual doctor, or any radical flattening of the hierarchy of status and income within the medical profession.

(2) The allocation of resources between different services and settings has not changed drastically either. The practice of acute medicine in hospitals continues to absorb the lion's share of NHS expenditure. There has been no flowering of preventive public health schemes, while the growth of local health centres (supposed, in 1946, to be a major feature of the new service) took 15 years really to get going. Since the late 1960s the DHSS and its successive ministers have articulated a policy of giving priority to the 'Cinderella services' (geriatrics, mental handicap and mental illness) over acute hospital care, but this has been painfully slow in taking effect as table 4.2 shows.

(3) The formal organization of the NHS, though twice 'improved', has always retained certain key features. Doctors have always been free to conduct private practice (though the precise terms and conditions for this have varied). Hospitals have always been overseen by at least two tiers (local and regional) of *appointed* members. Repeated attempts to give elected local authorities more control over the NHS have been opposed by the medical profession and successfully resisted by the DHSS and its predecessor department. GPs have retained the status of independent contractors, and have always had their own administrative machinery within the service. (The latest, 1982, reorganization has made their separateness even more marked).

(4) The wide disparities in the ill health experienced by different social classes have persisted, and in some cases grown. Making access to the NHS free and equal has not made any dramatic impact on these inequalities (Department of Health and Social Security, 1980). For example, using mortality (death) rates, it has been shown that *if* social classes 4 and 5 (partly-skilled and unskilled manual workers and their families) had enjoyed the same life expectations as social class 1 (professional workers and their families), *then* over three years 1970–72 there would have been 74,000 fewer

TABLE 4.2 HOSPITAL AND COMMUNITY HEALTH, CURRENT EXPENDITURE, ENGLAND (PERCENTAGES OF TOTAL HOSPITAL AND COMMUNITY HEALTH CURRENT EXPENDITURE)

Service	*1977/78*	*1980/81 (provisional)*
Acute	46.7	46.2
Geriatric	9.1	9.4
Obstetric	5.3	5.2
Mental illness	11.3	11.3
Mental handicap	5.2	5.1
Community health	8.4	8.8

Source: House of Commons Debates, 15 March 1983.

deaths. (This inferior life expectancy afflicts the lower social classes at all ages. In the sample referred to above, nearly 10,000 of the 'excess deaths' of class 4 and 5 were children under 15.) Note, though, that comparisons of this type have to be treated with caution because the relative sizes and make-up of the official social classes 1 to 5 have themselves changed considerably over time, so one is not comparing like with like. What is more, they do not tell us *why* there is an association between health status and social class; further evidence would be required here and it certainly should not be *assumed* that the reason is inferior available medical care. It could also have a great deal to do with life styles (chosen or otherwise) or 'other factors'.

(5) *Evaluation* of the *efficiency* and *effectiveness* of medical care has remained patchy, and largely a private matter for the medical profession. The social ownership of the NHS has not generated any major independent attempt to investigate the fundamental question of how much good medical care actually does. (Indeed, of late there has probably been more and more thorough research into this in the 'private' US system than in the NHS). The assumptions have been that doctors know best and can be left to evaluate their own performance (Klein, 1982). The basic belief still seems to be that the more medical care is available, the better the health of the community will be. Yet academic research has shown quite convincingly that, overall, medical

> care may be quite a small influence on a community's health, compared with, say, diet, sanitation, work environment and education (the best single exposition of this argument is probably to be found in McKeown, 1979).

Of course much *has* changed since 1946, and the NHS has many achievements to its credit (not least that people no longer have to worry about finding the money to get medical attention – though there may well remain other barriers to prompt care). But I have chosen to stress these broad continuities because they are both important elements in the contemporary NHS and particularly germane to an examination of the role of the state. In many respects, therefore, the 'nationalization' of health care, while greatly broadening access to medical care and crucially stabilizing its financing, did not much alter the *modus operandi* of the medical profession. They retained extensive independence, and used it to further the cause of 'scientific', hospital-based specialist medicine, and successfully to defend the mysteries of 'clinical freedom'. Only in the early 1980s, under a determinedly 'economizing' Conservative government, did a serious attempt begin to develop 'performance measures' for the NHS. And, at the time of writing, it seemed that even these would be principally directed at 'saving' public money rather than improving the *effectiveness* of medical care.

Theories of state intervention: a preliminary assessment

Looking back at the foregoing history, what insights can be gleaned by application of each of the three theories introduced in the second section? First, it may be useful to examine what kind of things government spokespersons *said*, at least during those periods when major changes in the extent of state activity were actively contemplated. In general terms two major justifications have been offered. In 1911, and particularly during the debates of 1946–8, there was a major emphasis on the state's role as a force for *rationalization*. In 1946–8, for example, the Labour government made much of the scope for rationalizing the haphazard pattern of local authority and voluntary hospitals. Again, in 1962 the then Minister of Health, Enoch Powell, introduced a Hospital Plan for England and Wales. The Plan had this same aim of systematically matching hospital resources to population needs. In 1911 'national efficiency' was a rallying cry, and most recently, under the

Conservative administrations from 1979, 'efficiency' and 'rationalization' have been the key terms used to justify a series of measures aimed at tightening control of NHS resource management and encouraging the private sector to assume a larger role in the overall provision of health care.

The second major argument used is that state intervention is necessary in the interests of *social justice*, particularly in order to lessen gross inequalities of access to medical care (e.g. by socio-economic class or geographical locality). Bevan minuted the post-war Labour cabinet with the proposition that 'We have got to achieve as nearly as possible a uniform standard of service for all.' Conservatives, too, have called on social justice as reason for state intervention: during the 1970s Conservative ministers were as active as Labour in the application of resource allocation formulae designed to reduce geographical inequalities in the distribution of NHS facilities. Overall, however, there remains a difference of emphasis — even if it is more noticeable in rhetoric than in achievement — between the Labour and Conservative Parties. With Labour 'social justice' has been closely identified with lessening *inequality*, and its pursuit has usually been seen as a matter of extending first, the range of health care facilities and services provided from within the public sector and, second, central or local government control over those services. For Conservatives, however, the concept of social justice has also included a strong commitment that both doctors and patients should have freedom of choice as between public and private sector provision. Gross inequalities are to be tackled, and the NHS should remain in being, but the simultaneous existence of a prospering private sector is seen as complementary, rather than subversive, to the nationalized service.

What is striking about governmental claims in respect both of rationalization and of lessening inequality is how little the state itself (whether in the shape of government or the NHS) has ever done to try to assess whether it is achieving its stated aims. Even in the mid-1980s the amount of reliable evidence linking the health of communities to state health care provisions is slight.

Liberal-democratic theory

How useful, then, are the three identified theoretical perspectives? As far as liberal-democratic theory is concerned, it is true that the setting-up of the NHS followed an unusually decisive electoral victory by a party responding to 'manifest pressure by a broad constituency of citizens'. Furthermore it is apparent that governments (of all hues) have *presented* their actions as responses to citizens' rational and legitimate interests in good health. But in many other respects this perspective is unilluminating. It does not explain why governments did so little as the network of 'voluntary' and local authority hospitals stumbled through the 1930s, providing a less and less adequately financed or co-ordinated service. Equally, it is difficult to understand why, in 1946, the government moved so decisively not merely to co-ordinate, rationalize and regulate the existing situation but actually to *nationalize* most hospitals. Nor can the Conservative efforts after 1979 to expand the private sector be seen as a response to popular demand – most polls have shown and continue to show very extensive support for the NHS and for *its* expansion and improvement. Finally, liberal-democratic theory seldom clarifies or anticipates those (not infrequent) occasions when the state actually *suppresses* private, voluntary initiatives. Mary McIntosh's chapter offered several examples of such attempts at social control. I will merely add two more. During the writing of this chapter a man was prosecuted by the state for (successfully) delivering his wife's baby at home instead of seeking professional help. And a company was prosecuted by the DHSS for importing drugs which it sold to the NHS at less than the manufacturer's list price (thus cutting the NHS drug bill but undermining the DHSS's pricing agreement with the big pharmaceutical companies.)

In sum, while useful in drawing attention to the occasional importance of public opinion, liberal-democratic theory leaves a great deal unexplained. It does not tell us where public opinion comes from; it does not tell us why governments sometimes take notice of it, while for long stretches of time they appear able to ignore it; it does not explain the evident power of the medical profession; and, crucially, it does not seem to provide an adequate account of the sheer extent of state intervention.

Pluralism

Pluralism, at least in its more recent forms, offers a way of tackling at least some of these *lacunae* in liberal-democratic theory:

(1) it draws attention to the institutional and group structures and processes which 'intervene' between 'raw' individualized

public opinion and the authoritative decisions and non-decisions of state officials;

(2) through these same institutional and group processes it begins to offer a theory of how attitudes may be shaped and patterned (for example, the way in which doctors' attitudes are influenced by the powerful processes of professional socialization built into medical training);

(3) by referring to (1) and (2) it gives a better account of how the state agencies may act on their own initiative: how they may develop a momentum and direction of their own which may not be at all connected to any popular mandate;

(4) it highlights (following Weber) competition *between* states.

In fact each of the four points listed are borne out by the historical evidence. Nationalizing hospitals; allocating resources more equitably between different regions; negotiating doctors' contracts; fixing drug prices – these and other activities take the state far beyond the role of 'referee'. Inter-state competition – or at least copying – has also been common. Before the 1911 National Insurance legislation, Lloyd George and his officials studied Bismark's German insurance scheme. In the 1980s, the Conservative government asked DHSS officials to 'bone up on' US Insurance schemes, in the hope that they might offer some way of increasing the flow of funds into health care without increasing general taxation.

But it is not enough for a group with demands merely to exist. Different causes are more or less easy to organize, and the state has active interests of its own (rather than being just a neutral or passive guardian of the book of rules for group bargaining). Thus one needs to consider:

(1) the resources available to the group (doctors' groups tend to find it easier to raise resources than 'client' groups);

(2) how well *organized* it is;

(3) how crucial a position it occupies in the state's performance of its essential functions (for example, it is probably not a coincidence that the state usually moves to provide direct health care for its armed services before other categories of employee, such as civil servants);

(4) whether a group can ally itself to (or even 'capture') groups *within* the state apparatus;

(5) how strongly the proposed intervention is resisted by other groups (for example, the medical profession's resistance to the salaried employment of GPs within the NHS).

Recent work within the neo-pluralist perspective has been particularly concerned with the role of professional groups, overlapping (as they often do) public and private sectors. The medical profession, with its staunch defence of its 'independence' and its freedom to practice privately, is a good example of this. Klein (1983, p. 57) says 'While it did not dominate the NHS in terms of getting what it wanted in a positive sense, it did succeed in asserting its right of veto in specific policy spheres.' 'There is one criterion by which as a profession we can measure these matters . . .' pronounced the BMA's journal early in 1948. 'It is whether these proposals do or do not bring us closer to a whole-time salaried service of the state.' This, above all, they wished to avoid. State employment thus carried a very negative image for (some) doctors. (The 'some' is important here: many doctors were already virtually full-time salaried employees of the state, for example, some of those working in the municipal hospitals, those working in the armed forces, and so on. It was the GPs that the BMA had particularly in mind.) A variety of stated reasons can be found, reiterated in editorials and public statements over a number of years preceding the 'Appointed Day' and the 1946 Act. The BMA — and other institutions representing doctors — were very suspicious of the Ministry of Health in particular and 'bureaucratic control' in general. In September 1943 the BMA had adopted 'fourteen principles' which they said should govern any post-war reorganization. Six of these will give you the flavour of medical attitudes:

3 The State should co-ordinate and augment resources, and not invade the freedom of the patient or the doctor.
4 A salaried service was against the public interest, and local authority control was rejected.
5 Free choice was basic, and any public service must preserve and encourage it.
6 The State should not invade the doctor-patient relationship.
7 The method of remuneration should reinforce free choice by being related to work done or patients accepted by the doctor.
8 Everyone should be free to consult his doctor within the service or privately.

(Pater, 1981, pp. 67–8)

The link here with liberal notions of consumer sovereignty is obvious, though the doctor-patient relationship has in practice always been a far cry from the ideal consumer going from shop to shop seeking a best buy. (The patient, unlike the ideal consumer, usually has little or no information about the nature or relative efficacy of the medical 'products' on offer; is frequently in pain or discomfort; and is commonly of lower social status than the 'seller'/doctor. Not uncommonly, also, there may be only one practicable source of professional medical help – a 'local monopoly'.) But, in the case of the medical profession, the ideology of free consumer choice is – to a possibly unique extent – married with a philosophy of professional autonomy. The practice of medicine is seen as anything but shopkeeping: rather it is presented as 'science', the precise and delicate application of which will be rapidly endangered by an intrusion from medically ignorant bureaucrats, cost-cutting public Treasuries or ambitious, mud-stirring politicians. Thus, both the patient and the doctor should be left alone, with the significant exception (principle 3) that the state is permitted a background servicing role of 'co-ordination' and the augmentation of resources (i.e. providing money).

The veto power of the medical profession helps account for many continuities in health care which are not easily explicable from within a liberal-democratic perspective. Equally the more active, autonomous role which pluralists accord to the state better 'fits' the historical evidence than the residual, responsive-rather-than-initiating role it tends to play in liberal-democratic interpretations. This initiating role is particularly obvious when there is a perceived military threat to the state's territorial integrity. Concern with military failure (Boer War) and competition with Germany were major motives for the creation of the school medical service (1907) and the introduction of National Health Insurance (1911). Then, from 1939, the Emergency Medical Service both demonstrated the administrative feasibility of state co-ordination of all hospitals and showed even more clearly the ineffectiveness and irrationality of the previous system.

Even when there is no threat of war, the state's initiatory powers remain considerable. In the mid-1970s the DHSS's implementation of a geographically-equalizing formula for NHS resource allocation resulted from an 'internal', politico-bureaucratic initiative, not from any noticeable popular pressure or direct demand from a powerful external group.

The historical record also lends support to contemporary pluralists' observations that the state is especially sensitive to the need of business corporations to make 'reasonable' profits. I cited the example of the DHSS's prosecution of the company which tried to undercut the DHSS's pricing agreement with the multinational pharmaceutical corporations. I might equally have referred to the extremely cautious and 'gentlemanly' approach the state has taken to health-threatening pollution by industry (see, for example, Attenborough, Pollitt and Porteous, 1977).

Finally, pluralism helps us understand how the state is often in conflict with itself. The processes by which different departments or public agencies, set up with different 'missions', can fail to communicate with each other, develop conflicting interests and procedures and directly clash (even in the courts) are well-documented in pluralist literature. Health care is no exception. Health authorities criticize the DHSS. Doctors criticize NHS administrators. Treasurers bewail financially 'irresponsible' doctors. Poorly-paid nurses agonize over whether to ally themselves with 'unskilled' ancilliary workers, or to cling to 'professional' status and distance themselves from strikes and public demonstrations. Few theorists of any hue now cling to the assumption that 'the state' is a monolithic, closely co-ordinated instrument acting as a unitary force.

Yet there are limitations to the pluralist approach. It usefully directs our attention to the resources and tactics of the main institutions and groups involved in any given issue but it yields no clear *overall* pattern of development. History can easily come to seem no more than a patchwork quilt of chance, opportunity, manoeuvre and decisions. Unless one is careful (some pluralist writers are, others less so) one's attention becomes so mesmerized by the surface play of events that deeper continuities may be lost sight of. Stability requires as much explanation as conflict; what is *not* on the political agenda (and why not) is frequently as significant as what is.

Marxist theories

In some ways Marxism complements pluralism. Marxism – in most of its varieties – does offer a 'big picture'. It foregrounds the underlying continuities (and correspondingly backgrounds – in my judgement sometimes too dismissively – 'surface' tactical or institutional factors). Thus the Marxist approach commonly focuses on such features as:

(1) The (almost universal) relative neglect of preventive public health programmes (aimed at seeing that the mass of people

enjoy proper diets and safe working and domestic environments) in favour of hospital-based, 'after the event' medicine. From the Marxist perspective hospital medicine does not pose the threat to capitalist employees that would be entailed by a full-blooded preventive strategy. What is more it provides profits for construction, pharmaceutical and medical equipment companies.

(2) The relative neglect of the economically less 'useful' groups, that is, the mentally handicapped and mentally ill; the elderly and (to a lesser extent) the woman at home without paid employment.
(3) The much poorer health experience of the lower, relative to the upper, classes.
(4) The ways in which receipt of state-controlled medical care may be made dependent on 'good behaviour', for example, on a record of contributions as an employee or on residence or even respectful behaviour towards the doctor.
(5) The absence of any real democratic control of the type of level of health services provided.
(6) The continued – privileged and state-protected – existence of private medical care in Britain, the USA and every other western capitalist state. Access to this type of care is principally determined by patient wealth rather than patient need.

These are powerful insights which help us find some pattern in the 'potted history' given earlier. It came as no surprise to Marxists that, faced with a business slump, Mrs Thatcher's administration firmly shelved a major report on health inequalities between the social classes (Department of Health and Social Security, 1980); imposed tight financial controls on the NHS; and encouraged the growth of private medicine. Furthermore, the emphasis some marxists put on health and welfare services as *legitimators* of the political system (and, by implication, capitalism *in toto*) is a useful clue to understanding bipartisan support for the basic concept of the NHS. As one (non-Marxist) writer succinctly puts it: 'whatever its strengths or weaknesses as an instrument for delivering health care, the NHS has . . . been a successful instrument for delivering support for the political system' (Klein, 1983, p. 146).

But there remain problems with Marxist theory. Without getting down to a more pluralistic analysis of the relative resources of various groups and institutions, it is difficult for Marxists to account for the vastly different development of the state's role in, say, the

USA and Britain (both, after all, advanced capitalist societies). And, once the analysis does reach down to this more detailed, empirical level, tensions begin to arise between the predominantly *structural* cast of Marxist philosophy and a quite different mode of explanation based on the more or less reasoned *actions* of individuals. Or, to be more specific, why should the big breakthrough in state intervention in the USA be in favour of the *old* (Medicare) and *poor* (Medicaid) where in Britain, West Germany and elsewhere the adult (male) worker has tended to be the first target for state assistance? If one of the main purposes of health care is to supply the capitalists with a fit workforce why, even in the NHS, are almost two-thirds of all beds in acute hospitals occupied by persons over 60? Or again, where do state bureaucracies, rolling along under their own momentum, spreading an ever broader and more intricate web of regulations, inspections and inducements fit into the Marxist account? Are they (as Marx himself seemed to indicate in one of his writings) merely an instrument of the ruling class? If so, why do such bureaucracies frequently breed reforms which are resisted — not always successfully — by that class? And what of the medical profession: can its evident strength be fully explained by an analysis founded on categories of social *class*, or do Weberian notions of *status* and *expertise* as independent sources of power have to be given more room? How, finally, is 'health' to be produced anyway? Is there either the weight of evidence and/or a basis of democratic support for a radical move away from a hospital-and-doctor dominated concept of health care towards something else? The Marxist critiques (for they are self-consciously critiques as well as theoretical analyses of the status quo) are far from having a well worked-out and agreed position on these important questions. Their boldness and explicitly normative intent make Marxist approaches both exciting — by offering a sweeping integration of many diverse events — and disappointing — because, infuriatingly, however the pieces of the puzzle are arranged, there are always some which do not quite seem to fit (not to speak of the awkwardly shaped new pieces which are thrown up by the passage of time). There is also a tendency — not, perhaps, with the best marxist authors, but with many others — to treat most individuals most of the time almost as residual features of analysis, as units pushed and pulled and moulded and duped by larger forces beyond their control or understanding. This tendency has ethical as well as analytical difficulties associated with it.

So which theory is best? The experienced reader will already know better than to expect an unqualified, one-line answer. Even *Which?,* the Consumer Association magazine, is rarely *that* straightforward, and it deals with relatively simple things like cars and washing machines, not the societies which give rise to them. But I will try to be as brief and direct as my own degree of understanding – and my educator's conscience about over-simplification – permit.

None of these theories seems wholly satisfactory, but pluralism and Marxism – in their contemporary, more flexible and critical forms – perform better than does liberal-democratic theory. As between neo-pluralism and neo-Marxism (the use of 'neo' here marks off the contemporary variants from their generally more simple and mechanistic ancestors) it is very difficult to decide. There is some evidence of recent convergence and overlap between exponents of the two schools of thought. Nevertheless, the theoretical and methodological foundations of the two approaches remain genuinely different, and the writing within each tends to *read* quite distinctively. So there is a real choice to be made here: it is not really acceptable to believe that the rival theories can eventually just be fudged together.

There is one final point about theory – choice. I do not believe anyone can hope to 'choose' between Marxist, pluralist or liberal-democratic theories *in general* on the basis of a study of 75 years of health policies in one country. What you have in this chapter is a sort of test drive over a short section of track. Before you actually buy a particular vehicle you would be well advised (1) to look under the bonnet and (2) to think hard about what kind of journeys you are expecting to make. Under the bonnet you may want to ask questions about the basic components. Is the Marxist concept of class really sufficiently 'heavy duty' to bear the explanatory load of the whole social engine? The pluralist battery of 'individual preferences' and 'organizational resources', seems to send a good current surging round the system, but where exactly does the battery get *its* energy from and what determines variations in the strengths of the current? As for journeys, is a Marxist Rolls, sweeping over huge landscapes of social change, quite the most appropriate means for analyzing specific contemporary decisions?

My own interests have lain in the direction of finding reasons for specific differences of belief and practice between different places and different times. For this purpose, I have sometimes found the Marxist vehicle too ambitious – it flashes past, blurring the detail at which I wish to pause. Furthermore, I am uneasy at the attempt many Marxists make to categorize individuals' beliefs and perceptions as *caused* by their socio-economic circumstances, and to assume a high degree of predictability in the actions and reactions of groups and state agencies. Unless one 'cheats' (for example, by generous applications of hindsight) the historical record seems to me to contain much more uncertainty than many Marxists will allow. Thus pluralism's relative indeterminacy may appear as virtue, instead of vice. On the other hand, I remain unhappy about the lack of interest many pluralists display in the detailed processes by which beliefs and perceptions grow and change. Both Marxist *and* pluralist scholars seem to have over-concentrated on crude motivational factors and under-concentrated on *cognitive* biases in their searches for explanations. The diagrams of *both* types of engine are seriously incomplete.

Thus the usefulness of a given theory is inevitably connected to the questions for which answers are sought. And one's choice of questions, in turn, is not arbitrary, but extensively influenced by the questioner's circumstances. Comparing theories should be a rigorous, painstaking process, but this is very different from pretending that it can be wholly 'objective' and value-free.

References

Attenborough, K., Pollitt, C. and Porteous, A. (1977) *Pollution: The Professionals and the Public*, Milton Keynes: Open University Press.

Barrett, M. and Roberts, H. (1978) 'Doctors and their patients: the social control of women in general practice', chapter 3 in C. Smart and B. Smart (eds) *Women, Sexuality and Social Control*, London: Routledge and Kegan Paul.

Chaplin, N. W. (ed.) (1982) *Health Care in the United Kingdom: Its Organization and Management,* London: Kluwer Medical.

Department of Health and Social Security (1980) *Inequalities in Health: Report of a Research Working Group, London.*

Doyal, L. (1979) 'A matter of life and death' in J. Irvine, I. Miles and J. Evans (eds) *Demystifying Social Statistics,* London: Pluto.

Dunnell, K. and Cartwright, A. (1972) *Medicine Takers, Hoarders and Prescribers,* London: Routledge and Kegan Paul.

Eyer, J. (1977) 'Prosperity as a cause of death', *International Journal of Health Services*, Vol. 7, No. 1, pp. 125–50.

Foot, M. (1973) *Aneurin Bevan* (two volumes), London: Poynter-Davis.

Hay, J. R. (1975) *The Origins of the Liberal Welfare Reforms, 1906–1914,* London: Macmillan.

Hodgson, C. R. (1982) 'Health policy and health service reforms in the 1970s' in J. Woodall (ed.) *Politics in Contemporary Poland,* London: Francis Pinter.

Hood, C. (1976) *The Limits to Administration*, London: Wiley.

Jessop, B. (1982) *The Capitalist State: Marxist Theories and Methods,* Oxford: Martin Robertson.

Klein, R. (1982) 'Performance, evaluation and the NHS: a case study in conceptual perplexity and organizational complexity', *Public Administration,* Vol. 60, No. 4, Winter, pp. 385–407.

Klein, R. (1983) *The Politics of the National Health Service,* London: Longman.

Lindblom, C. E. (1977) *Politics and Markets*, New York: Basic Books.

Maxwell, R. J. (1981) *Health and Wealth: An International Study of Health Care Spending,* Lexington: Lexington Books.

McKeown, T. (1979) *The Role of Medicine: Dream, Mirage or Nemesis?* (second edition), Oxford: Basil Blackwell.

Navarro, V. (1978) *Class Struggle, the State and Medicine: An Historical and Contemporary Analysis of the Medical Sector in Great Britain,* New York: Prodist.

Ogus, A. I. (1982) 'Great Britain' in P. A. Kohler, H. F. Zacher and M. Partington (eds) *The Evolution of Social Insurance 1881–1981: Studies of Germany, France, Great Britain, Austria and Switzerland*, London: Francis Pinter.

Pater, J. E. (1981) *The Making of the National Health Service,* London: King Edward's Hospital Fund for London.

Seldon, A. (1980) 'Why the NHS must fail' in A. Seldon (ed.) *The Litmus Papers: A National Health Dis-service*, London: Centre for Policy Studies.

Thunhurst, C. (1982) *It Makes You Sick: The Politics of the NHS,* London: Pluto.

Wadsworth, M. E. J., Butterfield, W. J. H. and Blaney, R. (1971) *Health and Sickness: The Choice of Treatment*, London: Tavistock.

Widgery, D. (1979) *Health in Danger,* London: Macmillan.

Wildavsky, A. (1979) *Speaking Truth to Power: The Art and Craft of Policy Analysis*, Boston: Little Brown.

5

'A conspiracy of silence'. The state, the BBC and public opinion in the formative years of British broadcasting, 1922–39

PADDY SCANNELL

Introduction

In his influential study of the British political system, Keith Middlemas has argued that the modern state has made the avoidance of class conflict its first priority (Middlemas, 1979, p. 18). The extension of the vote to the whole adult population in 1918 and 1928 was a strategic compromise made to avoid political breakdown and to rescue the authority of the state. The masses should be enfranchised, it was argued at the time, 'as a substitute for riot, revolution and the rifle. We grant the suffrage in order that we may learn in an orderly and civilised manner what the people who are governed want' (Lord Russell, 1917. Quoted in Schwarz, 1980/1, p. 141). In this context the monitoring and management of public opinion became crucial. It was *the* means through which the poison of extremism might be drawn from the body politic and the poultice of national consensus applied, based on respect for the parliamentary process and the rule of law.

In the inter-war period decisive investments were made in state propaganda. The techniques of crisis management, censorship and the routine control of official information to the media were systematically developed and applied by central government (cf. Middlemas, 1979, pp. 337–70). These discreet skills were backed up by a series of acts curtailing civil liberties, which culminated in the Incitement to Disaffection Act (1934) and the Public Order Act of 1936 (Anderson, 1983). This legislation tightened the Official Secrets Act (1911), enhanced the powers of government over organized labour, isolated the police from the trade union movement and underlined its role as a repressive force to be used by the state against extremist politics. The management of opinion meant patrolling the boundaries of legitimate political activity and expression, and the tactical use of force — direct and indirect, open and covert — to maintain the coherence of the system and to paper over the cracks in the consensus.

The formation of the National Council for Civil Liberties (1934) is one indication of alarm at the concentration of power in central government and the erosion of civic freedoms. The 1930s was a period when British society was politicized at every level, and in sharply conflicting ways, against a national government which, bereft of leadership and direction, seemed to have no effective solutions to any of the major economic and political problems which it faced. On unemployment and housing, on fascism in Britain and Europe, on peace or war there was silence, in public, from official quarters and an irrepressible surge of activity in the private sphere across all classes. The organization of public platforms, campaigns and marches; the explosion of social documentation concerned to get at the facts and make them known; the politicization of the intellectuals and the radicalization of the arts — all point towards the widespread mobilization of voluble opinion publics busily trying to fill the vacuum at the heart of public life created by the official control of information and the stifling of public discussion on the urgent matters of the time.

This general crisis of information came to a head at the time of the Munich Agreement (1938). It prompted a major internal debate in the BBC about the extent to which broadcasting had been drawn by the government into a conspiracy of silence on Chamberlain's policy of appeasement towards Mussolini and Hitler. In the accounts that follow I trace the largely hidden processes that had, by the late 1930s, effectively put broadcasting in pawn to the state, compromising its constitutional independence and its political responsibilities to the general public.

Putting the nation together

The BBC began life in 1922 as little more than an administrative convenience imposed by the Post Office on the British radio industry. It was a commercial monopoly in the private sector serving manufacturing interests and much resented by other competing interests, especially the newspaper industry. But the power of radio was recognized in official reports (Sykes, 1923;

Crawford 1925) which recommended that the state should retain regulatory control over such a potential influence on public opinion and national life. At the end of 1926 the Charter and Licence transformed the British Broadcasting Company into the British Broadcasting Corporation, situated in the public sector under the auspices of the state. As it crossed the political threshold the BBC became, in Middlemas's phrase, a governing institution in the cultural sphere, committed to co-operation with the state, sharing its assumptions about what constituted the national interest and accepting aims similar to those laid down by the government (Middlemas, 1979, pp. 372—5). The co-option of the BBC into the state domain proceeded, on the whole, with the support of the broadcasters until it began to dawn on them that they were being manipulated in ways that compromised their credibility and good faith with the audience. The Corporation's own sense of responsibility to the general public always set the limit to the processes of incorporation, and tested, in moments of crisis its own interpretation of the national interest as defined by government and the public interest as understood by itself.

As it became a centralized, national institution the fundamental task undertaken by the BBC, in its programme service, was the mediation of class differences in the name of a higher national unity. The presentation of royalty was the cornerstone of this work. Broadcasting revitalized the power of monarchy as a transcending value, above the levels of social and political strife, which united all classes. Not only through its coverage of spectacular ritual occasions (cf. Chaney, 1983), but especially through its Christmas Day broadcasts, the BBC forged a new intimacy between monarchy, people and nation. From the very beginning Christmas on radio was a celebration of 'Home, Hearth and Happiness' (*Radio Times*, 18 December 1924), and the royal broadcasts, which began in 1932 after years of diplomacy by Reith, seemed to put a crowning seal on the work of binding the nation together by giving it a particular form and content: the family audience, the royal family, the nation as family.

That sense of community was expressed in many other ways (Cardiff and Scannell, 1984). Broadcasting transformed a whole range of public events and ceremonies from being isolated events available only to particular publics into moments available to all. They took their place in the BBC's calendar as broadcast events that recurred regularly, year in year out, at the appropriate time. Civic and sacred ceremonies, sporting and cultural events, entered into a new relationship with each other, woven together in the

National Programme (commenced 1930) as idioms of national identity, moments in which the whole of society was able, for the first time, to participate. They became unobtrusive landmarks which organized and defined the unfolding of the broadcasting year.

Innocently and naturally the BBC appeared to be uniting both ends of the great chain of social being, connecting individuals to the centres of national life, town to countryside, region to region. By the end of the 1930s what had begun to mesh together in the National Programme was the orderly regulation of social time in relation to the social space within which listening took place. Favourite programmes like *Bandwagon*, *In Town Tonight* or *Monday Night at Seven* recurred as predictable enjoyments in the humdrum routines of daily life (cf. Frith, 1983), which were punctuated by that calendar of public events with their ebb and flow of seasonal climaxes. The blending together of these different temporal rhythms seemed to anchor and structure daily life, affirming the pleasures of privacy while joining it in new but familiar fashion to the great public world beyond the immediate environment of home and neighbourhood. Their combination in a single national channel worked to stabilize the national culture, the British way of life, as a knowable settled organic community.

The BBC constructed its national audience as individual family members with private pleasures and public duties as citizen-members of a democracy. The nation-state was distinguished from government and its values and loyalties, embodied in the monarchy, transcended politics. Both were presumed to be in harmony with each other. If government and people had a common interest in the effective and efficient working of democracy, then this secured the preservation and continuity of the nation in unity. Together they constituted the national interest in which rulers and ruled had a common stake. That was the ideal but, as we shall see, it never worked like that in practice. The BBC had a high degree of freedom and considerable success in constructing the nation-as-family by rigorously excluding class and politics from the programmes that mediated such values. But it encountered all sorts of difficulties in those regions of programming which addressed themselves to the pressure points in society, to the moments of crisis, to social, economic and political divisions within the nation.

The containment of news and controversy, 1922–7

From the very beginning political broadcasting was a site of struggle between the government and broadcasters in which the stake was public opinion. It has been said that the BBC was founded on the denial of politics (Curran and Seaton, 1981, pp. 135–58) but for this John Reith – its first Managing Director (1923–6) and Director General (1927–38) – was not to blame. He had a clear conception of broadcasting as an instrument of democratic enlightenment. He was well aware that the new listening public was also a newly enfranchised mass electorate, and he believed that only a fraction of it had any real knowledge of the vital political issues of the day (Reith, 1924, pp. 18–19). Radio might remedy that deficiency by claiming a right of access for its listeners to accurate impartial information, and to reasoned argument and discussion of public affairs. Thus listeners would be able to exercise their political rights at the ballot box in a rational manner. The basis of a healthy democracy was a properly informed public opinion.

Traditionally it had been argued that this was the role of the press which should act, ideally, as an indispensable link between the state and the public. By the late nineteenth century it was comfortably assumed, by legitimate opinion, that an independent press, as the Fourth Estate, was the watchdog of government, the guardian of the public interest and the informant and guide of public opinion (Boyce, 1978, for a critical analysis of this concept). But by the 1920s such reassuring assumptions had been eroded. The prestige and incorruptability of newspapers were tarnished by Lloyd George's antics in press manipulation and his purchase of the *Daily Chronicle* in 1918 as a means to advance his own political causes. At the same time charges were laid against the relentless triviality of the new popular journalism, its sensationalism and its irresponsible evasion of the serious issues of the day (Angell, 1926). Against this Reith wanted radio to foster the growth of an independent and informed public opinion, but the BBC had no control over the two key areas of political broadcasting – news and 'controversial' talks and discussions.

Even before the BBC was formally constituted in 1922, the Post Office had made a deal with the press who feared that an independent radio news service would seriously damage their industry. The Post Office had a vested interest in the press agencies who serviced the newspapers, since it drew substantial annual income from their use of Post Office wires. So to protect the newspapers, press agencies and its own interests the Post Office told the Company-to-be that it could not set up its own news service but must pay for a daily news summary supplied to it by the press agencies. This could not be broadcast before seven in the evening so as not to compete with the evening newspapers. These pre-emptive arrangements delayed for many years the full development of broadcast journalism.

The licence granted to the Company by the Post Office in 1922 required it to broadcast programmes to the reasonable satisfaction of the Postmaster-General. What did this mean? It soon became clear that it did not include dabbling in the clash of ideas and opinions. In March 1923 an objection was raised in the House of Commons to a BBC talk about a strike in the London building trade transmitted while the strike was continuing. The Postmaster-General declared that it was undesirable for broadcasting to be used to allow speculation on controversial matters and that he had made his view known to the BBC. A month or so later the Sykes Committee attempted, on several occasions, to unravel the implications of the Postmaster-General's response. Some members took the view that it amounted to a censorship far more severe than was exercised during the war by the Censor's Department. If not censorship it amounted to an influence, perhaps intimidation. Post Office officials made plain their view that the BBC could be as controversial as it liked, but if it took no notice of directives from the Postmaster-General it was most unlikely to have its licence to broadcast renewed. In its report the Committee stated that it was undesirable to rule out everything that was controversial, but the Postmaster-General should retain the final say on what was acceptable.

Reith pressed hard in the next two years to extend the political scope of broadcasting. He wanted to relay the public speeches of leading politicians and eminent men on matters of topical concern. He wanted to develop studio debates between representatives of the political parties in and out of election times. There was a sustained though short-lived campaign to broadcast daily the proceedings of the House of Commons (eventually realized some 50 years later). Reith promised absolute impartiality in the presentation of political issues and equal scope for all sides of the question, if only the Post Office would grant permission. But in nearly every case the Post Office refused, after long delays and masterly inactivity.

In 1925 Reith presented the Crawford Committee with a sharp protest at the present situation in which the BBC was cramped and restricted in its immense potential 'for helping towards the aim of a more enlightened democracy'. Radio would offer no support either to those who saw progress in terms of profit for the few and deprivation for the many, or to those who believed in the doctrines of revolution. But the present rigorous censorship without regard to the eminence of the talker was hampering the development of one of the most important aspects of broadcasting (Reith, 1925, pp. 4–6).

By now Reith had come to believe that the only way to establish the independence of the BBC, both from commercial interests and the restraints imposed by the state, was to change its constitution. Opinion in the Post Office was tending in the same direction and, after the Crawford Report recommended that broadcasting be run as a public corporation, Post Office officials began to prepare the documents for the changeover.

In the meantime though, there was a major crisis for the government and the BBC. The general strike of May 1926 is discussed below. Here it is worth noting that this crisis came at the most awkward possible time for the Company. The BBC had no option but to act with great caution while its own future was in the balance. In the aftermath of the strike Reith tried once more to pry open the oyster of controversy. Surely now, having proved its responsibility during the emergency, the BBC might be allowed, with all due regard to impartiality and balance, to present the discussion of issues of national concern. To no avail. But worse than that, to Reith's great anger, the draft proposals from the Post Office for the new constitution included a clause explicitly forbidding the BBC to broadcast programmes on controversial matters. On top of that the financial arrangements were even more punitive than the present ones.

The Charter and Licence (1926) confirmed the power of the state over broadcasting. The Corporation was to be granted no licence to broadcast in perpetuity. It received a ten year licence subject to review and renewal. The process whereby government-appointed committees periodically examine the activities of broadcasting to date and make recommendations about its future conduct and development, continues through to today. Its effect is perpetually to remind the broadcasters that their continued existence depends on their good conduct as approved by the state. The new arrangements not only confirmed Post Office control over administrative, technical and financial matters; they included clauses that gave the government the right to veto *any* material to be broadcast by the BBC if it so chose. But the BBC was not to be controlled directly by the government. The Postmaster-General made it clear that while he was answerable in the House of Commons on matters relating to broadcasting, in practice he expected the Board of Governors (whose members were all government appointees), as the supreme body representing the new Corporation, to be responsible and accountable for all day-to-day matters concerning its broadcasting activities.

Reith fought hard to reverse the ban on controversy and the financial arrangements for the Corporation-to-be, but without success. The Postmaster-General simply went behind his back and pressurized the elderly Lord Clarendon, Chairman-designate of the new Board of Governors, into signing the Charter and Licence with the simple threat of sign or be sacked (Briggs, 1961, pp. 356–7; cf. Stuart, 1975, pp. 140–1). When, in the House of Commons, the Postmaster-General declared that the Charter and Licence were agreed documents, accepted by the BBC, Reith's indignation knew no bounds. On the matters of finance and controversy the Charter was the denial of all he had worked for in the past three years.

BBC news and government 1926–35

Much has been written about the general strike so there is no need to rehearse again the details of those days of May (cf. Tracey, 1977; Farman, 1974; Morris, 1976; but Briggs, 1961 is still the best). Instead I wish to summarize its implications for state-broadcasting relations. The strike set the limits of the BBC's independence of government in a crisis. The BBC was not subject to direct control, though the government had that power and there were those who wished to use it. But the price of its fragile independence was co-operation with the state. The BBC accepted the government's view of the strike as unconstitutional. In so doing it sought to justify itself as a national asset in the national interest, and to win prestige and support from government and the general public.

The BBC news bulletins were balanced and impartial, it was claimed, in that they contained information from both the government's *British Gazette* and the TUC's *British Worker*, though not in equal proportion. Briggs concludes that what was included was usually right though much was omitted. There was no attempt to twist, distort or fabricate. Nevertheless, in his view,

BBC news helped the government against the strikers by its steadying effect on public opinion, by dispelling false rumours and by trying to spread 'good cheer' among the middle-class public not involved in the strike. What was absent from the bulletins were the views of the working class and their reasons for action. In one sense the BBC could not have done more to present the case of the strikers, since its hands were tied by government. The more damaging charge is that there were few, if any, in the BBC who even understood the causes of the strike, 'the realities of working-class life, the sense of solidarity, struggle and occasional triumph which the strikers felt' (Briggs, 1961, p. 374).

The strike set a potent precedent for subsequent 'national emergencies', a pattern of managerial co-operation between the state and the BBC in the sphere of news. Previously the BBC had been regarded as small fry by the authorities. Thereafter they began to supply the BBC with information, using the bulletins for their own purposes. After 1926 the BBC began to be absorbed into the corporate apparatuses of government, a process which it willingly encouraged. The general strike was the BBC's political apprenticeship, its rite of passage into the state domain.

After the strike things got back to normal and the BBC had to continue with the bulletins ready-made for them by Reuters. But by 1930 Reith, after tortuous diplomacy with the press agencies, had won the right for the BBC to prepare its own bulletins from the wire service they provided for a flat annual fee. In that year a handful of people in the Talks Department, with no journalistic experience, began to prepare the nightly bulletins from agency and official sources. Their first big test came with the economic and political crisis of 1931, when a run on the pound in the summer led the Treasury to produce emergency economies, including a 10 per cent pay cut in the public sector and in unemployment relief. This was unacceptable to a majority of the Labour cabinet who resigned, leaving MacDonald to form a hasty national government with a cabinet dominated by Conservatives to approve what Labour had been unable to stomach. The cuts produced the first mutiny in the navy (at Invergordon) since 1797. Within a couple of months there was a general election and a national government was returned with a huge majority.

If 1926 had, under pressure, educated the BBC in the rudiments of crisis management, 1931 was the first occasion that the lessons then learnt were voluntarily applied. Looking back over the year the News Section's second annual *Review of News* claimed:

> There is no doubt that the Corporation may claim not only to have maintained its high position as a supplier of unbiased information, but also by means of its news service to have contributed materially to the steadying of public opinion during the financial crisis. During this dangerous period the public received, in the News Bulletins, without any comment, the first notification of the formation of the National Government, the official statements of the Government on the course of events, and objective non-sensational accounts of the results of the crisis on the pound and on the country's economic life. (BBC Written Archive)

While the popular press had carried wild stories about the Invergordon Mutiny, BBC news had exercised 'a steadying influence by its reports of the unrest in the Atlantic Fleet'. At the height of the discontent the Admiralty released a detailed explanation of the cuts in naval pay to the press agencies and at the same time phoned a request to the BBC News Section asking it *not* to broadcast this statement. It was not included in the news. Two weeks later the Ministry of Labour asked the News Section to broadcast a notice of the reduced rates of unemployment relief, thoughtfully providing a specially condensed version of the new terms for transmission. It was included in the bulletin. After the resignation of the Labour cabinet, Downing Street phoned through the names of the new cabinet members as they were being appointed, for inclusion in the main evening news bulletin. This gave the BBC a notable coup over the press (much resented in Fleet Street) who were unable to run the story until the following morning.

These are fragmentary instances, in a moment of crisis, of the management of opinion and the steadying of national morale by government and broadcasters. But this was part of a more long-term development in which the state was moving into the continuous, routine management and control of information to the media. By the early 1930s most state departments had their own press and publicity officers to release information, organize publicity and promote the policies and aims of the department. This was an unprecedented departure from the ingrained tradition of anonymity and secrecy in the permanent bureaucracy. But now it was accepted that, 'under present day conditions when administration touches individual and community life at so many points, administrative and legislative responsiveness to public opinion is of fundamental importance; and it can scarcely be regarded as less desirable that public opinion should be fertilized by the most intimate possible contact with the facts' (quoted in Middlemas, 1979, pp. 356–7). This new kind of liaison with the public via the media was based on the doctrine that 'all this work, being in the national interest, was politically and ideologically neutral' (Middlemas, 1979, p. 356).

Routine press releases; ministerial briefings; the advanced circulation of official reports and white papers; the arrangement of press tours and visits; the supply of information to journalists on request – these were the means whereby continuous contact with the media was normalized. And, as the *Report on the Press* (1938) noted, only the last of them favoured the journalist. The rest placed the initiative firmly with government. The report summarized its views on these developments as follows: 'the Government tends to regard publicity as its own prerogative, and when a newspaper seeks to throw light on any department's activity the characteristic reaction is too often that the newspaper is up to no good' (Political and Economic Planning, 1938, p. 200). It is not a paradox to argue that official secrecy and control of information became more stringent as the state became more liberal with the flow of information to the media. The latter, we might say, protected the former more effectively.

By the end of its first year's work News Section could boast that it had established good relations with the Foreign Office, the Treasury, the Prime Minister's Office, the India Office, the Department of Overseas Trade, the Ministry of Agriculture and Fisheries, the Meteorological Office, the Air Ministry, the Home Office and Scotland Yard. It had looser contacts with the War Office, the Ministry of Health and the Post Office. By the end of 1931 the Board of Trade, the Ministry of Mines, the Ministry of Labour and the Admiralty had been added to the list. In spite of these successes the new arrangements usually favoured the press. Lacking any special correspondents of its own before the war the BBC had no access to press visits or ministerial briefings. Departmental publicity releases frequently carried an embargo on their use in BBC bulletins ahead of the morning press. Throughout the 1930s the BBC worked to establish, with press agencies and the government, an agreed code of practice for the classification of official publicity and news releases, but with little effect.

The News Section, it was stated in 1931, was, and would continue to be, 'sympathetic towards suggestions made privately to us by Government Departments about our handling of news material'. On 1 November 1932 the Home Office queried the inclusion in the previous night's bulletin of a protest from the Metropolitan Police

Federation about proposed cuts in police pay. Reith replied immediately that the item came from the usual agency sources but that he had issued instructions that 'no stuff from agencies re cuts in pay, protest etc is to be broadcast . . . . only HMG's official statements in future'. He added by way of reassurance that the bulletin had also included a request from the Commissioner of Police, specially phoned through to News Section, asking people not to go out and watch demonstrations.

Four days before this exchange of letters the national hunger march of the unemployed had arrived in London. It was organized by the National Unemployed Workers Movement and led by Wal Hannington and other leading members of the British Communist Party. The marchers were greeted with a massive display of support by sections of the London working class, and a massive display of force by the London police (cf. Hannington, 1977). From the start the march had been kept under close surveillance by the authorities. All along the roads to London the marchers were secretly checked out to discover if they had criminal or political records, while reports flowed in from workhouse masters and public assistance officers about their physical condition and whether they were armed (e.g. with walking sticks). Meanwhile working-class districts of London, and especially the haunts of the Communist Party and the NUWM, had been infiltrated by plain clothes police and informers and fine-combed for evidence of Moscow gold behind the march (Kingsford, 1982, pp. 139–65 for details).

By 30 October the newspapers were baying for the arrest of Hannington and his co-plotters of revolution. Subversive leaflets and stickers had appeared: 'Policemen! Defeat your own pay cuts by supporting Tuesday's demonstration against the Economies!' On the day the Home Office contacted the BBC, Hannington had appealed to the police, in Trafalgar Square, not to use their batons against the marchers and the huge supporting crowd. 'Let the working class in uniform and out of uniform stand together in defence of their conditions' (Kingsford, 1982, pp. 157–8). But violence broke out, and two days later Hannington was arrested and charged with attempting to cause disaffection among members of the Metropolitan Police contrary to the Public Act 1919. This incident was one of the factors leading to the Incitement to Disaffection Act (1934) and the formation of the National Council for Civil Liberties (Anderson, 1983, p. 76).

In 1934 a rather nonplussed Cecil Graves, then Controller of Programmes, was invited to attend a secret meeting at the Board of Education. It was called by the Secretary of the Board, wearing his other hat as publicity officer to the Chief Civil Commissioner. The purpose of the meeting was to ensure that the mechanisms for the control of information during an 'emergency', first used in the general strike, were still in good working order. In a comprehensive review of the whole supply, control and dissemination of information, the role of the BBC was discussed and it was agreed that a BBC official should be attached to the Board of Education (whence any future emergency would be co-ordinated) with a direct line to Broadcasting House. Present were representatives from the Stationery Office, the Post Office, the Colonial and Foreign Offices, the Board of Education and Graves for the BBC. The point to note is the significance of the uninvited guest. There was no press representative there. By now the state understood the importance of radio news: in a crisis it could control broadcasting more easily than the newspapers (assuming they were still running). The moment this truth began to dawn on the BBC was to come in 1938.

Controversy, talks, unemployment, 1927–35

'If once you let politics into broadcasting, you will never be able to keep broadcasting out of politics', the Postmaster-General had sagely declared in the House of Commons in November 1926. Reith, though angry at the veto on controversy in the Charter prudently allowed a year to lapse before trying to get it revoked. Early in 1928 he wrote to the Post Office with assurances that if the Corporation were allowed to introduce controversy to its programme it would do so with care. There could be no expression of views contrary to the interests of the state or on subjects liable to offend religious or moral sensibilities. Subjects would be so presented as to ensure adequate safeguards for impartiality and equality of opportunity. And all this might be safely left to the broadcasters since 'it appears from universal experience that the broadcaster himself is the most important censor of the form and extent of controversial matter, and that even where Government control is so remote and loose as to be negligible, the self-interest or sense of responsibility of the broadcaster require that controversy should be prudently and tactfully introduced' (Reith to the Post Office, 16 January 1928). Within two months Reith received a reply. After commending the BBC's good behaviour the Post Office advised the Corporation that the ban was now lifted.

Responsibility for this new freedom would devolve solely on the Governors and the Postmaster-General did not intend to fetter them in this matter. The government reserved the right to modify its decision in the light of further experience. Provisions for the direct control of broadcasting in a national emergency were to remain in full vigour (Post Office to Reith, 5 March 1928).

The Talks Department, set up in 1927, now faced the delicate task of finding ways of presenting controversial issues at the microphone. A range of techniques were tried out, all designed to provide the balance and impartiality that Reith had promised the government (cf. Cardiff, 1980). But the preferred method was the symposium – a series of talks by eminent public persons, expounding their licensed views on everything. Balance was not sought within each talk but across the representative spread of opinion within the series as a whole. Even so there were complaints. *Points of View* (1929) was thought by some Conservatives to be more inclined to socialist and Liberal viewpoints than those of their own persuasion. A series on *The National Character* (1934) created momentary uproar in the BBC and in the nation when one of the speakers, William Ferrie, representing 'the working man', wished to take issue with the previous speaker, Sir Herbert Austin. Austin, speaking on modern industry, had stressed the beneficial effects of mechanization on working conditions, standards of living and the mental life of the nation. In his draft script, Ferrie vigorously opposed such arguments, speaking of the economic exploitation of the working class, the rise of fascism in Europe and in Britain and declaring that he and his mates looked to Russia for a solution. All this got the blue pencil from the Talks Department and Ferrie apparently agreed to their deletion. But when he came to give his talk, which was, of course, broadcast live, he immediately abandoned his script, protested that he had been gagged and refused to say anything more. The left had a field day with this incident. It was proof of the censorship they had long suspected (cf. Postgate, 1935). The *Daily Herald* and the *Daily Worker* printed substantial portions of the original text including all the bits that had been cut.

If there was no room at the microphone for militant working-class points of view, the Talks Department was genuinely concerned in the early 1930s to convey to its largely middle-class audience on the National Programme the social effects of the recession. Well before such documentary classics as *The Road to Wigan Pier* (1936) or *Housing Problems* (1935), the BBC had produced three major talks series – one on the slums and two on unemployment. *Other People's Houses* (January 1933) used Howard Marshall, a BBC commentator better known for his cricket commentaries, to visit the slums in Glasgow, Tyneside and the East End, and give eyewitness accounts of what he had seen – the first example of documentary reportage on radio. *S.O.S.* (January 1933) used the same technique to describe the results throughout the country of the recent appeals on radio made by the Prime Minister and the Prince of Wales for voluntary aid schemes to help those who were, unfortunately, out of work. The next series on unemployment, *Time to Spare* (March 1934), brought the unemployed to the microphone for the first time, to describe in their own words what it was like living on the dole (for fuller accounts of these talks, cf. Scannell, 1980).

The talks gave rise to conflicting responses from the listening public and political groups. Howard Marshall was denounced by one angry listener as 'either the world's biggest liar or else as trying to play the funny man'. *S.O.S.*, coming as it did in the wake of the hunger march, was regarded by Wal Hannington and the NUWM as 'an astute and subtle change of tactics by the ruling class designed to deflect the unemployed from active political protest and to hold them more securely in their grip' (Hannington, 1936, p. 197). Hannington, on his release from jail had tried to persuade the BBC to let him speak in the series as the spokesman of the unemployed. His request was, of course, turned down. The BBC made it plain that it wanted to avoid controversy, and the *Daily Worker* commented (20 January 1933): 'In other words they want only one point of view, a point of view acceptable to the captalist class and directed against the mass organization of the unemployed.'

Time to Spare, though in intention not much different from *S.O.S.* – simple reports on the facts, an appeal to the conscience of the nation – had a different impact. It started at the same time that the Commons was debating the Unemployment Bill (1934), in the course of which extracts from some of these talks were quoted by Labour backbenchers as evidence of the inadequacy of the dole and the meanness of the Means Test. The Ministry of Labour replied that the whole truth had not been given, and that the circumstances of the individuals quoted were not as desperate as they made out. This exchange was taken up in the press (left-wing papers now praising the BBC for allowing a faint glimmer of the truth to be known), and a war of words ensued between the Ministry and the BBC. *The Daily Herald* carried a front page story that the effect of the series on public opinion was such that the government was thinking of stopping it. Indeed, though it was not known publicly at the time, Reith was summoned to Downing Street and asked by the Prime Minister to discontinue the series. To his credit Reith replied that though it was in the government's power to compel him to do so, he would instruct the BBC announcer, at the time the talk was due to be given, to declare that the Corporation had been ordered by the government to stop the series and so there would be silence for the next 20 minutes. Faced with this threat MacDonald backed down and the series continued.

By now there was a groundswell of muttering among Conservative politicians and the right-wing press that the Talks Department was run by a bunch of lefties. The Department had had a troubled history. Hilda Matheson, its first head, had resigned in an atmosphere of intrigue and bitterness in 1932, and Reith had become increasingly suspicious of Charles Siepmann, her successor. In 1935 a complete reshuffle of the Department promoted its leading lights to posts that took them a very long way from Broadcasting House. Siepmann was given a newly invented post – Director of Regional Relations – and sent to tour the provinces. Others were sent to New York, Palestine, India. Hilda Matheson called it 'a dispersal and disintegration unparalleled in any other department'. Writing a few months after this diaspora she recorded her impression of widespread arrested development in the work of the Department (Matheson, 1935, pp. 512, 514). As Lionel Fielden, one of the most imaginative talks producers, put it before his long trek to India: 'The programme was no longer the thing. It was wiser in the BBC of 1935 to be a good administrator than to have any original ideas; better to spend your time cutting down artists' fees than rehearsing the artist; more paying to use a blue pencil than your mind' (Fielden, 1960, p. 142).

In the early 1930s the form and content of programmes had not yet been systematized and routinized, and neither had their producers. But by 1935 an internal division of labour had been installed, separating policy making from programme making. Self-censorship could not after all be left to the discretion of individual producers. It had to be institutionalized in a hierarchy of power that flowed downwards from the Director General, through the Controller of Programmes and his assistants, through Heads of Department to the programme makers. They in turn were expected to refer upwards through the system for guidance if in doubt about the consequences of their activities. This whole process has since become deeply embedded in the managerial structure of the BBC (Burns, 1977; Schlesinger, 1978). It was the means whereby a corporate definition of public service was imposed across the whole range of output. Not that it was then or since established easily or completely. There were wayward elements and awkward individuals, and departmental heads often protected their staff against the administrators. But there were ways of marginalizing dissent; by 'promotion' or posting individuals elsewhere, by the fear of dismissal when there was nowhere else to work in broadcasting. Caution became inbred. In the initial stages of an ambitious social survey of Britain planned by Talks in 1936 all the participants were warned that 'we do not want to get into the difficulties such as a couple of years ago when we were doing a series dealing with the actual conditions of the unemployed' (Memo to Regional Directors, 12 February 1936).

This social survey by broadcasting was not completed. The hazards were too great. It is indicative of the growing crisis at the heart of public life in Britain that at the same time as the BBC's attempted inquiry into the state of the nation failed, two young graduates were launching an independent fact-finding movement called Mass Observation. The immediate impulse behind it was the abdication crisis and the realization, as Tom Jeffery has argued, that 'ordinary people were being misled by a complacent press and indifferent government, both deeply ignorant of the needs of working people and the desires of "people of goodwill". Against this people needed to know the facts about international affairs, government policies and about themselves; only if people were given the facts could democracy work' (Jeffery, 1977, p. 3). The Left Book Club, founded in May 1936 had a similar aim: 'to help in the terribly urgent struggle for world peace and for a better social and economic order and against Fascism, by giving all who are determined to play their part in this struggle such knowledge as will immensely increase their efficiency' (Reid, 1979, p. 194).

'Facts were wanted about everything and everybody — cross sections of society, symptomatic opinions and observations, detailed investigations and statistics' (Malcolm Muggeridge, quoted in Stevenson, 1977, p. 47). They were gathered in all kinds of ways: by workers' film, theatre and photography groups; by Grierson, Rotha and the middle-class film movement; in Penguin books and *Picture Post*; in the documentary writings of Priestley and Orwell. Social surveys were undertaken by philanthropic individuals, private trusts and independent research groups like Political and Economic Planning. The information they generated nourished the ferment of radical opinion publics, the ebb and flow of public platforms, campaigns and mass marches (against unemployment, against fascism: for peace, for the republican cause in Spain) — all indicating a widespread mobilization of public opinion as the noise of history grew louder and more implacable. A sense of being hounded by the pressures of external events dogged the Auden generation (Hynes, 1976). As British culture was radically politicized the gulf between the public and the private, government and people, rulers and ruled became more starkly apparent. The BBC was to confront this problem head on during the Munich crisis of 1938. Its difficulties in the presentation of foreign affairs from the mid-1930s to the outbreak of war bring together all the major themes in the relationship between the state, broadcasting and society in terms of news, political discussion and public opinion.

Broadcasting and foreign affairs, 1935–9

In 1931 the Talks producer A. E. Harding had put together a brilliant documentary account of the abdication of Alfonso XIII and the establishment of the Spanish republic (*Crisis in Spain,* National Programme, 5 June 1931). This bravura piece of radio, written within weeks of the events, was the first attempt at what we would now call current affairs documentary. It was also, for some time, the last. There were no more major programmes on European politics until war had been declared and a six part feature, *The Shadow of the Swastika* (November 1939), tracing Hitler's rise to power was hastily put together.

One critical incident in 1935–6 which contributed to the BBC's silence about the gathering crisis in Europe was a hidden confrontation with the state over an educational talks series called *The Citizen and His Government* (cf. Briggs, 1979, pp. 199–201, Scannell, 1984). The plans for this series on the British political system included not only speakers representing Labour, Liberals and Conservatives, but also Oswald Mosley (Fascist) and Harry Pollitt (Communist). The proposal had the unanimous support of the Board of Governors, and the Controller of Programmes informed the Foreign Office of the scheme in outline. The Foreign Office took exception to Mosley and Pollitt and a long drawn out struggle ensued over their fate as broadcasters. Eventually the matter went to cabinet. Anthony Eden, the Foreign Secretary, outlined the story so far and concluded:

> Though it is still desirable that the BBC should withdraw the objectionable items of their programme without bringing in His

> Majesty's Government, it seems impossible to induce them to do so; and if the talks are, in fact, withdrawn through Government intervention, it would seem difficult, and in fact undesirable, to refuse to permit them to say so. It would however be neither true nor desirable to state publicly that the talks would be 'an embarrassment to the Government' at the present time; but it would be true to say that 'they were not in the national interest'. (12 February 1936, BBC Written Archive)

Baldwin, with full cabinet agreement, ordered the Postmaster-General to make it clear to the BBC that the government would not permit the broadcasts. A week later he was able to report that the BBC had agreed to withdraw Pollitt and Mosley and that no public reference would be made to government intervention. The cabinet formally recorded its congratulations (Briggs, 1979, p. 200).

The Ullswater Committee's Report on Broadcasting was published four weeks later (16 March 1936). It declared that 'We have no reason to suppose that, in practice, divergent views of the lines of public interest have been held by the Corporation and by government departments, or that the Corporation has suffered under any sense of restraint or undue interference.' Its praise of the BBC for exercising the responsibility for controversy confided to it by the state 'with outstanding independence' seemed a hollow mockery.

In the wake of this affair the BBC maintained an extremely low profile on all political issues. The Talks Department, after its recent dismembering, was still in a state of shock. There was 'a period of anarchy' until Sir Richard Maconachie was appointed as head of the department in 1936. Maconachie had been British Minister at Kabul from 1930–6 and his appointment was seen as a swing to the right, a further retreat into caution (Briggs, 1965, pp. 148–9). The News Department was set up in 1935 following the appointment of Professor John Coatman from the London School of Economics, who was brought in as 'a right wing offset' to balance the direction of talks and news (Briggs, 1965, p. 147). Under his guidance the department grew rapidly as the BBC began, tentatively, to establish its own news gathering service.

There were continuing pressures on its handling of foreign issues. The Spanish Civil War was its first political minefield. Foreign Office scrutiny increased. The exact terminology to describe Franco's troops ('insurgents' rather than 'rebels') was a matter of exquisite nicety. And at one point R. T. Clarke (Foreign News Editor) marched into Reith's office and declared that the pressures on his boys must stop. For this he was nearly sacked (Dimbleby, 1975, pp. 76–7).

As the government turned towards conciliatory diplomacy with Hitler and Mussolini surveillance of the media increased. In January 1938 Chamberlain ordered a special watch to be kept on the BBC after it had broadcast a news item stating that no further steps were intended towards improving Anglo-Italian relations in the near future. This was corrected on the order of the Prime Minister, and denied in the BBC's main news bulletin the following day. There was a flurry in the press a couple of weeks later as Germany denied stories of unrest in its army, blaming Polish Jews and the BBC for the story. On 3 March 1938 the British Ambassador in Berlin told Hitler that on the same day the Foreign Secretary (now Lord Halifax) had arranged a press conference with responsible newspaper editors, the Newspaper Proprietors' Association and senior BBC officials. To all he had emphasized their responsibility in the maintenance of peace. A week later, just before Hitler annexed Austria, the Foreign Office warned the press that personal attacks on the Nazi leadership would make the Foreign Secretary's negotiations more difficult. As the Führer marched into Austria the BBC Talks Department was running a series called *The Way of Peace.*

In the autumn the Czechoslovakian crisis came to a head. In those anxious days, when Chamberlain flew to Munich to return with his scrap of paper promising peace in our time, the BBC appeared to play the same role that it had learnt in 1926. But within the Corporation the crisis produced a deep unease that over the last year or so, and particularly now, it had signally failed to provide its listeners with anything like an adequate understanding of what was really happening. The most fundamental issue – that of government control of BBC news – was raised by John Coatman, who had moved from News to be Director of North Region earlier in the year. The core of his remarkable memorandum must speak for itself:

> I say, with a full sense of responsibility and, since I was for over three years Chief News Editor, with a certain authority, that in the past we have not played the part which our duty to the people of this country called upon us to play. We have in fact taken part in a conspiracy of silence. I am not saying for a minute that we did this willingly or even knowingly. . . . In view of our history and our peculiar relationship to the Government, and also the very short time, comparatively speaking, that we have been at work, I think

> even the sternest of our critics can hardly have expected us to behave differently. But now things have changed. The position of this country is infinitely more dangerous than it ever has been in modern times, and the past few weeks have invested the BBC with a new importance, given it a more vital role in national life, and have, therefore, laid a new responsibility on us who are its servants. . . . We would, of course, keep full liaison with the Government, but we would never allow ourselves to be silenced except when we are taken into that confidence which our position and sense of responsibility entitles us to, and are given specific, valid reasons for not following out some course of action on which we were decided. (BBC Written Archive)

Coatman gave a number of examples of how, in the preceding years, the BBC had been drawn into the web of silence spun by the government. But his objective was not a review of the past. The Munich Agreement had given the country a breathing space, not a permanent peace, which the BBC should use to rethink its responsibilities to the people and to the government. His memorandum was widely circulated and discussed, and the substance of his argument was generally accepted at senior levels of the BBC. What were the consequences?

Outwardly the most noticeable change was in the tenor of the news bulletins. In November 1938 a letter was received from the offices of the cabinet ('a private letter – or at any rate a very semi-official one') complaining of the tendentious nature of the bulletins and the predominance of commentators who in the past were of a pacifist nature but had lately become ultra-bellicose. By early 1939 listeners had grown used to 'actual recordings of fiery foreign dictators making their speeches' in the nightly bulletins, which prompted a letter to *The Times* complaining that:

> Some of us ordinary citizens are troubled and perplexed that while our Prime Minister and Foreign Secretary do all in their power to bring about friendly cooperation between this country and the peoples of Germany and Italy, we are subjected every evening in BBC news bulletins to hearing only those words from abroad which must aggravate ill feelings and exasperate tired minds, so that nightly we can go to bed more certain that war must come. (*The Times*, 2 February 1939)

There followed an avalanche of letters in which the critics far outnumbered the supporters of the BBC. The popular press joined in; 'The fat boys of the BBC who try to make our flesh creep are under fire . . . and rightly so, for the manner and substance of much of the news broadcast is deplorable' (*Daily Mail*, 15 February 1939). As this commotion died down there was another as the press splashed stories of an outbreak of 'BBC suicides' said to have been caused by hearing bad news on the radio. There were no reported cases of newspaper suicides.

Behind the scenes the Chairman of the Governors had renewed efforts to bring to the microphone the opponents of Chamberlain's policy of appeasement – above all Churchill and Eden. His best chance came when the Prime Minister was asked in the House of Commons why he was entitled to state on radio his views on foreign affairs as he chose, and why no other leader was entitled, on any occasion, to make any reply (Sir Richard Acland MP, 27 March 1939). Chamberlain left the reply to his Postmaster-General, who answered with the classic ploy that the question of who should broadcast was a matter for the BBC Board of Governors to decide. This gave Normanbrook, the Chairman of the Governors, a pretext for writing that although this was undoubtedly the correct constitutional doctrine, the practices that had grown up with regard to political broadcasting hardly squared with dogma. It was uncomfortably near the truth to say, like Acland, that who should speak at the microphone was in the hands of the Prime Minister. It was not right that the British people, at a time like this, could not hear a Churchill, Lloyd George or Eden. It was essential that they be heard. The Postmaster-General's reply was as curt as it was short. He noted that Normanbrook would shortly be stepping down as Chairman and thanked him for his views. The efforts of the BBC to bring the opponents of appeasement to the microphone between Munich and the outbreak of war were completely thwarted (cf. Scannell, 1984, for a full account).

There was one last thing the BBC attempted to do in the spring and early summer of 1939, and that was to mobilize the nation for a major war. Again they were constantly hampered by Whitehall inefficiency and by different state departments blowing hot and cold. In exasperation the BBC went ahead on its own initiative, and by the end of May it had prepared a two week propaganda programme for early July to boost enrolment in the armed forces, to appeal for volunteers for air raid precautions and so forth. There would be talks by leading statesmen including Churchill and Eden, and Gracie Fields to encourage female recruitment. There would be special features and talks on home defence. All that was needed was the official green light.

On 5 June there was a meeting at the Ministry of Labour between that department, the Lord Privy Seal's Office and two senior officials from the BBC. It soon became apparent that the spokesman for the Lord Privy Seal had been briefed to squash the whole idea. He was very grateful etc. for the BBC's efforts, but it was rather like taking a hammer to crack a nut. He objected to having all the big guns — for example Churchill and Lloyd George — since it would make people think the government was in a hole and must have mismanaged its recruiting campaign in the past. The truth was that the campaign was already proving most successful, and the Lord Privy Seal feared that a crisis propaganda drive might give people the idea that they could be at war in a few months time — by, say, September. Someone interjected that to date the campaign had recruited less than half the target set. This, he was told, was better than alarming people.

The BBC had no option but to cancel almost all its plans. Basil Nicolls, Controller of Progammes, who had attended the meeting, sent a memo round thanking all concerned for their efforts and telling them that most would be dropped as a result of political or other extraneous motives of the government. He was angered at the BBC's waste of time and effort, and was no longer prepared to put the BBC to any expense or inconvenience for a government that saw no need for urgency.

It was a glorious summer. In July and August the BBC did all the things it usually did at that time of year. There was much tennis, cricket and golf and the August Bank Holiday seaside special features. Stephen Potter produced a programme from Oxford — *Undergraduate Summer* — from its backwaters to its common rooms; and John Pudney produced *A Modern Pastoral* about the coming of electricity to 'a remote Essex village'. J. B. Priestley began reading instalments from his new novel, *Let the People Sing*, before it was published. There were new quizzes and parlour games — *Noah's Ark, All in Bee* and *For Amusement Only*. *Radio Times* carried details of what autumn had in store for listeners by way of talks, music and variety. At last this hypnotic trance — as if warm days should never cease — was broken when, on 3 September, Chamberlain came to the microphone he had so jealously preserved as his own to declare that this country was now officially at war with Germany.

*　　*　　*　　*

After the general strike, Reith had rationalized the role of radio in the matter by arguing that 'since the BBC was a national institution, and since the Government in the crisis was acting for the people . . . the BBC was for the Government in the crisis too' (Briggs, 1961, p. 365). Munich was the first test of that syllogism as a precedent for the role of broadcasting in a national crisis. The BBC was confronted with the fundamental dilemma as to whose interests it had a prior duty to serve and it rightly decided that its final responsibility was to society, not the state. But what compounded its difficulties in breaking the deafening silence was its own absorption within the state domain. The Corporation had become the simulacrum of a state bureaucracy: a public institution, a private world (Burns, 1977).

As for society and public opinion, Munich was the last and perhaps most striking proof of the extent to which it remained confused and uninformed by the state before war was declared. *Britain by Mass Observation* (Mass Observation, 1939) contains a survey showing the uncertain and volatile state of public opinion before, during and after Munich. 'The urgency of fact, the voicelessness of everyman, and the smallness of the groups which control fact getting and fact distribution' was the motivating thrust behind the book. This pioneering study of public opinion identified two kinds of focus in society: 'One is the ordinary focus of the ordinary man or woman which centres on home and family, work and wages. The other is the political focus, which centres on government policy and diplomacy. What happens in this political sphere obviously affects the sphere of home and work. But between the two there is a gulf – of understanding, of information and of interest' (Mass Observation, 1939, p. 25). It is this gulf, and its critical implications for democracy, that I have explored in the formation of state-broadcasting relations before the war.

Note on Sources

Most of the material in this article is drawn from the BBC Written Archive Centre, Caversham, Reading. It is open to researchers and is the indispensable source of information on all aspects of broadcasting up to about 1955. I have not given detailed references to archive sources, since I did not wish to strew the text of a general article with footnotes. Briggs (1961 etc.) is, of course, the essential guide to broadcasting history.

References

Anderson, G. D. (1983) *Fascists, Communists and the National Government. Civil Liberties in Great Britain, 1931–1937*, Columbia and London: University of Missouri Press.

Angell, N. (1926) *The Public Mind*, London: Noel Douglas.

Boyce, G. (1978) 'The fourth Estate; the reappraisal of a concept', in G. Boyce *et al., Newspaper History from the Seventeenth Century to the Present Day,* London: Constable.
Briggs, A. (1961) *The History of Broadcasting in the United Kingdom,* Vol. I, *The Birth of Broadcasting*, Oxford: Oxford University Press.
Briggs, A. (1965) *The History of Broadcasting in the United Kingdom,* Vol. II, *The Golden Age of Wireless,* Oxford: Oxford University Press.
Briggs, A. (1979) *Governing the BBC,* London: BBC.
Burns, T. (1977) *BBC, Public Institution: Private World*, London: Macmillan.
Cardiff, D. (1980) 'The serious and the popular; aspects of the evolution of style in the radio talk, 1928—1939', *Media, Culture and Society,* Vol. 2, No. 1.
Cardiff, D. and Scannell, P. (1984) 'Broadcasting and National Unity' in J. Curran *et al., The Impact of the Mass Media*, London: Constable.
Chaney, D. (1983) 'A symbolic mirror of ourselves; civic ritual in mass society', *Media Culture and Society*, Vol. 5, No. 1.
Crawford Committee Report (1925) *Report of the Broadcasting Committee,* London: HMSO, Cd. 2599.
Curran, J. and Seaton, J. (1981) *Power Without Responsibility: the Press and Broadcasting in Britain,* London: Fontana.
Dimbleby, D. (1975) *Richard Dimbleby*, London: Hodder and Stoughton.
Farman, C. (1974) *The General Strike*, St Albans: Granada Publishing Ltd.
Fielden, L. (1960) *The Natural Bent,* London: André Deutsch.
Frith, S. (1983) 'The pleasures of the hearth; the making of BBC light entertainment', *Formations of Pleasure*, London: Routledge and Kegan Paul.
Hannington, W. (1936) *The Problem of the Distressed Areas*, London: Gollancz, Left Book Club.
Hannington, W. (1977) *Unemployed Struggles,* London: Lawrence and Wishart.
Hynes, S. (1976) *The Auden Generation. Literature and Politics in England in the 1930s,* London: Bodley Head.
Jeffery, T. (1977) 'Mass observation: a short history', Birmingham University, Centre for Contemporary Cultural Studies, Stencilled Paper.
Kingsford, P. (1982) *The Hunger Marchers in Britain, 1920—1940,* London: Lawrence and Wishart.
Mass Observation (1939) *Britain by Mass Observation,* Harmondsworth: Penguin Special.
Matheson, H. (1935) 'The record of the BBC', *Political Quarterly,* Vol. 6, No. 4.
Middlemas, K. (1979) *Politics in Industrial Society: the experience of the British system since 1911,* London: André Deutsch.
Morris, M. (1976) *The General Strike*, Harmondsworth: Penguin.
Political and Economic Planning (1938) *A Report on the Press,* London.
Postgate, R. (1935) *What to Do with the BBC,* London: Hogarth Press.

Reid, B. (1979) 'The Left Book Club in the thirties', in J. Clark *et al.*, *Culture and Crisis in Britain in the 30s,* London: Lawrence and Wishart.
Reith, J. (1924) *Broadcast over Britain,* London: Hodder and Stoughton.
Reith, J. (1925) *Memorandum of Information to the Crawford Committee,* Caversham: BBC Archive.
Scannell, P. (1980) 'Broadcasting and the politics of unemployment, 1930–1935', *Media Culture and Society,* Vol. 2, No. 1.
Scannell, P. (1984) 'Broadcasting and foreign affairs, 1935–1939', *Media Culture and Society,* Vol. 6, No. 1.
Scannell, P. and Cardiff, D. (1982) 'Serving the nation; public service broadcasting before the war', in B. Waites *et al., Popular Culture: Past and Present,* London: Croom Helm.
Schlesinger, P. (1978) *Putting Reality Together: BBC News,* London: Constable.
Schwarz, B. (1980/1) 'Conservatism and class struggle: Politics in industrial society', *Capital and Class,* No. 12.
Stevenson, J. (1977) *Social Conditions in Britain Between the Wars,* Harmondsworth: Penguin.
Stuart, C. (1975) *The Reith Diaries,* London: Collins.
Sykes Committee Report (1923) *Broadcasting Committee Report,* London: HMSO, Cd. 1951.
Tracey, M. (1977) *The Production of Political Television,* London: Routledge and Kegan Paul.
Ullswater Committee Report (1936) *Report of the Broadcasting Committee,* London, HMSO, Cd. 5091.

6

Science, planning and the state

FRED STEWARD AND DAVID WIELD

The late 1930s in Britain witnessed the emergence of an influential movement which advocated a far-reaching interventionist and planning role for the state. It was a movement of scientists. But scientists who were to leave their laboratories and lecture theatres to advise government: they did this both during the Second World War (a war once fashionably called the 'Boffins' war'); and after the war with the development of Harold Wilson's policy to 'forge a new Britain in the white heat of the scientific and technological revolution' in the 1964 general election. The activity of this group raises important questions about:

(1) the need for, and level of, state intervention in industry and the economy;
(2) the place of science and technology in industrial and economic change, and the role of the state in planning science and technology for social and economic objectives;
(3) the extent to which 'scientific' or 'rational' planning is possible in a capitalist state, and
(4) the role of scientific experts and expertise in planning.

'Science and the Nation'

At the end of the Second World War a book was written by this scientists' movement, most of whom were members of the Association of Scientific Workers (AScW). The book, *Science and the Nation* (AScW, 1947) was a comprehensive blueprint for the planning of science and for the increased role of the state in co-ordinating the expansion and application of scientific effort. In the light of history the themes it discussed are now well-known, but at the time they were new and a part of the strong desire for a change in peacetime British society.

The book was about the organization of science, but it advocated a vastly increased and planned role for science in Britain's post-war recovery

> Today everyone knows something about the part played by science and scientists in winning the war: in the development of weapons and ways of using them, in industry, medicine, agriculture, nutrition and many other fields. It is also generally realised that during the war Britain achieved new forms of organisation and planned direction of scientific effort which have built up, from limited resources of scientific man-power and facilities, a powerful and effective scientific service. (AScW, 1947, p. 15)

> The idea of writing this book originated during the last year of the war. It seemed obvious that if Britain's science could be so effectively planned for war, so likewise it could be for peace. (AScW, 1947, p. 5)

The book criticizes the lack of co-ordination and planning by the state and advocated the establishment of a central body to plan scientific effort in all parts of British society. It advocated not only strong state co-ordination of scientific research, but also similar co-ordination of its use in industry and the economy. For example nationalization of basic industries (such as fuel and power) was to be the key to the regulation of the economy in the interest of the whole community.

The book saw science not only as a key factor in industrial and economic development but also as the means by which social life might be organized on a more 'rational' basis. 'The real lesson which the development of "scientific" weapons should make as clear as daylight is: when sufficiently large resources of finance, organisation and scientists are used there are few problems of the control and exploitation of Nature that cannot be solved, and often with unexpected speed' (AScW, 1947, p. 243).

This fascination with planning was related to the scientists' interest in, and knowledge of, developments of central economic planning in the Soviet Union. Central planning was seen by some of these scientists as an alternative to the chaos and unemployment in British industry during the depression. 'In the USSR, admittedly with a different organisation of society, it has been possible, through the centralised planning of scientific research and development, for the community to set long-term objectives of application whose achievement will involve much scientific research of the most fundamental character' (AScW, 1947, p. 150).

This view first formulated in the late 1930s, was dramatically confirmed by their wartime experiences with operational research. Blackett, the President of the AScW who wrote the foreword to *Science and the Nation,* had been prominent in the development of operational research techniques for military affairs. In the book, science is seen to have a fundamental role in the process of control and regulation. *Science and the Nation* advocated the application of scientific procedures in policy formulation and decision-making. The solutions to social problems are to be posed in scientific terms.

This view, together with advocacy of an increased role for scientists as experts in government and state administration, gives the impression that experts could objectively determine the needs of the population. The role of the scientific expert is not seen as problematic in this respect, or at odds with the democratic aspirations of many of the authors. *Science and the Nation*, then, promoted two themes:

(1) the advocacy of state control and planning both of science and of its application in Britain's post-war regeneration, and
(2) the nature of planning itself: the need for 'scientific method' in organization of the economy and social life, and the role of scientists as experts within the state advisory and administrative structures.

The formation of this perspective on planning lies in the inter-war period and the Second World War.

State intervention and the planning of science movement in the inter-war period

State intervention

Recognition of the need for state support for science and technology in Britain was evident from the middle of the nineteenth century onwards. The aftermath of the Great Exhibition of 1851 had been marked by a growing concern about British science and industry slipping behind its major international competitors, Germany and the United States.

The backwardness of British science and industry had been exposed during the First World War when the inadequacies of areas such as dyestuffs and optics manufacture compared with Germany had become apparent. A government White Paper announced in 1915: 'There is a strong consensus of opinion among persons engaged both in science and in industry that a special need exists at the present time for new machinery and for additional State assistance in order to promote and organise scientific research with a view especially to its application to trade and industry' (HMSO, 1914–16, p. 351).

The Department of Scientific and Industrial Research was established by government followed by the Medical and Agricultural Research Councils. Although this greater intervention by the state represented in one sense a major departure from the tradition of individualism and amateurism characteristic of British science, in another sense this new framework still bore the marks of this approach. Haldane's report on the machinery of government in 1918 established a principle (the 'Haldane principle') that research sponsored by government should be insulated from immediate political pressures by, for example, giving considerable autonomy to the research councils, staffed by representatives of the scientific community, to determine research goals and objectives. In some of the most acutely undeveloped areas of industry more drastic government intervention was pursued. For example the state took a public stake in a number of private chemical interests to form the British Dyestuffs Corporation Limited in the immediate post-war period. Although the form of involvement varied, two researchers on this period, Roy and Kay MacLeod, conclude that overall, 'mediated by the State, research bearing on national and corporate economic interests became a hallmark of scientific activity in Britain and Western Europe' (MacLeod, 1977, p. 319).

The period following the First World War was marked by the expansion of two particular types of institution – the government laboratories of which a variety were established and the research associations which were set up as co-operative bodies in particular industries with financial contributions by individual companies and by the state. Implied by the choice of these mechanisms was a gap in the research effort undertaken in Britain if left to the initiative of private companies alone. Nevertheless the decision to channel state resources into this sphere was tempered by a reluctance to develop a very directive approach to industrial research in general.

The 1924 Labour government made little headway in the introduction of change. In fact it was the subsequent Conservative administration which, operating under more favourable economic conditions, expanded investment in scientific research, establishing a Committee on Civil Research which (between 1925 and 1930) investigated a range of problems including the state of the iron and steel industry, and the co-ordination of government research.

To summarize, it is apparent that there was an impetus for state support of science and technology, both in the late nineteenth century in response to international industrial competition, and in the aftermath of the First World War, as the result of weaknesses discerned in strategic industries. Such industries established new forms of scientific organization with state involvement. But overall their impact was limited.

The planning movement

It has been observed by Roy and Kay MacLeod that 'with this structure and co-ordination came also the association of scientists in collective economic and later, political, action on an unprecedented scale' (MacLeod, 1977, p. 319). This included not only professional bodies such as the Association of University Teachers and the Institution of Professional Civil Servants but also a National Union of Scientific Workers and the British Science Guild. It was these later organizations which professed a broader interest in issues of national science and technology policy within which the political pressures for the planning of science began to manifest themselves. Although a radical tendency was present in the NUSW from early on, represented for example by Hyman Levy who saw the union's activities as linked organically to a socialist perspective and the harnessing of science and technology for socialism, the mainstream of the NUSW and the British Science Guild (including the editor of *Nature*) were primarily committed to a consolidation and extension of the mechanisms introduced in the aftermath of war.

At the end of the 1920s, two factors combined to shift the focus of debate about the planning of science in a more radical direction. The first of these was the deepening economic depression signalled by the Wall Street Crash of 1929 which resulted in a set-back to the growth of scientific research with scientists being put out of work. There was also a view among some scientists that the existing social order was proving incapable of realizing what was technically possible in terms of the alleviation of poverty and the improvement of social conditions. The second was a growing debate on the social desirability and consequences of the technological changes which were underway in the period. The implications of automation and military technology attracted public attention. In addition, the whole notion of an increasingly technical society in which experts played a more prominent role became subject to political debate. The literary polemic between H. G. Wells who in *Men Like Gods* expressed optimism and enthusiasm for a technocratic ordering of social affairs and Aldous Huxley's pessimistic vision of a dehumanized scientistic society in *Brave New World* captures the essence of these concerns.

Soviet visit to Britain, 1931

This was the context in which an unexpected and dramatic input to the British debate among concerned scientists occurred. The occasion was the International Congress for the History of Science and Technology held in London in June 1931. At the last minute a high level Soviet delegation led by Nikolai Bukharin, one of the Bolshevik leaders, then in charge of industrial research in the Soviet Union, flew to London to present a marxist approach to the role of social and economic forces in scientific and technological development. Their perspective and the information they brought concerning Soviet policy on the planning of science had a major impact on a group of up and coming 'radical' British scientists: J. D. Bernal, P. M. S. Blackett, Hyman Levy, Joseph Needham, J. B. S. Haldane and Lancelot Hogben. Subsequently described as the 'Visible College' by Werskey (1978), they came to dominate the movement for the planning of science over the next two decades. The themes discussed by the Soviet delegation which impressed themselves on these scientists were that science is shaped by social relations and capitalist society is unable to realize the full benefits of science and technology. Consequently it was argued that science must be planned within a socialized economy and research directed to social welfare. The Soviet Union was presented as the socialist model of scientific planning.

Ironically, these ideas – a product of the post-revolutionary construction of a large-scale research effort in the Soviet Union (by the early 1930s the Soviet Union was spending a higher proportion of its GNP on science than either Britain or the USA) – subsequently attracted more attention in Britain than in the USSR where Bukharin's fall from power and the repressive climate instigated by Stalin in the 1930s prevented their further development.

The beginnings of organization

The main organization in which the radical scientists participated was the NUSW, renamed the Association of Scientific Workers in 1927. The involvement of many of the scientists in the Cambridge Scientists Anti-War Group in the 1930s led to a transformation of the AScW. In 1934 Bernal was elected to the National Executive committee and the Cambridge branch drafted a new policy document which pledged the Association to ensure that:

> (a) scientific research is adequately financed;
> (b) science should be intelligently organised both internally and in its application to ensure the maximum initiative and minimum waste and confusion;
> (c) scientific research should be directed primarily to the improvement of the conditions of life.
>
> (Goldsmith, 1980, pp. 78–9)

The publication in 1935 of a book *The Frustration of Science* marked the beginning of a determined effort to link the sense of social responsibility in science to the great political conflicts of the day. In it P. M. S. Blackett argued:

> Unless society can use science it must turn anti-scientific and that means giving up the hope of the progress that is now possible. This is the way capitalism is now taking, and it leads to Fascism. The other way is complete Socialist planning on a large scale; this would be planning for the maximum possible output and not a restriction of output. (Hall *et al.*, 1935, p. 139)

It is apparent that this interest in planning by the 'radical' scientists was part of a more general intellectual current concerning both the economy and social affairs. However, this interest in planning was not the sole preserve of socialists.

Leruez, in his study of economic planning in Britain, points out that:

> . . . during the thirties, planning created a new line of political cleavage cutting across traditional party lines. Nevertheless, among the 'planners' one could distinguish two main schools of thought, reflecting their socialist or non-socialist origins. For some, planning was a way of overcoming the most flagrant deficiencies of capitalism, which had been highlighted by the economic crisis; others wanted

> to replace the capitalist system with a planned socialist system. Yet in the immediate run the aims of these two schools very largely coincided, and particularly where they shared a belief in political democracy — which meant the immense majority of cases — there was very considerable common ground. (Leruez, 1975, p. 7)

Although there were obvious tensions between these 'radical' and 'reformist' wings, among the scientists, too, by 1938 there was considered to be sufficient common ground to make a broad alliance for the planning of science. This was expressed in the formation in that year of a new Division for the Social and International Relations of Science of the British Association for the Advancement of Science which included prominent members of both 'radicals' and 'reformists'. In 1939, on the eve of the Second World War, J. D. Bernal's major book, *The Social Function of Science,* was published. The work combined a critique of the consequences of the *laissez-faire* tradition in British science policy and a detailed blueprint for an enhanced role for the state in planning research set in a political context of socialist change.

An extract illustrates Bernal's criticisms of British industry's lackadaisical approach to science and technology:

> There is a tradition in British industry which is definitely inimical to science and consequently to the scope and freedom given to industrial scientific research. Few results of fundamental importance have in the past ten years emerged from any British industrial laboratory, whereas many such have come from German and American laboratories . . . Co-ordination of industrial research is virtually non-existent. This in itself leads directly to inefficiency, as there is no guarantee against overlapping. (Bernal, 1939, pp. 56—7)

But there were also critics of planning. The deep ideological hostility to increased state intervention and the planning of science, which still permeated established circles in Britain, was demonstrated by the reaction of a group of intellectuals including J. R. Baker, an Oxford scientist, and M. Polanyi, a Manchester chemist, who organized themselves into a Society for Freedom in Science (McGucken, 1978). Baker argued (echoing Orwellian themes in *Nineteen Eighty Four*):

> An ugly new god called the state demands worship. Nourishment, shelter, health and leisure are falsely regarded as ends in themselves . . . Science is equated with technology and decay. Individualism and free inquiry both are ridiculed. Everything is planned from

> 'above'. A dreary uniformity descends. Each person is a cog in a vast machine, grinding towards ends lacking all higher human value. (Baker, 1942, pp. 7, 133)

Bernal protested at the misrepresentation of his views on planning, in which he conceded considerable autonomy for fundamental scientific research and a lively polemic on 'planning' and 'freedom' ensued throughout the 1940s.

In spite of this group's opposition to any idea of planning, there is little doubt that the trend in the 1930s was toward an acceptance of the need for some sort of planning and state support of science. The proponents of planning covered a wide ideological spectrum; yet by the end of the decade there had emerged a substantial consensus in favour of state support and involvement in science.

Science and the Second World War

The turning point for state involvement in science and technology

Vig has described the Second World War as 'the great turning point in government-science relations' leading to what he terms 'a non-partisan consensus on scientific and educational expansion which emerged by 1945' (Vig, 1968, p. 14). Although this is partially true, it was also the case that the differences in political conception of an enhanced role for the state, already evident in the 1930s, persisted through this period. In practical terms the Second World War revealed greater willingness by the British state to employ scientific expertise in the furtherance of the war effort than had been the case earlier.

A variety of scientific and technical activities were developed in connection with the particular requirements of war. In the 1930s these were primarily concerned with issues such as defence against air attack, and provision of adequate food supplies for the population through the newly formed Ministry of Food. With the onset of war itself projects to develop new weapons systems became central. The work associated with the development of an atomic bomb was marked by new levels of organization and complexity in a totally novel field of technical endeavour. A general consequence of the application of science to war was a new awareness of the importance of expertise within the affairs of state and new relationships between experts, civil servants, politicians and military staff.

The institutions through which state support of science was channelled remained rather fragmented and *ad hoc*, linked to different ministries and branches of the services. Co-ordination remained weak. Although the period is marked by a significant expansion of state support for scientific activity, this was not matched by the development of a strong, centralized planning mechanism. As a consequence, strong pressure continued for this during the war.

Scientists and planning during wartime

The onset of war had three distinct consequences for the members of the 1930s planning of science movement. First, many of the prominent ones became directly involved in the activities of the state itself. Second, the pressing needs of war were considered particularly appropriate for the implementation of some of the ideas developed by the 'planners' in the 1930s. Third, the experience of state involvement in wartime science was used as a basis and model to argue for the introduction of planning machinery in peacetime.

The outsiders move inside

It was a supreme irony of history that the onset of war provided the opportunity for the sustenance and practical implementation of many of the ideas and proposals of the 'planners' of science. Although imbued with a spirit of anti-militarism and a desire to harness science and technology to peaceful objectives of general social benefit, the 'outsider' radical critics of government policy were to be adopted as key 'insider' specialists and advisers in the development of Britain's war effort. Though morally repelled by war they considered its anti-Fascist nature as politically just.

As early as 1934 Patrick Blackett had been a member of the Committee of Research on Air Defence. It was this committee which in 1935 took the decision to launch a major research programme into the development of radar to provide early warning of air attack on Britain. The radar research programme headed by

Watson-Watt became a practical example of the success to be gained by large-scale government sponsored and planned research. By 1939 the eastern approaches to Britain were protected by a string of 20 radio location stations. Many thousands of scientists and £10 million had been used in the development of the new technique. Watson-Watt himself, as a consequence became a forthright proponent of ideas of planning.

J. D. Bernal was appointed scientific adviser on civil defence to the Ministry of Home Security in 1939. This followed his involvement with the Cambridge Scientists Anti-War Group which in 1937 had severely criticized existing government policy on air raid precautions. His official appointment as government adviser arose from a meeting at All Souls College, Oxford, with Sir John Anderson, government minister responsible for civil defence. After hearing Bernal's persuasive criticisms of existing measures and having been warned by his advisers of Bernal's political orientation Anderson insisted on appointing him as an adviser even if 'he is as red as the flames of hell' (Snow, 1966, p. 29). At the Research and Experiments Department at the Ministry of Home Security, Bernal, together with Zuckerman, later to become scientific adviser to post-war governments, transformed the study of bombing and its effects from rumour and guesswork to a policy based on scientific and practical principles.

Although in the initial years of the war the 'outsiders' had made their way 'inside' in connection with matters concerning defence, by 1941 they had become even more centrally involved in the war effort. One striking feature of this was the development of operational research. As we saw earlier the 'planners' had made one of their central demands the application of scientific methods to the conduct of the affairs of the state itself. Again, it was the planning of military operations that provided the opportunity for developing these ideas in practice. In August 1940 Blackett became head of the Anti-Aircraft Command Research Group. 'Blackett's Circus' as it became known, pioneered techniques for evaluating and improving military performance. Blackett then moved to Coastal Command, to develop an operational research section there. Operational research became established as an organized feature throughout the British military forces.

In 1942 Bernal was appointed scientific adviser to Combined Operations under Mountbatten where he played a key role in the planning of Operation Overlord (the D-Day landings in Normandy) and many other projects. These examples were simply part of a general process of extending scientific activities under the auspices of the state, developing an extensive scientific structure and opening up the mechanisms of the state and the military to a wider range of scientific and political opinion than would have been conceivable hitherto.

The AScW and war planning

Despite these innovations the scientist 'planners' saw them as merely hints of what would be possible with a fundamental transformation of the relations between science and the state. Pressure was sustained through the public forum of the Association of Scientific Workers for such a change in policy. The intimacy of the relationship between AScW's activities and the military application of science is illustrated by the fact that both Robert Watson-Watt and Patrick Blackett were wartime presidents of the organization (Horner, 1981).

In the Penguin book *Science in War* (Anon., 1940) a group of the scientist 'planners' who met informally with Zuckerman as the 'Tots and Quots' dining club, argued for the application of scientific method throughout the war economy and in the conduct of military affairs. The AScW described its message as: 'that science had to be brought into close and active touch with every department of the war in order to avoid blunders that could be seen and difficulties that could be evaded' (*Scientific Worker*, 1942, p. 28).

Shortly after the outbreak of the Second World War, the Association's executive committee had issued a statement calling for the national co-ordination of scientific resources. The proposal was in effect a call for the establishment of a Ministry of Science. The Association sought the support of the Royal Society and the British Association for this proposal. However, neither body responded favourably, arguing that the time was not ripe for such a development and a centralized authority at this time was inappropriate. The Association pursued the idea of a National Council through the Parliamentary and Scientific Committee which initially consisted of an all-party group of 24 MPs, but by the end of the war had risen to over 100 – a reflection of the growth of interest in matters scientific which the war generated.

In the September of the same year, the AScW had a resolution accepted at the TUC annual conference which similarly demanded the setting up of a Central Planning Board with executive authority. The General Council referred the matter to the National Production Advisory Council, a joint union and government body.

The official response to the proposal, coming from the Ministry of Production, complacently indicated that the problems of co-ordination were being dealt with and did not require any major change.

The memorandum, *Scientists and Production* (1943a), reflected a long-running campaign of the Association and other staff unions for participation on Joint Production Committees (JPCs). These bodies consisted of manual unions and employers' representatives whose task was 'to consult and advise on matters relating to production and increasing efficiency in order that maximum output might be obtained'. Staff unions had been consistently excluded from such arrangements. The AScW saw the contrast between private ownership and control of pre-war days with the wartime need for maximization of the use of both material and manpower resources in which everyone had a part to play. Thus not only did the Association see participation on the JPCs as a key issue for wartime but also for the post war period: 'The frustration of science i.e. its application to the pursuit of private profit rather than the common good, and the misuse of it that was common before the war, can only be prevented by continual watchfulness and control by its producers, the scientists themselves' (AScW, 1943, p. 7).

Proposals for science in the peace

Parallel with the efforts by the AScW to secure more effective state intervention in the pursuance of war were the efforts made to draw lessons for future policies in peacetime. A series of conferences and publications were promoted with this end in view. The alliance forged before the war between 'radical' and 'reformist' scientists extended yet further during the war itself. In 1941 the British Association sponsored conference on Science and World Order addressed the theme of science in post-war reconstruction. It was a prestigious gathering including the luminaries of the scientific community, ambassadors, governments in exile and cabinet ministers. The terms of reference, however, were defined by the radical critics and presented as a major theme the idea that scientific planning could only be wholly successful under an economic system which replaced the profit motive by the criterion of social need.

In a publication *The Development of Science* in 1943 the AScW also expressed the view that capitalist production seemed to restrict scientific progress with a consequential waste and frustration of material and manpower resources in science: 'Scientists will be aware that there are still today powerful interests which cannot afford to permit certain technical advances to be used. Monopolisation of industry reduces the competitive urge to technical advance.'

The AScW promoted a campaign on the implementation of central planning of science. A conference on the Planning of Science, held by the AScW in January 1943, attracted the interest of both the scientific and political establishment. Stafford Cripps gave the opening address outlining the current organization of science and the problems of co-ordination. His approach, however, reflected the generally complacent and uncritical attitude of the coalition government.

The significance of the conference in terms of its impact on the scientific community may be judged from the extensive coverage it received in *Nature*. A long editorial criticized Cripps's contribution: 'Nothing in his address, however, goes far to resolve the doubts as to whether we can safely rely on advisory bodies . . . or whether it is necessary that there should be some Central Scientific and Technical Board with executive, rather than advisory powers' (*Nature*, 1943, p. 203). As to policy for peacetime it argued more cautiously: 'It is not a question of planning or not planning, but of the extent to which we will plan, and the limits which are placed on our planning by the necessity for preserving a free society and the freedom of investigation and utterance essential to scientific advance' (*Nature*, 1943, p. 205).

It is apparent, then, that the scientists' pre-war ideas were convincingly confirmed for them during their war work. Not only were they successfully integrated into military work, but their promotion of the ideas of planning gained support. AScW conferences were important events, their publications well read, and their attempts to put their ideas were listened to by parliament and government. However, the 'radical' elements of their ideas, involving central planning and far-reaching transformation of private industry met greater resistance. A powerful body of opinion favoured the adoption of elements of planning which enlarged the role of the state but did not alter in any fundamental way the existing social and economic order.

The AScW itself recognized that there were different options for state planning short of revolutionary change. Policy on planning will emerge from a political struggle in which 'a clear distinction should be kept between changes and improvements which can be envisaged within a given political environment and those that may depend on far-reaching political change' (AScW, 1943b, p. 8).

Science and production in war

As we have seen, much of the movement's pressure for greater state support and planning of science was directed to more effective social control of industry. To what extent were the new roles taken on by the state in relation to science reflected in government's relationship with the economy?

There was a major increase in employment in the engineering industries and a decrease in consumer industries. Industries geared towards war production expanded rapidly, so that by 1943 employment in the 'munitions' industries reached 5.2 million. Government controls over these industries were strong. Government became the sole purchaser of these industries, and also co-ordinated the supply of raw materials, but did not take over ownership of producers.

> The private 'sector' was thus very large, but the extent to which it was wholly private must not be exaggerated. Firms did not compete for orders and were all but safeguarded from loss. Decisions of individual managements could no longer be as independent and autonomous as in peace. At the same time the responsibilities of the state for the affairs of private firms grew to the same extent to which the independence of private firms declined. (Postan, 1952, p. 434)

Given that the state was the sole customer of war industry and prices were settled under contract as sufficient to avoid loss, competitive marketing was removed in many areas. What effects did this have on concentration and organization of production?

Postan views the situation thus:

> Did British production suffer from its dispersed structure and less specialised equipment? . . . a large number of firms in the engineering and allied industries fought shy of the methods of modern large-scale industry and did not fully master the more advanced arts of modern manufacture, such as the scientific organisation of the 'production line', the economical 'break-up' of operations, or even efficient cost-accountancy and store-keeping . . . the early records of aircraft production abound with examples of stubbornly persisting small-workshop methods. (Postan, 1952, pp. 408–9)

Changes in industry there were, and state involvement certainly increased. But 'radical' advances along the path to centralized planning (involving state ownership, and state control and co-ordination of private enterprises) were certainly less than the scientists were advocating from their experiences in the military sphere. There was state encouragement for technical change, and support for this, but no direct intervention in company management. An additional factor seeming to disturb the traditional government-industry relationship was that posed by the rise of dramatically new areas of technology.

The emergence of the nuclear industries showed the complex problems associated with the emergence of technology of unprecedented novelty and scale. In the early days of the nuclear industry in the early 1940s private companies took a leading role. Margaret Gowing, the historian of the UKAEA wrote: 'The project . . . was anxious to enlist private industry. It has frequently been suggested firstly that the decision to make a government organization responsible . . . was taken on dogmatic grounds, and secondly, that private industry played little part in the early part. Both these propositions, however, are wrong: the project depended heavily on private industry from the outset' (Gowing, 1974, p. 154).

ICI attempted in 1941 to take on full responsibility for the development of nuclear energy. But this proposal was turned down mainly because of the political problems in British–US relationships posed by the involvement of a British company in a field of great long-term economic significance. But at the end of the war when government attempted to involve private companies, none could be found to take on large parts of the nuclear power programme.

> The Government became sole entrepreneur not by expressed intention but because private industry refused the role . . . When in the last months of 1945, the Ministry [of Supply] contemplated the task . . . its instinct was to use private industry as main agency contractors, just as the United States project had done . . . the whole complex of plants belonged more obviously to the chemical plant industry than to any other . . . Sir William Akers . . . the peace time Director of Research at I.C.I. wrote in May 1945 that the board of I.C.I. had agreed in principle that the company should accept a contract for this work . . . In October Akers was authorised to approach I.C.I. officially . . . The I.C.I. board had now changed its mind and refused the contract for both practical and political reasons. (Gowing, 1974, pp. 155–8)

The practical reasons included the need for secrecy which would mean a separate department, the lack of design staff and 'What Akers could also see, and so could others, was that this would be an enormous task. . . . It would severely strain I.C.I.'s engineering resource at a time when I.C.I.'s natural field for profitable development, the chemical industry, also badly needed attention' (Reader, 1975, pp. 293–4). Politically also, 'it was generally believed that ICI feared that entanglement in such a potential "commanding height" of strategy and of the economy would lead to nationalisation' (Gowing, 1974, p. 157).

Overall, then, it is apparent that although the exigencies of war did force the state to adopt new functions concerning research and technology this was coupled with a reluctance to alter drastically traditional patterns of ownership and control. Where this did occur as in nuclear power it arose not from a particular ideological commitment, but in response to the very real limits in the private sector's capacity to take on a technology of enormous scale, with long-term and uncertain prospects, and of key national importance. In spite of the opening up of the state to scientists with radical views on planning, the overall pattern of research remained fragmented and unco-ordinated. The features of planning which were so successful in individual military research projects were neither applied in a general fashion to government research nor to the wider economy in spite of the evident weaknesses in the existing structures.

The post-war period

Government policy

The election of a Labour government in 1945 appeared to offer the opportunity for the implementation of the planning proposals developed during wartime. According to one commentator on science policy: 'When the war ended, government officials and scientists were equally impressed by the part research and development had played in winning the war, saw clearly their potentialities for peace-time development, and were determined that a new and permanent partnership between government and science should be constructed in the national interest' (King, 1974).

Herbert Morrison who, as Lord President of the Council, was responsible for civil science, informed the House of Commons that: 'The Government attach the very greatest importance to science. We recognise the contribution which science has made to the prosecution of the war and the achievement of victory, and we are no less desirous that science shall play its part in the constructive tasks of peace and of economic development' (Vig, 1968, p. 14).

Thus the prospects of the transformation of the organization of science in the direction which the Association of Scientific Workers had been campaigning for seemed propitious. This was even more so the case given Labour's ideological commitment to planning. However, while there was general agreement that the state should adopt a major role in peacetime science there were differences over the form this should take. In October 1945, Herbert Morrison appointed an *ad hoc* Committee on Future Scientific Policy whose principal task was to advise on the supply and use of scientific manpower. There was clear representation of the lobby for the centralized planning of science in the form of Blackett and Zuckerman. Three main lines of argument were to emerge in its deliberations.

One position closest to the 'radical' demands of the AScW was characterized by a belief in the need for a strong central scientific staff with wide advisory and executive powers. Zuckerman, proposed the formation of such a 'scientific general staff' criticizing the wartime Scientific Advisory Committee for its lack of initiative and authority. Zuckerman wanted a scientific secretariat located at the centre of government with wide executive powers. It would oversee all aspects of scientific endeavour from manpower to planning of private and public research in both military and industrial fields.

A moderate position put by the senior civil servant, Sir John Anderson, sought to balance the need for a central staff with the traditional boundaries of ministerial responsibility. There would be a standing advisory committee with a somewhat wider representation than the existing Scientific Advisory Committee, but no central specialist staff which would rival the department staffs. More conservatively still, Sir Alfred Egerton, one of the secretaries of the Royal Society, felt that even Anderson's proposals went too far down the road of centralization. He was anxious to avoid too definite planning of research by a board or committee or even the direction of it into definite channels' (Gummett, 1980, p. 219).

It is apparent that the broader issues of social need and democratization did not feature significantly within the terms of this debate. The principal issue was the degree of centralization of the structures in the state concerned with government support for science. Nevertheless, the reluctance to develop such a central mechanism arose from: (1) those ideological positions hostile to centralized planning as such; and (2) from the lack of a strong political commitment in the Labour government to challenge entrenched interests which the implementation of the more radical proposal would have involved.

The result of the early post-war deliberations was the establishment of two new advisory bodies: the Advisory Council in Scientific Policy (ACSP), and the Defence Research Policy Committee (DRPC). These were a limited attempt to introduce co-ordination but the powers of the ACSP were few and it had only a small secretariat. A scientific civil service was also established on a proper footing in 1946 and the National Research Development Corporation was set up in 1948 to encourage the industrial application of government sponsored research.

Vig, in assessing the impact of the ACSP, has argued that 'its vague terms of reference restricted it to occasional advice on general problems . . . it had no authority in budgetary matters or overall scientific planning' (Vig, 1968, p. 23). He continues: 'If scientific co-ordination was not appreciably improved neither was the position of scientists in administration . . . Although scientists were "established" in an external network of advisory committees and the Scientific Civil Service . . . scientists were still excluded from high administrative positions in most departments' (Vig, 1968, p. 23). Overall Vig characterizes the post-war Labour government policy for science as one of expansion rather than reform.

Essentially, the conflicting approaches promoted in the immediate post-war period were resolved in two ways. First, the desire for an expansion of the state resources allocated to scientific research which was common to all of the different groups of scientists, administrators and politicians was implemented in practice. Second, the introduction of a limited degree of administrative reform, coupled with the political marginalization of the radical planners after 1947–48, served to defuse the pressures for more fundamental change.

The post-war fate of the planners

Following the end of the Second World War, the AScW was

anxious to secure a firmer position within the trade union movement as a whole. Blackett, in his presidential address of 1946, saw the victory of the Labour Party as leading to greater participation by trade unions in government: 'The increasing complexity of modern industrial life not only demands a greater extension of education, but also necessitates the much more active participation of the workers and technicians at all levels in the machinery of government.' He saw the Association as the major representative of scientists and technicians as having a special role in ensuring that Labour's nationalization programme had a major effect in raising the scientific and technical level of industry.

As the Association's delegate at the 77th TUC Annual Congress in 1945, he moved the resolution which led to the formation of the TUC Scientific Advisory Committee. Blackett stressed the role of 'planned conscious co-operation' in the application of research to social ends. He presented the problems raised by atomic energy as representing both the promise and the threat of scientific discovery. The function of the Scientific Advisory Committee was thus to provide 'first class scientific advice' to the General Council to enable it to negotiate with government on equal terms.

Parallel with this formation of stronger links with the trade union movement was the fuller expression of the aims of the AScW through its comprehensive blueprint for the planning of science, *Science and the Nation* (1947). Blackett writes in the introduction to the book: 'The subjects treated are variously the concern of private industry, or of numerous, largely unco-ordinated, government departments. There is no central body yet in existence which could be officially entrusted with the task of making such a survey as have been attempted here.'

On the assumption that the Labour government would continue wartime controls and extend them into a network of planning mechanisms, *Science and the Nation* proposes a corresponding structure for the centralized planning and co-ordination of science. However, the onset of economic crisis in 1947 and the change in the political context of the Cold War was to demonstrate such optimism to be misplaced. The initial effect of the economic crisis was to resharpen the AScW's planning posture. The AScW renewed its calls for centralized planning.

Sir Robert Watson-Watt criticized the continuing high levels of expenditure on military research and development. Bernal argued that the economic crisis 'required a similar organisation . . . to that of the operational research teams during the war. In addition men of science are needed at Cabinet Office level working with the Joint Planning Staff' (*Nature*, 1947, p. 512).

In the following year, the AScW attempted to win TUC support in its campaign against excessive concentration on military research by government. However, the call for far-reaching proposals to adjust the balance between military and civil research to ensure the economic independence of the country (from United States economic aid) and to maintain its standard of life, were not adopted.

The cooling of receptivity within the labour movement to the radical proponents of planning reflected a more general change in the political climate. Politically, the onset of the Cold War led to the isolation of the left from the mainstream. As Vig writes: 'After government organisation and policy was again settled (in 1947–48), the activity and influence of the scientists' unions rapidly declined. Moreover, the development of cold war tensions and the overwhelming pre-occupation of scientists with the new-found power of atomic energy contributed to a renewal of political divisions' (Vig, 1968, p. 26).

The weakening of the left was reinforced by the general hostility to shortages, restrictions and controls and a growing disillusionment with the results of public ownership coupled with a marked indifference amongst organized labour toward the democratic control of industry. In this context, the proposals of the AScW for centralized planning, with its echoes of the Soviet model, were increasingly at a distance not only from the labour movement but also from its own membership.

The ideas of planning along socialist lines lost the popular support they had enjoyed at the end of the war. This was to some extent the fruit of a growing ideological counter-offensive. Hayek, for example, had published, in 1944, *The Road to Serfdom*, which had presented a vigorous defence of bourgeois political economy as a basis for political freedom. The same trend is evident in Jewkes's *Ordeal by Planning*, published in 1948. Jewkes concentrated his fire on how attempts at planning in the immediate post-war period led to bureaucracy and inefficiency; his target was the remaining controls which the government had retained from the war.

Developments in Soviet science rebounded to the movement's detriment. Werskey writes that 'more than anything else, it was Stalin's sudden decision in July 1948 to put T. D. Lysenko in charge of Soviet biology that seemed to catalyse the decline of the scientific left' (Werskey, 1978). Lysenko was a Soviet agronomist who challenged the mainstream of genetic science. The promotion of a 'two sciences' policy in the Soviet Union (bourgeois and proletarian) at this time underpinned his endorsement by Stalin as 'ideologically correct'. The result was a severe blow to the leading figures of Soviet genetics research and set back Soviet agrarian research for a number of years. Haldane, a geneticist, himself resigned from the British Communist Party as a result of his disagreement with Soviet policy.

The Lysenko episode was taken as an illustration of the dangers of the centralized and political control of science which the critics of central planning had been advancing for ten years. The hegemony of the left within the scientific community had lasted for about a decade from the late 1930s to the late 1940s. The key figures who had moved from the position of 'outsiders' to 'insiders' in this period began to be eased outside once more. Blackett's position on the important Advisory Committee on Atomic Energy was ended in 1947 after differences of view with government policy on atomic weapons. Haldane was asked to resign from the Medical Research Council in 1950 following pressure from the Admiralty (Clark, 1968). Bernal was removed from the governing body of the British Association in 1949.

In some ways, the state incorporated elements of the demands of the planners but within a political context aimed at preserving the existing social and economic order. After the war, research expenditure increased dramatically and scientific advice became a much more widespread feature of state policy formation. It has been suggested by writers such as Hilary Rose and Steven Rose that this reflected not only the changes in the political and economic environment but also limitations in the perspective of the planning movement itself. An overly optimistic view of the progressive potentialities of science and a rather uncritical attitude to the role of the 'expert' – an approach that they characterize as 'techno-economist' – are considered to have lent themselves to appropriation by the state and thus facilitated the isolation of the radical planners in the post-war context (Rose and Rose, 1976).

The divisions within the AScW and the exclusion of the radicals from the government advisory sphere certainly facilitated this process. Although science had become much more conspicuously identified as a sphere of state activity this was heavily oriented to military objectives and many of the basic problems concerning science and the modernization of the British economy remained unresolved.

Industrial policy in the aftermath of war

The Labour government's attempts at planning in the post-war period never seriously confronted the power of private enterprise in any other than a number of basic and unprofitable industries. There was, however, an increasing trend towards tripartism with management, trade unions and government involved in the establishment of joint bodies such as the National Production Advisory Council.

The war had made private industry aware of the benefits of some forms of state intervention. As a historian of the Federation of British Industry (FBI) says:

> Industry . . . had benefitted greatly from the intimate war-time relationship with government . . . few [industrialists] urged that the system of war-time controls be removed before the essential tasks of rebuilding much of the nation's economic structure had been fully completed. Many in industry realised, too, that . . . the responsibilities and powers of the state in the economy and even in the affairs of individual industries would have to be much greater than ever before in peace time. (Blank, 1973, p. 16)

Even state ownership was acceptable in some cases:

> . . . so long as nationalization was confined to ailing, inefficient industries or to public utilities and services, opposition from the major industrial associations remained muted . . . But the nationalization of the iron and steel industry was a different matter . . . to the FBI there was a world of difference between nationalization of iron and steel and of an industry such as coal which was sick. . . . The steel industry was neither sick nor particularly inefficient. (Blank, 1973, pp. 83, 85)

So private industry accepted a certain level of state support but not state direction of private industry. The 'backwardness' of private industry which Bernal had written about in the 1930s was not overcome by the war. Industrial investment in scientific research and development was very uneven and very low in some industries. State expenditure, though increasing rapidly, was highly concentrated in the military sector. Britain kept relatively well up in scientific expenditure in a few sectors but the 'older' industries and civilian (including consumer) industries in general did less well.

The planners' postscript

As a result, there were renewed attempts by the Labour Party in opposition in the late 1950s and early 1960s to develop a strategy for modernization with particular attention to the economy. Two prominent members of the earlier movement, Bernal and Blackett, became part of a group of informal advisers to the Labour Party. The policy proposals in *Science and the Future of Britain* (1961), still embodied a notion of planning but in a narrower political and economic context of improving international competitiveness. A policy to expand and co-ordinate was contrasted with the existing 'near anarchy in the administration of science'. The proposals for a Minister of Science accompanied by a Scientific and Technical Planning Board consisting 'largely of scientists' are made once more. The concern is primarily with the administration of government science and few proposals are made for greater intervention in the private sector.

By the early 1960s, a 'science group' headed by the Labour politician, Richard Crossman, provided the back-up to Wilson's notable call at the Scarborough Labour Party conference in 1963 to 'forge a new socialist Britain in the white heat of the scientific and technological revolution'. On the platform during the delivery of this speech was Patrick Blackett, the only major figure from the earlier planning of science movement still close to the centres of political power.

Accompanying the election of a Labour government in 1964 were a set of changes incorporating the setting up of the Ministry of Technology which assumed responsibility for much government research, and the establishment of the Department of Education and Science, responsible for the research councils which included the new Science Research Council. During the Labour administration of the 1960s, although new co-ordinating mechanisms such as the Council for Scientific Policy and a government Chief Scientific Adviser were introduced, there was again a reluctance to embark whole-heartedly on a democratically accountable planning strategy for science and technology.

Blackett was appointed Deputy Chairman of the Advisory Council on Technology and scientific adviser to the Ministry of Technology. The Ministry did not accomplish as much as initially hoped. At the end of 1965 Blackett concluded: 'The problem of the efficiency of British industry, which we were set up to do something about, is much more serious than was generally thought at the time, and a great amount of Government action is needed to put matters right.' He was critical of the low level of government investment in industry. In the late 1960s he became preoccupied with the issue of restructuring British industry to achieve larger units through merger and was a significant force behind the setting up of the Industrial Reorganisation Corporation. By implication, this placed the direction of research as a secondary consequence of such structural change. Government research itself became subject more to narrower criteria of financial accountability than to social planning.

Blackett, even though he became President of the Royal Society, is here operating alone rather than as part of a group. The AScW itself merged to form ASTMS, a large union marked by its vigorous pursuit of better rewards for managerial and technical employees rather than its promotion of policies for the planning of science.

Conclusions

Our account demonstrates a reluctance by the British state to intervene in the planning and co-ordination of science and technology. But during the period considered there were strong pressures on the state to increase its planning of science and technology which the state accommodated by gradually increasing its involvement. The most important problems which led to increased state planning were: (1) national strategic problems such as the two world wars, and (2) the relative performance of British industry. With respect to one theme, economic planning, the state responded to specific weaknesses by taking on increased functions for science and technology. One of our conclusions is that there was a marked reluctance on the part of the state to undertake planning in a centralized form.

For the 'radical' scientists, the two problems, of war and of Britain's industrial performance, were problems they analysed carefully and critically. They were able to point to weaknesses in the present system and to argue cogently for fundamental changes to it. The group of radical scientists linked to the AScW was one of the most successful groups, both in articulating and achieving a measure of political support for an alternative form of planning: one based on strong state intervention and centralized co-ordination of science and technology, and more generally of the economy. The reasons why they were relatively successful for a period is, we think, *both* because of the breadth of support they mobilized and gained among their scientific colleagues, *and* because key members of the group were involved in the state itself.

This relates to another theme, that of power and expertise. Part of the success of this group rested on the power which can fall on all specialist groups, in this case a group of eminent scientists. This power came because at certain moments (and particularly during the war) the state depended on these scientists for its survival. It seems to us that the relationship to the capitalist state that their expertise gave these scientists also limited their power for exercising the radical changes they were advocating. After their experiences as wartime scientists working with operational research, the scientists did tend to argue that solutions to social problems could be posed in scientific terms. And given the benefit of hindsight (using theories on the complexity of the relationship between basic science, invention and innovation), we can say that the scientists took a very optimistic view of what could be achieved in British industrial performance through further spending on science. In their policy proposals, they had a relatively straightforward, linear view of the relationship between science, its application through innovation, and economic growth.

Finally, on the theme of the state and economic change, the radical scientists in the 1940s still put a stark emphasis on the impossibility of capitalist industry's taking up technological advances – a claim belied by post-war change. They did seem to generalize their experiences inside the military sphere in wartime, to argue that there was no alternative to fundamental social transformation: that is, that capitalist society was incapable of producing and using scientific advances to maximum effect.

In spite of the power of this movement, the state showed a strong capacity to adapt and to expand its support of scientific effort without centralized co-ordination of science or the adoption of a planned approach to industrial change, and without the profound change in Britain's capitalist economy which the more radical scientists advocated. The movement underestimated the state's ability to adapt and this was certainly a reason for their decline as a group and for its division. Some kept top advisory positions after the war, but under narrower 'reformist' terms than they aspired for. Others, more 'radical', were frozen out. Because there was no profound change in British society, their most radical ideas for the regeneration of British industry were never tested.

References

Anon. (1940) *Science in War,* Harmondsworth: Penguin.
Association of Scientific Workers (AScW) (1943a) *Scientists and Production,* London: AScW.
AScW (1943b) *The Development of Science,* London: AScW.
AScW (1943c) *The Planning of Science*, London: AScW.
AScW (1947) *Science and the Nation,* Harmondsworth: Penguin.
Baker, J. R. (1942) *The Scientific Life*, London: George Allen and Unwin.
Bernal, J. D. (1939) *The Social Function of Science*, London: Routledge and Kegan Paul.
Blank, S. (1973) *Industry and Government in Britain: The Federation of British Industries in Politics, 1945–65,* Farnborough, Hants and Lexington, Mass.: Saxon House and Lexington Books.
Clark, R. (1968) *JBS – The Life and Work of J. B. S. Haldane,* London: Hodder and Stoughton.
Goldsmith, M. (1980) *Sage: A Life of J. D. Bernal,* London: Hutchinson.
Gowing, M. (1974) *Independence and Deterrence: Britain and Atomic Energy 1945–52,* London: Macmillan.
Gummett, P. J. (1980) *Scientists in Whitehall,* Manchester: Manchester University Press.
Hall, D. *et al.* (1935) *The Frustration of Science,* London: George Allen and Unwin.
HMSO (1914–16) *Scheme for the Organization and Development of Scientific and Industrial Research,* Cd. 8005, 1.
Horner, D. (1981) *The AScW and the Social Relations of Science, (1939–1949),* Aston University: MSc thesis.
King, A. (1974) *Science and Policy, the International Stimulus,* London: Oxford University Press.
Leruez, J. (1975) *Economic Planning and Politics in Britain,* Oxford: Martin Robertson.
MacLeod, Roy and Kay (1977) 'The social relations of science and technology 1914–1939', in C. M. Cipolla (ed.) *The Twentieth Century,* Glasgow: Fontana.
McGucken, W. (1978) 'On freedom and planning in science: the society for freedom in science 1940–46', *Minerva*, Vol. 16, pp. 42–72.
Nature (1942) No. 149, 7 March, p. 253.
Nature (1943) No. 151, 20 February, p. 203.
Nature (1947) No. 159, 12 April, pp. 511–12.
Pollard, S. (1969) *The Development of the British Economy 1914–1967,* London: Edward Arnold.
Postan, M. (1952) *British War Production,* London: HMSO.
Reader, W. J. (1975) *History of ICI,* Vol. II, *The First Quarter Century,* London: Oxford University Press.
Rose, H. and Rose, S. (1976) *The Political Economy of Science,* London: Routledge and Kegan Paul.

Snow, C. P. (1966) 'J. D. Bernal, a personal portrait', in M. Goldsmith and Alan Mackay (eds) *The Science of Science*, Harmondsworth: Pelican.
TUC (1945) 77th Annual Report, pp. 402–4.
Vig, N. T. (1968) *Science and Technology in British Politics,* Oxford: Pergamon.
Werskey, G. (1978) *The Visible College*, London: Allen Lane.

7

The family, regulation, and the public sphere

MARY McINTOSH

Four general perspectives

Introduction

A study of the family is central to any exploration of the relations between the modern state and civil society in Britain. Civil society refers to all those social institutions and relationships which arise, through voluntary association, outside the sphere of *direct* state control, and which belong to the domain of 'society' rather than the state. When first used by Adam Smith and the early political economists, the term 'civil society' most precisely designated the realm of private economic transactions outside the state (for example capitalist market relations, the private ownership and transmission of property, the production and sale of goods, the free sale and purchase of labour, etc.). But historically, many societies have recognized a broader distinction between things that pertain to the state and the affairs of 'public life' and the things that do not – 'private' relations. Roman law, one of the foundation stones of the modern state, made a very clear distinction of this kind. And since the sexual division of labour between men and women – differentiating their tasks and responsibilities on the basis of gender differences – is one of the earliest forms of the social division of labour in general, the distinction between 'public' and 'private' has existed in different forms for a very long time, with the family, women and the domestic sphere very commonly assigned to the latter.

In many societies with relatively simple social organization, the family has *not* been so clearly differentiated out from other so-called 'public' institutions as it is in capitalist societies. For example, family networks – kinship – have often overlapped with political relationships. But in more developed societies, and especially in societies of a capitalist type, the sexual division of labour is very advanced; the family has become more clearly designated, in contrast with work and public life, as a 'separate sphere' and the division between home and work – largely unknown, even today, in many rural societies where women have always worked in similar tasks alongside men – has become much sharper, with profound consequences for the position of women.

Under these modern conditions the family and public life have become clearly demarcated along gender lines. Accordingly, the family has acquired a particular, strong set of social connotations (haven, retreat from the bustle and pressures of the competitive public world, the 'little kingdom' of private virtues, feminine qualities and concerns and the realm of domesticity). It has become, in many ways, the *essentially* private institution, the heart and centre of everything we associate with what is *not* the state. Within the individualistic and competitive ethos of early capitalist development, the 'home' became associated, for men, with the antithesis of the public world of social affairs and the state: guarded over by women and the domestic virtues, and signifying a safe retreat from public life's stresses and strains. The taboos against state interference or state intervention in the economy, which came to be associated with classical liberal and *laissez-faire* doctrine in the eighteenth century and nineteenth century, were also erected around the family. Indeed, the family came to stand as a key metaphor for the rights of competitive and possessive individuals *against* the state: 'An English*man*'s [sic] home is his castle.'

However, as we have seen, the boundaries between 'state' and 'society' are not fixed by Nature but socially and historically constructed. They have constantly changed – and go on changing. Hence, as we might expect, the gradual emergence of a more collectivist and interventionist state towards the end of the ninteenth century was accompanied by the increasing regulation by the state of the family sphere. The moment when the state begins to have an open and direct stake in the family, extends its powers of legal and administrative regulation, begins to develop policies which have the family and family life as their object, is thus a critical one in the development of the modern state. The boundaries between state and society are constantly being redrawn; in this way society is constantly reconstituted by the state. In general, the state is therefore often seen as enlarging its sphere of action at the expense of the family. It is this process which we will be examining in this chapter: asking not only where and how these transactions between family and state now take place in Britain, but more significantly, *why* they take place.

A recurrent theme in discussions of 'the family' is how – and whether – it has declined or become eroded in modern western societies. Since its supposed decline is often attributed to the growth of institutions associated with the state, as well as to other social changes, it is worth examining this discussion in the context of this chapter. The usual argument is two-fold: (1) that in the past the family was a large grouping of kin whereas in modern industrial societies it has become pared down to its basic nucleus of a married couple and their dependent children (often called the 'nuclear family'); and, along with this, (2) that, in the past the family carried out a wide range of activities, including producing its own livelihood, whereas in modern societies it has very restricted functions, serving only as a unit of consumption, intimate sociability and for the bearing and rearing of children. All the other functions, it is argued, have been devolved to other institutions. Factories have taken over production, so that food, clothes and household necessities are no longer made at home. Television and other media have taken over recreation, so that people no longer tell stories or make music at home. Most relevant for our purposes, the welfare state has taken over provision for such contingencies as old age, disablement and unemployment and provision of education and training of the young, health care of the sick, and the mentally sick; it has provided a plethora of social workers and other paid helpers so that people no longer turn to their kin when in need of support or care.

Alongside this sociological argument has run a moral one, that the old family values are in decline under the pressure of secularization, sexual premissiveness and a new egalitarianism that undermines paternal authority. Some, however, have countered this by claiming that family values are changing but in ways that do not herald the family's demise, only its modification.

Discussions about the family are seldom dispassionate or objective. It is a topic that arouses deep and contradictory feelings. The family is at one and the same time the favoured cultural image for security, trust, warmth and intimacy and the commonly blamed source of boredom, burdens, unavoidable pressures and relationships that are wished on you rather than chosen. So it is a topic about which we all feel deeply ambivalent. There are also widely divergent political positions about the family. Some hold that it is 'the basic building block of society' and that everything possible must be done to preserve it, to encourage families to look after their own members, to discourage people from living together outside marriage or getting divorced, to strengthen parental and particularly paternal authority. Others hold that family life, and perhaps particularly that of the modern nuclear family, is oppressive to women and children and fundamentally individualistic and selfish in that it excludes those who are outside the family and seeks to pass on whatever privileges the parents may have to their own children and not to others. (See for instance Cooper, 1972; Leach, 1967).

My own sympathies are with the anti-family position (see Barrett and McIntosh, 1982), but my purpose here is not to argue that view; it is rather to explore the relation between the state and family patterns and to consider certain analytical questions. The choice of questions is no doubt influenced by my own views, and indeed reflects the problems that femininists have drawn attention to over the last decade. But I have tried to present the material and the arguments in such a way that you do not have to agree with my views in order to engage with them.

It is possible to detect, within writings on the relation between the state and the family, four different perspectives. These can be summarized in the following way:

(1) the interventionist state expands its activities and spheres of influence and increasingly intrudes upon areas that were once private family matters and thereby erodes and weakens the family (associated with this is the growth of interventionist professions such as teaching, medicine, social work, psychiatry, which although formally autonomous operate mainly within state institutions);
(2) the family is a bastion against state control, protecting an arena of personal life and individual freedom against impersonal outside forces;
(3) the family policy of the state provides for the functional needs of the economy/society, by supporting those aspects of the family that function well and by taking over those aspects that are not functioning adequately;
(4) the family policy of the state serves the interests of particular groups within the society (such as women, or men, or children, or the ruling class, or the working class).

It will be apparent that these general positions are not necessarily mutually exclusive and that the first and second, and the third and fourth, form two pairs representing different emphases in a similar analysis.

State intervention in the family

The first view on the relation of state and family is that the state is increasingly interfering in family life. The image is of 'the family', which was once an independent and self-governing unit, being subjected to so much regulation and control that it has lost its autonomy and become a mere creature of the state. Legal restrictions on parental rights limit the ways parents can chastise their children, the ways they can educate them, can forbid them even to give birth to their babies without medical supervision. The tax authorities pry into the gifts that family members make to each other. A phalanx of professionals – midwives, health visitors, social workers, doctors, psychiatrists, priests, police concerned with juveniles, school care officers, social security officers – not only come a-visiting the family home but even, some writers have suggested, enlist women as their allies and agents within the home. And behind them are the mass media pumping out their nostrums and blueprints for family life from pop-psychoanalysis to soap-opera marriage guidance to consumerist housecraft.

The image of the interventionist state that I have just presented is obviously a popular one. But it corresponds to the underlying assumptions of much of the more academic discussion of the family and family policy. Its analytical essence is that the family was once a part of civil society, arising organically from people's own needs, and is now so transformed that it is little more than a product of state interventions, whether or not these are sufficiently co-ordinated to be described as a state *policy*. The underlying political character of this argument is nearly always anti-statist, coupled with a regret for the demise of the supposed independent, 'natural' family form.

An interesting recent development of this sort of analysis is the book by Jacques Donzelot, *The Policing of Families.* Following the ideas of another French author Michel Foucault, Donzelot traces the growth in France during the nineteenth century of a whole set of strategies in the spheres of education, medicine, childcare, delinquency, psychiatry that were concerned with the regulation of everyday life and health. He sees these strategies as unified by their common function — 'policing'; that is to say, by the fact that they are all 'methods for developing the quality of the population and the strength of the nation' (Donzelot, 1980, pp. 6—7). So, for instance, in one fascinating chapter he traces the development of what he calls 'the tutelary complex': the juvenile courts with their objective of treatment rather than punishment; the social inquiry by social workers where children are no longer brought before adult courts and treated as responsible criminals to be punished, but appear at special juvenile courts where the objective is the treatment of the child rather than the punishment of the crime. There they and their parents come into contact with social workers, a social inquiry report is presented to the magistrates and frequently the probation or social service departments are made responsible for the child's treatment. Child psychiatry, too, has become a regular institutionalized part of the assessment and treatment of juveniles. The delinquent child therefore provides educators, social workers and psychiatrists with an entrée into the family since the delinquency of the child marks the failure of the family. So these agencies all practise in such a way as to *regulate* families by bringing any that fall out of line under coercive tutelage.

According to Donzelot, this is the culmination of a process which began in the early nineteenth century with medical concern over the 'preservation of children'. Doctors began to propound their principles of hygiene and child rearing and enlisted mothers as their allies within the family. These modern mothers, with a respect for medicine, rejected both the old male oriented structures of education, such as religious discipline and (in France) the boarding school and also the 'old wives tales' of domestic servants, wet nurses and midwives. So these bourgeois women gained status by submitting themselves to a medical surveillance that co-opted them as its agent within the family. Among the working class, the 'preservation of children' took the form of combating the abandoning of babies, encouraging marriage, restricting prostitution, limiting women's and children's employment, providing sanitary family homes and eventually establishing domestic hygiene as part of the school curriculum for girls. Again as in the bourgeoisie, the women became the agents of regulation, so that for Donzelot the substitution of 'government through the family' for 'government by the family' is also the substitution of women's power (albeit as agents of outside forces) for men's power. The defeat of the family as an autonomous power is represented vividly by the absence or the helpless silence of the father when his child appears before the juvenile court.

Donzelot weaves this story into a complex and ambiguous analysis, but much of what he describes has been recognized by other writers. For instance another French book published in the same year as that of Donzelot (*The Child and the State: The Intervention of the State in Family Life* by Philippe Meyer) also discusses 'the policing of families' in relation to delinquent children. It makes similar points, such as that, despite its declared liberal intentions, the modern therapeutic approach in the children's courts gives the courts even more effective control over children and their families than the traditional punitive legal approach (Meyer, 1983, p. 79). And the idea of the social worker as 'social policeman' was a strong theme in the radical critique of social work, social policy and criminology in Britain in the late 1960s (see for instance the work of the National Deviancy Conference).

Philippe Meyer takes this critique to the point of writing of 'the progressive destruction of society by the state' (p. 111), but he sees a paradoxical cause for optimism in the fact that this process of the regulation of families has constituted in the family a form of sociality which may be too dense to be monopolized by the state and may in the end be the basis for resistance and for a revitalization of the autonomous social sphere.

Starting from a similar observation, Eli Zaretsky (1983) comes to a very different conclusion. He writes: 'Far from the state "invading" or "replacing" the family, a certain kind of alienated public life and a certain kind of alienated private life have expanded together. The form in which the welfare state expanded was public, the content private' (Zaretsky, 1983, p. 303). So it is the state's demarcation of the 'public' realm that sets the boundaries and the character of the 'private' world of the family. Family privacy does not, as it were, exist from time immemorial before the state comes along to challenge it; it is constituted historically – in large part by the state itself.

The family as a bastion against state control

This leads us to the second perspective on the relation of state and family. While writers such as Meyer and Donzelot emphasize the way the state destroys the old family form and constructs in its place a colonized form designed to serve the needs of the state, this second perspective sees the family as a sturdy, enduring and popular way of life that persists despite rather than because of the state. In a sense, then, it is just the reverse of the coin of the interventionist perspective with which it usually shares a pro-family political stance, differing in being more optimistic about the ability of the family to resist intervention.

Ferdinand Mount offers a good recent example of this position. His book is called *The Subversive Family* and it argues that the western family has shown remarkable tenacity, surviving in the face of attempts by Church and state to subordinate it to 'higher' aims than those of people's earthly aspirations and search for a social form for 'the procreation and protection of children and the mutual help and affection of the couple' (Mount, 1982, p. 255).

The family, he argues, stands for privacy and individualism against the Christian and statist view that 'we are all members one of another'. His position involves the anti-statist conception of liberty associated with neo-liberalism. In a central chapter on 'Privacy and the Working Class' he claims that socialist intellectuals have been mistaken in seeing ordinary people as the helpless victims of wider social forces. For, he says, the working man remains independent and critical of the establishment; he chooses to devote himself to providing a better life for his family and to the protection of his privacy in the family. He speaks of 'the family's permanent revolution against the State, and of the working-class family as the only truly revolutionary class'.

Thus, although Mount presents a picture of state intervention that is not unlike that of Donzelot or Meyer, he sees the family as capable of an active resistance rather than as a mere 'point of intersection of forces' (as Donzelot puts it). He portrays vividly the ambivalent role of those agents of the state who are 'only there to help', but 'who come armed, all the same, with statutory powers and administrative instruments: education officers, children's officers, housing officers, architects, planners, welfare workers. . . . What is always affronting, offensive and distressing is the fact of their *intrusion* into our private space.' He points out that the health visitor is 'an inspector as well as an advisor'. But these officials do not go unchallenged.

> There is . . . an undeclared war between the [public and private] domains . . . On the one hand, an overclass, bossy, acquisitive of power and security, intermittently guilty about both; on the other an underclass, bossed, gulled and harried, intermittently aware of its situation and resentful. In all the revolts against big government and high taxes – which have swept the Western world in the past couple of years – this resentment has played its part. Domain-consciousness – the feeling that the State is intruding into private

> space more and more and ought to be stopped – is growing. The Visitor is being made to feel unwelcome. His or her claim to moral superiority is being disputed. What few have yet grasped is that the working class is the true defender of liberty and *privacy*, because it has no ulterior motive. The material triumph of the masses – the access they have finally gained to a decent standard of living – is not to be used for making society more public and collective. On the contrary, it is to be used for dispersing the delights of privacy to all. (Mount, 1982, pp. 174-5)

The 'subversive family', in Mount's view, thus resists effectively the commands of state, church and the public world.

From a quite different political position a Marxist, Jane Humphries, argues that the family in capitalist societies retains a 'primitively communal core' (Humphries, 1977a, p. 247) by providing for mutual support. 'According to this perspective the endurance of the family reflects a struggle by the working class for popular ways of meeting the needs of non-labouring comrades within a capitalist environment' (p. 250). She also claims that the system where a wife and child are dependent upon a man's wage enables the working class to resist the downward pressure on wages that would result from all of them going out to work, as happened in some areas in the early industrial period when wages were forced down by the huge supply of female and child labour. And she sees the family as playing 'a vital role in maintaining working-class autonomy and integrity' by reducing dependence on poor relief or state aid and passing from generation to generation a culture of communal loyalty and of resistance to external authority.

Jane Humphries explicitly rejects the Marxist-functionalist approach which sees the family from the point of view of capital. She argues against the one-sided emphasis by Marxist feminists upon the way in which the arrangement whereby women do unpaid housework serves to reproduce labour power cheaply for capitalist production. The family form cannot be explained, she says, by showing how functional it is in the capitalist system. For the working class have defended and strengthened the family as it helped them to protect their standard of living and their class cohesion against the ravages of capitalism. Capitalism tends to universalize the market principle and turn all relations between people into market relations; the preservation of non-market relations within the family enables the working class to resist this total subordination to capital.

Jane Humphries's position thus has some formal similarities with

Ferdinand Mount's (though he is an adviser to Margaret Thatcher and she is a revolutionary socialist). But where he emphasizes the family's resistance to a Church and a state that are seen as broadly similar throughout history, or at least throughout the history of Christendom, she focuses upon the specific form of capitalism and the capitalist state and the nature of the family in a specific class.

The state, the family and functional needs

The third perspective derives from a long tradition in the functional analysis of the family. In its simplest form, the argument runs that the family exists in all societies and performs certain basic functions that are essential to any social life. G. P. Murdock (1949), for instance, specified four basic functions – sexual, economic, reproductive and educational – each essential to carrying on the life of human beings and passing on culture from generation to generation. He claimed that the 'many-sided utility' of the family meant that it was an inevitable and indispensable feature of any society. However, he did not in fact explore very carefully whether these social needs could be fulfilled by other institutions or indeed whether there was really much similarity between, say, the economic or the educational functions (or even the sexual function) in simple hunting-and-gathering societies and in complex industrial societies.

Another sociologist, Talcott Parsons (1955) offered a much more elaborated version of the way in which the family performs its function of socialization (what Murdock has called 'education'). Primary socialization, especially in the pre-school years, structures the child's personality in terms of the particular culture of its society. Drawing on psychoanalytic theories, Parsons argued that in order to carry out this primary socialization effectively the family needed to provide a context of warmth and emotional security and that women embodied the warm and expressive qualities of this home, while men as breadwinners saw to its economic security and formed a link with the realities of the outside world of adulthood. Having been reared in such families, people have a need to live in them again as adults in order to 'stabilize their personalities' and this, according to Parsons, is the second major function of the family in modern industrial societies.

Another major theme in the analysis of the family has been the historical tendency for the family to become more specialized, performing only these basic functions and shedding others, such as production, social control, education, health care, recreation. In particular, it is argued, the welfare state has taken over some of the non-productive economic functions of the family, the provision of financial support and care for those in need. But it has not done so by simply stripping the family of these functions. What has happened has been that the family still has primary responsibility, but that state provision exists as a kind of safety-net, catching the casualties that escape family care. Later, we shall explore how this substitution of state for family works out in practice. In particular we shall look at the way that the conditions under which state welfare provision is offered structures the responsibilities of the family and the pattern of family life.

Like the welfare state, the development of the education system provides another example of how the state now replaces the family in providing for the functional needs of the society. Universal education was only provided by the state from 1870 onwards, though the introduction of schooling for working-class children had begun on a piecemeal basis much earlier. Before that, families had been responsible for bringing up children. Children got such socialization and training as they did either in the parental home or else in someone else's home as a servant or a farm servant or an apprentice. So the emergent education system took over part of what had been a function of the family. In the process, the way that function was performed became elaborated. The family became responsible for socializing the child in its early years and training it in basic social skills and obedient habits; the school became responsible for more specific training in skills relating to work and public life.

It is argued that the state-supported system of schooling served to bridge the gap between home and work by performing the function of differentiating school leavers into a hierarchy of qualification appropriate for different levels in an hierarchical occupational structure. At the same time, the schools did this in such a way as to redefine and then reinforce an area of parental responsibility. Parents are expected to produce five-year-olds ready and able to start school; they are expected to feed, clean and clothe them appropriately; they are expected to motivate them and to co-operate with the school if there are any problems. The school does not assume responsibility for bringing up the children, but it asserts its right to control some areas of their training and socialization. Thus is developed a new, differentiated, 'partnership' between home and school which serves well (or fairly well) a variety of functional needs of a highly differentiated industrial society. The state's educational policy is therefore also a family policy in the sense that it directs and defines the nature of the family's socializing function.

Now, many writers would be prepared to agree that state policies around the family can be understood in part as functional – providing for the functional needs of the economy and the society. Thus, for instance, there is a whole structure of family law relating to marriage and divorce, the mutual obligations of husband and wife, the duties of parents, illegitimacy, adoption, wardship, inheritance and so forth, and that these laws do much to favour and establish a particular pattern of family life. They favour long-term monogamous heterosexual relationships; they favour the economic dependence of those who have no income (e.g. wives) on those who have (e.g. the male family breadwinner); they favour a situation in which very few children are born into the world without at least a mother and usually a mother and father, to care for them and give them a place in the social structure. In short, particular state policies help to form and maintain particular family based relationships in society. On the other hand, it is agreed that although the state promotes a family form that provides for mutual support and caring, it also offers some state financial support and state care when such family support fails. But though some agreement may exist at this very general level, there are profound disagreements when it comes to specifying in any detail what those functional needs are. Writers ranging from some of the most conservative sociologists (such as Talcott Parsons) to fairly orthodox marxists have shared a functional view of state and family, but, as you can imagine, the actual analyses they offer are widely different in content.

For one thing, the language of traditional sociological functionalism is rather different from that of Marxist 'reproduction' theory. Whereas the sociological functionalists talk of society as a set of functionally interrelated institutions, all contributing in their different ways to the integration and stability of the whole society, the marxists talk of the 'reproduction of the social conditions of capitalist production' and explore the ways in which different social patterns and institutions like the family contribute to this. Typically, the Marxist approach is not integrative. Instead it tries to explain how even apparently progressive institutions (like education, social welfare, medical care, collective bargaining) can have their dark or contradictory side in that they are instituted in such a form that they serve to reproduce the conditions of capitalism and shore up the capitalist system. Furthermore, for

Marxists, this is not an accident or a result of the action of blind evolutionary forces, as it is to some degree orchestrated by the purposive action of a state which acts on behalf of the class that benefits from the continuance of the capitalist system.

Marxists emphasize specific features of the family and the functions they serve for a *specific* social system. So, for instance, there was a lot of interest among Marxist feminists in the 1970s in the ways in which the family served the *social* reproduction of capitalism. In particular, women's unpaid domestic labour – especially housework and childcare – was singled out for detailed study. It was argued that this work serves the function of reproducing a vital element of capitalist production, namely labour power, by servicing, refreshing and training both today's workers and the workers of the next generation. Of course, in other types of society too, the reproduction of people's ability to engage in productive work is vital. But because production is not located in privately owned industries organized by capitalists rather than the workers, this reproduction does not need a separate location in a family devoted to care and consumption. Similarly, in societies where production is not organized around the wage system (where people's subsistence depends on having a cash income in return for their work), the unpaid nature of housework is unremarkable.

To be unpaid only becomes significant in a wage-based society. In so far as women's domestic responsibilities go along with a marginal and intermittent involvement in work and low pay in their own employment, the unpaid nature of housework is significant because it involves partial or complete dependence on someone who has a wage, that is a husband. So there is a neat functional fit between a division of labour at home in which men are breadwinners and women homemakers and a division of labour in paid work in which men have the best and most secure jobs commanding a family wage and women have the poorer jobs that enable them to contribute only a subsidiary income to the household. And this functional fit helps to reproduce and maintain the social relations of a capitalist mode of production. This analysis, then, is a classically functionalist one, though there are many disputes as to whether unpaid domestic labour is really an essential and inevitable part of capitalist society or merely a highly convenient arrangement. Could capitalism survive without it?

Another functional analysis of the family derives from Louis Althusser's (1972) identification of the family as an 'ideological state apparatus'. The idea here is that, far from being the antithesis of the state, the family functions ideologically along with institutions like education and the media to contribute to the reproduction of the relations of capitalism. In particular, the individual self-supporting families provide an important motivation for regular hard work, especially for men who have the responsibilities of breadwinners, and the type of individualized child rearing that they offer helps to produce the individualistic personalities appropriate to life in capitalist society. Some would add that the paternal authority within the family provides the model for state authority and the experience of childhood submission establishes the basis for the submissive adult citizen. Others would emphasize the way in which the elaboration of privatized family life, especially in the form of consumerism, serves to divert the working class from a concern with exploitation at work and reduce the need for a more overtly repressive state. Again these are classically functionalist analyses, not so much explaining the form of the family as showing how it fits in with the specific society in which it is located.

But although functionalist analyses can explain the relationship between different processes well, they are much less useful when it comes to dealing with historical change. Usually we have to turn to much less systematic or holistic accounts for this. One exception among sociological functionalists, however, is Neil Smelser who followed closely the ideas of Talcott Parsons to develop an explanation of the way the form of the family changed in adapting to the major social upheaval of the industrial revolution, which, though it relies entirely on the operation of blind evolutionary mechanisms, nevertheless sees state legislation as playing an important part in establishing the new institutional form of the family.

In his book *Social Change in the Industrial Revolution* (1959), Smelser does not question the universality of the family, but he does see it as changing in form as the development of the factory system of production displaces the earlier cottage industry where the family formed a productive unit. Writing of the Lancashire cotton industry between 1770 and 1840, he describes how at first all the members of the family, including children, went to work in the factories and the strains that this put on the working-class family itself, in particular on its ability to perform its functions of socializing children and handling adults' tensions. The functional adaptation took the form of a differentiation between the sphere of production and the sphere of the family, with the family becoming a more specialized non-productive unit, segregated from its traditional productive roles. At the same time there developed a differentiation of occupational roles within the family: instead of all working together within the home, men became the chief factory workers, young children ceased productive work and women tended to stay at home more, engaged on 'domestic' work rather than working alongside their husbands. The historical process involved, according to Smelser, was not simply a smooth adaptation, but involved protests, struggles, campaigns, attempts to implement all sorts of solutions to the problems as they were experienced by the people involved and as they were interpreted in the light of the culture and expectations of the day. But Smelser sees legislation, and particularly the factory legislation that restricted the hours of women's and children's work and eventually excluded children from the factories altogether, as part of the process by which men's and women's involvement in production, and hence roles in the family, became differentiated.

The model of explanation that Smelser is using is one that sees social change as producing stresses in the existing social arrangements. In overcoming these, institutions like the family gradually become adapted and a new functionally integrated equilibrium is established. This reveals the potential circularity of any exclusively functionalist or evolutionary account of historical change: it assumes that whatever the struggles and false trails along the way, the social pattern finally arrived at will be the one best adapted to the new social situation.

Zaretsky (1983) offers an account that is, in some ways, the marxist equivalent of Neil Smelser's sociological account. Zaretsky sees the distinctive character of the family in the advanced capitalist USA as being economically and socially private: economically in the sense that it is a self-supporting unit and socially in the sense that it is sustained by an ideology relating domesticity, personal life and individualism. More generally, Zaretsky has argued that personal life, in the sense of subjective experience as the major source of meaning in people's lives, is peculiar to capitalist society, being made possible only by the split between work and home, public and private, that capitalism brings (Zaretsky, 1976).

The general picture that Zaretsky presents could be described as one of the 'functional adaptation' of the family to the advance of corporate capitalism. Most of this work can be read as a rejection of the thesis of the family as a bastion as well as of the thesis of state intervention weakening the family. For instance, he does not see the family as existing in the same form in all societies and historical periods, and he notes that 'the American political system, overall, has sought to foster independent, self-supporting units (individuals or families)' (Zaretsky, 1983, p. 291). So, for Zaretsky, the state's parental authority is not understood in terms of a struggle of state versus family in which the family was defeated and disarmed, but in terms of a functional reconstitution of the family.

> Rather than the state undermining the family, it is difficult to imagine how any form of the family could have survived the enormously destructive uprooting that accompanied industrialization without some intervention from the state. The issue is not whether the welfare state eroded the family, but rather in what form it preserved it. My argument is that the family has been preserved as an economically private unit and that most of the normative aspects of state policy are based on that. (Zaretsky, 1983, p. 292)

But Zaretsky is not strictly a functionalist, and he attaches much more importance than does Smelser to the political struggles in the course of which state policy around the family emerged.

One of the failings of functionalism is that it tends to oversimplify the state. For sociologists like Parsons the state merely serves to institutionalize functional social arrangements. It establishes stable social patterns and helps to maintain them. Its role is not a particularly active or important one. For functionalist marxists, on the other hand, the state reproduces the social and political conditions for the continued existence of capitalist production and the capitalist social formation.

What interests are served?

But some sociologists and most Marxists would say that the social arrangements assumed by the state not only meet the needs of the social system as a whole for stability and reproduction over time, but also – perhaps in the course of doing that – satisfy the interests of some groups within the society rather than others. For the way the society is arranged suits some groups more than it suits others.

For instance, Smelser ultimately explains the development of the Factory Acts which restricted women's industrial work during the nineteenth century in terms of the social disorganization produced by the indiscriminate drafting of men, women and children into the early factories. There was a crisis in the institution of the family in the textile areas where the previously bustling and productive homes were deserted during a long factory day until the exhausted workers came home to snatch a few hours sleep. The ending of child labour and the restriction of women's working hours helped reconstitute the family on a new basis, with children dependent to a later age and women devoting themselves to caring for the home. Thus a new social equilibrium was established and the state's contribution was towards reintegrating and stabilizing the social system. Smelser's concern is with the needs of the social system as a whole.

But the 'protective legislation' has also been much debated in terms of *whose* interests it served. At the time, many argued that it served the interests of working-class women by protecting them against the punishingly long hours and harsh conditions in the mines and factories, by freeing them to give their time and attention to childbearing and caring for the home and family and by enabling men to claim a 'family wage' and so support the whole family without the need for all its members to go outside to work. Others have said that it served the interests of the most advanced employers, who no longer needed such a huge mass of workers but who needed workers in better physical condition and with more developed abilities and skills. Mothers who did gruelling work before and after childbirth were producing puny infants who were in turn becoming crippled and stunted by a childhood of factory labour and unwholesome home conditions. The solution that suited the capitalist class as a whole, though often it did not suit individual employers, was that the main workforce should become an adult male one, childhood should be a period of education and healthy physical development, and that women should feed, clothe, warm and care for the male workers and their children. (The interests of the capitalist class may be thought of as coinciding with the functional needs of the capitalist system, so that those who believe that this particular interest has been paramount often couch their arguments in the functionalist terms of our third perspective.)

Others again have said that working-class men were, also, the beneficiaries of the protective legislation since it eliminated much competition in employment and enabled them to consolidate trade unions and more advantageous pay and conditions, based on their new responsibilities as family providers. At the same time, it enabled them to keep their wives at home to do all the work needed to give men a more comfortable home life in which they were the undoubted masters. Yet others, like Jane Humphries whose ideas I mentioned earlier, claim that the protective legislation was in the interests of the working class as a whole, reducing the cut-throat competition between men, women and children in employment and enabling the construction of a family life that protects people against the rigours of capitalist society.

The most developed part of this debate has been between those who say it was in the interests of capitalists and those who say it was in the interests of working-class men. This has been an important question to feminists because of its political implications for the relationship between feminism and socialism. But debates about the whole range of competing interests that may be served by state policies in relation to the family come to the surface time and again. Zaretsky's work is a good example of an historical analysis that explores how these various interest groups were mobilized and what programmes they pursued. He is well aware, as we should be, that there may be a difference between the goals that a social group's political representatives pursue at any particular time and what we as observers may see as the true interests of that group.

This is perhaps most poignantly true in relation to women and the family. Historically, some feminists have sought to improve and defend women's special position as wives and mothers arguing for policies like 'the endowment of motherhood' in the 1920s and 'wages for housework' in the 1970s and for greater respect for the feminine qualities of caring, co-operation and conciliation as against masculine impersonality, competitiveness and confrontation. Others have sought to rescue women from the confines of their domestic role and from the narrow current definition of femininity and give them a place in a wider public world, arguing that the home is not just a separate sphere that could be 'separate but equal' to men's sphere, but that it is a necessarily restricted and subordinate one. My own view, as I have mentioned, is closer to the latter, but it is certainly not the only current view on the matter. For this reason it is very hard to say whose interests are served by the prevailing family set-up, because much depends on where you think that women's true interests lie: in living within a family in which they specialize in cooking and caring for the home and the other people in it, or in abolishing the current division of labour between men and women, whether within the home or outside it.

However unresolvable these issues may be, we can list in summary form the various candidate interest groups which *may* be said to benefit from state policies that relate to the family:

(1) dependent people: the family is encouraged to look after children, others who need care, women who care for

children and others within the family. So active wage earning adults are encouraged to look after a circle of dependants. (A negative aspect of this is the idea of 'the manipulated male' – that women ensnare men into marriage and then sponge off them for life);

(2) men, since state policies encourage the dependence of women and their vocation as carers not only for children, the old and the handicapped but also for servicing their husbands themselves;

(3) the ruling class, whose ability to intervene in the family has greatly enhanced its ability to control the people at every level;

(4) the working class, who are protected by the definition of the family as private against more serious depredations by the capitalist state.

Each of the four broad perspectives examined illuminates a fresh aspect of the state/family relation. Yet applying them directly to what is actually going on in modern Britain is not easy, because the state impinges on so many aspects of family life. The aim here is to select and briefly discuss two of those aspects, and to look at recent policies and debates with a view to putting some flesh on the rather bare bones of the theoretical perspectives. The two aspects of family life that we shall look at are:

(1) responsibility for children, and in particular the relations between parental responsibility and the local authority social service departments;

(2) caring: personal care within the family and by the state health and welfare services.

Responsibility for children

An issue that highlights very dramatically the problematic relationship between the family and the state with respect to children is that of child neglect and child abuse, where there is endless doubt and dispute about the criteria for removing a child who is considered 'at risk' from its parents. This has been the subject of much debate in the press, parliament, and among the social work professions. The aim here is not to arrive at any policy conclusions but to examine the debates in order to see how the four general perspectives are represented in policy discussions.

Child neglect and abuse

The debate about whether children should be 'taken into care' by the local authority (whether to be placed in a children's home or fostered with a family) is frequently dramatized around cases where a child has actually been beaten to death by a parent. Although social workers are constantly working with families that are thought to be inadequate in the way they care for their children, this is mostly personal and confidential work where social workers exercise their professional discretion to a high degree. The only cases that hit the headlines are those of most severe neglect, beating or death, whether in a family or in a children's home or hospital. According to official figures, in 1978 42 children died as a result of homicide or injury inflicted by others and 88 died in circumstances where their injuries might have been intentionally inflicted. There were about 11 million children under 15 in 1978.

Yet these cases tend to dominate thinking about the issue and to have a considerable effect on policy. Indeed, Valerie MacLeod has written:

> Two events . . . have occurred in the past fifty years which have had profound effects on child care legislation. Denis O'Neil a foster child in the care of the local authority died in 1946 and Maria Colwell died at the hands of her step-father in 1973 while under local authority supervision. It could be said that the first event heralded an era where most families were to be encouraged and helped to care for their own children in their own homes whereas the second event was used to point out possible dangers in 'natural family' life, to enhance the rights of foster parents and to limit the rights of parents to reclaim children whom they had 'voluntarily' placed in care. The first event had the effect of bringing to light the importance of both the natural home and the child's own parents to his or her development. The second event was seen to demonstrate that natural family life was a risky affair needing scrutiny because of the damage parents could do to their own children. Even though, during this latter period disasters occurred in both foster and adopting homes they were seen, in comparison to natural homes, to be safe, well-tested havens. It was fashionable to speak of those who pointed out the advantages of natural parents to their children as 'unduly wedded to the blood-tie'. (MacLeod, 1983, p. 8)

The case of Maria Colwell contained many of the elements that were later to figure in all the debates about children in danger.

Social workers had been involved with the family almost from the start of her life, as her father died when she was four months old and soon afterwards she and her four brothers and sisters were put into various foster homes at the instigation of the National Society for the Prevention of Cruelty to Children. Maria was happily fostered with her father's sister, Mrs Cooper and East Sussex County Council had the legal parental rights. However, when Maria was six, her mother, now married to William Kepple and with three more children, began to apply pressure to have her back and to complain that she was not being allowed to see Maria enough. It became what is sometimes called a 'tug-of-love' situation (though this term is more often applied to a dispute between a separated mother and father). Diana Lees, the County Council Childcare Officer, wrote in her case notes: 'Maria cannot have both Coopers and Kepples — adults will not tolerate this. Therefore one or other must be rejected. . . . Given personalities and relationships . . . no happy solution possible. Maria bound to suffer' (DHSS, 1974, p. 126). Maria was very unhappy when she left her foster mother for trial weekends with her mother and would come back dirty and ill-cared for. She began bedwetting and the doctor diagnosed depression. In the end, though, Diana Lees believed that the tie with the natural parent was the most important one and the County Council did not oppose the revoking of the care order and Maria's return to her mother.

From then on, the picture of neglect and cruelty is sadly familiar. It was known to the police, the school and the social workers that the parents went out at night leaving the children alone. Maria lost weight dramatically and was said by the neighbours and school friends to have been beaten at home and locked in a cupboard. She was often late for school and eventually stopped going at all. In nine months there were 30 complaints about Maria to various welfare agencies and 56 official visits to her home. But the Kepples usually kept Maria out of sight of these callers and failed to take her to medical appointments. After a little over a year of this, at the age of seven, Maria was beaten to death by her step-father, though it was clear from the state of her body that she had been severely beaten and injured on earlier occasions.

Social workers and other officials are now highly conscious of baby battering and child abuse. Doctors, for istance, often treat a bruised or burnt child as a possible victim and are sceptical of its mother's account of a fall or an accident in the kitchen. They will question her in such a way that she feels she is being accused at best of neglect and at worst of wilful injury to her child. Social services departments now maintain an 'at risk register' of all children in their area who are considered in danger from parental neglect or abuse and senior social workers collage information from health, educational and police agencies to determine whether these children should be taken into care. When a child dies at home, social workers are often blamed and there are lengthy official enquiries producing bulky reports.

Childcare policy

In 1975 the legislative framework was altered in a Children Act that has been dubbed 'a charter for children'. It was felt that cases like the Maria Colwell one showed that too much heed was paid to the rights of natural parents and not enough to children's own views and interests. The 'welfare of the child' was to become the guiding principle and the courts were empowered to appoint a guardian *ad litem* to safeguard the interest of the child or young person at a court hearing if it was felt that there might be a conflict of interest between parent and child. Although at the same time parents were granted the right to separate legal representation and to Legal Aid if they could not pay for it, in general the balance was shifted against the parents who could not, for instance, appeal against a care order. Furthermore, the rights of foster parents were strengthened by the fact that they were given the right to an adoption hearing if they had cared for a child for five years or more and that the natural parents' refusal of consent to the adoption of a child in care could now be overruled. If parents had voluntarily placed their children in care — as is often the case at a time of illness or housing crisis — a time limit provision stated that after six months they could not remove the child from care without prior warning. And after three years the local authority could take over parental rights and duties.

All of this has immensely strengthened the hands of the local authority social services departments, not only in dealing with children like Maria Colwell, whose lives are in danger, but in a huge range of other cases where the parents may be felt to offer inadequate care. Behind it lies a view that children need secure and continuous care. There was evidence that once young children have been in care for as long as six months they are in fact unlikely to return to their parents (a one in four chance according to one study in 1973). So social workers tended to believe that unless a child's family can get itself organized to care for it fairly quickly, permanent alternative arrangements should be made as soon as possible. One book (Goldstein *et al.,* 1973) went so far as to argue that apart from separations of predictable and short duration each child placement should be final and unconditional, like a newborn baby's 'placement' with its own parents.

Inevitably, perhaps, there has been a backlash and the arguments against the current policies are being voiced and finding more support. Most obviously, there is the argument based on parents' rights that sees the power of the social workers as a threat to family life and a weakening of the natural ties between parent and child. Social workers are accused of pursuing an utopian dream of organizing a perfect childcare system and flouting both natural justice and the 'natural', though sometimes imperfect, family form of provision. Recently, there have been some horrific cases of parents who were forced to let their children go into care at a time of crisis and have then found they were unable to get them back again. At the same time many social workers are becoming aware that their extensive powers to make draconian decisions on child removal do not necessarily enable them to promote the best interests of the child. What they need is more staff and resources to help with rehabilitation so that parents who have to place children in care can keep in touch with them and prepare to take them back again, rather than the power to cut and run by giving up hope on 'inadequate' parents and simply relocating the children elsewhere.

The current policies encourage blaming parents for failure rather than helping them to succeed. In particular they do not take account of the fact that the children who are taken into care tend to come from socially and economically deprived areas, rife with poverty, overcrowding and poor housing. There is also evidence that they are disproportionately children with only one parent, or a large family, or parents who are unskilled manual workers with a low household income or from inadequate housing or actual homelessness (Holman, 1976, pp. 7–8). So it is argued that socially deprived parents are more at risk of losing their children. Some emphasize that this means there is a class bias in the existing childcare policies, which do not usually threaten middle-class families or erode their parental rights. Others point out that the policy of simply removing children again blames the parents, who are social victims, and distracts attention not merely from the need to provide better social casework to help these parents, but also to do something more fundamental to eliminate the social deprivation that lies at the root of their inadequacy as parents. Yet others would claim that the definitions of inadequate parenting that social workers use are middle-class ones that do not correspond to the ideas of the people they are dealing with, so that social workers are imposing alien standards upon people.

The main overt theme in this debate seems to be state intervention in the family and the question of rights. Some of the participants justify this intervention by appealing to a paramount concern: the interests of the child. Others, especially in the press reports, criticize state agencies for not intervening enough, for respecting family privacy and thereby letting killers go unpunished and other children remain in danger. Others deplore intervention, and especially the removal of children, as inappropriate to the problem involved and as tending to weaken family ties. Overtly, then, the debate is about which interests should prevail.

But underlying this overt theme is a less explicit assumption that children are a national asset and a social responsibility. This emerges less clearly in these either/or discussions or parental *vs* state responsibility than it does in more general discussions of social services for families and children. There we find articulated the idea that state policies must *support* families so that they can perform their social function adequately and that proceedings to take children into the care of the local authority should only be a minor and extreme part of the social worker's armoury. This functional approach comes through very clearly if we look at the historical origins of the childcare services. Caroline Rowan (1982) has argued that a 'rhetoric of National Efficiency' played an important part in developing the climate for the introduction of child welfare services in the first decades of this century. She has gathered together a number of telling quotations:

> For long, we have been accustomed to speak of children as the most valuable of Imperial assets . . . The child of today . . . will be the citizen of the coming years, and must take up and bear the duties of statesmanship, defence from foes, the conduct and all other, necessities for the perpetuation of an imperial race. (1916)

> Empire cannot be built on rickety and flat chested citizens. (1905)

An explicity functionalist vision of society as made up of mutually interdependent parts also played a role:

> The movement for the protection of children has also been inspired by a growing sense of social solidarity which regards the welfare of the community as depending upon the welfare of the children so intimately that any injury inflicted upon the children is transmitted to the whole community. (1907)

And the new relationship between state and family has a distinctly functionalist hue:

> the state 'has not lightened the load of responsibility which should properly fall on the parent; on the contrary it has fixed upon the parent new obligations for which it holds him responsible under pain of penalty'. (1907)

At that stage, the main state concern in relation to children was with health and nutrition. The registration of midwives, school meals, school health inspections, infant welfare centres, health visitors were all introduced. But rather than displacing the mother, the plan was to educate women for good motherhood, to harness them to serve the functional needs of the society.

The perspective that appears very little in these discussions is that of the family as a bastion against state intervention. The image is rather of the home as a castle that has been sacked by the invading forces of the state. The reason for this, I think, is that when we come to consider children there are the most important functional reasons and the most important justifications for state intervention. These tend to be couched in terms of 'the best interests of the child'. Since the child cannot speak for itself (or if it can it is usually ignored) the state becomes the representative of the child's interests. As we have seen, Jacques Donzelot argued that it was this concern with 'the welfare of the child' that laid the family open to all sorts of judicial, social work and medico-hygienic surveillance. Families — and perhaps especially the families of the poor — have found themselves unable to resist interventions on behalf of their juvenile members.

There are, however, legal limits to state intervention and legal safeguards of parents' rights. Even the Children Act of 1975, which restricted the rights of parents very considerably, nevertheless left the presumption that children should be in the care and control of their natural parents unless something had occurred to justify transferring what remained of parental privileges and obligations to some other person or institution (see Fitz, 1981). Families themselves may be unable to erect effective barriers against state intrusion, but the state guarantees some rights in much the same way that a colonial power establishes paramount chiefdoms ruling according to tribal law: it is cheaper and can often be more effective than direct rule.

It is worth noticing that all sides in the debate appear to take for granted that *family* care of some sort is what children need: the main question is, which family? Thus the whole debate serves, at one level, to emphasize and elaborate the ideology of the family. For instance, in two separate press reports from *The Times* (13.11.82) the ideal of the family as a completely satisfactory environment for a child is implicitly or explicitly present. In the first one, 'Miss Linda Gates' is presented as a 'strikingly incompetent mother', in implicit contrast to what everyone knows a good, caring mother is like. In the second, the theme is more overt, as the mother is 'ideal and caring' and her son 'well looked after and dearly loved'. Only her mental illness led her to stab him in the chest on one occasion and her heavy drinking to kill him in a later suicide attempt.

Caring

The theme of 'caring' brings us back to the point made at the start of this chapter: that the family is often seen as being in decline, with family values eroded or at least pared down to the bonds of the nuclear family during the time when children are young, with inter-generational links attenuated or non-existent. Social commentators often remark that old people and the handicapped can 'no longer' rely on care from relatives and neighbours. The image is one of a golden age when village and extended kin formed a network of mutual care. In the functionalist view, caring for dependent people is a 'non-essential function' of the family which has been taken over by specialized state (and charitable) institutions.

It is certainly true that new specialized institutions have developed over the past century: old people's homes, mental hospitals and a variety of institutions for the physically and mentally handicapped. Yet it is not clear *either* that more of the old and handicapped live in institutions *or* that family care has been reduced.

Indeed, the theme of the decline of family care is a venerable one that has been reiterated by each generation for at least 150 years. Moroney quotes the 1832 Report of the Royal Commission on the Poor Laws: 'The duty of supporting parents and children in old age or infirmity is so strongly enforced by our natural feelings, that it is well performed, even among savages, and almost always so in a nation deserving the name civilised. We believe that England is the only European country in which it is neglected' (Moroney, 1976, p. 8). Comparisons with the past are hard to make because the changing age structure of the population means that there are relatively more old people, especially in their eighties and nineties (and possibly there are also more other disabled people surviving than there used to be). Yet Moroney is able to present evidence to show that whereas in 1911 about 5.2 per cent of all elderly people were living in institutions, in 1973 only 2.9 per cent of the much larger and older group were doing so.

In part, this has been because of a strong revulsion in official and social work thinking against institutional care and the development of an ideal of 'community care'. This revulsion and this new ideal extend far beyond the care of the elderly: the mentally ill and the mentally handicapped, the physically handicapped, neglected children and delinquent children, even adult criminals, are all thought to regress in an institutional setting and to need the more stimulating and relatively normal setting of the community if they are to improve or make the best of their capabilities. The image of the state institution as a massive, depersonalizing place, totally enclosed and cut off from the rest of the world is counterposed to an equally exaggerated image of 'the community' as a local area of organic interdependence in which each individual has a valued place. Such imagery has, as Elizabeth Wilson (1982) has pointed out, deep roots in nineteenth century conservative thought but little relation to the realities of the social policy preference for community care.

Community care

In the post-war period, the emphasis was on care 'in' the community, especially in small-scale local residential accommodation. Beginning in the late 1960s, however, the idea of care 'by' the community caught hold. The idea was that the state services should provide support for the disabled, the elderly, and their families with day centres, domiciliary services like 'meals on wheels' and nursing visits and aids to mobility and adaptations to homes.

Terms like 'shared care' and 'partnership' were used to denote the relationship between the state, the community and the family. Since the mid-1970s, the emphasis has shifted again, this time towards voluntary participation such as the good neighbour schemes supported by several local authorities, with a revival of interest in the role of well-established voluntary bodies like the Women's Royal Voluntary Service, Task Force, Age Concern and the Royal National Institutes for the Deaf and the Blind. More optimistically, perhaps, there has been much talk of 'informal caring networks' of family, friends and neighbours.

In practice, community and neighbourhod social networks are far from corresponding to the stable village community that would be needed to support so many semi-dependent people. Some writers have detected a modern 'neighbourhoodism', not based on traditional local ties but on the 'attempts by newcomers (and in principle we are all newcomers now) to create a local social world through political or quasi-political action' (Abrams, 1980, p. 18). Such social networks, not based on kinship, are familiar to many of us living in new suburbs or other changing areas. But they are a fragile basis for responsible caring for the old or disabled, let alone the mentally ill, delinquent youth or drug addicts.

There is evidence that the elderly do get some help from neighbours, friends and social services. For instance, Audrey Hunt (1978) found that 11 per cent of the housebound people in her sample had help with the shopping from friends or neighbours and 13 per cent from a local authority home help. But 64 per cent were helped by someone in their household and 21 per cent by relatives outside. In practice, then, it is usually to kin that people turn when they become old or disabled, and it is to kin that social workers turn when they want a client cared for in 'the community'.

Often these people live alone or with their spouse, though elderly women are much more likely to live alone than elderly men, with over half of women over 85 living alone. A number of surveys suggest that they often get a good deal of help with meals, shopping, laundry, and cleaning from their relatives and that relatives will come in to look after them if they are ill (Rossiter and Wicks, 1982, pp. 41–8). But the more disabled they are, the more likely they are to live with relatives. Among those over 85, 43 per cent of men and 39 per cent of women live with relatives (Central Statistical Office, 1982, tables 13–18). On the whole, it seems, people do not enter residential institutions because their relatives will not look after them, but more because they have no relatives in a position to care for them. The official view is:

> Whatever success is achieved in improving community care there will always be a significant minority of elderly people who cannot continue to live in their own homes. Where relatives and friends are not able to look after them and where their degree of mental or physical disability is insufficient to require hospital facilities, the right answer may be care in a residential home. In the past, people entered residential homes while they were still in their sixties. Now, with the expansion of community care and sheltered housing, the age of admission has been steadily rising, and the average is approaching 82. (Department of Health and Social Security, 1981, pp. 44–5)

But the same White Paper also states that 'as people grow older they do not necessarily wish to lose their independence', and it seems likely that among those who can afford a pleasant private residential home where they can take some of their own furniture into a room of their own, this will be preferred to the loss of independence involved in living with relatives. In the nineteenth century, family care for the elderly often involved an unmarried daughter or sister living in the old person's home; nowadays it is more likely to involve the old person moving into the home of a married son or daughter, with a consequent loss of independence and authority.

Thus although since the Second World War local authorities have had statutory responsibility for the comprehensive care of the old and the disabled, in practice this has been exercised through a very heavy reliance on family care. The Secretary of State for Social Services in 1981 described the community and family as the 'front line providers of social care' and saw the government approach as being based on this 'simple fact' (quoted in Equal Opportunities Commission, 1982).

Recently there has been an increasing awareness that it is not simply 'families' that are the 'front line providers' but women relatives. Those who care for the elderly are usually married daughters and daughters-in-law; those who care for the disabled are daughters, mothers, sisters and daughters-in-law. People without such relatives are more likely to be found in institutions or living alone. Over three-quarters of those caring for elderly dependent people are women and elderly people are more likely to be living with their daughters than their sons. So the impact on the family is first and foremost an impact on women within the family.

The impact of these responsibilities can be quite considerable.

The women who care are usually not young; their own children are often well on in school if not already away from home before their parents become dependent. They frequently have to give up their jobs, often for long periods and, unlike with childcare, for quite unpredictably long periods. Their loss of income can be quite considerable. It has been estimated, for instance, that people with handicapped children lost an average of £42 a week by giving up work and by reducing their hours of work (Baldwin, 1977). To some extent state policies take this into account by providing an Invalid Care Allowance as a small income for those responsible for primary care. But married women, like people over retirement age, are not eligible for this allowance, it being assumed that they are housewives in the first place, rather than paid workers.

Caring for disabled dependants is often extremely hard and emotionally unrewarding work. It can involve heavy lifting, dealing with double incontinence and a 24-hour presence as well as ordinary household care like meals and cleaning. Recently the problem of 'granny battering' has attracted attention: the result, often, of the unbearable frustration of the unremitting responsibility for a needful but demanding old person.

The Equal Opportunities Commission, then, calls for more support both practical and financial for these women who are providing care 'on the cheap'. The official policy is 'shared care' and the main policy dispute at present is about whether the state is really doing its share. The major demands are for more support services and better income benefits to all who take on caring, including married and cohabiting women. And most discussion is about the relative success of particular schemes of government sponsorship and initiative in developing voluntary and social services support: networks of carers, 'holiday beds' in hospitals and 'relative relief' schemes so that carers can have a break, more flexible housing arrangements, paid 'foster-care' by non-relatives.

The main current debates about care for the old and the disabled all take it for granted that family care is the best. But how do we explain why family members, and especially women, provide this care for each other often at enormous cost to themselves? The idea of the family as a bastion would suggest that family members care for each other because they prefer it to any more collective, public form of care. Yet this may be because state policy makes state-provided institutional care unattractive as part of a policy to construct a relationship between state and family that ensures that family members do most of the caring. This would fit in with the functional view that as the state arranges for the functional needs of the society to be met, so it encourages, and to some degree assists, families to care for dependants. This is clearly the cheapest form of care.

Caring is one of the few facets of the state/family relation where the concept of intervention is seldom invoked. All the argument seems to be the other way, with requests for more rather than less outside involvement in this aspect of family life. One does not read accounts of intrusive and controlling social workers or medical staff. Yet there is an often unrecognized intervention in the way that social workers turn to a married female relative to take over care and the social security system so takes this for granted that it does not make them eligible for an Invalid Care Allowance.

Conclusion

For this study of the state and the family, I have selected two topics: childcare policy and caring for the old and disabled. I chose these because I think that they bring out certain problems very sharply, but there are other central topics which we might have considered. For instance, the obligation of husband and wife to maintain each other, juvenile delinquency, mental illness, education, child health, housing, income tax and so on all have important implications for the family and play a part in establishing a complex state/family relationship. Each of them seems open to diverse interpretations.

(1) You could see the family as resisting state control by providing a network of mutual support and caring, but as unable to resist effectively the state's claims to supervise its upbringing of children. This interpretation becomes less plausible if we consider how many mothers would like to go out to work and have their child placed in a nursery or their elderly parent in a day care centre or sheltered housing if such state provision were available. Nor does it account well for the resentment that unemployed women or full-time students feel about being forced into dependence upon their husbands or their fathers. But it gains strength from the fact that support and care are often given open-heartedly and much preferred to the care, however skilled, of professionals or to social security.

(2) You could see the state as intervening by defining who should look after whom and how and by reserving the right

to take children and the mentally ill into its care if the family is not thought adequate. Furthermore, state agents concerned with social security, with children or with the old and handicapped often have the right to visit people's homes and the authority, if not the formal power, to supervise the way family life is organized, how budgeting is done and so forth.

(3) Or you could see state policies as playing a part in constructing a family system that serves as well as possible the functional needs of the economy or of society, and providing a functional alternative only where the family system fails. It serves to distribute wages around among a wider circle of people than the wage-earners themselves, so that wages can support more people than just the wage workers. It provides for a high standard of child upbringing at low cost, with parents being made responsible for the physical development and the socialization and disciplining of their children to meet society's standards. And it provides care for many of those who cannot look after themselves and who would otherwise need more expensive institutional care.

(4) One thing these three interpretations have in common is that they all recognize that the family is constructed as a *private* sphere. As a bastion or as an object of intervention this privacy is taken for granted as natural: the family is private as opposed to the public concerns of the state. In the functional interpretation this privacy is seen not so much as pre-existing and natural but as being in part a product of state (public) policies. The state (public) defines and supports private obligations to maintain, parental rights and private caring by kin. The state does not question how much support a man gives his wife or children — that is their private matter; the state simply assumes that such support is given. The state is reluctant to intrude upon parental authority and often requires arguments about children's lives being at risk before it is willing to intervene in this private matter. The state assumes that families will want to provide private care for their dependent members and leaves it to them how they manage in the privacy of the home.

From this perspective, then, the very notion of 'intervention' becomes a problematic one. It only means that the state is intervening in areas that it had hitherto defined as being private.

The concern of a social worker for a child who is 'at risk' can only be called intervention in the context of a prior definition of parent-child relations as private. If children were considered social rather than private property, the social worker would simply be supervising the parent as a production worker may be supervised by a foreman. (I do not, of course, want to deny that social workers' concern can be experienced as intervention and that there may be a good case here for more workers' control.)

The pervasive definition of the family as private has often obscured what goes on inside families and the possibility that different family members have divergent interests. If the relations between husbands and wives, parents and children, are private they are also personal and not thought to follow any social pattern. As far as society is concerned the family is a private unit and what goes on within it is not a social concern. Yet the state policies we have examined do have different implications for different family members. In particular, women and children tend to be more locked within the family than men, more confined to this private sphere, and to have less opportunities for recourse to public forums.

It is interesting to consider the application of T. H. Marshall's notion of citizenship to women and children (Marshall, 1950). Children do not have legal, political or social citizenship. Any rights that they may have are exercised on their behalf by parents, guardians, guardians *ad litem,* anyone but themselves. Women may be seen as having acquired citizenship historically at three paces behind men. The civil citizenship of married women was only gradually established during the course of the nineteenth century. For a long time a married woman did not have a separate legal personality from her husband and it was even doubted whether women were 'persons' in the legal sense of the word (see Sachs and Wilson, *Sexism and the Law,* 1978). The Married Women's Property Acts eventually gave them the right to control their own property and to enter contracts and so on. Political citizenship was not gained until women got the vote – in 1918 for women over 30 and in 1928 for women over 21, the same as the voting age for men at the time. But it may be argued that women have not yet achieved *social* citizenship, in the sense that when married they have limited rights to social security and are expected to turn (privately) to their husbands for support rather than claim it directly from the state. They are defined as their husband's dependants first and foremost rather than as independent members of the society at large.

Separating out the members of the family in this way runs counter to the whole idea of the family as a solidary unit. Indeed, the very method that I have adopted here, of separating out the various aspects of the family, like economic support, rearing children, caring for the dependent, runs counter to the prevailing idea of the family as an organic and solidary unity. But it is only separating out the members of families, and noticing how many people are not in families, that enables us to consider whose interests are served by the family as a privileged institution.

Having spent most of the chapter looking at the family in a fragmented way, it is perhaps worth ending by considering how a unity is constructed out of these fragments. My brief answer is that the unity only exists in ideology, and that the state plays a key role in maintaining that 'family ideology', both as ideal and through particular practices.

Most people do not reside in a family for most of their lives; yet the term 'family' is often used as if it were synonymous with 'household'. There are immense differences between family relationships in different social classes. For instance, inheritance of wealth colours father-child relationships among the wealth-owning class, investment in education among the professional class, while the need for practical aid plays a strong part in mother-daughter relationships in the working class. Yet the family is thought of as a cross-class phenomenon, with the royal family experiencing the same joys and sorrows as any family on a run-down council estate. There is no necessary link between economic maintenance, love and affection, and the kind of servicing involved in housework or caring for children or old people. Yet the ideology of the family represents a fusion between these diverse elements and links them inseparably with kinship and marriage.

Furthermore, the unifying ideology of the family itself provides a very important unifying image of the *nation state*. Parental authority, and especially paternal authority, is a favourite model for *all* social authority. The king is the father of his people; the country is the motherland; the country's sons go off to war or to work in foreign lands; compatriots are brothers; expatriates are kith and kin. Indeed, the link may be more than one of mere imagery. It is sometimes suggested that a patriarchal family, where the father's power is absolute, produces a typical personality well suited to an authoritarian state. Certainly, the image of social harmony is the image of the well-run home, in which everyone has a particular part to play, and in which there are tensions but ultimate resolution, and everyone is cared for. The Home

Secretary, like the mother, is concerned with a varied assortment of tasks — from licensing to prisons — designed to secure order and good relations within, while the Foreign Secretary, like the father, sallies forth to enhance and preserve the country's standing in the world outside.

Family ideology has many facets, but all reflect the theme of the family as the focus of good things that are close to people's hearts and of family relationships as warm and deep, privileged in a way that other relationships can never be. These images come across most clearly, perhaps, in the media, where advertisers associate the family, family responsibilities and the rewards of family love with purchasing their products; humourists get endless laughs out of people who do not live up to family ideals, like the interfering mother-in-law, the shrewish wife, the gay man, the dried-up spinster; romantic magazines present variants of the will-she-won't-she-get-her-man story; while women's magazines give us variants of the she-tried-to-be-independent/adventurous-but-realized-the-boy-next-door-was-best-for-her story.

But, of course, family ideology is not just a product of the current mass media. Ideology is always materialized in and through particular social practices, institutions and opportunities. It has deep roots, a long and changing history. Of course, it is fed from many sources other than the state. But, as we have seen, the state plays a key role, and its role has expanded considerably in recent years, parallel with the growth of a more interventionist state, and is likely to go on growing, despite trends to 'roll back' state interventionism. It does so through all its forms of action — by administration systems (e.g. benefits), taxation policies, legal and other regulation, and even by the very forms of its supports. What this chapter has done is to explore some concrete relations between the state and the family. Now I want to point out that in each case the relation has an ideological, as well as a practical aspect. As well as being concerned with who is responsible for financial maintenance, for children and for the care of the dependent, the state is concerned with the ideology of family responsibilities, though this does not necessarily mean that its role is purely one of sustaining a family system that is functional for the society as a whole.

References

Abrams, P. (1980) 'Social change, social networks and neighbourhood care', *Social Work Service*, No. 22, pp. 12–23.

Althusser, L. (1972) 'Ideology and the ideological state apparatuses' in *Lenin and Philosophy and other essays,* London: NLB.
Baldwin, S. (1977) *Disabled Children: Counting the Costs,* London: Disability Alliance.
Barrett, M. and McIntosh, M. (1982) *The Anti-Social Family,* London: Verso/NLB.
Central Statistical Office (1982) *Social Trends,* 12, London: HMSO.
Cooper, D. (1972) *The Death of the Family,* Harmondsworth: Penguin.
Dale, R. *et al.* (eds) (1981) *Politics, Patriarchy and Practice,* Brighton: OU/Falmer Press.
Department of Health and Social Security (1974) *Report of the Committee of Inquiry into the Care and Supervision Provided in Relation to Maria Colwell,* London: HMSO.
Department of Health and Social Security (1981) *Growing Older,* London: HMSO.
Donzelot, J. (1980) *The Policing of Families,* London: Hutchinson.
Equal Opportunities Commission (1982) *Caring for the Elderly and Handicapped: Community Care and Women's Lives,* Manchester: EOC.
Fitz, J. (1981) 'The child as a legal subject' in R. Dale *et al.* (eds), pp. 285–302.
Giddens, A. and Held, D. (eds) (1982) *Classes, Power and Conflict,* London: Macmillan.
Goldstein, J., Freud, A. and Solnit, A. (1973) *Beyond the Best Interests of the Child,* Glencoe, I.U.: Free Press.
Holman, R. (1976) *Inequality in Child Care,* London: Child Poverty Action Group, Poverty Pamphlet Number 26.
Humphries, J. (1977a) 'Class struggle and the persistence of the working-class family', *Cambridge Journal of Economics,* Vol. 1, No. 1, pp. 241–58 (reprinted in A. Giddens and D. Held (eds) *Classes, Power and Conflict*).
Humphries, J. (1977b) 'The working-class family, women's liberation and class struggle: The care of nineteenth-century British history', *URPE,* Vol. 9, No. 3, pp. 25–41.
Hunt, A. (1978) *The Elderly at Home,* London: HMSO.
Land, H. (1978) 'Who cares for the family?', *Journal of Social Policy,* Vol. 7, Part 3, pp. 257–84.
Leach, R. (1967) *A Runaway World,* London, BBC.
MacLeod, V. (1982) *Whose Child? The Family in Child Care Legislation and Social Work Practice,* London: Study Commission on the Family, Occasional Paper No. 11.
Marshall, T. H. (1950) *Citizenship and Social Class and Other Essays,* Cambridge: Cambridge University Press.
Meyer, P. (1983) *The Child and the State: The Intervention of the State in Family Life,* Cambridge and Paris, Cambridge University Press and Editions de la Maison des Sciences de l'Homme.
Moroney, R. M. (1976) *The Family and the State,* London: Longman.

Mount, F. (1982) *The Subversive Family: An Alternative History of Love and Marriage,* London: Jonathan Cape.

Murdock, G. P. (1949) *Social Structure,* New York: Macmillan.

Parsons, T. and Bales, R. F. (1955) *Family, Socialization and Interaction Process,* New York: The Free Press.

Rossiter, C. and Wicks, M. (1982) *Crisis or Challenge? Family Care, Elderly People and Social Policy,* London: Study Commission on the Family, Occasional Paper Number 8.

Rowan, C. (1982) 'Motherhood and the early welfare state, 1900—1920', Critical Social Policy Conference Paper.

Sachs, A. and Wilson, J. H. (1978) *Sexism and the Law,* Oxford: Martin Robertson.

Smelser, N. (1959) *Social Change in the Industrial Revolution,* London: Routledge and Kegan Paul.

Walker, A. (ed.) (1982) *Community Care: The Family, the State and Social Policy,* Oxford: Basil Blackwell and Martin Robertson.

Wilson, E. (1982) 'Women, the "community" and the "family"' in A. Walker (ed.) (1982) *Community Care.*

Zaretsky, E. (1976) *Capitalism, the Family and Personal Life,* London: Pluto.

Zaretsky, E. (1983) 'The place of the family in the origins of the welfare state', in D. Held *et al.* (eds) (1983) *States and Societies,* Oxford: Martin Robertson.

8

The contours of British politics: representative democracy and social class

GREGOR McLENNAN

Introduction

In this chapter, I examine the connections between the political process and social structure in Britain. My aim is twofold. In the first place I want to present some information and argument which is essential for a serious assessment of contemporary politics. Secondly, I want to look at some of the concepts and assumptions which lie behind many such discussions. In particular, as my subtitle suggests, the notions of democracy and class are central. Democracy might be thought of in the 'classical' sense of the rule of the common people, embodied in some kind of direct participation in the political system. Or democracy could be seen as a *representative* process in which formal elective procedures are held to constitute the main feature of a 'democratic' regime. In the *liberal*-democratic tradition, popular channels of access are thought important, since they serve to check the powers of monarchy or government. But direct accountability and participation are not strictly necessary. The first main section of the chapter therefore analyses the two components of the well-known phrase 'representative democracy', then considers in what sense the formal procedures and powers of the British parliamentary system embody democratic values.

In the third section, I turn to the second question of the ways in which electoral democracy reflects social inequalities in the wider society. Here we have to pay attention to the nature of class divisions and to the influence of class on British party politics. But class — like democracy — is not a simple empirical issue. Arguments about its definition and influence affect the way we perceive the class-party relationship. And the extent and character of class politics in turn poses questions about the effectiveness of political democracy in capitalist societies.

Representative democracy

The concept of representation

The state is often (though misleadingly) associated with the actions of government. And governments in liberal democracies are formed by political parties which aim to convince electorates that they are distinctively suited to 'represent' the interests of the people who constitute civil society. How explicitly they seek to further those interests is a matter of the amount of participation and accountability that they think 'democracy' entails. Indeed, the parties will have competing notions of the public that they serve or represent: a collection of self-interested private individuals, perhaps; or social classes with identifiable collective interests; or a national moral majority. It is thus of considerable importance to dissect the whole idea of political representation and its relation to democracy — particularly as defined in the 'classical' manner. Though at times somewhat abstract, differences as to the meaning of these concepts are pivotal for the different political programmes. Such a discussion is therefore as important for the understanding of British politics as the electoral facts we will be looking at in detail later on.

In fact, representation is not an easy term to define, nor is it easy to establish how much democratic content it must involve. As a relationship, political representation has two aspects: the type of representative, and the nature of the constituency. One conception of the representative is that of trusteeship. In this model, the MP is elected for the personal qualities which make her or him (usually the latter) suitable to represent the country — but according to *his* own lights. MPs are the trustees of the electorate's interests, but this role is expressed in wise and independent judgement. Some such conception is contained in the Tory ethic of responsible government. Rulers should be *responsive* to an electorate without being *accountable* to them. A notion of trusteeship also lies behind arguments for a second parliamentary chamber. Opponents of the

British House of Lords regard the symbolic trusteeship embodied in that institution as undemocratic and spurious, given that its basis lies in wealth and status rather than in free election. Supporters of the Lords, by contrast, maintain that it is only if some people have the education and leisure, free of a strict mandate from a constituency, to exercise judgement on matters arising from the adversarial politics of the Commons, that the 'excesses' of the latter can be checked, in accordance with liberal principles.

A second conception of the representative's role is that of delegation. Here the idea is that MPs should represent the interests of constituents and that in some way the MP should be clearly accountable to them. It might further be argued that representatives as a body should be as far as possible 'typical' of the people as a whole, reflecting the predominant distribution of class, gender, and ethnic factors in society. Of course, what is typical may be open to dispute, and even 'typical' MPs can appear wholly remote from constituents when in office. For example, whilst many would agree that black people, or women are under-represented in virtually every deliberative body, it cannot be guaranteed that individual black or female representatives will always work for specifically ethnic or gender interests. So it is difficult to imagine the representative managing perfectly or coherently to mirror those who are being represented. And this may be true even if (as in models of 'direct democracy') representation is strenuously decentralized, power being spread amongst community bodies. In this sense, there is always some necessity for the representative to initiate and lead as well as to reflect his or her constituents' interests. Overall, though, the conception of representation active in this strong idea of delegation is used to support arguments for a greater degree of participatory democracy than is allowable in the trustee's role.

Notice that whilst these two conceptions of representation are usually to be identified with, respectively, right and left political views of democracy this is not exclusively the case. The neo-liberal thinker F. A. Hayek, for example, advocates a second legislative chamber consisting of elected representatives who are recognized to have valuable experience in everyday life, aged between 45 and 60 years old. This is in no sense conceived by Hayek to be a relationship of delegation, but the chamber *is* meant to reflect something of the composition of society at large (Hayek, 1982, p. 113). And it is also true to say that left-wing advocates of accountability and delegation are as concerned as Hayek is for the preservation of civil liberties. It is a common radical stance to defend the rights of immigrant 'guest' workers, ethnic and political minorities, homosexuals or those with unorthodox attitudes to gender from the 'tyranny of the majority'. Mechanisms would have to be found in any representative system for the expression of minority as well as majority concerns.

Turning now to the nature of constituencies, there are similarly a number of options, ranging from 'society as a whole' to a variety of local criteria. One main contrast in deciding *what* is being represented is between territorial and functional principles. Territorial representation, of course, has always been a definitive part of the parliamentary seat in Britain, even when only a handful of people occupied a huge geographical area. However, it was well into this century before the qualification to vote ceased to be based on property and became based principally on residence within a given territory. (I say 'principally' here because there are yet other criteria in operation – age being the most important, and changing, factor.) The territorial principle of representation is perhaps the most familiar to us. Yet questions about the extent of its 'representativeness' can legitimately be raised. Territoriality, of itself, is an inadequate notion, since it is not clear that geographical area alone is a coherent principle of selection. More obvious would be a system of electoral districts comprising the same *number* of voters. However, this alternative is in its turn countered by the argument that the character of a specific locality should be reflected in the definition of constituencies. So a simple numerical division of seats might be thought to lose that aspect of locality and social composition which gives representative politics some of its best qualities.

That point raises another criterion of representation: functional representation. Here, representation is held to be desirable according to the social and economic role or function played by groups of people in society. Thus a conception of functional representation might comprise recognition of the separate interests of the business class and the working class. As we will see later (and in chapter 3) 'corporatism' is a system of negotiation based on the recognition of functional representation of this sort. Nevertheless, 'function' is a rather vague term, so it is arguable that divisions of interest along 'functional' lines other than economic class are conceivable – for example the contrast between the public and private sectors or between producers and consumers. In this wider conception of function, the 'territorial' boundaries of constituencies in Britain are already dependent upon at least one 'functional' principle, namely the urban/rural division.

Clearly, then, representation takes a number of forms. Some writers have tried to argue that representation is best fulfilled when the people directly participate in the political system (e.g. Pitkin, 1967), but there is no necessary or privileged content to be deduced just from the notion of representation as such. All forms require that a certain constituency is literally 're-presented' in another medium – that of the meeting of representatives. However attractive, then, a system whereby the constituency is in every respect faithfully represented is extremely unlikely and may in some ways be quite impracticable. There is, logically, always a distance between the thing being represented and the manner of representation. (This is also true of other forms of representation: think of the various ways in which an object can legitimately be photographed, sketched, or depicted in a diagram.) So arguments for participatory democracy take their power not from the concept of representation, but from the intrinsic merits of democratic participation. Conversely, a system can be said to be representative without encouraging participation or embodying democracy. In fact, whilst Britain has long had representative and parliamentary institutions, its democratic credentials are relatively recent, and indeed these can be contested even today.

Democracy in Britain

In medieval times, a 'parlement' meant the meeting of the king in council together with some representatives of counties and boroughs. In time, this became the forum in which members of parliament would present the 'grievances' of his subjects prior to the monarch's fiscal needs being met. None of this could be said to be very democratic, but the origins of the British parliament do show a long concern for establishing checks and balances against arbitrary rule. Representation in Britain thus develops steadily as a liberal tradition (checking absolutist tendencies), rather than as a democratic one. The eighteenth century was the heyday of trusteeship as a form of representation, in which Whig landowners formed exclusive parliamentary cliques, sometimes founded upon quite spurious constituencies. Prior to the first serious (if minimal) moves towards a democratic constitution with the 1832 Reform Bill, 'old Whig parliamentarism' (Beer, 1969, chapter 2) was considered by its beneficiaries to be both effectively liberal and entirely representative of worthy opinion in the country. To its radical opponents it merited the tag of 'Old Corruption'. The fitful progress of democratic representation is indicated in table 8.1. One particularly notable fact is that all adult women were only enfranchised as late as 1928.

TABLE 8.1 ELECTORATE AS A PROPORTION OF THE ADULT (i.e. OVER 21) POPULATION

Year	%
1831	4.4
1868	16.4
1914	30.0
1921	74.0
1931	96.6

I mentioned that even today the nature of democracy in Britain is problematical. There are four dimensions to this argument. In the first place it is important to see that the definition of political sovereignty is a matter of political debate, not of constitutional fact. And sovereignty, of itself, may not be connected to democracy – as in the case of the absolute monarchies. So although the sovereignty of the British parliament, for example, is cited as the embodiment of the democratic system in the west, the equation between the two is not as simple as it sounds.

Democratic government, on the classical reading, suggests that the people are sovereign, and that parliamentary and governmental powers are valid only in so far as this is recognized. Labour's Tony Benn, for instance, has strenuously advocated this idea of popular power. A different view is that sovereignty lies directly with parliament itself as the embodiment not of classical but of representative democracy. This view corresponds to the liberal conception of democracy, and is symbolically incarnated in the mace – an ornate staff which lies on the table in the centre of the House of Commons. In 1976 Tory MP Michael Heseltine physically wielded the mace as a constitutional gesture of defiance against the Labour government's proposals to extend nationalization. This rather theatrical notion that the authority of the mace can be asserted against undesirable political developments has also been canvassed by a prominent political scientist (Rose, 1982). In Rose's case, the keeper of the mace – and thus the keeper of sovereignty

– is the ruling cabinet of government. This is again slightly different from the other interpretations mentioned, and Rose's particular political worry is that unless the mace is asserted as the symbol of national unity, Britain may slide into regional disintegration.

The second set of reasons for concern about British democracy stems from the fact that parliamentary power is weak in relation to government; and government may not be in full control – or even full cognizance – of the activities of other branches of the state. Being more a means of enacting legislation than deliberating issues, parliament is tightly organized on party lines. The main governmental departments (Home Office, Treasury, Foreign Office) are not subject to cabinet scrutiny, far less that of the Commons. More specifically, the Prime Minister has enormous powers of patronage through ministerial appointment and the annual honours list. The careers of hundreds of junior politicians are advanced or stalled by prime ministerial decision, and in the era of highly developed communications media, the public eye is increasingly trained upon the leaders of the parties. In 1982, Prime Minister Thatcher established a close-knit inner cabinet to conduct the Falklands war, recalling Anthony Eden's decision, without consultation, to throw Britain's might against Egypt after the Suez crisis in 1956. Whilst it is plausible that Conservative administrations have a closer relationship to the establishment than do Labour, and whilst the Tories are certainly, as a party, openly hierarchical in structure, Labour cabinets have not for their part markedly changed the practice of 'closed' government. This is well illustrated in ex-ministers' published cabinet diaries, and going back further, Clement Atlee committed Britain to nuclear arms production in the late 1940s. So many government measures, particularly on 'security' matters – though they may be rationalized in terms of popular assent – are seldom arrived at with an eye on inner-party or extra-party democracy.

At the same time, formal government control of the security services, police, army, and civil service cannot disguise a substantial autonomy in these areas of the state. Both the powers of government and the powers of state have been subject to serious and accumulated criticism as their scope has widened over recent years. Arguments against the former have been couched in terms of the need for a Bill of Rights to curb the encroachment of government legislation in matters previously watched over by an independent judiciary. This point of view, whilst potentially many-sided has become part of a right-wing argument against the moves of specifically Labour governments to adjudicate over civil contracts and extend nationalization. By contrast, the wider concern for the erosion of civil liberties at the hands of a technologically advanced state is more directed against Conservative administrations. Under their auspices, the annual scrutiny of army budgets has lapsed, the discretion and armoury of the police force has been considerably enhanced, and the activities of the 'secret state' in political and personal surveillance has increased. In all these matters concerning state activities and individual citizens, Britain lags considerably behind other capitalist democracies, such as Sweden and the USA, in upholding democratic rights of access to information and state accountability. This situation has led some critical political commentators to include a slide to state authoritarianism as one worrying but entirely possible direction for future British politics to take (Miliband, 1982; Hall, 1980).

A third case against parliamentary claims to democracy concerns growing evidence that the public has neither much knowledge of, nor interest in, the national 'talk shop' at Westminster. This disaffection takes several forms. For one thing it could be said that whatever democratic life there is *inside* parliament takes its vitality from social movements *outside* parliament. Apart from the long-term influence of industrial relations, the growth of 'issue politics' — exemplified by the Campaign for Nuclear Disarmament, environmentalism, the women's movement, or consumer councils — seems to indicate that democratic participation requires strong independent movements in civil society. In that sense, the often-heard claim that 'extra-parliamentary' politics is undemocratic seems seriously mistaken.

There is, in fact, a growing sense that it is national parliaments that are extremely unwieldy and distant from the everyday concerns of the electorate. Elected on a minimal programme at long intervals, it seems that centralized governments must (inevitably perhaps) find it hard to become familiar with or reflect people's needs and aspirations. There is thus some force to the view that more local forms and forums of decision-making are necessary to give context to national processes, whether in the traditional shape of regional and local administration, or in ideas of neighbourhood councils, workplace committees, or village assemblies.

Finally on this point, the failure of large numbers of people to be interested in any form of politics is an observable trend in the western democracies. There has been an increase in those failing to vote in elections (a quarter of the electorate in the general election of 1979, anything up to three-quarters in local and by-elections). The Minority on the Kilbrandon Royal Commission on the Constitution which reported in 1973 indicated that 55 per cent of the people showed fairly deep dissatisfaction with British governments. A similar US Senate survey showed a jump from 29 per cent in 1966 to 55 per cent in 1973 in those who felt 'alienated and powerless' (Hart, 1978, p. 69). Moreover, amongst those who are suspicious and resentful of the careerism and remoteness of elected representatives are considerable numbers of poor people, the relatively 'inarticulate', the young, the unemployed, and the ethnic minorities (seven million out of 17 million black people were *not* registered to vote in 1982 in the USA). That this underswell of unrepresented opinion must be taken seriously by politicians becomes clear in outbreaks of disturbances or riots, such as those which swept through US cities in the later 1960s, and in Britain in the summer of 1981.

The fourth and last procedural criticism of British democracy I wish to discuss is the view that the electoral system itself is grossly unfair. Indeed many of the more general problems of defining the role of the representative, and the boundaries of constituencies, arise in this controversy around proportional representation (PR). The case for PR arises because of regular discrepancies between the relative numbers of votes cast for different parties and the overall proportion of seats gained. In a non-proportional system, just making changes to the geographical boundaries of the constituencies can make a significant difference to the outcome of an election, yet there would be no difference in the distribution of votes going to each party. Thus, for example, we can 're-run' the results of the 1979 general election according to the new boundaries established in 1982, as in table 8.2.

If boundary-tinkering reveals a disturbing discrepancy, the results are more dramatic when we consider the results of the 1979 election as compared with an estimation of results, were PR to be adopted; that is where party *seats* are directly proportional to the popular *vote* cast for each party (table 8.3).

Those who support PR think that the territorially-based system where the first candidate 'past the post' wins the seat is unjust. Some argue that PR would put a brake on the tendency for the dominant party system to swing sharply between right and left policy. They hold that the 'adversarial' politics of Tory and Labour is destructive of continuity. It is also of dubious legitimacy, given the distortions of representation in the 'first past the post' system. This line is strongly advocated by the Liberals and Social

TABLE 8.2 THE EFFECT OF BOUNDARY CHANGES

Party	*Actual Result*	*New boundary result*
Con	339	360
Lab	268	257
Lib	11	10
Plaid Cymru/SNP	4	5
Ulster	12	17
Speaker	1	1
Total	635	650

Source: R. Waller, *The Almanac of British Politics*, 1983.

TABLE 8.3 SEATS IN 1979 AND UNDER PR (PROJECTION)

Party	*Share of vote*	*Seats*	*Seats under PR*	*Difference*
Con	43.9	339	279	−60
Lab	36.9	269	234	−35
Lib	13.8	11	88	+77
SNP	1.6	2	10	+ 8
Plaid Cymru	0.4	2	3	+ 1
Other	2.8	12	18	+ 6

Source: S. E. Finer, *The Changing British Party System*, 1980.

Democrats, who would together have many more MPs under PR. A rather different argument for PR is that minority political or ethnic or regional opinions must be squeezed out and ignored *unless* their small but significant clusters of votes receive the proportional representation they deserve. Active minorities might therefore be in a better position from which to make others familiar with their views. The argument here, therefore, is that PR entails greater effective democracy in that each and every vote actually counts as equal.

Opponents of PR might argue in two directions. The first has been mentioned already: some of the distinctiveness of British society, embodied in territorial constituencies, would disappear in PR. A second line of approach is to say that PR would introduce the plurality of society into the legislature, and this would make the implementation of distinctive party programmes that much more difficult. Far from getting closer to the people, PR would encourage further disenchantment with the fudging of issues by politicians. And the sense of stability under PR would be misleading given the probability of an endless succession of unstable coalition governments. Yet other critics of PR say that successive coalitions make for boringly immobile politics.

I do not want here to try to resolve this debate about PR, since it is one which is likely to remain on the political agenda in Britain for some time, and since it appears to divide people across the entire political spectrum. Indeed, as an issue, PR has become more controversial since the 1983 general election. The Conservatives were returned to power, having trebled their parliamentary majority, and this victory was considered a 'landslide' by sections of the press. Yet the Tory vote actually *declined* slightly in comparison with 1979. Not surprisingly, Prime Minister Thatcher declared her opposition to PR. The Alliance of Liberals and Social Democrats, on the other hand, showed the only 'positive' endorsement in terms of the popular vote, gaining some 25 per cent. However they received only 23 seats in parliament, the same number as the Liberals polled on their own in 1979 on 13.8 per cent of the vote. One newspaper estimated that if votes were translated directly into seats the result in 1983 would have been approximately 285 Conservative seats, 180 for Labour, and 160 for the Alliance. Under the 'first past the post' system, the ratio was actually 397:209:23. A PR system may thus have resulted in a coalition scramble: the real result produced the biggest government majority since 1935.

As an electoral mechanism PR can take several forms (see McLean, 1976, chapter 2), none of which is perfectly democratic. Yet it seems clear that PR must entail greater democracy at the ballot box. Some right-wing opponents of PR fear that it might intensify chaotic pluralism and thus prevent governments carrying out their proper leadership function. Some left-wing opponents indeed also share this criticism of PR, but others see it as encouraging yet further undemocratic bargains and manoeuvres amongst the parties of the governing coalitions, or as denying the electors real choice (Benn, 1982, pp. 63ff.). These reservations are each cogent, but they are not as they stand arguments against the intrinsic democratic merits of PR as a method of electoral choice.

They are either arguments *against* democratic electoral choice, or warnings that the absence of democracy (for good or ill) in *other* parts of the political system will render PR inefficient or ineffectual.

Class and politics in post-war Britain

The existence of class

So far I hope I have sketched out some reasons for thinking that the British political system may be less democratic than is customarily claimed. Nevertheless, governments *are* re-elected or rejected periodically by way of a free popular vote. Society thus retains an important democratic grip on what can be done by the state in the name of the people. But a further question now arises about the nature of that social influence. What are the key characteristics of the democratic vote? In voting, do individuals register preferences according to personal whim, private calculation, or as a reflection of their social position? In particular, the influence of social *class* on British politics is a staple issue for political analysis.

> Class is the basis of British party politics; all else is embellishment and detail. (Pultzer, 1972, p. 102)

> From 1931-74 . . . identification of parties was largely a function of class and attitudes towards class. (Bogdanor, 1981, p. 4)

These statements might appear rather stark in the context of a cultural climate which has striven hard to ignore or deny the existence of class divisions. In the 'affluent' 1960s with a general increase in living standards, and again today in the presumed antechamber of a world of microchip production and endless leisure prospects for all, the notion of class conflict and of separate class interests has appeared somewhat outdated. It is as well, therefore, to give some broad indications of the persistence of class as a central social division in British society. For it is by reference to social inequality as well as to procedural mechanisms, that the effectiveness of British democracy must be judged. I would note in passing, however, that there are several ways of defining class, each of which carries analytical disadvantages. We will return to this question in a later section. For the moment, let me roughly summarize some of the findings of the recent sociological literature on class.

One obvious indicator of class division is private property. According to Westergaard and Resler (1976, p. 112) the richest 1 per cent in Britain in 1971 owned 26 per cent of private property, and the next 2–5 per cent owned a further 21 per cent. This contrasts with the fact that the remaining 53 per cent of property wealth was shared amongst 95 per cent of the population. In terms of the capital stock which can be attributed to individuals, 1 per cent of the population owned 80 per cent of capital and 93 per cent of all adults held no shares or government bonds at all.

This perspective sets out not so much to show the (perhaps increasing) gradations of class in modern Britain, but to highlight the (also increasing) polarities between the very highest class and the 'broad mass of ordinary earners', which Westergaard and Resler reckon as 75 per cent of the population. Today, we would want to highlight too those who due to unemployment have little opportunity even to become 'ordinary earners'. Indeed, using certain scales for calculating poverty, there is an identifiable and growing group of people at the *bottom* of the class structure. According to Department of Health and Social Security figures for 1982, there were in 1979 4 per cent of the population below the poverty line (estimated at supplementary benefits level). This amounted to 2.1 million people. Taking a level of 140 per cent of the SB figure as an indication of those in need, or close to poverty, the proportion rises to something over one in four, or 12 million people. This degree of relative poverty – which almost certainly has increased in the 1980s – has probably trebled in extent since the 1950s and is amply documented in a new generation of investigations into the extent of the British 'underclass' (e.g. Townsend, 1979).

Notice that calculations of personal wealth are not the same as proportions of the national income or, even less, estimations of personal incomes. Arguably, the first criterion is the most appropriate, and it sheds an interesting light on the widely held idea that redistribution of the assets of the few would not go far amongst the many. The Central Statistical Office estimates that if the personal marketable wealth of the top 1 per cent were redistributed, the wealth holdings of the poorest 50 per cent could nearly double (Westergaard, 1984, p. 34). That estimation would *not* include business wealth.

This kind of computation suggests why, after much preoccupation with the divisions (or apparent *lack* of divisions) between the working class and the middle class, sociologists are once again turning their attentions to the upper class and business classes (often left out of a mysteriously topless hierarchy in popular parlance). John Scott has argued that the 'core' of the British business class must only be around 0.1 per cent of the population, and that even after adding top professionals, retired magnates, and the higher managerial fringes, the percentage size of the wealthiest and most powerful capitalists cannot be much more than 5 per cent. This is important in an era where business is becoming even larger and more concentrated: in 1970 the largest 100 companies controlled 45 per cent of all corporate assets. Scott is prepared to be quite concrete about the upper class in Britain, pointing to 30 or 40 'really big' landowners and, amongst powerful 'finance capitalists', an elite of 282 directors who sit on two or more of the boards of the largest 250 companies (Scott, 1982, chapter 6).

Another common index of class structure is social mobility. In the major study on this topic John Goldthorpe operates with rather wider class brackets than Westergaard or Scott. He collapses the official occupational classes 1 and 2 into a compound category embracing top and middle businessmen, professionals, and administrators. This device is open to criticism, since it seems to blur over vital distinctions such as those between core capitalists, hired managers, and bureaucrats. Even so, this rather generous estimation of the upper middle class, or 'service class', is not thought to exceed 15 per cent and may be closer to 10 per cent (Goldthorpe, 1980, pp. 39–42; Scott, 1982, p. 130). One of Goldthorpe's most accurate and novel calculations is that mobility out of the working class (defined in terms of manual labour background) and into the service class, is quite high – some 15–20 per cent (1980, p. 266). Despite considerable 'upward' fluidity, though, there is no corresponding 'downward' movement. The working class remains large and homogeneous, and it is likely that with nearly a decade of recession since Goldthorpe's initial study, the growth of the service class – and consequent upward mobility – has eased.

We may conclude that whilst a focus on mobility study may serve to encourage the sense that class is disintegrating as a meaningful social category, even here broad class divisions persist and are undeniable. Goldthorpe insists that although *relative* mobility has increased, absolute mobility remains fixed. Indeed neither economic growth nor the social-democratic post-war effort to ameliorate class inequalities through supposedly progressive taxation, and programmes of welfare and education, has succeeded in transforming Britain into a more 'classless' society (1980, pp. 57, 85).

As I mentioned, there is plenty of scope for further theoretical debate about the conceptualization and calculation of class. But broadly speaking, according to the miscellaneous criteria of income, wealth, poverty, and social mobility, Britain remains unambiguously a society divided into social classes. If there is any ambiguity in the class structure, it is the relation between, roughly, the 'upper working class' and the 'lower middle class'. Changes in technology, and the decline of traditional industries have reduced the number of 'blue collar' workers – from 62.5 per cent in 1961 to 53.6 per cent in 1978. Non-manual grades have increased from 37.5 per cent to 46.4 per cent in the same period. Whilst this is clearly an occupational change, it is questionable whether it is a class change, unless classes are defined solely on occupational grounds. This latter equation is especially problematic when examining 'class voting'. Similarly, it can be argued that 'white collar' tasks *by themselves* are little indication of middle-classness (think of the status and income of typists, clerks, computer punchers, service workers, sales people and so on). Nevertheless, the changing composition of class is significant and some aspects of this can be cited in relation to the issue of working-class 'desertion' from the Labour Party.

The classes and the parties

It is important to register the extent to which the main British political parties have been based on class interests or class movements. The Labour Party was formed in the early years of this century specifically to represent working people *as* working people. From the beginning it has depended upon the financial and political backing of the wider labour and trade union movement. As part of the cultural experience of the working class, Labour was an integral part of its symbolic and material universe, embracing unions, working men's clubs, close-knit communities, and so on. Despite a widespread temptation to exaggerate the extent and depth of this local culture, there is no doubt that for many working-class people the slogan 'I've always been Labour' expresses a quite deep social allegiance. Even today, three-quarters of Labour voters in Glasgow give class-based reasons for their electoral decisions, as do half of Labour Londoners (Budge *et al.*,

1983, p. 84). From 1918–35 72 per cent of Labour MPs were of manual work background. The trade unions account today for 89 per cent of Labour Party conference votes, 80 per cent of the party's income is derived from union sources, and the latter drummed up over £2.5 million for Labour's 1983 election campaign. The basis of the party – enshrined in its very name – is sometimes so obvious as to be considered purely nominal, but it should not be underestimated.

The Conservative Party cannot be class-based to quite the same degree as Labour. As one writer has said, 'the social structure would doom the Conservatives to unending defeat if the party became identified as the protagonist of the middle class and the adversary of the working class' (Rose, 1980, p. 36). Working-class Tory voters have often been described as 'deference' voters as if cowered respect for upper-class leaders prevented them perceiving their true working-class interests. This may contain a degree of truth, and would – in a 'deviant' form – confirm the class basis of the parties. It seems fairly plain that the Tories are supportive of the capitalist order, sometimes militantly so: 'Whatever else the Conservative Party stands for, unless it is . . . the party of capitalism, then it has no formation in the contemporary world, then it has nothing to say to modern Britain' (Enoch Powell MP quoted in Leys, 1983, p. 155).

Indeed it is no secret that big business funds the Tory party by a greater amount – though not by a higher proportion – than the unions back Labour. In the 1970s, two-thirds of Tory MPs held business directorships as they sat in the Commons, and since 1945 a vast majority of Conservative members have been either in business or in business-related professions such as accountancy or law (Scott, 1982, p. 175; Grant, 1980, p. 155). In the build-up to the 1983 election, the City responded to opinion polls which placed the Conservatives comfortably ahead of Labour, by pushing the Index of share prices to record levels.

Yet the class basis of the parties cannot be taken too far. The Labour Party has never been a party of working-class people only, or for that matter, of full-blooded socialism: it has not been committed to working-class interests to the point of challenging the capitalist system *as such.* Rather, its trajectory has been to improve the short-term interests of labour within a framework of managing the 'mixed economy' in which private enterprise has remained dominant. Nor has Labour sought to be an exclusively working-class party, even less one appealing to manual labourers alone. Certainly, this cannot be the future of Labour as a central political force.

As far as the Conservatives are concerned, their general commitment to the business interest does not preclude serious and significant divisions as to *which* sections of capitalism to favour. The interests of finance capital, for example, may well differ from that of manufacturing or commerce. Agriculture has different conditions of growth from industry, and *over time* the (in Marxist terms) 'general interests' of capital as a whole are a matter of argument and politics as much as questions of economic fact. Thus the Thatcher government earned the criticism of the Confederation of British Industry, and a split within Conservatism about the correct strategy for capital emerged in the late 1970s. The dissenters from Thatcherism, or 'wets', expressed concern that the re-invigorated capitalism advocated by Thatcher was neither in the Tory political tradition of fair government nor helpful to British manufacturing capital itself.

As far as working-class voting goes, a regular third have regularly signed up for Conservatism. The argument that 'deference' is wholly responsible for this apparanetly classless vote is questionable, as is the view that the deferential vote has been replaced by an individualistic or 'pragmatic' working-class attachment to Conservatism. Jessop (1974) has argued that working-class commitment of this kind is better described as 'traditionalism'. This is because the Tories have a tradition of appealing to a cluster of values such as respectability, order, and independence which have a real, material resonance amongst sections of working people. Whilst of course any ruling class has an 'interest' in social control, order, and thus (small 'c') conservative values, these issues have to be built into a political profile. By contrast, they have not been visibly part of Labour's programme for a secure and prosperous future. There is no *direct* link, in other words, between some popular conservative values and capitalist interests, nor are the former necessarily unworthy standards for working-class people to aspire to. The Conservative perception of this fact has enabled them to make a cross-class appeal without undermining their overall support for large-scale private ownership and class division.

Corporatism

One form of political negotiation which retains a clear class character is corporatism. This phenomenon is considered in more detail in chapter 3, particularly in its economic dimension. Here, I want only to indicate its nature and extent in Britain as a form of political representation. Corporatism refers to the procedures through which key economic interest groups establish a stable network of negotiations, and where these procedures are institutionalized at the level of the state itself. For example, business groups, labour organizations, and government ministers, in the advanced capitalist countries, frequently enter into tripartite discussions with a view to creating a framework for peacefully settling their respective socio-economic interests. These are said to be 'corporate' bodies, thus 'corporatism'. In Austria this interest-negotiation is in every sense part of the workings of state, and outlasts particular changes of government. In Britain corporatism is less secure. Attempts to harmonize relations between the CBI, the TUC, and governments have been mainly informal, and rival party policies approach the problem differently. Indeed, from 1979, the Thatcher administrations have clearly renounced any commitment to corporatist consultation as a serious avenue of policy-making. However, there continues to be corporate representation on a range of economic bodies (such as 'Neddy' — the National Economic Development Council), and corporatism will continue to be favoured by some politicians (including 'wet' conservatives) as a conceivable alternative to *laissez-faire* approaches.

Corporatism is thus an important form of the relation between social interests and the state. It is additionally interesting for our purposes, since it is the most significant contemporary example of a system of functional representation, which we discussed earlier. Now whilst there may be some tension between functional and territorial representation, they are also in some ways complementary. In states of a fascist character (such as Mussolini's Italy in the 1920s and 1930s), full state corporatism was achieved at the expense of democratic parliaments. But elsewhere, forms of corporatism thrive under conditions of electoral democracy. It is true that corporatist arrangements are often the result of backstage negotiations between the leaders of strong states and strong unions (in Austria and the Netherlands for instance). But the general legitimacy of particular corporatist policies depends on the normal representative channels of party opinion formation and parliamentary debate.

So the representative form of corporatism is not intrinsically inimicable to territorially-based democracy. Nor is the social content of corporatism. It has been argued that corporatism represents a new form of post-capitalist economy, and (from a certain kind of marxist perspective) that corporatism is always only a means of resolving capitalist crisis by way of disciplining labour through public sacrifice. Since no fundamentally novel form of economy has yet emerged in corporatism and since the extent and quality of corporatism vary enormously, the first view seems exaggerated. And, arguably, corporatism represents in some cases (for example, Sweden) an open compromise with the social and democratic strength of the labour movement. The interests of capital, in that sense, might be better served *without* state concessions to labour. The general conclusion must be that the content of corporatism will depend on the social balance of forces in each case. As a form of representation, corporatism is one way of ensuring functional participation in the economic system, for the most part running alongside parliamentary legitimacy.

The variability of corporatism raises the question of how far Britain itself has been corporatist. Yet for the same reasons of degree, no definitive answer can be given. In the period of the 'social contract' between Labour and the trade unions (1974–8) it seemed to many observers that a stride towards corporatism had been taken. Yet the ill-fate of several attempts in the last 20 years to deliver a prices and incomes policy, and the dramatic return to the constraints of the market under Thatcherism should give us pause. At best Britain seems to be a borderline case between 'medium' and 'weak' corporatism, even when a social-democratic government is installed (Lehmbruch and Schmitter, 1982, pp. 16–23).

From a historical perspective, Keith Middlemas has argued that the term 'corporate bias' best describes British attempts to resolve industrial relations problems. It cannot be regarded as corporatism in any full sense, since 'progress towards institutional collaboration, and the avoidance of economic competition and class conflict is a tendency, not an irreversible trend' (Middlemas, 1979, p. 372). Such progress was, according to Middlemas, one path by which Britain avoided, in the inter-war period, the lapse into authoritarian rule, and thus the state-corporatist fascist economies. Nevertheless, in ensuring by means of corporate bias a 'uniquely low level of class conflict' in the British system of the last 60 years, the major interest groups 'became governing institutions, existing thereafter as estates of the realm'. As a consequence, Middlemas regards the benefits of stability as having a democratic price. 'Corporate bias should be seen as having political substance in its own right, rather than being simply a matter of economic practice' (Middlemas, 1979, p. 378). And thus, 'the concept of democracy needs to be modified much further to account for participation by institutions in the governing process, and for the phenomenon of opinion management by the state in its bureaucratic aspect' (Middlemas, 1979, p. 381).

Middlemas's account is worth borrowing from, since it is a major analysis of the way in which class and politics interact as a historical process rather than merely as a series of electoral decisions by individuals. Yet whilst his sense of the ambiguity of corporatism, as far as parliamentary democracy is concerned, is exemplary, his characterization of the interest groups as part of the extended state strikes me as excessive. The labour movement in Britain has never reached that exalted status, and indeed the low level of class conflict in the inter-war period followed a decade of sharp class struggles which were lost by the working class and won by the state and the employers (culminating in the general strike of 1926). It was on this basis that the first formal 'corporatist' procedures were erected.

The problem of class dealignment

British elections

Tables 8.4 and 8.5 contain the salient facts about British elections since the war. Several important trends can be discerned from the tables. There has been a noticeable – though uneven and slight – decline in the numbers of people turning out to vote. No winning party has gained a majority of the votes cast. More importantly, the share of the vote (and the share of the electorate) going to the two main parties has dramatically decreased. The 1979 election checked somewhat the serious decline in Conservative support, but confirmed the marked erosion of Labour's base. This was signally confirmed in 1983, though the Tories' 'landslide' victory in terms of *seats* (an overall majority of 144) was hardly confirmed at the level of votes. Rather, the margin of victory was secured by the extent of Labour's decline, since the Conservatives' share of the vote was lower than in their much narrower victory result of 1970, which itself was the Tories' lowest winning total since Bonar Law. For Labour, 1983 saw its lowest poll for more than 60 years, and a decline of 9 per cent overall on 1979's bad result.

What these general statistics do not automatically tell us is what kinds of citizens vote for the various parties, and for what reasons. It is at this point that argument based upon opinion polls, political

TABLE 8.4 GENERAL ELECTION RESULTS AS PERCENTAGE OF VOTES CAST, 1945–79

Year	*Con*	*Lab*	*Lib*	*Other*	*Turnout*
1945	39.8	47.8	9.0	2.8	72.7
1950	43.5	46.1	9.1	1.3	84.0
1951	48.0	48.8	2.5	0.7	82.5
1955	49.7	46.4	2.7	1.2	76.7
1959	49.4	43.8	5.9	0.9	78.8
1964	43.4	44.1	11.2	1.3	77.1
1966	41.9	47.9	8.5	1.7	75.9
1970	46.4	43.1	7.5	3.0	72.0
1974 (Feb)	37.8	37.1	19.4	5.7	78.7
1974 (Oct)	35.8	39.2	18.3	6.7	72.8
1979	43.9	36.9	13.8	5.4	76.0
1983	43.5	28.3	26.0 (Alliance)	2.2	72.0

TABLE 8.5 % OF ELECTORATE AS A WHOLE VOTING FOR THE TWO MAIN PARTIES

Year	*Con*	*Lab*	*Together*
1951	39.6	40.3	79.9
1955	38.1	35.5	73.6
1959	38.9	34.5	73.4
1964	33.5	34.0	67.5
1966	31.8	36.3	68.1
1970	33.4	30.9	64.3
1974 (Feb)	29.8	29.2	59.0
1974 (Oct)	26.1	28.5	54.6
1979	33.4	28.0	61.4
1983	31.0	20.0	51.0

theory, and ideological preference comes to the fore. Moreover, there are two principal and quite distinct perspectives from which to analyse British electoral behaviour, and whilst these partly overlap, they also conflict with one another. For example, we might be interested in the relationship between individual voters and the *issues* over which the main parties do battle. This viewpoint conceives the electorate as an aggregation of rational individuals calculating the pros and cons of party programmes, then deciding how to vote. And indeed, the parties themselves can be regarded principally as competing units calculating for electoral victory. This general perspective treats parties as analogous to economic firms and voters as individual self-interested consumers. For this reason one of its most influential versions has been termed the 'economic theory' of democracy (Downs, 1957). From this perspective recent British trends are interesting mainly for the way in which the electorate seems less predictable and more volatile. People appear to vote less than in the past on grounds of traditional loyalties, and even amongst those who do still display 'affective' loyalties rather than pragmatic calculation, the strength of their political 'identification' with the parties is declining. According to one survey, only one in five of the 1979 electorate described themselves as very strong supporters of their party choice (Sarlvik and Crewe, 1983, p. 295). For this reason, volatility means, according to another British study, that 'each election is like a new shopping expedition' (Himmelweit, 1981, p. 14). So individual voters seem more pragmatic or self-interested on electoral issues, and their voting behaviour may fluctuate from party to party in elections.

The stability which characterized electoral politics until 1970 was thereafter shaken to some extent. In February 1974 the aggregate lead held by Conservative over Labour was reduced by 0.7 per cent from the 1970 situation. Yet, beneath this modest change, there was greater flux. In fact, all three parties lost about one third of their 1970 supporters. In the case of the Liberals, between the two elections in 1974, 48 per cent and three million voters were lost, but the party picked up another two million from elsewhere. In 1979, the Tories gained 33 per cent *new* votes (not necessarily *first time* votes) yet lost many previous Conservative voters of the 1960s (Sarlvik and Crewe, 1983, pp. 43–52). When commentators speak of increasing volatility in Britain it is to switches of these surprisingly large dimensions that they refer. On average, one in three electors changed voting allegiance in two elections in the 1970s.

However, the extent of volatility should not be exaggerated. In fact the rate of party-choice switch has not altered much in the post-war period, and in no election has an overall swing been an unambiguous benefit to any single party. The aggregate vote is affected by several different currents; so that for example Labour might gain from newly enfranchised young voters only to lose on the circulation of the Liberal vote. The Conservatives might gain from a higher abstention rate but lose on the dynamics of how one electorate replaces another in generational terms: this seems to have happened in 1979 for example. The main conclusion about 'volatility' is not so much that it gives a picture of individual rational voters in an increasingly whimsical or self-interested mood. Rather, it indicates a decline in overall support for the two main parties and a tendency for large numbers of people to favour a 'third force' in British politics. The Liberal surge of 1974 was checked by the 1979 result. But in 1983 the Alliance of the Liberals with the newly formed Social Democratic Party gained 26 per cent of the popular vote (though of course they received disproportionately fewer seats).

The other approach to electoral change I mentioned is a sociological approach. This perspective does not *deny* that individual and party calculation plays a part in election results and policy formation. Whatever else they may be, elections are formally no more than aggregate decisions. However, the 'calculative' approach presents politics as a business where collective, social and ideological aspects of voting behaviour can only be reflected in the prism of individual self-interest and party manoeuvre. In the sociological approach, it is the underlying social structure and patterns of collective beliefs which reveal most about political attitudes. This is not the place to contrast these perspectives in detail, and it is important to see that they must in some way be merged to provide an adequate assessment of the political process. But as types of analysis, they stand in a methodologically contrasting relationship to one another. It is the sociological approach which concerns us most in this book.

From the sociological standpoint, the interesting feature of recent decades is not so much the growth of electoral volatility, but the significant changes in the types of people who vote for the main parties. In terms of social class, there has been a 'dealignment' between the parties and their traditional base. In particular, the Labour Party has been losing working-class votes. As in the past, Labour's vote remains largely working class, but the working-class vote has ceased to be Labour.

The British Election Study survey for 1979 shows 73 per cent of Labour voters to be working class, but less than half the manual working class voted Labour. This historically novel development was emphatically confirmed in 1983, when the working-class Labour vote was a mere 36 per cent – the same figure as the working-class Conservative vote. In 1979 numbers of skilled manual workers in particular seemed to desert Labour, and in 1983 more of them (40 per cent) voted Tory than Labour (32 per cent). The unskilled manual working class seems to have followed suit: from 57 per cent Labour in October 1974 to only 41 per cent in 1983. Similarly, for the first time, a majority of trade unionists declined to vote for the traditional party of the labour movement, and more voted Tory than Labour. Even amongst the unemployed, less than half voted Labour, and first time voters (upon whom Labour can normally rely) cast more votes for the Conservatives and the Alliance. These losses by Labour have not directly been transferred to the Conservatives. The Liberal/SDP Alliance has gained too. But the pattern is clear enough for Labour radically to rethink its political appeal. Labour is still the main party of the less skilled, of poor and black people, and of council tenants. The party remains strong in northern centres of traditional industry: in Glasgow the Tories are a struggling minor force and there is no Tory MP for Liverpool. But in 1983 Labour held no seats south of a line from Bristol to the Wash and the new town areas were signal losses. Labour's strength in some areas, then, is increasingly insufficient for electoral victory across the class and geographical spectrum.

The extent of dealignment should not be exaggerated. Whatever the shifts, there is still a heavy class commitment in British politics. Two political scientists most concerned with the 'decade of dealignment' still allow that class divisions remain the principal 'lockgates on the vote' (Sarlvik and Crewe, 1983, chapter 3). Secondly, there has been a significant but under-advertised reduction in the middle-class Tory vote. The Conservative lead over Labour in non-manual occupational groups declined from 53 per cent in 1964 to 35 per cent in 1979. Thirdly, Labour's plight is not at all unique in Europe. The prosperous nordic countries with social-democratic governments since the war have moved in various degrees to the right, and working-class support for the staple issues of left-centre politics (for example, state intervention, welfare provision) has weakened. Fourthly, working-class allegiance to Labour *in the past* can itself be seriously overrated. There was no distinct working-class party before the First World War, and Labour has only been a leading party since 1945.

Moreover, the process of dealignment seems to have begun around 1964. And of course, whether due to 'deference' or not, a regular third of working-class people have always voted Tory. So we have to resist forcefully the idea that a long golden age has suddenly passed, one in which the working class unambiguously sponsored Labour governments or their policies.

Yet it is clear that these reservations about dealignment offer cold comfort to Labour. The SDP, though in some ways deserving its initial tag as a creation of the media and the middle class, has attracted a sizeable working-class vote. It has also diminished Labour's middle-class third of the electorate, since Tory dealignment seems to favour a 'third force' party or alliance. Whilst the success of the SDP is not guaranteed, it is clear that the electoral system itself has actually shielded Labour from further damage in the polls. And the manifest persistence of classes does not automatically mean that ordinary people will perceive the need to preserve the Labour Party, or that a 'classless' appeal such as is paraded by the SDP is bound to fail as an alternative to the Conservatives – who for their part have not gained significantly from the widespread disaffection with Labour.

Social class and political analysis

We have been examining the changing patterns of class voting in Britain, especially as it has affected the fortunes of the Labour Party. But at this point it is important to enter a note of caution into the very assumption that there is a precise or 'objective' relationship between electoral decisions and social structure. This is necessary because, first, 'class' is notoriously open to different interpretations, and secondly it is not obvious that political decisions should derive from economic or social position alone.

In the electoral analyses we have been considering, there are several criteria of class in play. For example, the distinction between manual and non-manual labour remains a basic category. Yet this seems increasingly inappropriate in today's economic structure. Routine white collar clerical work, for one thing, seems more obviously working-class than middle-class in terms of function and payment. This section make up some 24 per cent of the electorate (Sarlvik and Crewe, 1983, p. 108). Defining class in terms of occupation is another common assumption. But a plumber who runs his or her own business is arguably in a different class altogether from one hired by the Gas Board. These anomalies can easily be added to. The mobility studies we looked at, for example, defined class in terms not only of occupation and income, but of the amount of discretion and authority attached to a job. Here again, it is clear that some modestly paid working-class jobs contain important discretionary elements (garage mechanics, for example) whilst rich businessmen could, conceivably, suffer under stringent corporate constraints.

Another key weakness in the empirical studies of class and voting is their continued allegiance to survey work which takes the head of household to be male and assumes that his class can represent other family members accurately. Of course, women's role in society has not changed so drastically as to make these assumptions wildly wrong or necessarily 'sexist' — by and large the family structure remains patriarchal. Women's work continues to be subordinate to men's, often part-time, and a wife's occupation is unlikely to be vastly different in class terms from that of her husband (Goldthorpe, 1983). However, it does not follow from this that the family, taken as a single unit, is the most appropriate for class analysis. Nor does it follow from the subordination of women's work to men's, or from wives' relative deprivation within the family, that the class position of working women should be calculated through husbands' occupations. Taking the first of these common *non sequiturs,* many of our assumptions about family organization and extent tend to be inaccurate. Divorce rates are annually increasing and the chances of changing partners or staying single or living a shorter period of one's life in marriage are greater than is often considered 'normal'. The variability of individuals' work histories and perhaps class position — especially for women — needs careful attention. Only about one in four households conform to the typically 'nuclear' family of married parents with one or two children. And 54 per cent of adult couples of working age show both partners in work, whereas only in 32 per cent is the father the sole 'breadwinner' (*Social Trends,* 1983). So the idea of the family as being the 'natural' unit of class analysis stands in need of considerable justification.

The second dubious inference is to assume that because wives' earnings are normally less than husbands', and because there may be a cultural homogeneity within families, wives' relationship to the class structure is *indirect.* But class analysis is about the sources of people's income and the dispensation of their labour. The fact that a woman is married should have no bearing whatever on how her paid work is classified. Obviously, the *experience* of class will be mediated by family. Where the man is the main earner, his class location may be predominant, whatever that of the woman. Yet it is entirely possible that more women will become the principal earning partner. Where this is not so, it is clear that the contributions of working wives (both monetary and 'informal') to the family wage are central for material aspirations and perceptions of class.

In a workforce over 40 per cent of which is female, it may seem that a sizeable proportion of families are likely to be cross-class. If we take manual labour as the criterion, this supposition is confirmed. Yet the 'routine non-manual' work characteristic of much female employment does not differ greatly (in terms of earnings, mobility, or conditions) from many lower-manual male and female work tasks. On this basis, 88 per cent of working-class family men have wives in 'proletarian' class positions. This does not necessarily refute the existence of cross-class marriages, however, for by the same token, a sizeable majority of the wives of *service*-class husbands are *working*-class (Stanworth, 1984). In sum, it seems that wives are classified according to husbands' occupations as much for the easing of sampling difficulties in class surveys as for any cogent sociological reasoning.

In the light of these considerations, the Marxist conception of class seems more attractive than the standard measurement of class by occupation. Generally, a Marxist perspective consists in an emphasis on the ownership and control of the means of economic production, distribution and exchange rather than merely occupational gradations or claims to authority and discretion. However, within Marxist theory, class divisions have been argued about. A narrow view is that only workers who are responsible for producing economic surplus in material production ('surplus-value') are strictly speaking working-class. Accordingly, the size of the working class in, for instance, the USA would be about 20 per cent. Another Marxist approach is to argue that all those without ownership and control in companies constitute the 'collective labourer' in a complex capitalist society. The broadly defined working class, therefore, would amount to upwards of 90 per cent of the population. Between these arguments, some marxists maintain that whilst there is indeed a small ruling class and considerable working class, a significant (perhaps growing) number of people are not easily placed according to the twin criteria of 'ownership and control'. These people are thus held to be part of either a variegated '*petit bourgeoisie*' or to occupy 'contradictory class locations' (see Wright, 1980). So although the Marxist account plausibly returns the concept of class from simply occupation to ownership and effective control over production, there are ambiguities in the Marxist debates and Marxists confront parallel problems of definition to orthodox political science categorizations – including a tendency to concentrate on *male* workers.

For the purposes of this chapter, we can conclude that assessments of the politics of class are not matters only of fact but also of theory. This is important when judging statements to the effect that the working class no longer votes Labour or that the middle class is becoming less class conscious. Indeed, a second difficulty arises here: why should it be assumed that political decisions and beliefs can always be meaningfully connected to economic class positions *however* we choose to define class? This protest has often been made against sociological accounts of politics, particularly Marxist ones. Thus one recent theorist: 'before treating politics as a dependent variable, it behoves the political scientist to explore how much mileage is afforded by its autonomy' (Sartori, 1976, p. 10).

This assertion of the 'autonomy of politics' has received some support – perhaps surprisingly – from within the camp of neo-Marxist theory. Thus Barry Hindess says in a critique of 'vulgar' sociological approaches: 'What is at stake here is the treatment of important elements of political life as if they were determined by social conditions quite independently of the activities of parties, trade unions and other significant political actors' (Hindess, 1983, p. 3). This critique of determinism is trenchant. It reminds us that there is never any permanent or automatic connection between people's class or social position and their political ideas, far less their periodic electoral gestures. And from the sociological point of view it is all too easy to overlook the real strengths of the 'autonomy of politics' standpoint in explaining the mechanisms of change. In the 'calculation' model, for example, the growth of the SDP can be easily surmised from the fact that Labour, simply by moving leftwards (or in staying put while the entire political stage moved right), opened up a numerical space for a 'third force'. In the critical Marxist perspective, Labour's own reliance on the myth of spontaneous class allegiance led to its neglect of people's changing concerns and of the parties' own important role in *constructing* the very content of class and class interests. Finally, it is clear that party disunity and a lack of media sophistication aided Labour's defeat in 1983 – and one surely cannot put that down solely to factors external to political mechanisms themselves.

Nevertheless, there are fewer merits to the 'autonomy' position when seen as a self-contained alternative to 'sociology'. Political beliefs and ideas do not spring out of the air. Certainly, they are worked up, disseminated or stalled by various agencies and media at the political level. But this political process feeds upon the real experiences of workplace, home, and environment. In a society still governed by material need and social inequality, the multiple effects of social class remain central to those experiences. So the nature of politics is, broadly speaking, to do with the *interaction* of social existence and political discourse. The sociological angle, therefore, whilst not exhaustive by any means, is indispensible. This is especially the case when we recall that British politics is considerably wider in scope than its electoral dimension.

Returning to the problem of class dealignment, it is clear that an awareness of recent changes in the occupational structure and social conditions helps account for Labour's loss of electoral fortune. If the sociological approach in general is necessary, its exact terms of reference are subject to change and refutation. Manufacturing now accounts for just 28 per cent of jobs in the British economy. There has been a transfer of resources, managerial skills, and technological research out of traditional heavy industry and into electronics and services. In parallel, firms are moving from the large cities to the green belts. Particularly noticeable in this respect is the 'sunbelt' of new technology in the area from Southampton to Bristol to Cambridge (Massey, 1983).

These developments have left a core of unemployment and decay in the older cities, and an expansion of the 'new working class'. The extent of this new working class, working in new technology or services rather than in heavy industry or transport, based in new towns bearing little resemblance to the terrace-housed, close-knit old communities, is liable to be exaggerated. But traditional skilled workers have declined to some 18.6 per cent of the workforce, and trade unionism in manual work began to decline in the later 1970s after decades of growth. So along with significant occupational change has developed a cultural shift in working class aspirations and a growing contrast between the interests and economic capacities of those in regular new-industry employment and the poorer sections of the urban working class. Three further developments are worth briefly focusing upon. The first of these has already been touched upon, and that is the proportion of economically active women in the workforce. This amounts to 40 per cent and nine million people, 46 per cent of whom are in white collar occupations. Many of these women, however are part-time and relatively low-paid, the Equal Pay Act (enacted in 1975) having failed to achieve anything like parity for women workers.

The changes in the family and in women's employment, together with persistent gender inequalities gives rise to a cogent and thorough-going feminist critique of democratic theory and practice (cf. Pateman, 1983). In this chapter, I have been concerned with the influence of class on voting, and more generally with the social inequalities which render democracy in Britain at best partial. Yet the egalitarian critique of democracy and the Marxist conception of class as rooted in production require further 'radicalization' based on the facts about women's social role which have been highlighted by active feminists. True, women can only gain from a more participatory democracy; and they are certainly exploited along with other workers. But the fact is that wives' very citizenship remains restricted by their legal subordination to husbands, and that within the labour process working men are differentially advantaged over working women.

The second point is to do with the role of the state in the economy: the proportion of the labour force employed in the public sector by 1978 had reached 30 per cent. Thirdly, the role of industrial production itself has declined, and this must weaken the power of explanations based on *work.* Of course with Britain having experienced a period of severe recession it seems ironic and faintly luxurious to perceive a future where the organization, amount, and quality of work is likely to reveal some clear if gradual changes from the past picture of classic capitalism. Yet there may be an inexorable trend towards fewer working hours, to job sharing schemes, and to greater leisure opportunities. In this context, the importance of work experience and class divisions may weaken. Political demands and movements around consumption and community are likely to become interwoven with those of production. The decline of class as a production-based grounding for politics further qualifies the classical Marxist account of capitalist society. But the implications are not intrinsically inimical to socialist conceptions of the future. In one radical prescription an end to the tyranny of work (and therefore the end of the working class as such) opens up the possibility of autonomous and creative production outside 'work' for all individuals (Gorz, 1982).

Short of that somewhat iconoclastic socialist concern to bid goodbye to the working class, the British Labour Party's future seems dependent upon its coming to terms with the new structural conditions of class and capitalism. The differentiation of interests and cultural contexts within the working class itself seems central to such a recognition. Within the realm of production, a person's location within the public or private sphere may be as important for allegiance to Labour as the traditional manual/non-manual divisions. For example, the public sector now has the highest rate of trade union growth amongst both manual and non-manual workers (Dunleavy, 1983, p. 52). The Labour Party, as the party of the mixed economy and state welfare, gains support, some of it cross-class, on that very basis. However in order to recapture lost ground, it must also find ways of convincing those non-unionized manual workers in private industry that Labour's programme rather than free market Conservatism is really in their interest. This category make up 21 per cent of the electorate, and in 1979 44 per cent of those workers voted Tory. Similarly, the continuing aspirations of many people for home ownership, safety on the streets and efficient public services cannot be ignored. These aspirations are to do with consumption rather than production. And they are to some degree non-class issues which could be expected to arise routinely in any society. The achievement of Thatcherite Conservatism has been to bring together these immediate material and psychological concerns of the respectable British working class with an almost evangelical revival of the capitalist ethic. But these 'conservative' concerns are *not* necessarily linked to the rampant reintroduction of the free market, and in some ways may prove to be harmed by the latter. Labour's problem, on the other hand, has been to neglect some of these cross-class but extremely important issues, assuming perhaps that as they are cross-class they must be outside the brief of a reformist or socialist government. But this is not so, and the fact that nearly half of working-class home-owners voted Tory in 1983 (28 per cent of the whole electorate), has alerted the Labour Party to a weakness here, though it may continue to be addressed as a matter of pragmatic electoral calculation than as a serious political question poser for Labour.

To conclude, we can say that Labour need not give up its claim to be the party of the working class. Nor will the latter cease to be a major social category for the foreseeable future. And electorally, Labour continues to be supported for its emphasis on good and cheap public transport, and the public sector generally. Nevertheless, class is now experienced in a number of different ways: by women, in the private sector, in the south, in the new towns, and so on. The importance of questions of consumption is also unlikely to wane, and the problem of different cultural expectations within different parts of the working class is a complex one. A general appeal to classlessness – such as is offered by the SDP – is as unlikely in the long run to succeed as is a nostalgic appeal to the supposed golden age of working-class alignment for Labour. But Labour will have to pay attention to the shifting contours of class position and shed some of its unpopular association with electoralism as such, and with the paternalistic state, if it is to re-emerge as a dynamic mass party.

References

Beer, S. (1969) *Modern British Politics,* London: Faber.

Benn, T. (1982) *Parliament, People and Power,* London: Verso.

Bogdanor, V. (1981) *The People and the Party System,* Cambridge: Cambridge University Press.

Budge, I. and McKay, D. *et al.* (1983) *The New British Political System,* London: Longman.

Central Statistical Office (1983), *Social Trends.*

Downs, A. (1957) *An Economic Theory of Democracy,* New York: Harper and Row.

Dunleavy, P. (1983) 'Voting and the electorate' in H. Drucker *et al., Developments in British Politics,* London: Macmillan.

Finer, S. E. (1980) *The Changing British Party System, 1945–79,* Washington: American Enterprise Institute.

Goldthorpe, J. *et al.* (1980) *Social Mobility and Class Structure in Modern Britain,* Oxford: Oxford University Press.

Goldthorpe, J. (1983) 'Women and the class structure: in defence of the conventional view', *Sociology,* Vol. 17, No. 4.

Gorz, A. (1982) *Farewell to the Working Class,* London: Pluto.

Grant, W. (1980) 'Business interests and the British Conservative Party', *Government and Opposition,* Vol. 15, No. 2.

Hall, S. (1980) *Drifting into a Law and Order Society,* London: Macmillan.

Hart, V. (1978) *Distrust and Democracy,* Cambridge: Cambridge University Press.

Hayek, F. A. (1982) *The Political Order of a Free People,* Vol. 3 of *Law, Legislation and Liberty,* London: Routledge and Kegan Paul.

Himmelweit, H. (1981) *How Voters Decide,* London: Academic Press.

Hindess, B. (1983) *Parliamentary Democracy and Socialist Politics,* London: Routledge and Kegan Paul.

Jessop, B. (1974) *Traditionalism, Conservatism and British Political Culture,* London: George Allen and Unwin.

Lehmbruch, G. and Schmitter, P. (1982) *Patterns of Corporatist Policy Making,* London: Sage.

Leys, C. (1983) *Politics in Britain,* London: Heinemann.

Massey, D. (1983) 'The shape of things to come', *Marxism Today,* April.

McLean, I. (1976) *Elections,* London: Longman.

McLennan, G. (1984) 'Capitalist state or democratic polity?', in G. McLennan, D. Held, S. Hall (eds), *The Idea of the Modern State*, Milton Keynes: Open University Press.
Middlemas, K. (1979) *Politics in Industrial Society: The Experience of the British System since 1911*, London: André Deutsch.
Miliband, R. (1982) *Capitalist Democracy in Britain*, Oxford: Oxford University Press.
Pateman, C. (1983) 'Feminism and democracy' in G. Duncan (ed.), *Democratic Theory and Practice*, Cambridge: Cambridge University Press.
Pitkin, H. (1967) *The Concept of Representation*, Berkeley: University of California Press.
Pultzer, P. (1972) *Political Representation and Elections In Britain*, London: Allen and Unwin.
Rose, R. (1980) *Do Parties Make a Difference?* London: Macmillan.
Rose, R. (1982) *Understanding the United Kingdom: The Territorial Dimension in Government*, London: Longman.
Sarlvik, B. and Crewe, I. (1983) *Decade of Dealignment*, Cambridge: Cambridge University Press.
Sartori, G. (1976) *Parties and the Party System*, Cambridge: Cambridge University Press.
Scott, J. (1982) *The Upper Classes*, London: Macmillan.
Stanworth, M. (1984) 'Women and class analysis: a reply to John Goldthorpe', *Sociology*, Vol. 18, No. 2.
Townsend, P. (1979) *Poverty in the UK*, Harmondsworth: Penguin.
Waller, R. (1983) *The Almanac of British Politics*, London: Croom Helm.
Westergaard, J. (1984) 'Class of '84', *New Socialist*, January/February.
Westergaard, J. and Resler, H. (1976) *Class in a Capitalist Society: A Study of Contemporary Britain*, Harmondsworth: Pelican.
Wright, E. O. (1980) 'Varieties of marxist conceptions of class structure', *Politics and Society*, Vol. 9, No. 3.

9

'Rolling back' the state? Economic intervention 1975–82

GRAHAME THOMPSON

Introduction

The period from the mid-1970s is popularly characterized as one marking the defeat of the prevailing Keynesian orthodoxy with respect to economic management and its substitution by a radical 'monetarism', particularly in Britain and the USA. Along with this, it is suggested, goes a dramatic interruption in the manner of conducting state intervention in the economy. This chapter examines the 'ideology' of that set of theoretical economic arguments characterising 'monetarism', and related but different economic arguments which are sometimes confused with monetarism. The specific economic policy implications of these arguments will be discussed, particularly how they relate to state economic activity. Finally I will look at the manner of implementation, or not, of these policy recommendations in the context of the British economy. There will, however, be some switching between these three aspects as the argument of the chapter advances.

Monetarism: its popular celebration

> We used to think that you could spend your way out of a recession, and increase employment by cutting taxes and boosting government expenditure. I tell you in all candour that that option no longer exists, and that in so far as it ever did exist, it only worked on each occasion since the War by injecting a bigger dose of inflation into the economy, followed by a higher level of unemployment as a next step. (Labour Party, 1976, p. 188)

This widely quoted extract from a speech made by James Callaghan at the 1976 Labour Party conference is taken as one of the first public political admissions that 'Keynesianism' was dead. This heralded a spate of similar public pronouncements by leading politicians and policy makers of which the following was typical:

> It is here in Britain that pseudo-Keynesian policies of demand management and deficit financing coupled with socialist attitudes to wealth-creation have since the War been put most sustainedly into action. The result . . . can be summarised all too briefly: among industrial countries we have nearly always been at the top of the inflation and the bottom of the growth league. (Joseph, 1976, p. 12)

The lessons drawn from such attitudes about the appropriate levels of public expenditure soon became embodied into political manifestos. Thus the authors of *The Right Approach to the Economy* (the Conservative Party's manifesto on the economy for the 1979 election) write: 'Our intention is to allow state spending and revenue a significantly smaller percentage slice of the nation's annual output and income each year. We shall not be able to reduce state spending and manpower without rigorous cash limits for the total annual expenditure of all government programmes that can sensibly be controlled in this way' (Maude, 1977, p. 9).

By the time the Conservative government was installed at Westminster these ideas had become a fully-fledged economic philosophy. Sir Geoffrey Howe was able to lay out the following four main principles for economic policy in his first budget speech in 1979:

> . . . the need to strengthen incentives, by allowing people to keep more of what they earn, so that hard work, talent and ability are properly rewarded.
>
> . . . the need to enlarge freedom of choice for the individual by reducing the role of the State.
>
> . . . the need to reduce the burden of financing the public sector, so as to leave room for commerce and industry to prosper.
>
> . . . and the need to ensure, so far as possible, that those who take part in collective bargaining understand the consequences of their actions – for that is the way to promote a proper sense of responsibility. People have to understand and accept that the only basis for real increases in wages and salaries is an increase in national

> production. Higher pay without higher productivity could only lead to higher inflation and unemployment. (Quoted by Leon Brittan in Kay, 1982, p. 9)

This philosophy, coupled with the main objective of reducing inflation, has sustained the Conservative Party's economic strategy since 1979. Such a policy became embodied in what has since come to be known as the 'medium term financial strategy'. This is an innovative financial policy that tries to set targets for a range of monetary variables in the economy, particularly those of the money supply and of the public sector borrowing requirement (PSBR), and control the economy largely via these financial means. Fiscal or budgetary policy is allocated a secondary seat in this management policy framework. Formally, at least, it is subsidiary to financial or monetary policy.

Thus there are three main elements to this new strategy towards the economy: in the first place it involves an emphasis on reducing the level of state involvement in the economy. This has two aspects: (1) a reduction in the so-called 'burden' of financing state expenditures so that there is more 'room' for the private sector to flourish. This implies that public expenditure should be cut; (2) a reduction in taxation to improve incentives to work. These would lead to an increase in the amount of expenditure that is left in private hands, and this is meant to increase individual 'choice' about how people wish to allocate their incomes and to make the system more efficient.

The second feature involves the question of the labour market. Here the idea is that such a labour market should be left to regulate itself – that those involved in collective bargaining (both workers and employers) have to accept the consequences of 'excessive' wage increases which, it is argued, only lead to increased inflation and unemployment. The idea, then, is mainly to affect the monopoly power of trade unions by letting that 'monopoly power' manifest itself in increased unemployment when wage increases are struck which outpace productivity increases. But there is an implicit criticism of employers here too.

The third feature involves a change in emphasis with respect to what is seen as the main objective of governments in the economic field. Inflation has become the number one problem and employment levels are more a 'residual' difficulty of secondary importance. This third feature relates to the question of how this connects to 'monetarism'. What is demonstrated formally in the strategy is the necessity to deal with inflation (a 'monetary' phenomena) via the instruments of monetary policy in the first instance; namely by controlling the monetary level of public expenditures (so called 'cash limits' – discussed below – and the PSBR) and using the money supply as the main targeted variable to affect the levels of credit and money circulating in the private economy. A Keynesian 'budgetary policy' approach is displaced by a monetarist 'financial policy' one. This, at least, is the 'theory' behind and informing the economic strategy.

How did this seemingly dramatic and rapid transformation in the way policy towards the economy was to be conducted come about? In the next section we shall look at some of the economic theory that informs the new approach and later at the conditions in the economy. Before this, however, it might be useful to comment briefly on the context in which these developments were taking place and on some developments outside Britain.

One important point to emphasize here is that despite the British economy sharing in the world-wide boom of the post-war period its position in terms of economic growth, domestic investment, share of world trade, competitiveness and in terms of a number of other comparative economic features, declined relatively to other advanced economies.

Britain's particular economic difficulties stemmed from problems of structural readjustment which had their roots in the inter-war period or before. Capitalist economies are clearly subject to fluctuations in economic activity – the precise reasons for which are still the subject of intense debate among economists. In Britain's case the severe economic problems that arose in the mid-1970s had been building up for some time. And the events of this period provided the opportunity for the developing pressures to come to a head. The most important consequence of this was the rapid rise in the rate of inflation and a sustained recession. Attempts at controlling the latter through the traditional methods of demand deflation and incomes policies associated with Keynesianism, proved unsuccessful, providing the single most important stimulus for the emergence of 'monetarism' and its associate economic doctrines. We shall discuss some of the immediate effects of this below.

The second point to make about the context in which all these changes arose is of a more ideological character. The Second World War and its aftermath had seen a trend towards the bureaucratization and centralization of decision-making in a widening range of social and economic arenas. Such 'statist' tendencies encouraged widespread concern for both personal freedoms and, less dramatically perhaps, the quality of life on a day-to-day level. Disillusionment over the claimed benefits of centralized decision-making grew, especially in the area of state activity. Despite some undoubted over-exaggeration of these dangers and their (uneven) consequences in terms of the effectiveness of decision-making itself, the 1970s witnessed a reaction against centralization and moves towards various models of decentralized decision-making. The changed outlook was not confined to capitalist societies, but affected socialist ones as well.

It is important to recognize, however, that the serious economic events of the mid-1970s did not produce a uniformed *political* response in either the capitalist or communist countries. In western Europe for instance such diverse countries as France, Sweden, Spain and Greece elected socialist governments in the early 1980s. These continued to pursue policies supporting strong and active state involvement in the economy. So it is important to register a certain caution in discussing the way 'Reaganomics' or 'Thatcherism' as particular variants of a more generalized 'monetarism' are supposed to have swept away all other modes of economic management in advanced capitalist economies. It should also be remembered that in the USA itself, President Reagan's approach to economic management has in no way been a straightforward 'monetarist' one. Indeed, his Program for Economic Recovery inaugurated in February 1981 bore a closer relationship to what is known as 'supply-side' fiscal policy and to the 'economics of politics' tradition than it did to 'monetarism' proper. Let me try to indicate to what, specifically, each of these terms refers.

The theory of the 'new economic management'

In this section we shall be looking at the 'theoretical' precepts of that which is supposed to have replaced Keynesianism since the mid-1970s. In fact this is a fair characterization of the issue since 'that which has replaced Keynesianism' is just what it amounts to. It is not a coherent body of economic theory, I will suggest, but rather an amalgam of sometimes conflicting pieces of theoretical and policy advice. What unifies it, if anything, is the opposition to what *it* in turn constitutes as an ubiquitous and highly untrustworthy 'Keynesianism'. This too appears to be a catch-all category, synonymous with anything from state intervention to 'socialism'.

Monetarism

One of the forms of opposition to Keynesianism can be characterized as 'monetarism proper'. The basis of the idea has already been outlined above but it is necessary to extend this a little. There are even a number of variant forms of monetarism but here I try to give a minimum list of features with which most economists who call themselves monetarists would agree. Briefly these are:

(1) That monetary factors and particularly 'money' itself is central to the way the economic system functions; and that it is the quantity of the money stock that determines prices. This latter specification is crucial. It links the quantity of money directly with the determination of inflation, and provides the rationale for the central policy feature of monetarism which emphasizes the control of the money supply as a regulator of economic activity.

(2) A 'belief in markets'. The idea here is that markets work; they clear in the long-run so that economies with large private sectors or in which markets dominate the distribution and allocation of economic resources are inherently stable if left to operate by themselves. Keynesian 'underconsumption' or lack of demand is purely a short-term problem which will 'right itself' in the long-run if left to do so.

(3) Whilst there is a stable relationship on the demand side of the economy — the demand for money and money national income grow together if left to their own devices — the *supply* of money can fluctuate widely. This is because of the state's need to finance itself under differing economic constraints. The state must enter the privately controlled money markets as a seller of debt and this alters the amount of money that will circulate in the economy. Such activity 'disturbs' the natural rhythms of the private sector. Thus it is precisely state activity that sets up disturbances in the economy, which in turn call forth the need for stabilization policies which attempt to manage demand. Therefore the 'stop-go' character of the Keynesian demand management cycle and the government intervention that this implies is precisely a product of government itself.

The 'economics of politics'

This approach to issues of state economic activity develops out of the idea that the domain of politics can be analysed in a very similar way to that in which economists approach questions of resources allocation and distribution. Economics, it is suggested, is the science that studies human behaviour as a relationship between ends and scarce means that have alternative uses. This leads to an approach to economics which employs the idea of individual consumers or other agents with stable preferences maximizing their behaviour to reach an optimum. Applied to politics, parties and governments are supposed to seek to maximize their political support in the same way that economic agents maximize their personal utilities. Voters also act in this way, voting for the party they feel will maximize their own benefits. As a result, government expenditure is largely determined by parties' and governments' calculations about how they might maximize votes. Clearly, however, such expenditure has to be financed, largely by taxation. Thus there is a trade-off between the 'utility' of expenditures and the 'disutility' of taxation, which voters, parties and governments must take into acount in their calculations.

The general 'economics of politics' argument on this trade-off is that it leads to asymmetrical results with respect to expenditures and taxation. Because expenditures are highly specific in character, whereas taxation is general, the sentiment against paying taxes is likely to be 'dispersed' and felt less intensely than the advantages perceived to derive from the much more visible effects of expenditures. There is therefore likely to be a 'bias' towards greater expenditures by governments in relation to the taxation claims made to finance these (Buchanan and Wagner, 1977). This bias is confounded when the 'balanced budget constraint' is removed by the adoption of a Keynesian demand management policy. State expenditure is then in no way immediately or directly limited by its taxation consequences and this leads to further bias towards publicly provided goods and services and against privately provided ones. It creates the impression that publicly provided goods and services have become relatively cheaper than privately provided ones, and signals to voters how they might best allocate their vote among contending parties. Of course, the reverse side of this increased incentive for government expenditures is higher inflation, but this is heavily discounted by voters since the 'cost' of this only appears some time in the future, whereas the gain from expenditures is relatively immediate.

Largely as a result of this kind of analysis it is argued that increased government expenditure is a secular feature of the post-Second World War Keynesian period. This emphasizes the growth of nominal government expenditures as a percentage of total national income, the implication being that the public sector is engrossing private resources and leading to their 'crowding out' by government expenditure (see chapter 3). When this is combined with the idea that such government expenditures are largely *unproductive* a strong case can be made for the reversal of this trend. Such a case was actually made by Margaret Thatcher in the run-up to the 1979 General Election:

> First, if our objective is to have prosperous and expanding economy, we must recognize that high public spending, as a proportion of GNP, very quickly kills growth. . . We have to remember that governments have no money at all. Every penny they take is from the *productive* sector of the economy in order to transfer it to the *unproductive* part of it. That is one of the great causes of our problems. . . (Margaret Thatcher, Hansard, 25 July 1978, Col 1400; emphasis added)

While the 'economics of politics' position would seem at first glance to be abandoning the notion of 'economic ideas' as the main determinant of government expenditure levels in favour of the realism of voting, political parties and government calculations, in fact it just reproduces and reintroduces this approach by way of the back door. It is the abandonment of the Gladstonian balanced budgetary constraints with the adoption of Keynesian ideas that heralds the growth of unproductive, inflation-producing and socially wasteful government expenditure as a proportion of total national income. Instead of Keynes as the man whose theoretical advances set policy on the right road, we now have Keynes the disaster, whose ideas permeated policy and resulted in the present ills of the economy (see Tomlinson, 1981, p. 385).

Supply-side economics

One thing that is thought to have caught the imagination of policy-makers in the 'post-Keynesian era' is the supply side of the economy. In the USA a number of popular journalistic accounts of supply-side econmics became best sellers (Wanniski, 1979; Gilder, 1981) and were thought to have captured the attention of President Reagan during the period of economic-policy formation for his 1981 budget. Supply-side arguments are also closely tied into the economic philosophy of Mrs Thatcher's ministers and advisers as elaborated earlier in this chapter. What, then, is the more general background to supply-side economics?

Keynes, it is argued, stressed the demand side of the economy. Keynesian policy is focused on the components of aggregate demand. It is demand deficiency ('under-consumption') that leads to problems of economic management, requiring an injection of publicly induced expenditures to restimulate and reposition the economy for stable growth. What this ignores is the supply side of the economy. It presumes that the supply side will automatically adapt to the changing conditions of aggregate demand without severe inflationary consequences. A number of different elements comprise supply. At the aggregate level it involves the supply of appropriate factor inputs to the economic process, including the state of technological input, the character of the production process in terms of the combination of labour and capital, the supply of labour, the role of managerial and other expertise, the industrial structure and so on. Clearly this could raise the interesting and important issues of 'industrial policy' and the role of the state in intervening to encourage or direct this in various ways.

By and large, however, this is not the way that supply-side economics has been developed. It has concentrated almost exclusively upon the supply of labour input and upon conditions in the labour market. Simply put, the argument is one that concerns the necessity to lower taxes or wage rates in order to increase incentives and labour input. This is the central platform of supply-side economics. The crucial element in economic decision-making is the government stance towards the taxation side of budgetary policy. From this point of view monetary policy, and particularly monetarism, is chided. Inflation, it is argued, is caused by taxes, not by increases in the money supply. Milton Friedman is a 'demand-sider' — stressing the active role of money and supporting the 'quantity theory of money' (that it is the 'quantity of money' in the system that largely determines aggregate 'demand' and the health of the economy in terms of production brought forward and the level of inflation) whereas for supply-siders money is passive. Money automatically adjusts to the needs of trade; to restrict its growth will only dampen private sector growth and ultimately increase permanent inflation. Nor do supply-siders follow the 'economics of politics' position too closely, though they have some affiliation to it in that they want to 'economize on government'. But the stress of the 'economics of politics' position is again on calculations with respect to expenditures, and on demand for goods and services. For supply-siders, even though they may accept that the money supply can initially cause inflation, feel that it is tax *increases* which fuel it, and that it is the unremitting and relentless cultivation of the private supply of goods and services that provides the driving force to the economy which can offset tendencies towards their public provision. Full play must be given to private sector inputs and creativity. Incentives are the major problem and it is tax *reductions* that will provide just these necessary incentives. Such reductions should not be confined to personal incomes, however, but should be extended to all forms of taxation. Under these circumstances, the argument goes, firms will be willing to increase the amount of factors they wish to employ and those factors will be more willing to become employed.

Politics versus the market?

The theoretical arguments that inform the 'new economic management' approach to the economy are sometimes lumped together under the generic term 'monetarism'. My objective has so far been to show that they are in fact somewhat different in character, and that the policy advice they generate is not always consistent. Indeed it would be possible to add to this list of different approaches; the three discussed above do not exhaust possible arguments that can be brought to bear on the issue of state involvement. For instance, Hayek represents another strand of philosophical neo-liberalism with a somewhat distinct approach to economic policy advice. He would be suspicious of the kind of monetarism specified above as it puts an emphasis on the ability of governments to control the economy through controlling the money supply. But government action of anything but a limited kind is not thought desirable (let alone effective), least of all with respect to aggregate economic regulation. For Hayek, the main cause of inflation under contemporary conditions is the trade unions and the monopoly power they exercise over the setting of wages in the economy. He would call for a 'short sharp shock' of severe deflation to rid the economy once and for all of inflationary expectations, along with a legislative policy to dismantle the trade unions. For strict monetarists, however, trade unions are less of a problem. In the longer run they are the 'passive' element since they cannot push wages up faster than the money supply growth warrants, without undermining the strength of their very position. Hayek's arguments could therefore be included as yet another anti-state perspective (see Thompson, 1984 for further discussion of these differences).

However, this raises the question of whether these are simply variations on a more general theme. Might they not all be reduced to the invocation that it is the 'market' that is the only appropriate mechanism for economic management and that, as a result, any mechanisms of state intervention and involvement which overrule the market should be rejected? Clearly, all the approaches outlined above do invoke the 'market' as the prime virtuous mechanism which is to be stimulated at the expense of the 'public' or 'political' provision of goods and services. In fact some have seen this as the main issue of the current post-mid-1970s era. As Milton Friedman puts it:

> In the economic market — the market in which individuals buy and sell from one another — each person gets what he pays for. There is a dollar-to-dollar relationship. Therefore, you have an incentive proportionate to the cost to examine what you are getting. If you are paying out of your own pocket for something and not out of somebody else's pocket, then you have a very strong incentive to see whether you are getting your money's worth.

The 'political' mechanism, on the other hand, has a 'fundamental defect' in that:

> . . . it is a system of highly weighted voting under which the special interests have great incentive to promote their own interests at the expense of the general public. The benefits are concentrated; the costs are diffused; and you have therefore a bias in the political market place which leads to ever greater expansion in the scope of government and ultimately to control over the individual. (Friedman, 1976, p. 10)

Here are the familiar themes that seem to pervade *all* the approaches discussed above. The market dispenses benign *discipline* whereas the state dispenses ultimate *oppression*.

While there is obviously some merit in linking these all together through their celebration of the market mechanism, there are also some disadvantages. In the first place it is important to reiterate the point that there is no clear movement from economic ideas through to practical policy. While one may hold to a very general idea about the market and its virtues, this need bear little relationship to the actual policy course mapped out, let alone that actually pursued. The second point is that, in relation to this, actual economic policy suggestions are always accompanied by particular and detailed arguments. These particular arguments cannot be simply deduced as expressions of their more general counterparts and have to be confronted on their own ground and in their own terms. Thirdly the general idea of a 'market' itself is a dubious abstraction. Markets are highly specific in their character and operation – they are always set within the context of particular institutional mechanisms. The invocation of a general 'market mechanism' usually avoids the actual detail of how specific markets work and the constraints and limits that operate on them and through them. The final and related point concerns the presumed symmetry between the 'market mechanism' and the 'political mechanism' as embodied in Friedman's remarks. In fact, these are not simply alternative mechanisms which can be directly compared as though they had the same general objectives. The two mechanisms are quite distinct, both in terms of the purview and their mode of operation, which undermines Friedman's simple 'philosophical' juxtapositioning of their respective legitimacies in terms of a singular 'rationality'. They need to be judged by separate criteria, specifying the limits and appropriateness of each.

Bearing these points in mind, we can now move on to a discussion of some rather more detailed issues and arguments associated with the experience of the British economy over the post-1975 period.

The rolling back of the state: the British case

The question of the 'reversal' of the British government's or state's attitude towards economic intervention and regulation has a number of features and is something that would proceed at an *uneven* pace even if pushed consistently by a determined government. As mentioned earlier the benchmark for this change in attitude arises some time in the 1974–6 period, which can be seen as a turning point for both economic policy and economic ideology. From here on 'monetarist' ideas are supposed to take the ascendancy over 'Keynesian' ones. But I want to question both the sharpness of that supposed break, and the simplicity of the idea of 'monetarism versus Keynesianism' which suggests it.

The state and the management of the UK economy

Much of the important economic background to this debate has been sketched in chapter 3. There are perhaps two periods involved: one up until 1979 when the Labour Party was still in power and one after May of that year when the Conservatives gained office. However, many commentators would see the whole period as something of a continuum. Denis Healey, the Labour Chancellor of the Exchequer, is thought to have initiated the policies of monetarism which were only followed up and intensified by the Conservative Chancellor, Geoffrey Howe. In this scenario, both are the villains of the piece.

The severe economic problems facing the Labour administration in 1974–6 had a catalytic effect upon government policy. The Bretton-Woods system of fixed exchange rates collapsed in 1972, heralding the way for rapid and destabilizing fluctuations. The oil price explosion of 1973 led to continuous balance of payment deficits during the early 1970s. This resulted in heavy British overseas borrowing which culminated in a disastrous run on sterling in 1976. (It collapsed from a figure of $2.80 to the pound sterling in 1973 to below $1.60 at the end of 1976.) The International Monetary Fund (IMF) had to be called in to give a £3.9 billion loan to the government. This was made conditional on the introduction of limits on Domestic Credit Expansion ('money' creation, broadly speaking) which in turn had implications for acceptable levels of PSBR and thereby government expenditure itself. Such DCE targets and concern with the PSBR are seen as precursors of the more stringent money supply controls of the subsequent Conservative government. They implied a deflationary policy for the domestic economy. In fact these DCE limits were quietly forgotten when sterling recovered in the late 1970s, though concern with PSBR continued.

The PSBR and levels of government expenditure became *the* economic problem in the mid-to-late 1970s in Britain. The PSBR was a problem because it became difficult to finance. There were a number of reasons for this, one of which involved constraints on taxation increases. Some of the downward pressure on government expenditure and the PSBR could have been eased if taxation as an alternative revenue source to borrowing could have been developed. But the government found itself unable to increase taxation levels at a time when its expenditures were increasing rapidly. Its fiscal policy was constrained by a number of policies adopted during the Social Contract phase (discussed in chapter 3) which were designed to secure trade union co-operation over wage restraint. Any interests in indirect taxation (taxes on goods and services) would have affected the Retail Price Index and triggered renewed wage claims, whereas direct tax increases (taxes on incomes) were also constrained in the interests of public support.

At the same time government expenditures were spiralling for a number of reasons. These included (1) inflation in the 'prices' of its expenditures relative to prices generally (the so-called 'relative price effect'); (2) because of social policy changes, again dictated by the Social Contract, involving subsidies on consumer expenditures and income maintenance; (3) because of growing unemployment and the secular decline in the working population as against the dependent population (a growing 'ageing' of the population structure); and (4) finally, but not least, because of the lack of any serious and effective control over these public expenditures themselves.

All these tendencies came to a head in the period of 1975–6 and could be said to have coerced the government, perhaps against its 'will', to adopt stringent cash limits on public expenditures and to concern itself more centrally with the effects of inflation and of the financial conditions under which it could operate. This in turn produced some unforeseen effects upon a range of other policy instruments and variables, notably the difficulties encountered in financing the Public Debt. When the government tried to increase its borrowing to finance its expenditures the financial markets (lenders to the government) would not take its debt without forcing up interest rates. The subsequent rise in interest rates put continued pressure on the 'costs' of public expenditures and on financing the Public Debt. At one stage in 1979 for instance three-quarters of the PSBR was needed just to cover interest payments on the state debts.

What this discussion has highlighted is the importance of actual circumstances and constraints in the economy combined with the onset of a recession, rather than with the changes in ideological outlook on the part of policy-makers. It was this matrix of events that provided the conditions for a different ideological explanation to be given for the economy's decline and for a different set of remedies to be thrown up that would solve these problems.

During this period the whole area of 'public expenditure' came under increasing scrutiny and was constituted as the major problem of the economy. Such pressure on public expenditure has been kept up since then, as is indicated by the discussion earlier in the chapter. 'Public expenditure' has been successively accused of being 'unproductive' and hence a burden on the economy and on society more generally; of being the element that had 'crowded-out' wealth producing and productive private expenditure, having grown to such a high proportion of GNP that it posed a real threat to 'freedom and democracy'; and as being the cause of inflation and unemployment.

We might well be sceptical that such a range of economic effects should be attributable simply to high levels of public expenditure, but the task of reducing this level was a central justification for Margaret Thatcher's economic strategy after the election of 1979 and a crucial test for the 'disengagement of the state' argument.

Public expenditure has however proved very difficult to cut back, particularly as a percentage of overall GNP. The Conservatives inherited an overall public expenditure to GNP ratio of approximately 46 per cent in 1979–80 (see figure 3.2). Despite their determined attempts to bring this ratio significantly down it was 44.5 per cent in 1980–1, 45 per cent in 1981–2 and was projected to fall only to 44.5 per cent in 1982–3. The difficulty of bringing this ratio down can be attributed to many reasons: foremost amongst them are institutional rigidities which make cut-backs operationally difficult to organize; the growth of unemployment and other social benefits which push up the transfer element of public expenditures; and the general stagnation or decline in GNP itself. Government forecasts indicate that the ratio is likely to remain around the 45 per cent mark for the foreseeable future and may even increase *unless* something much more dramatic is undertaken such as dismantling the NHS and radically changing the system of educational finance in Britain (Report on the 'Think Tank's submission to the Treasury as cited in *The Economist* 18–24 September 1982).

One other way of reducing the size of the government sector would be to sell off some of the state's assets to the private sector. This became an active part of the Conservative government's industrial policy in the post-1979 period. The idea here was that the conversion of some of the nationalized industries into private businesses would help to revitalize the domestic industrial structure. This policy of 'privatization' deserves a slightly extended discussion as it represents a significant shift in the boundaries between the public and the private sphere and of the legitimate domain of state action with respect to the economy.

'Privatization' of the industrial structure

It was argued in chapter 3 that the nationalized industries had been progressively reintegrated into a mixed economy based upon rather orthodox commercial criteria of efficiency and performance during the post-war period. Initial financial criteria of 'breaking even one year after another' for the nationalized industries were progressively transformed into firm financial objectives and targets, investment appraisal techniques based upon market rates of return, and pricing policies that stressed a more commercial approach towards customers and demand. These were conceived as proxies for market forces given that the ownership and economic position of the industries precluded their direct integration into the private market economy.

When the question of public expenditure came into the foreground of political problems around 1975–6 the financial control of the nationalized industries was tightened even further by the introduction of external financial limits (EFLs) or 'cash limits' as they became popularly known. With EFLs, financial policy began to take precedence over planning the use of physical resources. An EFL is set for a nationalized industry which controls the amount of external finance it can expect either the Treasury to provide directly, or which the Treasury will back with a state guarantee if the industry wishes to borrow directly from the capital markets. Such EFLs were set with a target for the PSBR very much in mind.

Some industries (for example, British Rail) complained that their own EFLs were too tight during this period. Cutting an EFL puts pressures on capital spending which could damage the long-term prospects for the industry. The limits operate an overall cash control and do not discriminate between worthwhile capital investment, less worthwhile capital investment, and revenue account items. They are thus arguably rather crude mechanisms of control. In addition strict EFLs might result in pressures to raise prices 'unnecessarily' to generate non-constrained internal resources. In 1980 for instance nationalized industries' prices rose twice as fast as private sector prices (Redwood and Hatch, 1982, p. 94). Or they might be met by lowering standards to customers in terms of maintenance of infrastructure or service back-up.

What EFLs did rather effectively, however, was to lower wage expectations in the nationalized industries. They gave the management of those industries a means to limit wage increases that could be granted to employees since the industry was 'forced' to work within its financial guideline. All in all the EFLs imposed a discipline somewhat analagous to that imposed by banks on private sector companies. Within this framework it was expected that the internal efficiency and effectiveness of resource use would be encouraged.

In addition to this imposition of a more controlled financial environment the Conservative government embarked upon a radical programme of 'privatization' of state-owned productive activity. This was aimed explicitly at pushing back the frontiers of state involvement in the economy by selling assets to private sector interests. It was argued that the state had no place owning and running commercialized businesses where it was possible that private management could own and control these and where strict market criteria of operation could be introduced and become effective. The Conservatives thus embarked upon a programme of denationalization the early results of which are shown in table 9.1.

A number of points are worth making about the companies involved in the table. In the first place they represent activity which was reasonably buoyant under the depressed conditions of the early 1980s (electronics, computers, oil). Secondly a number of these organizations were either originally private ones taken into public ownership during the late 1970s because of temporary financial difficulties (ICL, Ferranti) or were ones developed around North Sea oil activity. They did not involve the traditional, immediate post-Second World War nationalized industries apart from rather marginal activities like BR hotels or the National Freight Corporation. The 'Old Guard' nationalized industries escaped relatively unscathed during this period. Finally, as can be seen, in a number of cases the state withdrew from a controlling interest in the companies but did not abandon its stake altogether. In fact it probably remained the largest single, and therefore dominant, shareholder even though it did not form a controlling 51 per cent of the capital stock. The near £2 billion raised by these sales probably had only a marginal impact on a PSBR that was running at well over £10 billion each year during this period.

What about the prospects for the other, more traditional, nationalized industries? The situation with respect to these at the end of 1983 is set out in table 9.2. To privatize these was proving something of a more complex and difficult task. It is not easy to dispose of very large sections of productive activity during a period of instability and depression. A great deal of discussion was underway. To privatize all of the industries included in table 9.2.

TABLE 9.1 PRIVATIZATIONS 1979–82

Company	*Date*	*Method*	*Yield £m*
British Petroleum (Oil)	Nov '79 and Sep '83	State holding reduced in stages from 51% to about 31%	817
ICL (computers)	Dec '79	State sells its 25% holding	37
Fairey (engineering)	May '80	Selling of a NEB Company	22
Ferranti (electronics)	July '80	State sells its 50% holding	55
British Aerospace	Feb '81	State reduces 100% holding to 48.4%	43
Prestcold (engineering)	Mch '81	Selling of part of British Leyland	9
National Freight	Oct '81	Firm sold to management and staff	5
Cable and Wireless	Nov '81	State reduces 100% holding to 49%	182
Amersham (oil)	Feb '82	State sells its 100% holding	65
Britoil (oil)	Nov '82	State reduces 100% holding to 41%	548
BR Scottish Hotels	Nov '82	Sold to private owners	40
Associated Brit. Ports	Feb '83	State reduces 100% holding to 48.5%	46
		Total yield 1979–82:	£1869m

Source: *Sunday Times*, 9 October 1983.

would however represent a radical withdrawal of state ownership over large sections of British industry, though whether this would herald a disengagement of intervention and regulation is another matter. It seems unlikely that the state could or would abandon regulation and intervention with respect to the kinds of activities included here given their central structural importance to the economy. The *forms* of intervention may change as ownership retreats. In fact as many financial problems may result from denationalizing *parts* of these industries as are 'solved' by the process. The question becomes how to finance the rump of the uneconomic but socially necessary activity left in public hands, when the more profitable side of the business has been sold off (Heald, 1983).

TABLE 9.2 PROSPECTS FOR PRIVATIZATION OF NATIONALIZED INDUSTRIES AS OF THE END OF 1983

Industry	*Prospects*	*Possible Yield at 1983 prices*
British Airports Authority	Selling of airports under discussion	£400m
British Airways	1980 Civil Aviation Act allows sale of share-holding but sale delayed until capital restructuring undertaken and performance improves	£500–1000m
British Gas Corporation	Minister orders sale of Wytch Farm Oil Field and progressive sale of showrooms over five years period. Beginning of this delayed and deferred	£600–1000m
British Rail	See table 9.1 on sale of hotels. BR Sealink Ferries to be sold when conditions permit	£100m
British Steel Corporation	Small shareholdings in other steel companies sold. Long-term prospects of complete denationalization when industry performance improves	

Electricity	Possible sale of CEGB generating capacity being discussed	
National Coal Board	No likely change in near future	
Post Office		
Postal Services	No likely change in near future	
Telecommunications	Possible future sale under active discussion	£4000m
National Bus	1982 Transport Act enables assets to be sold. Inter City coach business likely to be sold in near future. Possible complete denationalization in medium term.	£100m
British Leyland	Possible sale of Jaguar, Land Rover and Unipart businesses	£200m

Sources: *Sunday Times* 9 October 1983 and Redwood and Hatch, 1982, table 7.1.

Controlling the money supply?

Perhaps the centrepiece of the Conservative government's economic strategy and of monetarism more generally was the control of the growth of 'money supply'. This was to take the burden of regulating the economy in classical monetarist terms. However one problem here is that in any actual economy there is no one unambiguous place from which the money supply emanates. Rather, there are multiple places where money in the form of credit is created in an economy. The state does not simply create money at will — it does not print money and then distribute it such that this 'production process' could be interrupted and thereby easily controlled at the behest of the government. One of the early problems confronting the government was to find a reasonable *measure* of the money supply so that some attempt at controlling it could at least be organized. A measure called Sterling M3 was focused upon and then a target band for this produced. Needless to say, perhaps, this target was consistently overshot (1981–2 for instance targeted at 6–10 per cent, actual rise in £M3 14.5 per cent).

In part this overshooting of the rise in actual money supply was itself a result of the way the PSBR was found to be difficult to control and target properly. The PSBR comprises the difference between two very large aggregates of government expenditures and government revenues, all the components of which are highly sensitive to changes in underlying economic conditions – expenditures in particular proved difficult to reduce at a time of recession. The result was that forecasts of PSBR's tended to go very much astray from actual events (1980–1 forecast £7.5 billions, actual out-turn £10.6 billions), though the PSBR as a proportion of GDP was consistently lowered from a high of 9.4 per cent in 1976–77 to 4.4 per cent in 1981–2 (HMSO, 1982).

There was also considerable argument as to whether £M3 was the most appropriate measure of money supply to be targeted. In fact in the 1982 budget *three* targets were fixed for monetary aggregates. However the question here is not whether this or that particular target was appropriate but rather, if the state is not the sole source of the 'money supply' in an economy generally, can an economic strategy be rigorously based upon a policy of government-set monetary targets? (cf. Thompson, 1981). The main point of this brief discussion is to argue that attempts at controlling the money supply do not necessarily mean a *disengagement* of the state from all economic intervention. In the case under discussion the Bank of England continued to intervene significantly in the private money markets and on the international exchanges in its attempts to control the money supply targets and interest rates. In fact to some extent it increased its level of intervention on this score – defining and targeting a new and increasing range of policy variables. What monetarism means, then, in the limited sense of a policy with respect to the control of the money supply, is more a change in the forms, emphasis or direction of intervention rather than an abandonment of such intervention altogether. Equally it has meant more stringent and extensive sets of controls and 'interventions' with respect to the government's own expenditures.

At this stage it might also be useful to point out some of the institutional limitations to the pursuit of a full monetarist policy which exist at the level of the state apparatuses themselves. In the case of Britain the Treasury and the Bank of England did not have exactly the same attitude towards all aspects of the proposed monetarist policy. Whilst the Treasury was largely in favour of the policy, the Bank of England was rather reluctant to see some of its more radical implications pursued. This was particularly the case over the detail of exactly how the money supply might be controlled. The idea that absolutely 'free' market mechanisms could be allowed to set interest rates and determine the amount of money in an economy — the position advocated by some of the Treasury's monetarist advisers — was resisted by the Bank of England. The Bank wanted to maintain a firmer leverage over various monetary instruments and over the financial system in general, than was implied by the radical critics of its position (e.g. Griffiths *et al.* in HMSO, 1980). To some extent it could be argued that the Bank of England became a critic of the monetary policy adopted by the government during the early 1980s. In fact the Bank seemed to have successfully resisted the attempt to deregulate the money markets completely, at least up until 1983 (Fforde, 1983).

Interestingly enough, this disagreement between the two main institutions dealing with financial policy in Britain had a parallel in the USA, though with a different emphasis. It was mentioned earlier that President Reagan was influenced by supply-side economics in formulating the early budgets of his administration. However the Federal Reserve Bank — the American central banking mechanism — was not at all persuaded by this position. It resisted and criticized what it saw as the implications for the size of the Federal Budget deficit and advocated a conventional monetarist policy approach rather against the supply-side influence alone. In addition the Congressional Budget Office offered its own critique of the budget proposals which was based upon more conventional Keynesian approach (Rousseas, 1981—2). Thus a number of competing conceptions and approaches were in play within the state apparatuses themselves, which tended to undermine the single-minded pursuit of any one of the policy options proposed.

An incomes policy?

The issue mentioned above of the change in *form* of intervention implied by the new economic management is vividly demonstrated by the abandonment of formal incomes policies by 'monetarist' governments. One of the planks of a 'belief in markets' is that the labour market should be left to find its own equilibrium based upon the free collective bargaining by workers and employers.

Incomes policies organized by the state should thus be avoided since they only lead to more problems than they solve.

The point this raises, however, is whether in a highly advanced economy it is possible *not* to have an incomes policy of some kind or another. Here, then, is the central issue – an incomes policy of *one kind or another.* Take the 1982 situation as an instance. The public sector was working under a regime of very tight cash limits already discussed which severely constrained wage bargaining in this sector. This sector also accounts for some 30 per cent of total employment in the economy (see figure 3.5). In addition there was a highly orchestrated and government-supported campaign organized to define 'acceptable' and 'sensible' wages increases in the economy generally. This was aided by the severe – and possibly government-condoned – recession in the economy which provided a very effective mechanism for keeping private sector wage claims at low levels. And trade union legislation was proposed designed to decrease the effectiveness of picketing and the like. All in all this added up to a very effective incomes policy despite the official rhetoric against the idea. Clearly the *form* of incomes policy and the type of intervention that it implied differed from that of the period covered by chapter 3. The later measures seek to impose an incomes policy on the trades unions rather than negotiate one with them.

Monetarism or deflation?

The final point to make in this examination of the actual policies pursued by an ostensibly monetarist government is to ask how, in spite of everything, the government managed to reduce inflation to single figures by 1983. Does this not demonstrate that its commitment to the centrality of the 'fight against inflation' marked it as following a pre-eminently monetarist course? To answer this we need to look at exactly *how* the government might have brought this inflation down. The argument here would be that this was not predominantly achieved by monetarist policy recommendations but rather by the developing recession in the world and domestic economy generally, though this was heavily aided by the government through its fiscal stance and taxation policy. These were generally tight. What we had, then, was a rather old-fashioned recession in the economy accompanied one might add by fairly 'traditional' mechanisms of fiscal and monetary restraint (interest rate policy) rather than by monetarism proper. It was basically fiscal policy and the budgetary stance adopted by the government that 'deflated' the economy (Miller, 1982). To a large extent monetary policy was out of control, in the sense that targets set here were consistently overshot. Thus it is perhaps an exaggeration to suggest that the state had been 'transformed' in its functions with respect to economic management — and it had been far from fully 'disengaged'. As of 1983 it has been changed rather marginally on this score — a different emphasis and form with respect to its legitimate interventions. Whether it will be, or could be, so transformed in the future is, of course, another matter. (This argument is pursued at greater length in Thompson, 1984.)

Conclusion

The conclusion of this chapter is twofold. On the one hand, whilst there can be little doubt that a significant ideological change with respect to state involvement in the economy had been brought about largely by the changed circumstances of the world economy, this had yet to turn itself into a full blooded withdrawal of the state from involvement with the economy. There were institutional obstacles to this and other practical obstacles which worked to divert efforts away from disengaging the state apparatuses. Despite the hopes of many policy-makers, modern complex economies which are integrated into a myriad of international relationships, cannot be left to regulate themselves. 'New economic management' ideologies involve only a re-organization of the forms of legitimate interventions.

On the other hand it could be argued that the attempt to disengage the state apparatuses from both direct *and* indirect mechanisms of economic intervention have only just begun. The whole pattern of what used to be thought of as legitimate interventions and social relations more generally has certainly been disturbed and its scope redefined. Time will show whether further serious steps towards the perfect market can be achieved and justified.

References

Buchanan, J. and Wagner, R. (1977) *Democracy in Deficit,* London: Academic Press.

Fforde, J. S. (1983) 'Setting monetary objectives', *Bank of England Quarterly Review,* Vol. 23, No. 2, June, pp. 200–8.

Friedman, M. (1976) 'The fragility of freedom', *Encounter,* November, pp. 8–14.

Gilder, G. (1981) *Wealth and Poverty,* New York: Basic Books.

Heald, D. (1983) *Public Expenditure*, Oxford: Martin Robertson.

HMSO (1980) *Memorandum on Monetary Policy,* London: Treasury and Civil Service Committee, HCR.729, July.

HMSO (1982) *Financial Statement and Budget Report,* UK Treasury.

Joseph, K. (1976) *Monetarism is Not Enough,* Centre for Policy Studies.

Kay, J. (ed.) (1982) *The 1982 Budget,* Oxford: Basil Blackwell.

Labour Party (1976) *Report of the Annual Conference,* London: The Labour Party.

Maude, A. (ed.) (1977) *The Right Approach to the Economy,* London: Conservative Party.

Miller, M. (1982) 'Inflation – adjusting the public sector financial deficit' in J. Kay (ed.) *The 1982 Budget.*

Redwood, J. and Hatch, J. (1982) *Controlling Public Industries,* Oxford: Basil Blackwell.

Rousseas, S. (1981–2) 'The poverty of wealth', *Journal of Post Keynesian Economics,* Vol. 4, No. 2, Winter, pp. 192–213.

Thompson, G. F. (1981) 'Monetarism and economic ideology', *Economy and Society,* Vol. 10, No. 4, pp. 27–71.

Thompson, G. F. (1984) *The Conservative Government's Economic Policy 1979–1983,* London: Croom Helm.

Tomlinson, J. (1981) 'The "economics of politics" and public expenditure: a critique', *Economy and Society,* Vol. 10, No. 4, November, pp. 381–402.

Wanniski, J. (1979) *The Way the World Works,* New York: Simon and Schuster.

10

Power and legitimacy in contemporary Britain

DAVID HELD

In this chapter[1] I shall explore questions about power and legitimacy in relation to Britain since the Second World War. My objectives are threefold. I would like, first, to sketch the historical background of the period and to introduce some crucial dimensions of the British political system. Second, I want to assess some ideas and theories about the British state – many of which crop up in various forms in public debate. Third, I want to develop a model to help shed light on state power. The argument which runs through the chapter is that while the British state form remains a representative democratic system it has come to depend more and more in the post-war years on institutions of administration, constraint and coercion to ensure stability. This is the result, I believe, of multiple conflicts which have roots in economic, political and cultural domains.

The chapter is divided into a number of sections. After an initial statement of some key issues, I consider two sets of arguments. The first set is about the nature of the post-war years of social 'consensus' (the 'end of ideology' and 'one dimensional society' theses). The second set concerns the growing 'crisis' of the state and the erosion of its legitimacy from the late 1960s ('government overload' and 'legitimation crisis' theories). In examining each position I try to advance beyond the main competing perspectives by means of a combination of empirical inquiry and theoretical argument. In so doing, I also recount the story of the post-war years in particular periods (1945–early 1970s, mid-1970s–1980s). I conclude by looking at some central issues of power and legitimacy today.

The issues

The decade and a half following the Second World War has been characterized by many as an age of consent, faith in authority and legitimacy. The long war appeared to have generated both a tide of promise and hope for a new era and substantial changes in the relationship between state and society. The coronation of Queen Elizabeth II in 1953 — at least two million people turned out in the streets, over 20 million watched on television, nearly 12 million listened on radio — reinforced the impression of a social consensus, a post-war social contract. As one historian put it, 'the coronation was associated in many people's minds, however vaguely, with the idea of a new Elizabethan age in which through the Commonwealth, if not through the Empire, Britain would still retain a glorious place in the world' (Marwick, 1982, pp. 109—10). The monarchy signalled tradition and stability while parliament symbolized accountability. People seemed to identify with each other in and through the state: the patriotic allegiance of all citizens seemed to have been won.

During these early post-war years political commentators from right to left of the political spectrum remarked on the high degree of compliance to the central institutions of British society: private property, welfare, parliament and the monarchy. On the Labour front benches socialism was regarded ever less as a 'class movement'; and the front benches of the Tory party affirmed that the 'class war' was obsolete. In the early 1950s Anthony Eden declared the Tory objective as 'a nation-wide property-owning democracy' while in the late 1950s Harold Macmillan was sufficiently confident to make 'You've had it good. Have it better. Vote Conservative' the slogan for the 1959 general election. Reflecting mournfully on Labour's failure to win, Hugh Gaitskell declared: 'the changing character of labour, full employment, new housing, the new way of life based on the telly, the fridge, the car and the glossy magazines — all have had their effect on our political strength'. Moreover, the belief in 'free enterprise', a 'do-it-yourself' world, moderated and contained by the interventionist state, was reinforced by the political excesses of the right (Fascism and Nazism in central and southern Europe) and the left (Communism in eastern Europe). The Cold War was an immense pressure confining all so-called 'respectable' politics to the centre ground.

Commenting on this period in British politics A. H. Halsey wrote: 'Liberty, equality, and fraternity all made progress.' Full employment, growing educational and occupational opportunity marked it as a time 'of high net upward mobility and of slowly burgeoning mass affluence. The tide of political consensus flowed strongly for twenty years or more' (1981, pp. 156–7). The existence of this consensus – suggesting that the modern British state was widely regarded as a legitimate order – was strongly supported in the now famous work, *The Civic Culture,* by Gabrial A. Almond and Sidney Verba. *The Civic Culture,* conducted in the late 1950s and early 1960s, was the first nationwide sample survey of political attitudes in Britain carried out by academics. The study indicated that the British had a highly developed sense of loyalty to their system of government, a strong sense of deference to the independent authority of government and state, attitudes of social trust and confidence, and a deep commitment to moderation in politics.

Before proceeding any further it might be useful to clarify a 'family' of potentially very ambiguous concepts: consensus, consent, compliance and legitimacy. The meaning of this 'family' of concepts has been much discussed in philosophical and sociological literature.[2] An example might help to illustrate some of the problems. Citizens *obey* the commands laid down by rules or laws (concerning, for example, traffic regulation, sending children to school, respecting the property of employers, not 'taking the law into their own hands'). They *comply* with rules; they *consent* to them. In following the rule of law, they affirm a belief in legality. According to some political and social analysts, such a belief entails that the polity or political institutions are accepted, i.e. *legitimated.* But the difficulty with *this* concept of legitimacy is that it fails to distinguish between different grounds for obeying a command, complying with a rule, agreeing or consenting to something. We may obey or comply because:

(1) there is no choice in the matter (*following orders,* or *coercion*);
(2) no thought has ever been given to it and we do it as it has always been done (*tradition*);
(3) we cannot be bothered one way or another (*apathy*);
(4) although we do not like the situation – it is not satisfactory and far from ideal – we cannot imagine things being really different and so we 'shrug our shoulders' and accept what seems like fate (*pragmatic acquiescence*);

(5) we are dissatisfied with things as they are but nevertheless go along with them in order to secure an end; we acquiesce because it is in the long-run to our advantage (*instrumental acceptance* or *conditional agreement/consent*);
(6) in the circumstances before us, and with the information available to us at the moment, we conclude it is 'right', 'correct', 'proper' for us as an individual or member of a collectivity: it is what we genuinely *should* or *ought* do (*normative agreement*);
(7) it is what in ideal circumstances – with, for instance, all the knowledge we would like, all the opportunity to discover the circumstances and requirements of others – we would have agreed to do (*ideal normative agreement*).

These distinctions are analytical: in real life of course we often jumble many different types of agreement together; and what I am calling 'ideal normative agreement' is not a position we are likely to reach. But the idea of an ideal normative agreement is interesting because it provides a benchmark which helps us assess whether those whose acquiescence to rules and laws is, for instance, pragmatic *would* have done as they did *if* they had had better knowledge, information, etc., at the moment of their action. I will not make direct use of this particular idea until the conclusion of the chapter.

It is important to be aware for analytical purposes of the continuum of types of obeying/complying/consenting/agreeing. The types are represented on the scale below:

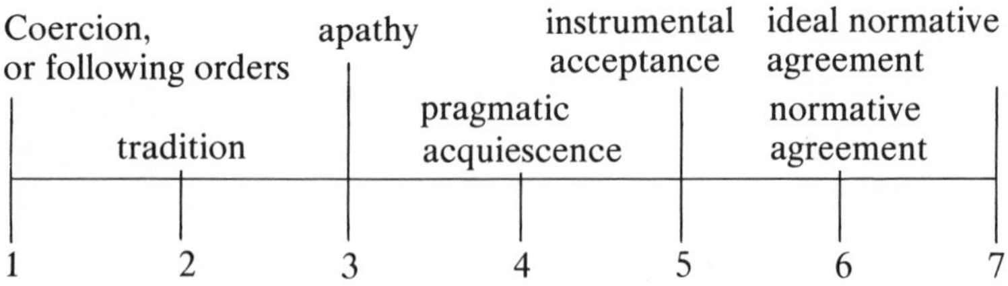

I shall reserve the term legitimacy for types 6 and 7 on the scale; that is, legitimacy implies that people follow rules and laws because they think them right, correct, justified – worthy. A legitimate political order is one that is normatively sanctioned by the population.

It is worth pointing out that category 5 on the scale is ambiguous;

it could be taken to imply a weak form of legitimacy. But because compliance and consent is instrumental or conditional I shall not take it to mean this; for when acceptance is instrumental it means that the existing state of affairs is only tolerated, or compliance granted, in order to secure some other desired end. If the end is not achieved the original situation will not be more agreeable – in all probability it will be much less so.

A legitimate state or a repressive regime?

Political analysts thinking about the extraordinary turmoil of the twentieth century industrial capitalist world – two colossal wars, the Russian Revolution, the depression of the 1930s, the rise of Fascism and Nazism – were impressed by the high degree of compliance to the dominant institutions of society and the striking absence of mass movements demanding revolutionary transformation of the political and social order in the years after the Second World War. American, British and continental political scientists and sociologists working in the late 1950s and early 1960s attempted to develop explanations of this state of affairs. One prominent group, arguing within the framework of a pluralist theory of power, developed the 'end of ideology' thesis. It is a thesis which was markedly in tune with views expressed during the late 1950s and early 1960s in the media, in the main political parties, in official political circles, and in many of the organizations of the labour movement. Another much smaller group expressed a radically dissenting view: they offered an interpretation of events which found little, if any, sympathy in the main institutions of state, economy and culture, although it had a major impact on students and the new radical protest movements of the 1960s. This second group, arguing within a modified Marxist framework, analysed the so-called 'end of ideology' as the realization of a highly repressive order: 'the one dimensional society'.[3]

By the 'end of ideology' Lipset, the best known exponent of this position, means a decline in the support by intellectuals, labour unions and left-wing political parties for what he calls 'red flag waving'; that is, the socialist project defined by Marxism-Leninism (Lipset, 1963). The general factors which explain this situation are the demise of Marxism-Leninism as an attractive ideology in light of its record as a political system in eastern Europe, and the resolution of the key problems facing western industrial capitalist societies. More specifically, Lipset argues that, within western democracies, 'the ideological issues dividing left and right have been reduced to a little more or a little less government ownership and economic planning', and that it 'really makes little difference which political party controls the domestic policies of individual nations'. All this reflects, he suggests, the fact that 'the fundamental political problems of the industrial revolution have been solved: the workers have achieved industrial and political citizenship; the conservatives have accepted the welfare state; the democratic left has recognized that an increase in overall state power carries with it more dangers to freedom than solutions for economic problems' (Lipset, 1963, pp. 442–3).

Arguing along parallel lines to Almond and Verba, Lipset affirms that a fundamental consensus on general political values – in favour of equality, achievement and the procedures of democracy – confers legitimacy on present political and social arrangements. Accordingly, the western democracies, particularly of Britain and the USA, will enjoy a future defined by progressive stability, convergence in the political views of economic classes, parties and states, and the steady erosion of conflict.

Butler and Stokes, focusing particularly on changes in Britain, have made analogous arguments (Butler and Stokes, 1974, pp. 193–208). One of their central themes is the declining relevance of social class to politics. Economic prosperity in the post-war years has brought within the reach of mass markets new types of goods and services, while the welfare state has substantially reduced the remaining 'pockets of poverty'. Differences between the living standards and social habits of working-class and middle-class people have diminished; and social mobility has 'added to the bridges over the class divide'. Accordingly, the 'electorate's disposition to respond to politics in class terms has been weakened'. This process of (apparent) class dealignment (see chapter 8) led Butler and Stokes to affirm a drift to the 'centre ground' in British politics. While the subsequent evidence of 'volatile' electoral behaviour (a point I shall come back to later) is also examined by them, there is little, if anything, in their work to suggest that the legitimacy of the state might be in doubt.

The theorists of the 'end of ideology', or the end of class politics, offer an interpretation of post-Second World War political life which Marcuse, who made famous the thesis of the 'one dimensional society', completely rejects (Marcuse, 1964). Yet curiously, as I have already noted, there is a common starting point: an attempt to explain the appearance of political harmony in western capitalism in the post-war years.

Marcuse's analysis begins by pointing to a multiplicity of forces which are combining to aid the management and control of the modern economy. First, he notes the spectacular development of the means of production – itself the result of the growing concentration of capital, radical changes in science and technology, the trend toward mechanization and automation, and the progressive transformation of management into ever larger private bureaucracies. Second, he emphasizes the increasing regulation of free competition – a consequence of state intervention which both stimulates and supports the economy and leads to the expansion of public bureaucracy. Third, he describes a reordering of national priorities by international events and the permanent threat of war – created by the Cold War, the so-called 'threat of communism', and the ever present possibility of nuclear catastrophe. In short, the prevailing trends in society are leading, Marcuse contends, to the establishment of massive private and public organizations which threaten to engulf social life.

A crucial consequence of this state of affairs is what Marcuse calls 'depoliticization': the eradication of political and moral questions from public life by an obsession with technique, productivity and efficiency. The single-minded pursuit of production for profit by large and small businesses, and the state's unquestioned support for this objective in the name of economic growth, sets a highly limited political agenda: it creates a situation in which public affairs become concerned merely with debating different means – the end is given, i.e. more and more production. Depoliticization results from the spread of 'instrumental reason'; that is, the spread of the concern with the efficiency of different means with respect to pre-given ends.

This state of affairs is further reinforced, according to Marcuse, by the way the cultural traditions of subordinate classes, regions and minorities (racial and ethnic groups) are swamped by the mass media producing 'packaged culture'. The mass media is shaped to a significant extent by the concerns of the advertising industry with its relentless drive to increase consumption. The effect, he argues, is 'false consciousness'; that is, a state of awareness in which people no longer consider or know what is in their real interests. The world of massive public and private bureaucracies pursuing profitable production corrupts and distorts human life. The social order – integrated by the tight interlock between industry and the state – is repressive and profoundly 'unworthy'; yet, most people do not recognize it as such. Marcuse does analyse counter-trends to this state of affairs but his general emphasis – at least in his book *One Dimensional Man* — is on the way the cult of affluence and consumerism (in modern industrial capitalist society) creates modes of behaviour that are adaptive, passive and acquiescent. Against the portrayal of the political order as one based on genuine consent and legitimacy, Marcuse emphasizes the way it is sustained by ideological and coercive forces. People have no choice or chance to think about what *type* of productive system they would like to work in, what *type* of democracy they would like to participate in, what *kind* of life they would like to create for themselves. If they wish for comfort and security they have to adapt to the standards of the economic and political system. They have to go to work, get ahead, and make the best use of the opportunities with which they are presented; otherwise, they find themselves poor and marginal to the whole order.

The post-war years: 1945—early 1970s; problems with the theories of the end of ideology and one dimensionality

The details of these theories are not as important as their overall general claims. For despite their many differences — differences which centre on whether the legitimacy of the political order is genuine or contrived — they both emphasize (1) a high degree of compliance and integration among all groups and classes in society and (2) that the stability of the political and social system is reinforced as a result. I shall argue that both these claims are false by, first, examining some pertinent research findings and, second, by sketching the mounting difficulties faced in the 1960s and early 1970s by the British state and the political system more generally.

The post-war consensus re-examined

An intriguing place to begin is Almond's and Verba's influential study, *The Civic Culture* (1963), which, as I noted earlier, was the first work of its kind on the British political system. According to Almond and Verba, 'the state of feeling of political emotion in a country is perhaps the most important test of the legitimacy of its political system' (Almond and Verba, 1963, p. 100). If a political regime is to survive in the long-run 'it must be accepted by citizens as the proper form of government per se' (1963, p. 230). Democracy, according to these authors, is accepted in this sense 'by elites and non-elites' (1963, p. 180). Almond and Verba arrive at this conclusion by taking as a suitable index for the measurement of legitimacy what individuals report as a source of pride in their country (1963, pp. 102–3, 246). But a number of things need to be noted.

First, only a minority, 46 per cent, of the British respondents expressed pride in their governmental, political institutions (1963, p. 102). Second, and rather more importantly, Almond's and Verba's measure of legitimacy is very crude; for it fails to distinguish between the different possible meanings of pride and their highly ambiguous relation to legitimacy. For instance, I can express pride or pleasure in parliamentary democracy without in any way implying that it operates now as well as it might, or that it is the proper, or best or most acceptable form of government. I can express pride in something while wishing it substantially altered. Almond and Verba do not investigate possibilities like this. Third, Almond and Verba seem so anxious to *celebrate* western democracies of the British type that they misinterpret their own data. Michael Mann (1970) and Carole Pateman (1980) have shown that a careful reading of the data presented in *The Civic Culture* shows that not only is the degree of common value commitment in Britain fairly minimal but that according to the only (and indirect) measure of social class used – the type of formal education of the respondent – working-class people frequently express views which Almond and Verba think 'reflects the most extreme feeling of distrust and alienation' (1963, p. 268). Almond and Verba fail to explain the systematic differences in political orientation of social classes and, cutting across these, of men and women which their own data reveal (Pateman, 1980, pp. 75–80).

That value consensus does not exist to a significant extent in Britain (and the United States) is confirmed by Mann (1970) in a survey of a large variety of empirical materials based on research conducted in the late 1950s and early 1960s. He finds that middle-class people (white collar and professional workers), on the whole, tend to exhibit greater consistency of belief and agreement over values than do the working class (manual workers). In so far as there are common values held by the working class they tend to be hostile to the system rather than supportive of it. There is more 'dissensus' between classes than there is 'consensus'. Further, if one examines 'political efficacy', that is, people's estimation of their ability to influence government, noteworthy differences are also recorded among classes: the middle class tend to assert far greater confidence than their working-class counterparts. Considerable distance from, and distrust of, dominant political institutions is indicated among working-class people (Pateman, 1973 and 1980). Strong allegiance to the liberal-democratic system and to 'democratic norms' appears to be correlated directly to socio-economic status.

It should be stressed that much of the research on value consensus is ambiguous and difficult to interpret; I will offer a fuller discussion of it later. What matters here and what we can say with confidence is that any claim about widespread adherence to a common value system needs to be treated with the utmost scepticism. But what of the immediate post-war years? Might not Lipset and the others at least find some supporting evidence for their claims during these years? The argument presented so far should lead one to be cautious about this as well.

It is hard to characterize with precision the political atmosphere of the immediate post-war years; surprisingly little detailed social history has been written about the period. In Britain, no doubt, a mixture of joy about the war's end, resignation to difficult economic circumstances and hope for the future intermingled in complex ways across social groups and classes. As the multiple restraints of war were relaxed popular radical sentiments became more clearly demarcated: newspaper commentators at the time, as well as historians and sociologists writing later, have emphasized how high people's expectations were and how these were marked, especially among the mass of working people, with egalitarian ideologies and a sense that things would soon get markedly better (Ryder and Silver, 1977; Middlemas, 1979; Halsey, 1981). Among the soldiers returning from war these aspirations were especially high (Middlemas, 1979, pp. 360–1). There were few illusions about the prevalence of class in Britain prior to and after the war (see Marwick, 1982, p. 48). That British society had been and was a class society, does not appear to have been in question.

If there was a widespread 'consensus' or 'common value system' adhered to by the working classes in Britain during the immediate post-war years it seems better interpreted in terms of what I called earlier 'instrumental consent': in this case, general compliance to dominant political and economic institutions linked directly to an expectation of a qualitatively new and more egalitarian life. As the Postal Censor noted in a (1941) report on working-class and lower middle-class aspirations for the future, they were 'looking forward confidently to a post-war levelling of class distinction and redistribution of wealth' (quoted in Middlemas, 1979, p. 361). 'Deep scepticism' about government propaganda along with signs of popular 'dangerous' radicalism noted by Mass Observation (a private research organization) as early as 1940 certainly seems to have lived on — perhaps because of the memories of the 1930s. There was a general sense that the 'rights and dignity' of ordinary people would be fully acknowledged in the period to come (cf. Morgan, 1984; Thompson 1984).

A sense of allegiance to Britain, tied to patriotism generated during the war, was also undoubtedly strong. But the post-war Labour government, and the Conservatives after them, were constantly anxious to emphasize that the state in Britain was the symbol of common values, justly attracting the allegiance of its citizens. Utilizing techniques of 'public information presentation', 'public relations exercises' and 'public opinion management' developed before and during the war, governments went to extraordinary lengths to try to manage opinion, to reinforce acceptance of the state's authority, and to create 'consensus'. Paddy Scannell's chapter on the state and broadcasting in this volume provides a vivid illustration of these themes. There seems little doubt that governments judged these efforts necessary — further interesting evidence of the unsteady state of consent.

The grounds for allegiance to the nation-state are of course complex. But one key factor should not go unmentioned. Victory in war against Nazi Germany had confirmed the importance of some of the freedoms that can be enjoyed in a political democracy like Britain. The Labour party seemed the 'natural heir' to the institutions which nourish such freedoms *and* to the aspirations which sought an extension of 'liberty, equality and fraternity'. The election of the Labour Party in 1945 confirmed a desire for a programme of change that might slowly establish a socially undivided nation. Labour politicians and later Conservative governments claimed to diagnose adequately the deficiencies in British 'old ways' and promised to rectify them.[4] In so doing they further enhanced expectations of change.

There is an important implication of such high hopes and aspirations: if political and social changes are not undertaken, or if changes are found inadequate, or if they fail perpetually, the scope for disappointment and disillusionment with government and perhaps the state more generally is great. Instrumental consent contains within it this possibility.

In short, neither a system of 'shared values' nor of 'ideological domination' simply conferred legitimacy on the British political system in the post-war years from 1945 to the 1960s. The situation was far more complicated. The complications can be highlighted further by examining the second major point of overlap between the theorists of the 'end of ideology' and 'one dimensionality', that is, the focus on the stability of the political and social order. For the biggest difficulty faced by all this literature on consensus, be it voluntary or contrived, is the sequence of events which followed its publication. With the prosperity of the post-war years it appeared that many, if not all, of the interests of social groups, elites and classes could be accommodated in the politics of the expanding welfare state. Prosperity helped sustain the illusion that the acquiescence of the mass of people meant legitimacy of the political and social order. A simple rosy picture of post-war political harmony and stable prosperity is heavily compromised, however, by a whole variety of economic, political and cultural developments.

The economy

The post-war revival of foreign trade provided almost ideal conditions for successive government attempts to manage economic growth and to redeem the promise of steadily increasing affluence. The idea of a managed economy working at full capacity with adequate provision for the welfare of all citizens seemed to fit reasonably well with the actuality of the immediate post-war years; increased prosperity and expanding opportunities were enjoyed by many. Although British industry had been damaged and severely disrupted during the war, the position of many of Britain's future major competitors (for instance, Germany, France and Japan) appeared much worse; and there was still a supply of relatively cheap raw materials from the empire, as well as special 'protected' markets for British goods. Britain's long commercial and trading history placed it in what seemed a strong international position.

The favourable economic conditions of the early 1950s, which made full employment, price stability and growth all seem possible simultaneously, soon, however, began to melt away. In practically all spheres the performance of the British economy was outstripped by its major competitors. Investment levels were chronically low, profitability was in decline, productivity poor, real wages – while slowly increasing – fell behind those of many other industrial capitalist countries. The terms of trade worsened, there were periodic currency crises, and markets were lost. A series of deepening political-business or 'stop-go' cycles – involving seemingly endless booms followed by sharp downturns in economic activity – became a marked feature of political and economic life.

Indicators of worsening economic difficulties were steadily declining rates of growth, progressively rising levels of unemployment and inflation and steadily declining company profits.[5] While problems of unemployment and inflation, among other things, were to become testing problems facing *all* western capitalist states from the 1970s, the particularly sharp decline of the British economy relative to its competitors is unmistakable (Glyn and Sutcliffe, 1972; Jessop, 1980; Bornstein *et al.*, 1984).

One of the distinctive features of the British economy is its extensive and deeply rooted overseas commitments which helped give Britain such a pre-eminent position in world trade throughout the nineteenth century. The City of London flourished in this context and became one of the world's leading financial centres. It is worth stressing certain aspects of the City's economic and political position; for it is crucial to understanding British politics and the place of the state in social and economic life (Rubinstein, 1976; Nairn, 1977; Ingham, 1982).

The significance of the City as an economic centre dates from the pre-industrial expansion of world trade. The City's commercial and banking activities developed partly through the financing of this trade and partly through the financing of the state itself, for instance, its armies and overseas exploits. From the outset, the City was oriented to the international economy, to the financing of commerce and debt. This orientation was reinforced, Geoffrey Ingham has shown, by several nineteenth century developments all of which led to the rapid 'expansion of London's management of international mercantile and monetary transactions'. Thus, the City's main interest became the 'buying and selling of money (in all forms); of stocks and shares; of commodities and commercial services such as insurance' (Ingham, 1982, pp. 219–20). This had major consequences for domestic industry in Britain and for employment prospects as well. Ingham refers to a 'disjuncture' of practices and interests between the City and domestic industry. On the one hand, the City is oriented toward short-term gains from a high volume and fast turnover of commercial transactions while, on the other hand, industry works for profitability on a longer time scale, since its investments take time to implement and mature. This disjuncture, moreover, has always showed itself in two ways:

> First, in the low level of long-term external finance for productive industry [that is, loans and credit available from sources other than productive industry itself], and secondly, the political implementation and defence of policies designed to maintain London as an

> open, unrestricted market place with a currency strong enough to be a basis for international mercantile and banking transactions. (Ingham, 1982, p. 220)

The influence of those in political life who still believe in the durability of the British state with its old world role (concerned with, for instance, the maintenance of a strong pound, defence of foreign investments and high expenditure on arms and military material) and City interests (concerned with, among other things, a strong pound to maintain the value of overseas investments, high interest rates to increase income levels and the free flow of capital for investment abroad) remains considerable and combines to help sustain the City's powerful position in British politics and economics.

The twentieth-century erosion of Britain's world economic and political position has had very uneven effects on different sections of the economy. While the output of Britain's industrial 'workshops', especially after the Second World War, became less and less significant in world manufacturing, the City of London retained a leading role. It is clear that the interests of the City — of banking, commerce and overseas trade generally — are not necessarily those of British domestic industry; and, in fact, British economic policy from the mid-1950s to the early 1970s was caught in a vicious circle — trying to satisfy first one then the other of these interests and, in the end, satisfying neither adequately. The point has been well put by Jessop:

> . . . since this attempt required a free flow of capital for portfolio and industrial investment overseas and entailed heavy expenditure on foreign aid to maintain the overseas sterling area, production of arms and military material, and defence of foreign investments, markets and vital sources of supply, governments were forced to concentrate their efforts on increasing the reserves and eliminating the deficit on visible trade. However, since the state was also operating in the context of the post-war settlement between capital and labour, it could not pursue these policies to the point where full employment and welfare expenditure were threatened. The overall effect of these complex structural and political constraints on the conduct of the government's policy was continual oscillation between deflation and reflation triggered in turn by sterling crises and rising unemployment. (Jessop, 1980, pp. 31-2)

Financial and overseas interests have been able, within the Treasury and the Bank of England in particular, to sustain concerns with sterling, currency reserves and balance of payments over and against increased public expenditure, full employment and economic growth (see P. Hall, in Bornstein *et al.*, 1984). Moreover, the complex (and often contradictory) pressures facing the state from the City and much domestic industry have not eased with time, although their form, as we will see later, has undergone change.

The steady decline in the fortunes of British industry was one of the key factors facing British politicians from the late 1950s. Although a variety of economic packages were presented by Conservative and Labour governments in the 1960s and early 1970s, a sense of the steady deterioration of the British economy was more marked by the early 1970s than it had been at the start of the 1960s.

Industrial conflict and strikes

The theorists of the end of ideology and one dimensionality, while they did not predict the end of all industrial conflict, certainly provided an inadequate framework for its comprehension. Far from waning or, as some put it, 'withering away', strikes remained a persistent and much discussed feature of British industrial relations. From the late 1950s to the 1970s, while strike rates varied, strikes were one of a variety of indicators of the low level of trust between both parties of industry (Fox, 1974). The data on strike volume (days 'lost' per 1,000 wage and salary workers) is represented in figure 10.1. After 1968 there was a marked increase in strike activity, especially during the Heath government's attempt in the early 1970s to restructure industrial relations legislation. This can be gleaned from the data presented in table 10.1.

One of the most significant features of strike activity is the way it is related to the state of the economy. In a variety of interesting studies Douglas Hibbs has shown how strike volume varies with, among other things, the demand for labour (Hibbs, 1976, 1978). Hibbs's analyses affirm what the historian Eric Hobsbawn has called 'the common sense of demanding concessions when conditions are favourable' (1952). As Hibbs explains: 'the working class exercises considerable sophistication in the use of the strike weapon. The pronounced inverse relationship between the volume of industrial conflict and the rate of unemployment demonstrates that on the whole strikes are timed to capitalise on the strategic advantages of a tight labour market' (Hibbs, 1976, p. 1057). Not

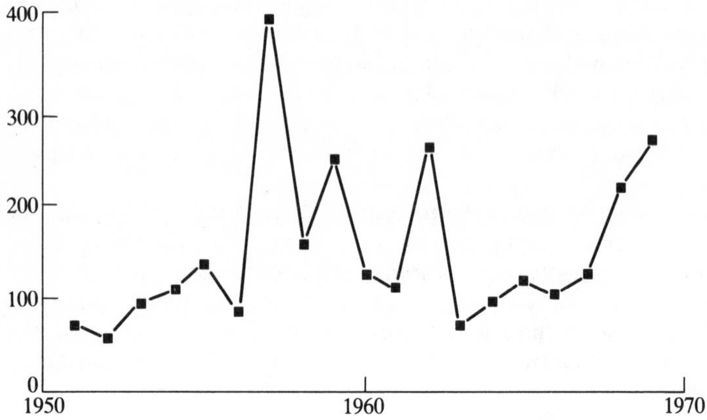

Figure 10.1 The volume of strikes (days 'lost' per 1,000 workers)
Source: Hibbs, 1976, p. 1041.

TABLE 10.1 STRIKE ACTIVITY, 1967–73/4

	1967	*1968*	*1969*	*1970*	*1971*	*1972*	*1973*	*1974*
UK								
Number of strikes	2116	2378	3116	3906	2228	2497	2873	2922
Number of workers involved (1,000s)	734	2258	1665	1801	1178	1734	1528	1626
Number of days lost (1,000s)	2787	4690	6846	10,980	13,551	23,909	7197	14,750
Economically active population 1971: 25,715,000, Population Census.								

Source: *Yearbook of Labour Statistics*, (1977) ILO.

only are strikes related to levels of unemployment — the lower unemployment is, the higher the strike rates tend to be — but they are also related to changes in real wages and profits. Hibbs concludes that far from being a simple 'reactive phenomena' strikes can be interpreted in no other way than as an expression of the struggle for power between social classes over the distribution of resources, especially over national income (1978).

Hibbs's analyses show how class conflict is an inextricable feature of the cyclical movements of the economy. The crises faced by the state's 'economic managers' (in government, the Treasury, etc.) are in part both a symptom of this conflict and a crucial obstacle to strategies for its resolution. The attempts by Conservative and Labour governments alike in the 1960s and early 1970s to reform the industrial relations system met with little, if any, success. The period under review in this part of the chapter ended, as is well known, with the fall of the Heath government at the hands of, among others, the miners.

Of course, strikes are only one of the more obvious manifestations of intense social conflict. In some sense they are the tip of the iceberg: resistance to changing work practices, absenteeism, high labour turnover, industrial sabotage are among a range of other symptoms. But perhaps one of the most remarkable features of the 1950s and 1960s was the growth of unofficial strikes and the shop stewards movement. This was not simply a result of changes on the side of management, although changes in the organization of production — its progressive rationalization and centralization — undoubtedly played a part. The biggest trade unions had got progressively bigger in the inter-war and post-war years. Increased size did not make the representation of local concerns and interests easier. Middlemas goes so far as to say that the biggest of the unions were engaged in a 'cult of size' and that this 'turned what had once been manageable institutions into sprawling, precarious empires vulnerable both to unofficial shop-floor revolt and employer's counter-attacks' (Middlemas, 1979, p. 392). Certainly, the growth of massive trade unions went hand in hand with another trend: those excluded from the formation of wage and other policies at the national level asserted their independence on the shop floor.

Throughout the 1950s unofficial stoppages increased and a marked trend developed toward superimposing local wage agreements onto national settlements. The attempt to control wages and especially local 'wage drift' (the difference between actual earnings and officially agreed rates at national or industry level) with incomes policies in the 1960s only further alienated rank and file workers. The prices and incomes policies of the Labour government in the middle and late 1960s had short-run successes, but each small success seemed to be followed by a crescendo of wage increases. Labour Party attempts in the late 1960s to reform the 'unofficial movement' of the shop floor (elaborated in *In Place of Strife*) – to make this movement more amenable to control by trade union officials and government alike – foundered, as did the Conservative attempt that followed (the *Industrial Relations Act,* 1971). Traditional management prerogatives, the policy-making capacity of government as well as the very rule of law were under challenge (Hyman, 1972; Lane, 1974; Middlemas, 1979; Jessop, 1980). The fragility of tripartite negotiations or 'corporatist arrangements' was clear: they were arrangements amongst formal leaderships who often perhaps shared more in common with each other than they did with their constituencies.

State expenditures and fiscal crisis

The post-war reconstruction involved the state in the finance of permanently high levels of expenditure. The key periods of growth in state expenditure and the changing commitment to various sectors are set out in chapter 3. By the early 1970s total public expenditure rose to over 50 per cent of GNP and the British state began to face a series of escalating deficits (see Gough, 1975). In the wake of the 'post-war settlement', the attempt to maintain full employment and to meet extensive welfare obligations imposed on the state rapidly escalating costs. In the context of the overall deterioration in Britain's economic performance the problems of meeting these costs through taxation and borrowing became ever more acute. The result has been the mushrooming 'fiscal crisis' of the state; that is, the tendency of state expenditures to outrun revenues (O'Connor, 1973).

The fiscal crisis of the British state is a symptom of a multiplicity of difficulties: foremost among these are problems which derive from the attempts to sustain a highly regulated economy with maximum employment possibilities while simultaneously meeting the demands and interests of, among others, domestic industry, the export sector, financial centres like the City and the various sectors of the labour movement. The pervasive dissensus between classes, the fragile nature of much working-class political consent, the risk that industrial conflict might spill over directly into challenges to government, law and the state, provided enormous pressures on successive governments to expand the range of the activities of state agencies. This was reflected not only in successive governments' expenditure on health, education and social security, but in a variety of direct financial aids (e.g. cheap energy from the nationalized industries), tax allowances and budgetary assistance to industry (Gough, 1975). A series of government attempts to advance the rationalization and re-organization of industry through, among other things, the introduction of planning experiments, was also a prominent feature of the time.

But the mounting pressures on state expenditure did not just derive from the immediate circumstances of the post-war years. Britain's past global role and politicians' seeming reluctance to adjust to 'second division' status meant continually high levels of military and related expenditures compared, for instance, to other European countries and Japan (Cambridge Political Economy Group, 1974). While at one time such policies had clearly been essential to the maintenance of overseas trade, markets and financial dealings, they were arguably at least – as they still are now – anachronistic, and another heavy burden on Treasury resources. Finally, it is worth mentioning the increase in expenditure on the police and judiciary, an item that has continued to grow especially rapidly – one more indicator perhaps of social and political tension.

Electoral scepticism and party politics

Rising standards of living throughout most of the 1950s, 1960s and early 1970s provide a somewhat paradoxical background to the deepening shadow of economic crisis and political difficulties. Successive governments accepted the credit for improvements in standards of living and, at every election, the political parties assumed the burden of responsibility for high aspirations (Moss, 1982, p. 151). But the responsibility assumed by these political agents has, as Middlemas aptly put it, 'contrasted unfavourably with the actual inability of the state . . . to accomplish its declared job of delivering a consistently better future' (Middlemas, 1979, p. 424). It is far easier to assess actual political performance when pretensions and promises are so clearly advertised.

There is evidence, discussed in chapter 8, of growing scepticism and disenchantment with traditional party politics throughout the period under review. The two major parties together have attracted (with the exception of 1979) an ever smaller proportion of the total vote, while the share of third party votes has increased. All winning parties had the support of only a minority of the electorate, support which has now dropped to not more than one third of the vote. Although electoral trends are hard to interpret accurately, these trends – along with huge swings in by-elections in the 1960s, the mixed fortunes of the Scottish and Welsh Nationalists, the marked decline of Labour votes in traditional Labour strongholds – combine to suggest growing disillusionment, uncertainty and volatility in support for the dominant parties. Electoral studies appear to confirm this suggestion (Butler and Stokes, 1974). The politics of the centre ground, 'Butskellism', or and what one might call the politics of 'crisis avoidance', appeared throughout the 1960s and early 1970s, to be less and less attractive to voters.

By the middle of the 1960s Harold Wilson's Labour Party claimed the mantle of 'the natural party of government'. Pursuing policies preoccupied with establishing 'national unity', Wilson sought (as did James Callaghan and Denis Healey in the late 1970s) to hold together the rapidly eroding centre ground of British politics. Labour became ever more the party of the status quo: the party of the regulatory state, the declining mixed economy – 'tightened belts' – and the massive inequalities which persisted in all spheres of life (see Panitch, 1976). It was on this ground that it was so easily out-manoeuvred by the Conservatives under Edward Heath in 1970 (and later by Margaret Thatcher) under anti-'big state', anti-bureaucratic, anti-corporate, anti-union banners – banners suggesting the possibility of radical change on behalf of the individual, the family and law and order.

While the declared ideologies of the major parties began to polarize in the late 1960s, the political achievements of both remained firmly on the centre ground. Edward Heath's famous 'U' turn in 1972 seemed to be just more evidence that party programmes meant relatively little in practice and that all government's 'changed direction' in office. In this context, widespread scepticism and cynicism about party politics is not perhaps too difficult to understand.

The authority of the state in question? 1968 and after

Increasing unemployment and inflation, the general decline in the performance of the economy compared to major competitors, rising levels of official and unofficial industrial conflict, challenges to the 'rule of law' during such conflict, mounting fiscal difficulties meeting the costs of the welfare interventionist state, growing signs of disillusionment with the two dominant parties, electoral scepticism in the face of the claims of politicians: all of these were signs indicating that within and underlying the state and the political system there were deeply structured difficulties. While the state had become immensely complex, it remained in general much less monolithic and much less capable of imposing clear direction than Marcuse had suggested, and less legitimate than the theorists of the end of ideology had thought. By the end of the 1960s few denied that dissensus was rife: the certitude and confidence of the middle ground (and largely of the middle and upper classes) was slipping away; and the instrumental consent of segments of the working class seemed to be giving way to progressive disillusionment and conflict.

The 1968–9 period represents something of a watershed (Hall *et al.*, 1978). The anti-Vietnam war movement, the student movement and a host of other political groups associated with the New Left began to alter the political pace: it was a time of astonishing political polarization. Demands for peace, the end of imperialism, resistance to racism, the extension of democratic rights to industry, sexual freedom, the liberation of women, were just some of the issues which produced unparalleled scenes of protest in (post-war) London and took France to the edge of revolution in May 1968. The new movements seemed to define themselves against almost everything that the traditional political system defended. They defined the system as rigid, regimented, authoritarian and empty of moral, spiritual and personal qualities. A mass rebellion against one dimensionality which Marcuse had thought possible but unlikely in 1964 (the year *One Dimensional Man* was published), appeared on the verge of development.

Widespread dissent was met by, among other things, the 'heavy hand' of state power: violent clashes involving riot police were frequently reported in the press. These conflicts were interlaced with further pressures on the state: the revival of nationalist movements in Wales and Scotland and, of course, the intensification of struggle in Northern Ireland. 'The Break-up of Britain', the title of one well-known book about the period, certainly seemed imaginable (Nairn, 1977).

Moral panics

The developments from the late 1950s to the early 1970s had a profoundly unsettling effect on the standard bearers of 'traditional' morality: those who in government, the media, schools, among other places, saw themselves as the arch defenders of the best of '*the* British way of life'. Tracing the history of this defence from its earliest manifestations, Stuart Hall and others have argued in a provocative work that it begins

> with the unresolved ambiguities and contradictions of affluence, of the post-war 'settlement'. It is experienced, first, as a diffuse social unease, as an unnaturally accelerated pace of social change, as an unhingeing of stable patterns, moral points of reference. It manifests itself, first, as an unlocated surge of social anxiety. . . . Later, it appears to focus on more tangible targets: specifically, on the anti-social nature of youth movements, on the threat to British life by the black immigrant, and on the 'rising fever chart' of crime. Later still – as the major social upheavals of the counter-culture and the political student movements become more organized as social forces – it surges, in the form of a more focused 'social anxiety', around these points of disturbance. It names what is wrong in general terms: it is the permissiveness of social life. Finally, as the crisis deepens, and the forms of conflict and dissent assume a more explicitly political and a more clearly delineated class form, social anxiety also precipitates in its more political form. It is directed against the organized power of the working class: against political extremism; against trade union blackmail; against the threat of anarchy . . . (Hall *et al.*, 1978, p. 321)

This analysis is important, for it reminds us how extraordinarily complex are the patterns of political and social change and reaction. The political events of the late 1960s and early 1970s cannot simply be characaterized by the emergence of radical movements. Reaction to them was also strong and this reaction was not simply located in 'the establishment', in the centres of 'patrician culture'.* Scepticism about politics, the demise of the centre ground in party affairs, fear about 'lack of direction', can

* By 'patrician culture' I mean, following Nairn (1977 and 1981, pp. 365ff.), adherence to the values of nobility, tradition and grace along with an emphasis upon independent action and private initiative in civil society.

become the basis of a call for 'new leadership', the firm application of 'law and order', the affirmation of the 'need for control' of all those who threaten the status quo. The anxieties of many – from all sorts of class, occupation and social position – can become a foundation for a massive defence of the state against all kinds of perceived threats, and the basis of a new 'strong state'.

It is time to take stock of the argument so far. Neither the theories of the 'end of ideology' nor 'one dimensionality' can account adequately for the relation between state and society, the instability of the economy and government policy, and the persistence and escalation of tension and conflict which emerged in the post-war years. The joint preoccupation of these theories with compliance, consensus and integration of social groups into the political order led them to overlook the different meanings of compliance and integration and the *conditional* nature of much acquiescence. Mass acquiescence to dominant institutions in the post-war years by no means entailed the mass legitimation of the British state. That this is so is amply borne out by the palpable lack of political and social stability in the 1960s and early 1970s. While this certainly did *not* add up to a major revolutionary attack upon the state, it constituted a severe test of the very foundation of the political order. A crisis of the state *seemed* to be developing.

What exactly was the nature of the crisis? How were its dimensions to be analysed? What were its origins and causes? Were the strengths and limits of state power really exposed?

Contrasting accounts of the crisis of the state: overloaded state or legitimation crisis?

What is a crisis? A distinction must be drawn between, on the one hand, a partial crisis or collapse and, on the other, a crisis which might lead to the transformation of a society. The former refers to such phenomena as the political-business cycle – involving booms and recessions in economic activity – which have been a chronic feature of the British economy. The latter refers to the undermining of the core or organizational principle of a society; that is, to the erosion or destruction of those societal relations which determine the scope and limits to change for, among other things, political and economic activity. A crisis of this second type – which I shall refer to as a 'crisis with transformative potential' – involves challenges to the very core of the political and social order.

In marked contrast to those political analysts of the 1950s and early 1960s who talked about 'integration', 'consensus', 'political stability', etc., those thinking about the late 1960s and 1970s were struck by almost the opposite. The work of recent political science and political sociology reflects preoccupations with 'British decline', 'a breakdown in consensus', 'the crisis of the state'. This section will set out briefly the arguments of two contrasting theories of crisis – theories which try to make sense of the events of the 1960s and early 1970s. The contrast is, again, between writers arguing from the premisses of a pluralist theory of politics, and authors arguing from the premisses of Marxist theory. Both groups of writers, it is worth stressing, are staunch 'revisionists'; that is, they have modified substantially the theories which they take as their starting points.

The first group – arguing from pluralist premisses – can be referred to as theorists of 'overloaded government'; the second group – arguing from Marxist premisses – develop a theory of 'legitimation crisis'. The writers who discuss 'overloaded government' include Anthony King (1976), S. Brittan (1975 and 1977), R. Rose and G. Peters (1977), Samuel P. Huntingdon (1975) and W. D. Nordhaus (1975). The theory of 'legitimation crisis' has been developed by, among others, Jürgen Habermas (1976) and Claus Offe (1984).[6] For the purposes of this chapter it is unnecessary to follow all the details of these writers' analyses, nor do we have to follow the differences in emphasis between, say, King (1976) and Brittan (1975). It will be enough to present broad general summaries of the two positions. I shall leave their appraisal until later.

It should be emphasized that both these contrasting accounts of the crises facing the modern state focus on the possibility of 'crisis with transformative potential'. But while theorists of overload are clearly warning of this as a danger and/or menace to the state (and suggest measures of containment and control), the theorists of 'legitimation crisis' see this as presenting both difficult political dilemmas and potentiality for decisive, progressive, radical change. It is also noteworthy that overload theorems have been influential in party political circles and much discussed in general ways in the media. Theories of legitimation crisis have remained by and large the province of some left-wing political analysts, although they have gained influence in more general academic circles recently.

To help comprehension of the arguments I have set out the key steps of each in diagram form: figures 10.2 and 10.3. I shall go over each of these steps briefly, connecting some of the major points to illustrations from British politics.

The overloaded government

(1a) A pluralist starting point: the theorists of the overloaded state frequently characterize power relations in terms of fragmentation – power is shared and bartered by numerous groups representing diverse and competing interests, e.g. business organizations, trade unions, parties, ethnic groups, students, prison officers, women's institutes, defenders of blood sports, etc. Hence, political outcomes are determined by democratic processes and pressures; governments try to mediate and adjudicate between demands.

(1b) The post-war market society plus the early successes of Keynesian economic policy generated rising mass affluence and the general prosperity of the post-war years, e.g. booms in consumer goods, new housing, spread of television and entertainment industries.

(2) Accordingly, expectations increased, linked to higher standards of living, e.g. annual increments in income and welfare, availability of schooling and higher education.

(3) Aspirations were reinforced by a 'decline in deference' or respect for authority and status. This is itself a result of, among other things, growing affluence, 'free' welfare, health and education which undermines private initiative and responsibility, and egalitarian and meritocratic ideologies which promised much more than could ever be achieved realistically.

(4) In this context, groups press politicians and governments hard to meet their particular aims and ambitions, e.g. higher wages (most employed groups), protection of jobs in declining industrial sectors (some trade unions), high interest rates (banks), low interest rates (domestic industry), low prices (consumer groups), higher prices (some business organizations).

(5) In order to secure maximum votes politicians too often promise more than they can deliver, and sometimes promise to deliver contradictory and therefore impossible sets of demands: competition between parties leads to a spiral of ever greater promises.

(6) Thus, aspirations are reinforced; political parties are seen by the general population as competing means to the same end, i.e. better standards of living.

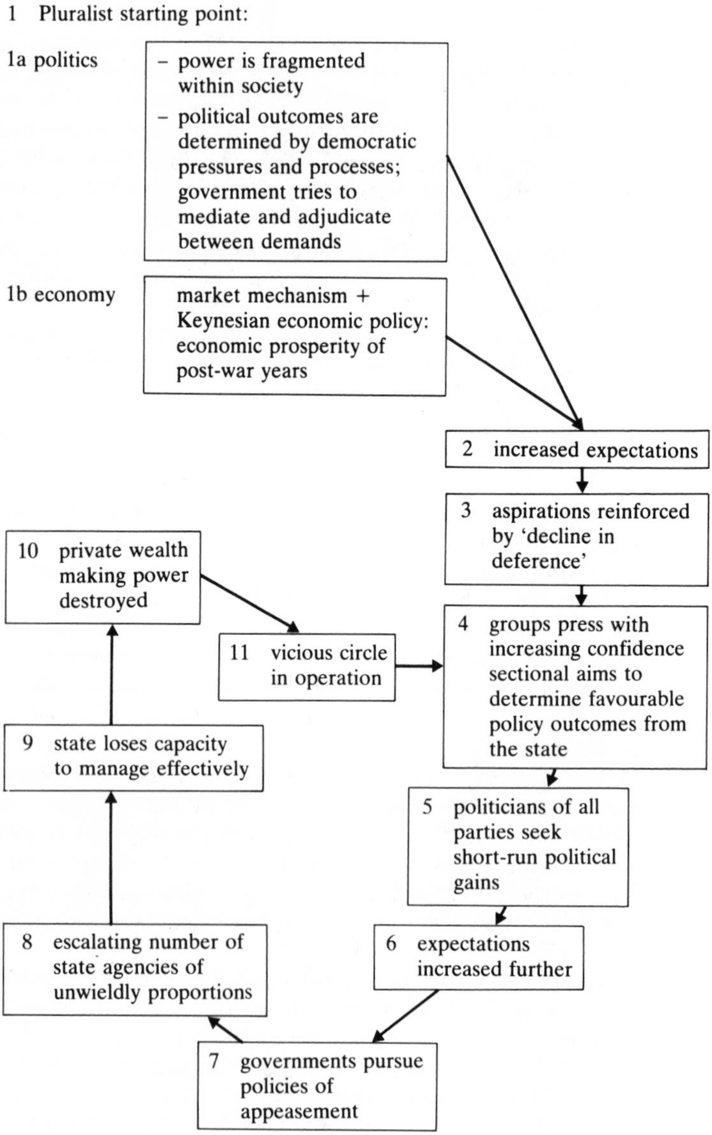
1 Pluralist starting point:
1a politics
– power is fragmented within society
– political outcomes are determined by democratic pressures and processes; government tries to mediate and adjudicate between demands
1b economy
market mechanism + Keynesian economic policy: economic prosperity of post-war years
2 increased expectations
3 aspirations reinforced by 'decline in deference'
4 groups press with increasing confidence sectional aims to determine favourable policy outcomes from the state
5 politicians of all parties seek short-run political gains
6 expectations increased further
7 governments pursue policies of appeasement
8 escalating number of state agencies of unwieldly proportions
9 state loses capacity to manage effectively
10 private wealth making power destroyed
11 vicious circle in operation

Figure 10.2 Overloaded government: crisis of liberal welfare state

(7) In government, parties all too often pursue strategies of appeasement for fear of losing future votes. 'Firm action', for example, to set the economy on the 'right path' or deal with 'young offenders' is postponed or never taken.
(8) Appeasement strategies and the pursuit of self-interest by administrators lead to ever more state agencies (in health, education, industrial relations, prices and incomes, etc.) of increasingly unwieldy proportions. 'Faceless' bureaucracies develop which often fail to meet the ends for which they were originally designed.
(9) The state is ever less able to provide firm effective management faced as it is with, for instance, the spiralling costs of its programmes. Public spending becomes excessive and inflation just one symptom of the problem.
(10) As the state expands it progressively destroys the realm of individual initiative, the space for 'free, private enterprise'.
(11) A vicious circle is set in motion (go back to circle (4) on figure 10.2 and carry on around!), which can be broken only by, among other things, 'firm', 'decisive' political leadership less responsive to democratic pressures and demands.

Legitimation crisis of the state

In contrast to the theory of overloaded government, I shall now set out legitimation crisis theory. Its main elements are as follows:

(1a) A Marxist starting point: while political parties compete for office through the formal rules of democratic and representative processes, their power is severely constrained by the state's dependence on resources generated to a very large extent by private capital accumulation. The state has thus a general 'interest' in facilitating processes of capital accumulation: hence it takes decisions which are compatible in the long-run with business (capitalist) interests. At one and the same time, the state must appear neutral between all (class) interests so mass electoral support can be sustained.
(1b) The economy is organized through the private appropriation of resources which are socially produced (i.e. produced via a complex web of interdependence between people). Production is organized for profit maximization. The 'Keynesian state' in the immediate post-war period helped to sustain two decades of remarkable prosperity.

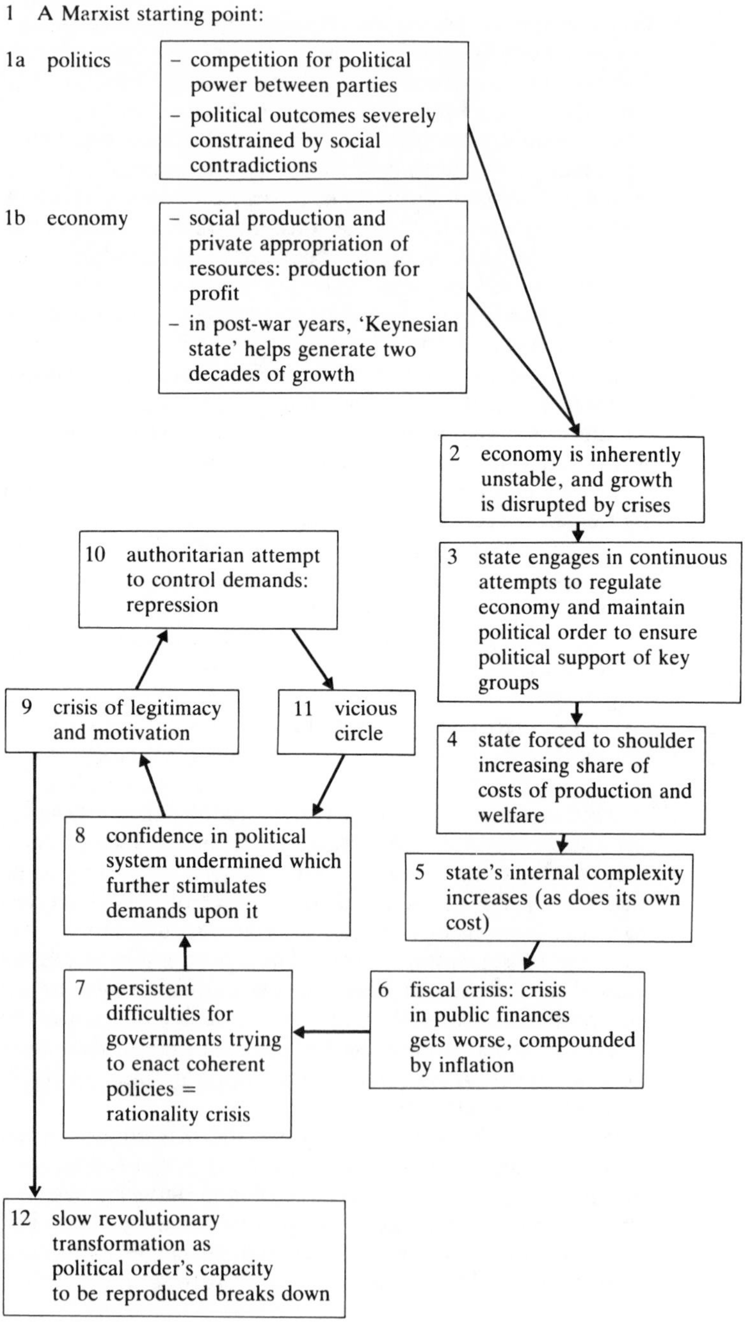
1 A Marxist starting point:
1a politics
– competition for political power between parties
– political outcomes severely constrained by social contradictions
1b economy
– social production and private appropriation of resources: production for profit
– in post-war years, 'Keynesian state' helps generate two decades of growth
2 economy is inherently unstable, and growth is disrupted by crises
3 state engages in continuous attempts to regulate economy and maintain political order to ensure political support of key groups
4 state forced to shoulder increasing share of costs of production and welfare
5 state's internal complexity increases (as does its own cost)
6 fiscal crisis: crisis in public finances gets worse, compounded by inflation
7 persistent difficulties for governments trying to enact coherent policies = rationality crisis
8 confidence in political system undermined which further stimulates demands upon it
9 crisis of legitimacy and motivation
10 authoritarian attempt to control demands: repression
11 vicious circle
12 slow revolutionary transformation as political order's capacity to be reproduced breaks down

Figure 10.3 Legitimation crisis: crisis of the democratic capitalist state

(2) But the economy is inherently unstable: economic growth is constantly disrupted by crises. The increasingly extensive effects of changes within the system (high rates of unemployment and inflation at the troughs and peaks of the political-business cycle) and/or the impact of external factors (shortages of raw materials as a result of international political events, for instance) have had to be carefully managed.

(3) Accordingly, if the economic and political order of contemporary societies is to be maintained, extensive state intervention is required. The principal concerns of the state become sustaining the capitalist economy and managing class antagonisms (through agencies, for example, of welfare, social security and law and order). The state must constantly act to ensure the acquiescence and support of powerful groups, especially the business community and trade unions.

(4) In order to avoid economic and political crises governments take on responsibility for more and more areas of the economy and civil society, e.g. the rescue of industries in trouble (British Leyland, British Steel, engineering companies, etc.). Why? Because a bankruptcy of a large firm or bank has, among other things, implications for numerous apparently sound enterprises, whole communities, and hence for political stability.

(5) In order to fulfil their increasingly diversified roles, governments and the state more generally have had to expand their administrative structures (e.g. enlargement of the civil service), thus increasing their own internal complexity. This growing complexity, in turn, entails an increased need for co-operation and, more importantly, requires an expanding state budget.

(6) The state must finance itself through taxation and loans from capital markets, but it cannot do this in a way which will interfere with the accumulation process and jeopardize economic growth. These constraints have helped to create a situation of almost permanent inflation and crisis in public finances.

(7) The state cannot develop adequate policy strategies within the systematic constraints it encounters; the result is a pattern of continuous change and breakdown in government policy and planning (e.g. stop-go policy, the fluctuating use of incomes policy). Habermas and Offe refer to this as a 'rationality crisis' or a 'crisis of rational

administration'. The state, controlled by a Conservative government, cannot drastically reduce its costs and spending for fear of the power of unions to cause large-scale disruption (e.g. the 'U' turn of the Heath government); the state, controlled by Labour, cannot efficiently pursue strong socialist policies, because business confidence would be undermined and the economy might be drastically weakened. Hence, governments of different persuasions come and go, and policy chops and changes.

(8) The state's growing intervention into the economy and other spheres draws attention to issues of choice, planning and control. The 'hand of the state' is more visible and intelligible than 'the invisible hand' of the market. More and more areas of life are seen by the general population as politicized, i.e. as falling within its (via the government's) potential control. This development, in turn, stimulates ever greater demands on the state, for example, for participation and consultation over decisions.

(9) If these demands cannot be fulfilled within available alternatives, the state may face a 'legitimation and motivation crisis'. Struggles over, among other things, income, control over the work place, the nature and quality of state goods and services, might spill beyond the boundaries of existing institutions of economic management and political control.

(10) In this situation, a 'strong state' may emerge: a state which places 'order' above everything else, repressing dissent and forcefully diffusing crises. Authoritarian states smashed most forms of opposition in the late 1930s and 1940s in central and southern Europe. One cannot rule out such attempts occurring again – or, much more likely, representative governments using progressively more 'strong arm' tactics.

(11) If one of the two scenarios in point (10) occur, a vicious circle may be set in motion. Move back to circle (8) (figure 10.3) and carry on around!

(12) However, the fundamental transformation of the system cannot be ruled out: it is unlikely to result from *an* event, an insurrectional overthrow of state power; it is more likely to be marked by a process – the continuous erosion of the existing order's capacity to be reproduced and the progressive emergence of alternative socialist institutions (e.g. state agencies taking more industry into public

ownership, state organization of ever more resources according to need not profit, extension of workplace and community democracy).

Crisis theories: initial assessment

How are we to assess these two contrasting theories of mounting political crisis? There are many significant differences between the theorists of overloaded government and legitimation crisis, some of which I shall discuss in a moment. Nonetheless, they also appear to share a common thread. First, governmental, or more generally state, power is the capacity for effective political action. As such, power is the facility of agents to act within institutions and collectivities – to apply the resources of these institutions and collectivities to chosen ends, even while institutional arrangements narrow the scope of their activities. Second, state power depends ultimately on the acceptance of the authority of the state (overload theorists) or on legitimacy (legitimation crisis theorists). Third, state power (measured by the ability of the state to resolve the claims and difficulties it faces) is being progressively eroded. The state is increasingly hamstrung or ineffective (overload theorists, points (7)–(9)) or short on rationality (legitimation crisis theorists, point (7)). Fourth, state power is being undermined because its authority or legitimacy is declining progressively. For overload theorists the 'taut and strained' relationship between government and social groups can be explained by increased expectations, excessive demands related to, among other things, the decline in deference. Legitimation crisis theorists, in turn, focus on the way increased state intervention undermines traditionally unquestioned values and norms and politicizes ever more issues, that is, opens them up to political debate and conflict.

Although the emphasis of Offe's and Habermas's work is more explicitly on legitimation, both overload and legitimation crisis theorists claim that state power is being eroded in the face of growing demands and claims: in one case these demands are regarded as 'excessive', in the other they are regarded as the practically inevitable result of the contradictions within which the state is enmeshed. But, on both views, state power and political stability alter with changes to the pattern of values and norms.

While these theories offer a number of important insights, they also raise some fundamental questions: is the authority or legitimacy of the state eroding to the point where we are justified in talking about a mounting political crisis with transformative potential? Is state power eroding in the manner depicted? Is the state increasingly vulnerable to political and social turmoil?

I have three fundamental objections to the 'common thread' which runs through overload and legitimation crisis theory. First, there is no clear empirical evidence to support the claim of a progressively worsening crisis of the state's authority or legitimacy. It is not that the authority or legitimacy of the state has collapsed; for, as I have argued, it could never be simply characterized (in the post-war years or before for that matter) as high. Rather, what has happened to stimulate these theories of crisis is that dissensus and hostility to 'the system' prevalent among many working-class people and some middle-class groups — leading to instrumental or conditional consent — has given way to greater expression of dissent as, among other things, comforts diminish and/or the promise of future benefits appear ever less meaningful and/or the pains of acquiescence increase. Second, it is not obvious that state power is eroding. Both overload and legitimation crisis theorists tend to treat the state as an 'empty' box through which things pass. This fundamentally underestimates, in my view, the state's own capabilities and resources which derive from, for example, its administrative and coercive apparatuses. Finally, while particular *governments* may be vulnerable when citizens fail to confer legitimacy, the *state* itself is not necessarily more vulnerable to collapse or disintegration. The question of the vulnerability of the contemporary British state needs to be looked at again carefully.

Accordingly, in the remainder of this section, I shall explore at greater length issues about forms of political orientation. In the next section I shall relate the discussion to contemporary British politics and argue that recent developments can only be properly understood in light of the way the modern British state developed in the context of both national and international pressures. I will then draw together many of the points made hitherto and present a model to help illuminate the way the political order coheres. The final section will offer a few brief concluding remarks.

Schism, antagonism and legitimacy

Many authors have been critical about claims that value consensus, or a common system of political attitudes and beliefs, is widespread in Britain: there is more 'dissensus' between classes than there is 'consensus'. But while the degree to which the political and social order is regarded as 'worthy', as legitimate, is to a significant extent related to class, the research on these issues has not been extensive, studies often leave a lot to be desired, and the evidence is not always without its ambiguities. With this in mind, I shall review the findings of a few key works.[7]

Some of the central issues have been explored by Nicholas Abercrombie, Stephen Hill and Bryan S. Turner (1980). They argue that there is little historical evidence to support the view that there is either a common value system, or a one dimensional ideology, or widespread legitimation. 'Bourgeois individualism', the secular ideology of a rising entrepreneurial class in the seventeenth and eighteenth centuries, did not diffuse downwards to the emergent class of wage workers. Their compliance in the series of changes that led to the ascendancy of capitalistic enterprise was secured, first of all, by their forcible expropriation from the land and then by the economic necessity of having to find paid employment. So far as contemporary capitalism is concerned, the authors accept the view of Mann and others that the bulk of the working class holds beliefs less coherent in character and, in some respects, substantially divergent from those of the middle and upper classes. Affirmative perspectives on the state and economy, they contend, secure the coherence of governing elites and classes. Clearly, some groups have to be integrated into the governing political culture to ensure a society's reproduction; what matters most — and what generally can be demonstrated — is the moral approval of existing institutions by dominant groups.

Examining the evidence from research based on interviews and ethnographic studies suggests, the authors further argue, that much more weight should be given to the autonomy of working-class cultural traditions than many authors have done — traditions which *tend* to emphasize the virtues of collectivism and community over and against 'bourgeois individualism' ('getting ahead') and the naked pursuit of private property ('the drive to accumulate') (Abercrombie *et al.*, 1980, pp. 140ff.). The evidence on attitudes to liberal-democratic institutions is less clear cut, but the fairly consistent findings of the 1960s and 1970s they note include:

(1) between half and three-quarters of working-class respondents to surveys suggest that 'big business has too much power in society', there is 'a law for the rich and another for the poor' and 'the upper classes are hostile to working-class interests';
(2) between two-fifths and one half of working-class respondents

did not think they had or could have 'any influence on government';
(3) only one-third thought that the British political system 'works for the interest of most of the people most of the time'.

These findings suggest that there is a majority of working-class people who deny that liberal democracy works as its advocates says it should – as, for instance, pluralists claim it does (Abercrombie *et al.,* 1980, p. 148). Noteworthy as this is, however, it only covers a fairly narrow range of issues which concern politics and the state.

Focusing more broadly on the latter, Dennis Kavanagh argues 'that the picture of political consent in Britain presented in textbooks – emphasizing the pervasiveness of the qualities of 'consensus, pragmatism, gradualism, tolerance, limited partisanship and deference' – is anything but borne out by his survey of recent evidence uncovered in political science (Kavanagh, 1980, pp. 124–76). He reports the findings under a number of headings, the most significant aspects of which I have summarized briefly below:

(1) *On pride in the system of government.* Widespread disaffection is noted. For instance, the large-scale *Attitudes Survey* conducted for the 1970 Royal Commission on the Constitution reported a 'general feeling of dissatisfaction' with the 'system of running Britain'. Nearly half (49 per cent) favoured some change while 'only 5 per cent thought things could not be improved'.
(2) *On partisanship between parties.* The evidence to the mid-1970s shows growing disillusionment with the two dominant parties; voters saw ever fewer differences between them. In 1951 only 20 per cent polled by Gallup thought the parties 'much of a muchness', by 1974 the figure was 45 per cent (although this figure is, I suspect, lower again today).
(3) *On trust in government.* While the 'totally cynical' about government and the political system amount to only between 10-15 per cent of those studied, on none of four conventional political science measures of trust in government does 'a majority offer a "trusting" response' in a recent work (see Marsh, 1978).
(4) *On a sense of belonging to a national community.* The sense of belonging to a 'British community' is weak outside England. Most Scots and Welsh people identify with their own respective nationalities, while people in Northern

Ireland divide their loyalties between Ulster and Ireland (Rose, 1974). The political movements in Northern Ireland amount, of course, to the severest challenge to the authority of the British government.

(5) *On influencing government.* In 1969 over 60 per cent of those sampled in an extensive study felt that government paid 'not much' attention to what ordinary people think (Butler and Stokes, 1974).

Relating such findings to phenomena such as the demise in support for the two major parties, demands for devolution, increased political violence, etc., Kavanagh asks whether the British political system is faced with a growing crisis of legitimacy (Kavanagh, 1980, p. 152). He stresses that it is important to distinguish attitudes to the state generally from attitudes to particular groups of leaders; and while much dissatisfaction is related to the latter, he believes that general political consent is unstable. Two reasons are given (p. 170). First, 'no great popular confidence exists' in political institutions (although the absence of a pronounced desire for 'radical change' is also noted). Second, traditional bonds, indicated by electoral voting patterns, are waning between class, party and nationality. The evidence highlights, Kavanagh contends, that people's relationships to party, government and the state are becoming ever more instrumental; that is, consent or loyalty is tied increasingly to the promise and actuality of better political and economic performance. Support for the political status quo is *conditional.*

Unlike Kavanagh I do not think that the phenomenon of extensive instrumental consent is new, but his review of the pertinent evidence certainly bears out the widespread nature of such attitudes. It also bears out something else that parallels Mann's findings: while legitimacy is not extensively conferred most people do not have a clear cut conception of what alternative institutions they desire. Hence, there is reason to suspect that the distance, remoteness or even alienation people experience in connection with dominant political and economic institutions might be the basis of further political uncertainty and volatility in the future. Before concluding this section, I want to spend a moment reviewing a study conducted in 1978 by Louis Moss.

Moss's study – based on extensive interviews with over 1,300 people in England and Wales – is perhaps the most elaborate survey of opinion on government yet conducted. Its results provide additional evidence for the claims presented so far about the prevalence of dissensus between classes, high levels of ambivalence about dominant political institutions, low levels of trust, acceptance and legitimacy, and hopes for change marked by a seeming absence of clear political direction. The advantage of Moss's study is that it focuses in more detail on the various institutions of government and state. I shall just mention a few of the pertinent findings.

Beginning with the rather diffuse (but intriguing) category of 'trust in government', the study reveals that only 24 per cent thought they could 'trust government to do what is right most of the time' (Moss, 1982, p. 64). Comparative data from the University of Michigan is interesting; for it reveals that 37 per cent of those sampled in the USA in 1974 felt they could 'trust government'. It is noteworthy that this US figure was recorded *after* the retreat from Vietnam and *after* the Watergate scandal! What people understand by 'government' and 'trust' here is very uncertain, but the British figure is nonetheless remarkably low. The data reported in table 10.2 adds further dimensions to the question of trust. Moss's comments on the findings are apposite: 'Parties and parliament become less important as one moves from [column] (a) to (b) and from (b) to (c). Whilst nearly 60 per cent of the sample see them as the corporate embodiment of the public face of government, less than one fifth of the sample put their trust in them as a guardian of their personal interests' (Moss, 1982, p. 69). The central representative function of British democracy seems not very highly regarded.

It is interesting that while local councillors are not thought of as very significant in the determination of political outcomes, they are conceived – in relative terms – as more 'reliable' to look after people's interests (see table 10.2 again). This and other aspects of the study bear out what might have been expected from earlier studies, that there is a clear preference for what is local: people claim to understand better local affairs and generally believe 'local representatives' are more aware of 'ordinary people's needs' – even if it is admitted that such representatives are powerless to do anything about them. These results are related to social class: the 'higher up the stratification hierarchy' one goes the more one tends to find both 'increased trust in general' *and* increased 'trust' in the central institutions of the state.

The government system based in London was widely conceived as distant and remote from 'ordinary people', and was widely reported as ineffective. Over 50 per cent of the sample claimed they did not understand the system of government 'very well'. A majority of the sample (58 per cent) thought that government had

TABLE 10.2 BRANCHES OF GOVERNMENT, TRUST AND INTERESTS

When you hear the word 'government', which one of these comes first to your mind?
Which of these would you say is most important in deciding what is to be done?
Which would you trust most to look after your interests?

	(a) *Comes first to mind* %	*(b)* *Most important* %	*(c)* *Most trusted* %
1 MPs	14.7	14.1	18.1
2 Political parties	22.2	9.2	3.7
3 Parliament	37.3	28.0	10.6
4 Government ministers	17.6	30.3	8.2
5 Civil servants	2.3	6.7	4.0
6 Local councillors	4.2	8.5	35.1
7 Don't know	1.7	3.0	7.6
8 None	—	0.4	12.9
	1,331	1,335	1,335
	%	%	%
2 and 3 Parties and parliament	59.5	37.2	14.3
4 and 5 Government ministers and civil servants	19.9	37.0	12.2
1 MPs	14.7	14.0	18.1
6 Local councillors	4.2	8.6	35.1

Source: Moss, 1982, p. 68.

little, or at best mixed effects, on their lives. Perhaps not surprisingly nearly 40 per cent sampled were either 'rather uninterested' or 'not interested at all' in the 'affairs of government in London'. But general interest in 'London government affairs', concern for who wins the next election (because it is believed it will make a considerable difference), claims to knowledge about politics are all related to class. It seems that, as Moss puts it, 'those who feel more assured of their place in the social scene (higher socio-economic groups) are much more consistently favourable to the institutions. Presumably this may help to explain, too, their greater certainty about the electoral system' (p. 177). Finally, Moss found a substantial proportion (over 40 per cent) in favour of 'substantial changes' to the system of government but a great deal of ambivalence about what sort of change was desirable. Even those against substantial change often expressed markedly negative views about many of the institutions of liberal democracy. This all seems, as Moss maintains, 'a poor return for the constant barrage of argument, assertion and denial to which the electorate is exposed' (p. 99).

It is interesting to note in passing that while Moss's study neglected what is clearly one of the most important aspects of the British state — the monarchy — the evidence collected by earlier studies fits well with some of the themes of his work. If surveys of public opinion restrict themselves to general questions about support for the monarchy, they find that the overall level of support is high by practically any criterion, although it is especially high among top socio-economic groups and among Conservative voters. However, if attention is turned from the monarchy as a general symbol to particular aspects of it, a more complicated picture emerges. As Jessop put it summarizing the findings: 'one third of the population believe royalty have too many privileges, one half believe the Royal Family has too much money and should mix more with ordinary people and two thirds believe the people around the Queen are drawn from too narrow a social class. Furthermore, agreement with these criticisms is strongest among the subordinate classes and among Labour voters' (Jessop, 1974, pp. 89—90). Disagreement between classes and ambivalence about the monarchy is revealed when attitudes to it are examined in a little depth.

Summary: Statement of the argument so far

There are many limits to the value of survey data: caution is required in its interpretation. But the various studies reviewed here are from a wide variety of research traditions and all rather significantly report fairly similar findings. I want to summarize the most important points now and connect them to the general concerns of the chapter.

The evidence reviewed highlights further the inadequacy of the terms of reference of both the end of ideology and one dimensionality perspectives. There is a striking absence of powerful consensual values (with the exception perhaps of a diffuse adherence to nationalism in England and, among some groups, in Northern Ireland) which might confer widespread legitimacy. There is also a striking absence of one dimensionality: the extent to which the state, parliament and politics are regarded as 'worthy' is to a significant extent related to class. Having said this, it should be noted that the widespread scepticism, cynicism, distrust and detachment of many men and women does not amount to pervasive evidence of revolutionary views either.

Pragmatic acquiescence or instrumental orientations and conditional consent appear common among the working classes, as does a mixed and sometimes fragmented or confused oppositional language – a 'dual' or 'divided' consciousness. Is this phenomenon new? And is this relevant evidence of a mounting crisis of the authority of the state (overload theorists) or of legitimacy and motivation (legitimation crisis theorists)? There does not seem much evidence to support these views. (1) As I argued earlier, instrumental attitudes are not new: legitimacy was never conferred widely in the post-war years. (2) While dissensus and conflict are rife, it is not apparent that a massive protest potential has *grown* demanding increased participation in political decision-making and developing extensive criticism of the existing economic and political order. (3) The pervasive scepticism, distrust, etc. documented has not given way to any clear demands for alternative kinds of institutions: there is a clear absence of images of alternatives, except among rather marginal groups. But, what of the signs of conflict, the severe challenges to the way resources and rights are distributed outlined in the third section of this chapter?

In a nutshell, it is *not* that the end of ideology has been 'reversed', or a one dimensional world has collapsed, or the authority of the state is suddenly in decline because demands have become excessive, or legitimacy is now undermined; rather, it is that the cynicism, scepticism, detachment of many people today fails sometimes to be offset by sufficient comforts and benefits as the economy and successive governments run into seemingly ever worse problems. The oft-expressed distrust, etc., has been, and can be, translated into a range of actions. The possibilities for antagonistic stances against the state – prefigured or anticipated in people's distrust of politicians, respect for the local and the common sense of ordinary people, rejection of 'experts' – are there, as indeed are germs of a variety of other kinds of political movements (e.g. the National Front). That there should be antagonism and conflict is not surprising: conditional consent or pragmatic acceptance of the status quo is potentially unstable precisely because it *is* conditional or pragmatic.

The evidence discussed above when linked to the material on the sustained difficulties of the British economy, on official and unofficial industrial conflict, on the fiscal difficulties of the state, on electoral absenteeism, on the variety of political movements stemming from the 1960s (women's movement, anti-nuclear groups, ecological protests) and on the tensions of the inner city areas, does suggest a number of fundamental questions. In the absence of marked consensual values how does the political order still hold together? It is clearly not simply legitimacy that provides the 'glue', that 'cements' or 'binds' the polity. On what does the 'cohesion' of the political system depend then?

Into the 1980s: the state at the intersection of international and national pressures

In this section I want to explore further the strength and vulnerability of the contemporary British state. I shall pursue the question of social compliance and state power but in closer relation to recent developments. Three points (which will be expanded upon throughout the section) are of particular importance to the analysis:

(1) The processes which shaped the formation of the modern British state created a situation which can be characterized as one both of structural weakness (primarily as a result of the extraordinary decline in Britain's world position as a political and economic power) and of growing political

strength (primarily as a result of the expansion of institutions of administration, constraint and coercion to contain, in part, the multiple economic and social difficulties linked to decline).

(2) Mounting economic crisis (indicated by massive unemployment, inflation, fiscal crisis and extensive bankruptcies) and the failure hitherto of political strategies to resolve it (e.g. the demise of James Callaghan's and Denis Healey's Social Contract during the 'winter of discontent', 1978–9, the extraordinary decline of the British manufacturing base under Margaret Thatcher's Conservatives) vastly increases the number of those who experience the worst effects of such crises. As the prospects for prosperity diminish and the political and economic system fails to 'deliver the goods' and 'delivery on promises', the potentiality of enhanced political conflict grows. The oft expressed distrust of centralized political institutions may be translated into action. The possibility is enhanced of antagonistic stances against the state.

(3) While there are extensive pressures and demands on the polity (as suggested by theorists of overload and legitimation crisis), the resources of state power generate sufficient scope to ensure that actual political outcomes (policies, coalitional arrangements, particular exercises of coercion) are not simply determined by socio-economic forces.

Parliamentary politics from the mid-1970s was marked by Labour's attempt, after the fall of Edward Heath's government in 1974, to reforge the centre ground in British politics and to mobilize a fresh coalition among powerful trade unions and business groups. The results of this 'corporatist strategy' are well known. Labour's claim to be able to establish a unique relation with both trade unions and industry was heavily compromised by the sustained strikes of 1978–9. At the time of writing it seems very improbable that the Thatcher government's almost 'anti-corporatist' strategy – the marginalization of the representatives of trade unions and, to a lesser extent, of manufacturing organizations – will do anything other than reverse for the shortest period Britain's economic and political difficulties including: crisis in public finances, inflation, dwindling employment prospects, industrial conflict, crisis of inner city areas and the overt sense of hopelessness and frustration among Britain's youth, especially among young blacks (Hall, 1979). The question is, how is this state of affairs to be explained? How are we to understand the trends in British politics and the contemporary position of the state?

Let me go back for a moment to theories of overload and legitimation crisis. In general terms, I think Habermas's and Offe's analysis of the way the state is enmeshed in contradiction and conflict is correct; as is their analysis of pressures that can create a 'crisis of rational administration' (see pp. 325–8, points (1)–(7)). But it follows from my argument in the previous section that I do not find convincing their subsequent focus on legitimation, and the spread of a legitimation crisis. While, in contrast, the theorists of overload are right to point to the many different *kinds* of groups pressing their demands on government, I find neither their starting point (pluralist premisses) nor their diagnosis of problems of state power and conflict satisfactory (see Held, 1983, pp. 40–1). Pluralism does not provide an adequate framework to explain the development and constraints on the state in Britain: the segments of the dominant class which have markedly shaped economic policy, and the class conflict over national income, among other things. The model sketched by Habermas and Offe rightly suggests the necessity for a very different starting point to pluralist premisses, while the evidence presented in the previous section highlights the significance of classes to the dynamics and instability of political life. However, I do not wish to discuss these two theories of crisis at greater length now. For I want to make a more fundamental criticism of them both and suggest that they are (1) too general and abstract and (2) inadequate in their attempts to relate developments within a nation-state to international conditions and pressures. I want to try to substantiate this by arguing that one can only really begin to advance our understanding of the contemporary British state if we grasp the political, economic and cultural structures which have developed over the long term. It is by following the state's development at the intersection of national and international pressures that we can proceed most fruitfully.

Structural weaknesses of the British state

The development of the modern British state led to a position of what we might call 'double dependence': on material resources generated at home through the largely privately controlled processes of manufacturing, trading and banking as well as on those resources generated from overseas activities. This relationship of double dependence – from which the state derives its income – contributed directly to economic vulnerability in the post-war years.

Britain's rapid demise as a world power has led to special difficulties. While severe political and economic problems faced *all* western nation states from the mid-1970s, those in Britain became especially acute. For too long Britain's supremacy rested on the might of an empire while all around it the economic and political map was changing. As new nations asserted their independence and as competition between 'advanced' industrial societies increased, the senior personnel of the British state continued to retain faith in its seemingly natural greatness. The cost of 'patrician hegemony' – that is, of an influential section of the dominant class still imbued with the values of tradition, loyalty, voluntary action, etc. – rapidly increased, no matter which party was in power (Nairn, 1981, pp. 365ff.). The very conditions which led to the early successes of the British state – extensive overseas commitments and a cohesive upper class – now were the basis of its rapid decline (in comparison with many other European countries). The British state is hamstrung by a profound structural weakness: dependence on changing overseas conditions to which an influential sector of the economy is still oriented, but which does not today provide the basis for general prosperity and employment.

The constraints and conflicts in which the state is enmeshed and which generate 'crises of rational administration' in Britain are, then, not merely those which derive from conditions internal to the nation-state: the division between the owners and controllers of industry and labour, electoral struggle, social conflicts of various kinds, etc. Rather, they are also the result of the constitution of the modern British state at the intersection of international and national conditions. But the political outcomes of this crisis are far from clear.

Party politics and international status

As the sun set over Britain's empire and competition among industrial nations intensified throughout the post-war years, politicians of nearly all persuasions placed hopes in general economic rejuvenation on strategies geared to the maintenance of Britain's international status either as an independent power, or in junior partnership with the United States or latterly with Europe (see Coates, 1984).[8] These strategies helped sustain the illusion that the decline in Britain's world position could be checked. By the late 1970s and early 1980s it was clear, however, that nothing of the sort had been achieved.

Successive Labour governments have, moreover, attempted to transform state-economy relations through strategies involving rationalizing, centralizing and modernizing industry. (Some of the pertinent issues are summarized in chapter 3.) But whatever good intentions Labour politicians may have had, the entrenched interests of the most powerful state agencies along with a segmented or divided economy proved insuperable obstacles to their policies for change. Margaret Thatcher easily outmanoeuvred the Labour government in the 1979 elections: the Labour government had become the party of the status quo, of existing institutional arrangements, of cuts in social expenditure and of the stagnating economy (cf. Held and Keane, 1984). The reasons for the decline in electoral support for the Labour party are of course complicated (and controversial). In 1979 Labour's room to manoeuvre was severely hampered both in parliament (the uneasy coalition with the Liberals) and in the economy (deteriorating international economic circumstances). But the government, I think, compounded the difficulties it faced by insisting on a tough 5 per cent pay norm (phase 4 of the Social Contract) after a long period of income restraint. The resulting 'winter of discontent' alienated many Labour supporters and provided extraordinary political ammunition to Labour's opponents.

Margaret Thatcher came to office promising something new and yet warning that her policy mix – aiming to redraw the boundaries between state and economy (pulling the former as much as possible out of the affairs of the latter) and reasserting the authority of the law – would take time to work. I shall return a little later to some aspects of this strategy. But one thing, above all, is remarkable: it provided an impetus, in conjunction with North Sea oil, to well-established trends (Nairn, 1981, p. 389ff.; P. Hall, 1984, pp. 34ff.). Within a short period of time in office, the Conservatives abolished all foreign exchange controls which meant that money could flow in and out of the economy at will. This opened vast new opportunities for the City which were quickly taken advantage of, e.g. investment overseas rapidly increased. Accordingly, British banks and financial institutions were in an even stronger position to manage the resources of, among others, the wealthy, multinational corporations and other countries (e.g. some of the OPEC nations). The effects on domestic industry included a loss of potential investment and further difficulties exporting (due, for instance, to the high value of sterling and/or fluctuating exchange rates). The problems facing the British political economy were compounded: unemployment, deflation, industrial bankruptcy, high prices — but these were some of the best years ever for the City and banks. As a result, the industrial decay of large areas of Scotland, Wales, Northern Ireland and the north of England accelerated, as it did in some parts of the south, particularly inner city areas.

Is growing political and social conflict inevitable under these circumstances?

Dispersing the effects of political and economic crisis and the limits of such strategies

As long as governments and states are able to secure the acquiescence and support of those collectivities who are crucial for the continuity of the existing order (e.g. City interests, vital industries, unions with workers in powerful economic positions), 'public order' can be sustained and is likely to break down only on certain 'marginal' sites. What I call 'strategies of displacement' are crucial here; that is, strategies which disperse the worst effects of economic and political problems onto vulnerable groups while appeasing those able to mobilize claims most effectively. I am *not* arguing that politicians or administrators necessarily desire or intend to displace the worst effects of economic crisis onto some of the least powerful and most vulnerable of society. But if politics is the 'art of the possible', or if — to put it in the terms used hitherto — governments will generally try to ensure the smoothest possible continuity of the existing order (to secure support, expansion of economic opportunities, enhanced scope for their policies), then, they will see little option but to appease those who are most powerful and able to mobilize their resources effectively. The quick settlement of the miners' pay claim in 1981 by Thatcher's government is a case in point: it was in considerable excess of what was tolerated of most other public sector workers. Successive governments have pursued strategies involving both appeasement and the uneven dispersal of the effects of economic crisis. As the crisis and difficulties facing the British economy have become worse, these strategies have come more to the fore (Bornstein *et al.*, 1984).

Many of those who for one reason or another are most vulnerable have suffered the worst effects of the crisis of the British political economy. They include: the young (whose opportunities have radically decreased); blacks (whose employment prospects, housing and general conditions of living are becoming ever more difficult); the disabled and sick (who have suffered a deterioration of services due to public sector cuts); the unemployed and poor (who have vastly increased in numbers) and those who live in regions particularly hard hit, for instance, certain major areas in South Wales, the north of England and Northern Ireland. It is perhaps not surprising that some of these groups become restless and active in 'street' and other forms of protest. The extensive riots in British cities in 1981 were just one symptom of feelings of hopelessness and frustration. It is in contexts such as these that Thatcher's Conservative government and many branches of the mass media, in particular, have sought to pin the responsibility for some of the present difficulties on the 'scrounger and the welfare state'. Stuart Hall has pointed out that their stories

> have been heavily embroidered with epithets drawn from the stock of populist demonology: the workshy, the feckless poor, the surly rudeness, the feigned infirmities, the mendacity, lack of gratitude, scheming idleness, endless hedonism and 'something for nothing' qualities of 'Britain's army of dole-queue swindlers'. So the Welfare State has been constructed in the media as a populist folk-devil: Britain's undeserving poor, the great majority of whom, if the *Mail* and the *Sun* are to be believed, spend most of their days, between signing on, lolling about on the Costa Brava. (Hall, 1979, p. 6)

Apart from the fact that proven fraud accounts for only a tiny proportion of claims for Supplementary Benefit (0.59 per cent in 1978), this attempt to blame particular individuals or types of individuals for their plight and thus to define Britain's problems essentially as problems of motivation, lack of self-restraint and discipline misses entirely the deep structural roots of Britain's protracted economic and political difficulties. Further, it is a definition of the problem which, I think, fewer and fewer people will find compelling. Why?

The difficulty for this 'definition' is, in fact, that the number of people affected by economic stagnation and the short-fall on successive government promises has increased as has the range of people affected: unemployment has soared (see p. 364) affecting nearly all occupations; officially defined poverty has spread (according to Townsend, 12 million people in Britain now live on or near the poverty line); young people from all social classes have found educational and employment opportunities diminishing; women have found themselves often the first to be sacked, shunted to part-time work and have had the scope of their potential activities radically reduced; more and more regions of the country have been subject to decline and urban difficulties (see e.g., Townsend, 1979; Smith, 1984; Bruegel, 1979; Lewis, 1984). While there are many sources of schism dividing groups against one another and undermining the possibility of united opposition to contemporary political and economic arrangements, in the changing circumstances of today it seems that, at the minimum, official political accounts of 'the state of the nation' will be treated with even more scepticism, cynicism and distrust than heretofore. Under these circumstances it is at least possible that British politics will become an arena of greater flux and change.

Social movements, representation and the state

Surveying British politics it is not hard to point to a variety of different types of conflict over wages, work, industry, race, gender, bureaucracy, the environment as well as over the nature and quantity of state goods and services. It is also not difficult to highlight widespread scepticism (or cynicism) about politics – generally understood as traditional party politics. Possibilities for antagonistic stances against governments, the state and 'the system' more generally – prefigured or anticipated in people's distrust of politicians, concern for local issues etc. – are realized in a variety of actions. The foundation of instrumental consent appears strained.

There are trends which enhance the possibility of a severe political crisis. The favouritism toward certain powerful or dominant groups expressed by corporatist strategies or 'special' bargains erodes the electoral/parliamentary support of the more vulnerable groups, which may be required for governments' survival. By placing certain issues high on the political agenda it leads inevitably to the systematic marginalization or exclusion of others. More fundamentally, such strategies, especially if successful for a short time, may further erode respect for, and the acceptability of, institutions which have traditionally channelled conflict, e.g. party systems and conventions of collective bargaining. Thus new arrangements may backfire, encouraging the formation of opposition movements to the status quo based on those excluded from key established political decision-making processes, e.g. the jobless, shop floor workers, those concerned with ecological issues, campaigners for nuclear disarmament (CND), the women's movement activists, and those in the nationalist movements within the 'United' Kingdom (Offe, 1980). Many of these latter groups have their origins in the 1960s and earlier. Some of them, above all perhaps CND and the women's movement, have continued to grow. Their significance lies not only in their growth – E. P. Thompson claimed that by 1983–4 CND had become the biggest mass movement in Europe since 1848 – but in their attempt to forge a new participatory politics, involving as many of their members as possible in, among other things, the crucial processes of decision-making.

Moreover, the attempts by successive governments to ensure the acquiescence, if not support, of powerful groups (especially key trade unions) are threatened by the failure of these governments to meet declared political and economic objectives and to manage crises successfully. Labour's 1976–8 Social Contract became ever more a vehicle for the management of sustained deflation rather than for, as promised, greater social justice and economic growth. Thatcher's Conservative government has broken with any such general arrangements, relying on the vulnerability and timidity of employees faced by mass employment. Nevertheless, even Thatcher's government has made a series of promises: her mix of policies was presented as the only way forward in economic and social terms. The distance between promise and actual performance has persisted: social opportunities have decreased, inequalities have been exacerbated and sustained growth is still elusive.

While there is widespread scepticism about conventional politics, there is also, however, considerable uncertainty about alternatives to the status quo; Cold War attitudes and, of course, Stalinism have discredited certain socialist ideas in the eyes of many. As I argued earlier, while legitimacy is not extensively conferred, there is considerable uncertainty not only about what kinds of institutions there might be but also about what general political *directions* should be taken. Thus there is reason to believe that the scepticism and remoteness many people feel in relation to dominant political institutions might be the basis of further political disaffection in the future. As possibilities for antagonistic stances against the state are realized, so too are the germs of a variety of other kinds of political movements, e.g. movements of the 'new' right. Anxiety about directionless change can fuel a call for the re-establishment of tradition and authority. This is the foundation for the appeal by the 'new' conservatives – or the new right – to the people and the nation, to many of those who feel so acutely unrepresented.

The New Right and strategies for state legitimation

The New Right is, in general, committed to the view that political life, like economic life, is – or ought to be – a matter of individual freedom and initiative. Only individuals can judge what they want and, therefore, the less the state interferes in their lives the better for them. Accordingly, a *laissez-faire* or free market society is the key objective along with a 'minimal state'. The political programme of the New Right (or neo-liberals) includes: the extension of the market to more and more areas of life; the creation of a state stripped of 'excessive' involvement both in the economy and in the provision of opportunities; the curtailment of the power of certain groups to press their aims and goals (for instance, trade unions); the construction of a strong government to enforce law and order.[9]

The Thatcher government's advocacy of the 'rolling back of the state' is on grounds similar to those of the New Right and of some of the theorists of the overloaded government: individual freedom has been diminished because of the proliferation of bureaucratic state agencies attempting to meet the demands of those involved in group politics. The Thatcher government is committed to the classical liberal doctrine that the collective good (or the good of all individuals) can be properly realized in most cases only by private individuals acting in competitive isolation and pursuing their sectoral aims with minimal state interference. This commitment to the market as the key mechanism of economic and social regulation has a significant other side in the history of liberalism: a commitment to a strong state to provide a secure basis upon which, it is thought, business, trade and family life will prosper (Held, 1983, pp. 16, 44).

It is essential to the Thatcher government's strategy of expanding the realm of non-state activities that the politics of the post-war settlement be fundamentally altered. The government is trying to break with the dominant trend in post-war decades toward a regulated mixed economy, a welfare interventionist state. The strategy is predicated both on an aversion to state intervention and control, and on a belief that the state has neither the management capability nor the responsibility to ensure the performance and effectiveness of the economy and its related institutions. Thatcher's Conservatives, and the new right more generally, have sought to attack the claim that the state and government are inextricably linked to the direct creation of expanding economic opportunities and social welfare.

The political success of the Thatcher regime to date (confirmed by its re-election in 1983) has rested, I believe, in large part on the uncoupling or separation of the instrumental or performative dimension of the state, i.e. the state as an instrument for the delivery of goods and services, from consideration of the state as a powerful, prestigious and enduring representative of the people or nation. Thatcher has sought to draw upon and reinvigorate the symbols and agencies of the latter while systematically attacking the former. The current success of this political project lies in its direct connection to, and mobilization of, that massive amount of cynicism, distrust and dissatisfaction with many of the institutions of the interventionist welfare state that has long existed. Her achievement, I believe, is to have recovered the traditional symbols of the British nation-state and made them her own (precisely those symbols associated with Great Britain, the 'glorious past', the empire and international prestige) while separating these from the idea of the state as a capable guarantor of economic and social opportunities. Sociologists and political commentators have often noted a diffuse and general commitment to the idea of the nation, to nationalism, to pride in being British (e.g. Nichols and Armstrong, 1976). There is good reason to think that this diffuse commitment has been – after some decades of relative dormancy – reactivated (at least in England) and brought once again to the foreground of British politics. How long this selective revival of symbols can be sustained is an open question. The argument in this chapter suggests that this new attempt to legitimize the state's authority rests on a fragile economic base. Whether this fragility will have a direct political consequence is, however, another matter.

Unfortunately, it is hard to test properly the interpretation of Thatcher's achievements I have just offered because insufficient time has elapsed and insufficient research has been conducted. Some very rough data is available from recent surveys of public opinion. This data gives us no information about how attitudes and beliefs might divide across socio-economic groups and classes and, therefore, has little direct bearing on the kind of argument presented so far. But it does indicate, and this perhaps is noteworthy, that in two time periods in 1981 and 1983 the only institutions out of ten to register the confidence of a majority of the population consistently were the police, the armed forces and the legal system (Gallup, 1981 and 1983).[10] The Falklands war was no doubt an important factor contributing to the expression of confidence in institutions like the army; it reactivated patriotic sentiment and brought it once again to the centre of British politics. But if my argument above is correct then the effects of the Falklands war have to be understood within the context of a wider political strategy – a strategy to bolster the legitimacy of the state's traditional authority while systematically discrediting its capability to assume responsibility for the management of economic and social affairs.

Political compliance and the 'strong' state

There are many factors which ensure compliance with existing institutions; and among these are the formidable resources of state power itself, especially those for the maintenance of 'law and order'. I should like to focus briefly on these resources and, then, in the last and final part of the chapter, I shall place them within a model of the many factors which lead to political and social compliance.

There is some evidence to suggest a massive reorganization of the apparatus for maintaining law and order in recent times (see, e.g., Jessop, 1980, pp. 62–5). This has involved a further concentration and centralization of state power developing considerable capacities for information storage, surveillance and pre-emptive control of, among other things, industrial conflict and political dissent. The tip of the iceberg involves new legal powers for the police (for example, the Prevention of Terrorism Act, 1975) and the introduction of specialized forces (for instance, Special Patrol Groups, Special Response Units, Anti-Terrorist Squads) all with fairly wide-ranging briefs. There has been, moreover, an increase in co-operation between the police and the military as both have acquired a wide range of weapons for use in civilian disturbances along with highly complex equipment for the surveillance and containment of disputes. For instance, the police are now able to draw on vast new computer facilities. The police national computer (which can support 21,000 requests for information per hour) has been designed in part to aid the trends towards pre-emptive policing supported by extensive information (State Research, 1982, pp. 107–8). Additional specialized computers include the 'C' division Metropolitan Police computer – the secret national police intelligence unit. It appears that its function is to store 'information on over 1.5 million people many of whom have not committed any crime but are "of interest to the police" ' (State Research, 1982, p. 113). The latest M15 computer system is immense: its storage capacity is two and a half times greater than the national police computer and is thought to be capable of storing information on up to 20 million people.

These facts alone might not be so important if it was not for the evidence which further suggests that extensive surveillance ability enables 'security' agencies to extend their control over hitherto ordinary civil and political activities. Of course, some of this capacity aids the protection of citizens from aggressive and violent attacks by groups whose objectives and methods we might all deplore. Additionally, the capacity by no means generates omniscience; and such capacities as do exist are frequently under-utilized. On the other hand, increased technological know-how allows potentially what one might call the 'logic' of surveillance to be realized: even allies and friends must be spied upon because one day they too may become enemies (Campbell, 1981, p. 16). Information on the activities of security agencies is, of course, hard to come by and one can never be certain of its reliability. But a recent survey by Duncan Campbell (1981) suggests that targets of surveillance have included:

(1) leaders of industrial disputes. In 1978, for example, the Grunwick strike committee's phone was tapped and long-range microphones were used by the Special Branch in an attempt to monitor conversations;
(2) embassies. According to an ex-intelligence official all embassies (including the US) are targets of bugging and tapping;
(3) journalists and politicians. Even ministers (for example, Judith Hart, in the last Labour government) have had their phones tapped.

As important as the range of monitored activities, are questions about the accountability of the security agencies. Campbell argues provocatively that the sovereignty of these powerful organizations lies with their 'top men' and there is minimum parliamentary control and little accountability even to ministers. This situation is apparently compounded by the extensive interlocking of the British network of surveillance with that of the United States's NSA (National Security Agency). Much of the British network is closely tied into the US operations. But it is, according to Campbell, a *dependent* allegiance — an alliance which links British security and, more generally, foreign policy to that of the United States — a link which would perhaps be hard to break, even, for example, for an elected Labour government mandated to ensure more independence in foreign affairs.

A sophisticated system of collecting and storing information is a prime source of state power and directly aids — through the control of communications, 'public' information and planning processes — the containment not only of crime but of all those who are considered civilian dissidents. (The military control of Poland in the 1980s is an example of the extreme application of such power.) These capacities comprise a formidable quantity of human energy and resources assembled and mobilized to help ensure compliance, law and order. For a country which has been held as a model of tolerance and consensus such a state of affairs is perhaps remarkable (cf. Halsey, 1981, chapter 7). It testifies to the claim of the previous section of this chapter: tolerance and consensus are far rarer qualities in Britain than many have heretofore claimed. This is clearly recognized, at least, by those who have built up the 'secret' strong state, accumulating the resources to manage subject populations. The apparatuses of coercion and administration have generated considerable capacities to contain opposition.

There are many factors which lead to political compliance. While this section has explored elements of the formation of the modern British state which have exacerbated economic and political difficulties, it has also explored some of the reasons why growing conflict is not inevitable. Strategies of displacement fragment and disperse the worse effects of crisis; new attempts are made to legitimize the authority of government and the state; and formidable resources exist to monitor and potentially to control many aspects of day-to-day life. Accordingly, although public order forces are highly visible in the lives of some groups (such as blacks, immigrants, unemployed youths, prostitutes, workers on picket lines), in certain regions (where industrial and urban decay is advanced, e.g. parts of Liverpool) and in political activities of various kinds (for instance, demonstrations, marches, civil rights campaigns in Northern Ireland), it remains the case that they can maintain a low profile in most situations. Moreover, a low profile is often more than sufficient as a reminder of the ultimate constraints on civil and political life.

Social compliance and state power: a model

In this section I would like to draw together several strands of the chapter and bring out a number of central ideas in a schematic model – a model of social compliance and state power. In order to explain the integration and reproduction of the political order we need to depart from the view that state power and political stability depend only upon things like legitimacy or respect for the authority of the state. Rather, I shall argue, compliance results from a complex web of interdependencies between people, collectivities and institutions – interdependencies which incorporate relations of power and dependence (Lockwood, 1964; Giddens, 1979). Three themes are of particular importance: (1) state power is only a part, albeit a very important part, of the relations of power or the power structure; (2) the resources of state power are themselves extensive and complex (more so than suggested by the theorists considered so far); (3) there are many overlapping and interlocking forces which fragment experience of the political and social world and constitute major hurdles to any movement seeking fundamental transformations in political life.

The model I will present here is of a rather different kind from those presented by the theorists we have discussed so far. Whereas they tend to focus either on political stability or on political crisis, the model dwells on neither exclusively. Rather, it focuses on the interrelation between state and civil society and on the resultant divisions and fragmentation of political and economic life. It is these divisions which constitute the basis of political stability today. The model concentrates on a set of elements which bear on the scope and limits of state action and then considers wider features of civil society. Taken together these elements delineate a series of trends or tendencies, but without a single clear-cut outcome. For all the elements in the model are parts of a process in which outcomes depend, above all, on the contingencies of political conflict.

Economic compulsion. Both Marxists and non-Marxists have recognized the distinctive elements of constraint and compulsion that emerge when people are separated from the means (land, technology, techniques, etc.) of production. Weber analysed the way the emergence of modern capitalism included the formation of a mass of propertyless wage workers, who have to sell their labour to owners of capital in order to sustain a livelihood (Weber, in Giddens and Held, 1982). Marx of course wrote at length about the way the worker is 'forced to sell his [or her] labour-power for a wage in order to live'. He called this 'the dull compulsion of economic relations'. If we wish to enjoy some of the comforts of life we have to participate in these relations; for nearly all working people there is no realistic alternative but to try to earn a living and comply with working arrangements dictated largely by others: 'dropping out', relying upon social security or being super rich are the only immediate ways out – and the latter only for a tiny minority. These processes in themselves constitute an immense pressure to conformist patterns of behaviour (Abercrombie, Hill and Turner, 1980, p. 166).

Transfer and concentration of the means of violence. Dependence on employment is the main basis of the power relation between employers and employees (a relation which, as I mentioned earlier (pp. 313–316), alters the state of the economy). The management or supervision of employees – which is of course extensive in all occupations – is not sustained by the immediate threat of the use of physical force, as it frequently was in the past. The 'means of violence' are concentrated in the hands of the state. Anthony Giddens elaborates a version of this idea as follows:

> The monopolisation of the means of violence in the hands of the state went along with the *extrusion of control of violent sanctions from the exploitative class relations involved in emergent capitalism.* Commitment to freedom of contract, which was both part of a broader set of ideological claims to human liberties for which the bourgeoisie fought, and an actual reality they sought to further in economic organisation, meant the expulsion of sanctions of violence from the newly expanding labour market. (Giddens, 1981, p. 180)

With the development of capitalism the state entered into the very fabric of the economy by reinforcing and codifying – through legislation, administration and supervision – its structure and practices. It thus constituted and complemented, as it still does, economic relations.

Partial and dependent state: the depoliticization of property. To the extent that private and public spheres are kept distinct, the state can, with certain justification, claim to represent the community or the general interest, in contrast to the world of individual aims and responsibilities. But the opposition between general and particular interests is, as Marx argued, to a large extent illusory. The state defends the 'community', and thus its own claim to legitimacy, as if fundamental differences in social class and interest did not largely define economic and political life. In treating everyone in the same way, according to principles which protect the freedom of individuals and defend their right to property, the state may act 'neutrally' while generating effects which are partial, sustaining the privileges of those with property. Moreover, the very claim that there is a clear distinction between the private and the public, the world of civil society and the political, is dubious. The key source of contemporary power — private ownership of the means of production — is ostensibly depoliticized; that is, treated by virtue of the differentiation of the economy and state as if it were not a proper subject of politics. The structure of the economy is regarded as non-political, such that the massive division between those that own and control the means of production, and those who must live by wage labour, is regarded as the outcome of free private contracts, not a matter for the state. But by defending private property in the means of production, the state already has taken a side.

The state, then, is a not an independent structure or set of institutions above society, i.e. a 'public power' acting straightforwardly for 'the public'. On the contrary it is deeply embedded in socio-economic relations and linked to particular interests. It is also to a significant degree vitally dependent. Its dependence is revealed whenever the economy is beset by crises; for economic organizations of all kinds create the material resources on which the state apparatus survives. State intervention in the economy has to be broadly compatible with the objectives of powerful economic interests, e.g. 'the City', financiers, industrialists; otherwise civil society (business and family life) and the stability of the state are jeopardized (e.g. fiscal crisis). The state is dependent on the process of capital accumulation which it has for its own sake to maintain. Charles Lindblom, who writes from a position closer to pluralism than Marxism, explains the point well (and in a manner compatible with the perspectives of Offe and Habermas).

> Because public functions in the market system rest in the hands of businessmen, it follows that jobs, prices, production, growth, the standard of living, and the economic security of everyone all rest in

> their hands. Consequently government officials cannot be indifferent to how well business performs its functions. Depression, inflation, or other economic disasters can bring down a government. A major function of government, therefore, is to see to it that businessmen perform their tasks. (Lindblom, 1977, pp. 122-3)

The system of private property and 'dull economic compulsion' is necessarily reinforced by the state, however much various governments may seek to balance this interest with welfare and other policies.

Sources of state power: the coercive and administrative apparatus. Weber's classic definition of the state placed emphasis upon its capability of monopolizing the legitimate use of violence within a given territory. Weber writes: 'Of course, force is certainly not the normal or only means of the state — nobody says that — but force is a means specific to the state . . . the state is a relation of men dominating men [and, generally, men dominating women], a relation supported by means of legitimate (i.e. considered to be legitimate) violence' (Weber, 1972, p. 78). The state maintains compliance or order within a given territory; in individual capitalist societies this involves crucially the maintenance of the order of property, and the enhancement of domestic economic interests overseas, although by no means all the problems of order can be reduced to these. The state's web of agencies and institutions finds its ultimate sanction in the claim to the monopoly of force, and a political order is only, in the last instance, vulnerable to crises when this monopoly erodes.

The significance of the institutions of force or coercion goes beyond the use of the military against 'national enemies', i.e. defensive policing of territories and aggressive exploits overseas. The quelling of the riots in Brixton and elsewhere in the summer of 1981 are just one example of the wide use of such forces to ensure compliance within the nation-state. Further, the police are deployed constantly (and the military occasionally) to manage not only crime but industrial and political dissent as well. In addition, the means for the enforcement of order and law include massive agencies of surveillance. Nobody has documented the dimensions of this source of 'administrative power' better in recent times than Michel Foucault. As he wrote:

> If the economic take-off of the West began with the techniques that made possible the accumulation of capital, it might perhaps be said

> that the methods for administering the accumulation of men (population) made possible a political take-off in relation to the traditional ritual, costly, violent forms of power, which soon fell into disuse and were superseded by a subtle, calculated technology of subjection. (Foucault, 1977, pp. 220-1)

In discussing forms of subjection it is important to distinguish two connected phenomena: the supervision of the activities of subordinates in organizations of all kinds and the accumulation of information which can be stored by an institution or collectivity (Giddens, 1981, pp. 169ff.). The collection and storing of information about members of a society is a prime resource for those who wield power and it is closely related to the supervision of subject populations; it directly aids the control of a range of activities (as I illustrated in the previous section). The computerization of information adds little that is qualitatively new to these operations, it merely aids them – extending the capacity 'to make tyranny total', as Frank Church commented in his Congressional investigations of the technology available to the US National Security Agency (which has extensive connections to the British secret service).

The state, thus, plays a massive role in enforcing political order through its many agencies. Clearly this role has changed over time: in the early ascendancy of industrial capitalism the direct use of force in economic and political life was probably far more frequent than it is now; but against this must be weighed the fact that the means both of information co-ordination and supervision are far more sophisticated today than they ever were. At the minimum it seems justified to say that if the political order was more extensively adhered to, there would be less call for such extensive apparatuses of 'enforcement': presumably the latter exist because they are judged by those in power to be necessary. There is a formidable concentration of resources – far more formidable than the theorists of overload and legitimation crises suggest – at the disposal of both the key executive branches of government (the Prime Minister, the cabinet and its offices) and the permanent senior officials at Whitehall in the national and international networks of surveillance. The resources for the successful exercise of political strategy should not be underestimated.

Capacity and limits of state administration. While the state has an interest in sustaining and encouraging commerce, business, etc., the criteria by which those in state agencies make decisions are distinct from the logic of market operations and the imperatives of profit maximization. Through administrative or legislative organs, policy alternatives can be presented to clients with conflicting interests, thereby creating a possible opportunity for compromise. State managers (those in powerful non-routine jobs) can formulate objectives and alternatives which respond to different pressures and in accordance with a government's strategy for electoral/parliamentary success. The power of governments and the pattern of state policy are, leaving aside international conditions and pressures, determined by four interlocking institutional arrangements: by formal rules which set the mode of access to governmental power (free elections, free speech, freedom to organize); by the institutional arrangements which determine the articulation and implementation of state policy (civil services, judiciary, police, etc.); by the capacity of the economy to provide sufficient resources for state policies; and by the constraints imposed by the power of dominant collectivities (for example, the willingness of corporations to invest limits the scope of intervention into the process of accumulation and appropriation of capital, while trade unions can block attempts to erode hard-won social benefits).

The state is not controlled *directly* by the various interest groups (the City, domestic industry, etc.) of the dominant economic class. In pursuing their own interests (the prestige and stability of their jobs, their futures and those of their kin, among other things) the state's managers are likely to have interests which are compatible with those of at least some leading economic factions (Crouch, 1979, p. 140). But, while the state is dependent on the process of capital accumulation, the multiplicity of economic and electoral constraints on policy mean that the state is not an unambiguous agent of capitalist reproduction. The history of the labour movement is the history of a constant effort to offset some of the disadvantages of the power differential between employees and employers. In response the state has introduced a variety of policies which increase the social wage, extend public goods, enhance democratic rights, and alter the balance between public and private sectors. Social struggle is 'inscribed' into, that is, embedded in, the organization, administration and policies of the state (see Poulantzas, 1978). The state's partiality and dependence is thus to a degree both masked (hidden) and offset by successive government attempts to manoeuvre within these conflicting pressures.

International constraints and politics. The pressures to which the state responds are international as well as national. International events like the oil crisis of 1973 are only the tip of the iceberg: the capacity and limits of government and state power are related systematically to international circumstances. External developments exercise a decisive influence upon the very constitution of the state. If, as was the case in Britain for well over two hundred years, a country enjoys extensive maritime and military dominance, many domestic conflicts of interest can be resolved temporarily with the help of materials plundered, extracted or exchanged at advantageous prices from colonies and dependent territories. But the erosion of this particular form of power – the speed of which escalated rapidly in the post-war years despite the fact that a key segment of the British economy remained substantially oriented to overseas operations – allows considerably fewer modes of this kind for alleviating conflict.

Today, the integration of Britain into Europe constitutes a crucial limit to state power. For it involves the partial loss of sovereignty to the central institutions of Brussels, as does membership of NATO and of a host of other international institutions like the International Monetary Fund. These phenomena, along with the internationalization of capital through the growth of multinational corporations and banks, take many decisions out of the hands of domestic institutions. The progressive development of the 'world economy' creates economic and political interconnections between nation-states which are beyond the control of any one such state (Wallerstein, 1974). As a result, opposition, for instance, to decisions to close down factories, to run down industries affecting whole regions, to proliferate nuclear weapons, can founder for want of being able satisfactorily to pin responsibility onto any central authority. The internationalization of economics and politics can, thus, displace national power centres and weaken the scope of protest and possible democratic control.

Displacement strategies of the state. The state, in its bid to sustain the continuity of the existing order, favours selectively those groups whose acquiescence and support are crucial: the City, oligopoly capital and some groups of organized labour. The hope is that representatives of these 'strategic groups' will increasingly step in alongside the state's representatives to resolve threats to political stability through a highly informal, extra-parliamentary negotiation process in exchange for the enhancement of their corporate interests (Panitch, 1976; Offe, 1980). These attempts to establish 'corporatist arrangements' (especially by Labour governments) constitute a desire for a kind of 'class compromise' among the powerful — a compromise that is, however, all too often at the expense of vulnerable groups, e.g. the young, the elderly, the sick, non-unionized, non-white, and those in vulnerable regions, e.g. areas with 'declining industries no longer central to the economy'.

The capacity of governments to manoeuvre is enhanced by their ability to displace the effects of economic problems onto vulnerable groups while appeasing those able to mobilize claims most effectively. By dispersing the effects of economic crisis unevenly, the basis is weakened for solidarity amongst those who might potentially oppose existing political and economic arrangements.

Further divisions: work and domestic life. The separation of the worlds of work and domestic life, and of the worlds of men and women, is another major source of schism and divided allegiance. The advent of industrial capitalism brings about a split between workplace and domestic life (Marglin, 1974; Giddens, 1981). The main phenomenon which establishes this division is recognition by traders and employers that control over labour can only be effectively achieved (and thereby profits maximized) if workers are located in factories. Thus the system that creates what Marx termed 'dull economic compulsion' also creates a vast split in everyday life between work on the one hand, and home, leisure and relaxation on the other. A private world of individuals and small families — a world in which consumption is paramount — is set off for the first time from the world of social or collective production. This is one (crucial) moment in the demise or fragmentation of community — the atomization and segmentation of life. To the extent that people displace both their hopes and their disappointments from work and political life onto the private sphere — seeking 'freedom', for example, only in patterns of consumption or in sexual encounters — the difficulties posed by political and economic crisis can be partially forgotten. The 'private sphere' can become the only sphere where people attempt to assert and fulfil themselves (Chinoy, 1965; Zaretsky, 1976).

Further sources of schism: the social and technical division of labour. In addition to the effects of the division between work and domestic life, the knowledge and orientations of working-class people, along with the consciousness of other social groups, is impregnated by the work process. Analyses by Marcuse (1941) and more recently by Braverman (1974), point to the significance of understanding the way in which the rationalization and standardization of production fragments tasks. As tasks become increasingly mechanized and automated, there are fewer chances for mental and reflective labour. Work experiences are increasingly differentiated. Knowledge of the total work process is hard to come by and rarely available, particularly for those on the shop floor. Most occupations (despite the possibility of greater exchange of functions) tend to become atomized, isolated units, which require for their cohesion co-ordination and management from above. With the development of the division of labour, knowledge and control of the whole work process are ever more absent from daily work situations. Centralized control mechanisms and private and public bureaucracies then appear as the only agencies which are necessary for, and guarantee, 'a rational course and order' (Marcuse, 1941, pp. 430–1).

The impact of the technical division of labour is compounded by social divisions in society based on ethnicity, race and sex (Aronowitz, 1973). These divisions can be the basis of intense antagonisms between people who might otherwise find a basis of common ground among themselves. For example, labour unions – the branch meetings of which are often organized at difficult times for women – have been used in some part by men in order to weaken the position of women in the labour market. The more privileged position of men with respect to job opportunities and income has been to a large degree at the expense of women and, ultimately, one might add, at the expense of both to defend their opportunities together (Hartmann, 1976). In short, occupational and social hierarchies threaten attempts to create a greater solidarity.

The media, formal education and official information agencies. The evidence presented above highlights both the general moral approval of dominant institutions by the politically powerful and mobilized (which is crucial to ensure the reproduction of a political order), as well as the prevalence of value dissensus and of pragmatic acquiescence and instrumental orientations among many working people. It reveals also that a substantial proportion of people claim not to understand the system of government, and claim little or no interest in what the government is doing or in the outcomes of elections. This is indeed, as Moss put it, a 'poor return' for the constant barrage of written materials, discussion and information presented by the media and other institutions. But the impact of the latter should not be underestimated. Marcuse's provocative work reminds us of the relentlessness of such institutions and their highly affirmative images of the status quo. Mann refers to their power, and especially that of the education system, to produce a dual or divided consciousness. Earlier sections of this chapter referred to attempts – explored also by Scannell in chapter 5 – to create political consent partly through the promulgation of images of national unity and the reinvigoration of the traditional symbols of the British nation-state. The reporting of the Falklands war is a case in point; through the use of D notices and a whole package of rules, conventions and laws pertaining to secrecy (going well beyond the 1911 Official Secrets Act), the government was able to keep a remarkable amount of information to itself, offering only a highly selective impression, and making it very hard to discern exactly what was happening and in whose interest. (A useful account of the rules, conventions and laws pertaining to secrecy can be found in May and Rowan, 1982.)

The power of institutions like the media can be exaggerated. It is clear that values, beliefs and the very framework of thought of many people do not simply reflect the stamp of the production system, the commercial preoccupations of much of the media, and the official agencies of information. But together their fairly relentless presentation of affirmative images constitutes, at the minimum, a systematic inhibition to reflection on alternative institutions, to the development of an oppositional or counter ideology to existing political and economic arrangements (Bottomore, 1980, p. x). There is little in the language and ideas of the media, for example, to encourage the critical views of those in marginal or subordinate positions. It is hardly surprising, therefore, to uncover a dual or divided consciousness and a lack of consensus. The views 'aired' in politics and the media intersect in complex ways with daily experience, local tradition and regional life. Fragmentation of cultural experience is one almost inevitable result.

Conclusion

Political order is not achieved through common value systems, or general respect for the authority of the state, or legitimacy, or, by contrast, simple brute force; rather, it is the outcome of a complex web of interdependencies between political, economic and social institutions and activities which divide power centres and which create multiple pressures to comply. State power is a central aspect of these structures but it is not the only key variable.

The precariousness of 'government' today is linked both to the limits of state power in the context of national and international conditions and to the remoteness, distrust and scepticism that is expressed about existing institutional arrangements including the effectivity of parliamentary democracy. The institutions of democratic representation remain crucial to the formal control of the state, but the disjuncture between the agencies which possess formal control and those with actual control, between the power that is claimed for the people and their limited actual power, between the promises of representatives and their actual performance is likely to become ever more apparent. But in the context of the many factors which fragment opposition movements, it is, of course, hard to predict the balance of political forces in the future: the 'balance' always depends on *political* negotiation and conflict – in other words, on a process which is underdetermined by socio-economic life.

The first section of the chapter introduced the notion of an 'ideal normative agreement'; that is, an agreement to follow rules and laws on the grounds that they are the regulations we would have agreed to in ideal circumstances – with, for instance, all the knowledge we would like and all the opportunity we would want to discuss the requirements of others (p. 302). I find this idea useful because it provides a basis for a 'thought experiment' into how people would interpret their needs, and which rules and laws they would consider justified, under conditions of unconstrained knowledge and discussion. It enables us to ask what the conditions would have to be like for people to follow rules and laws they think right, correct, justified – worthy. Surveying the issues and evidence explored in this chapter, we can say, I believe, that a state implicated deeply in the creation and reproduction of systematic inequalities of power, wealth, income and opportunities will rarely (the exceptions perhaps being occasions like war) enjoy sustained legitimation by groups other than those whom it directly privileges. Or, more contentiously, only a political order that places the transformation of those inequalities at its centre will enjoy legitimacy in the long-run.

Notes

1 Apart from the Open University State Course Team, I would like to thank Anthony Giddens, John Thompson, Bob Jessop, Bob Reiner and Michelle Stanworth for extensive comments on earlier drafts of this chapter.

2 The points below owe a good deal to a consideration of Michael Mann, 1970, and Jürgen Habermas, 1976.

3 Note that, unless indicated to the contrary, writers in both groups were writing about trends in western industrial societies generally.

4 The reasons for Labour's failure to consolidate their post-war triumph in the long-run are beyond the scope of this chapter. Among them I would include the way key Labour politicians helped undermine the popularity of socialist ideas by espousing uncritically the rhetoric of the Cold War and by diverting excessive funds into arms and defence expenditure. Cf. Morgan (1984) and Thompson (1984).

5 This state of affairs is shown in the table below, and the progressive rise in unemployment is charted in the figure.

Unemployment 1921 – 1980

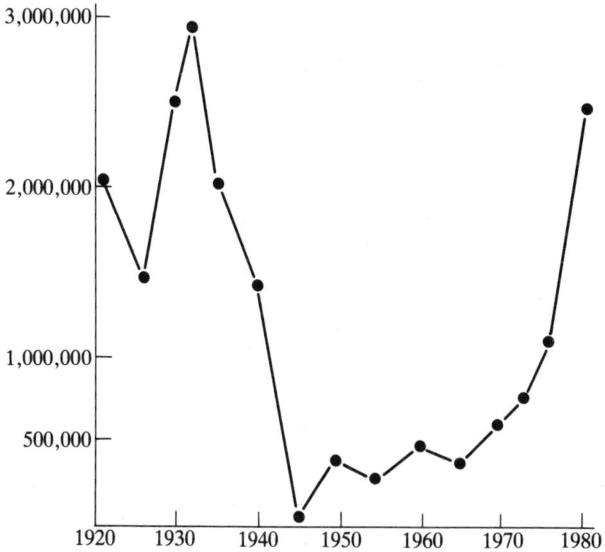

Source: Halsey, 1981, p. 30.

POST-WAR CYCLES

POST-WAR CYCLES	I	II	III	IV	V	VI
Period	1952–7	1958–61	1962–5	1966–70	1971–5	1976–8
Duration	6 yrs	4 yrs	4 yrs	5 yrs	5 yrs	3 yrs
Real GNP rise (%)	16.4	12.1	13.4	11.2	7.5	8.6
Peak Unemployment (av % adult in yr)	1.8 (1952)	2.0 (1959)	2.2 (1963)	2.3 (1968)	4.4 (1975)	5.7 (1977–8)
Peak Inflation (% RPI rise in yr)	5.3 (1955)	3.4 (1961)	4.7 (1965)	6.4 (1970)	24.1 (1975)	16.1 (1977)
Peak Payments Deficit (a) (% of GDP)	0.91	1.12	1.29	†	3.6	‡
Average Pre-Tax Company Profits (av % for cycle) (b)	15.9	15.4	14.5	12.1	5.5	n.a.

†Masked by 1967 devaluation (a) current account in calendar years.
‡Distorted by North Sea oil (b) share of company profits in GNP.

Note: Jay's table concerned incomes policy cycles, the table above concerns 'stop–go' cycles (no longer coincident from period V onwards).

Source: Jessop, 1980, p. 87 (originally adapted from P. Jay, *The Times*, 1 July 1974).

6 Legitimation crisis theory was not developed with special reference to Britain, but to the extent to which it is concerned with general developments in capitalist societies, it can be applied to Britain. The theory of overloaded government was partly developed with reference to Britain, although it as well is often thought to be applicable to many states in advanced liberal-democratic societies.

7 A fuller review can be found in my Open University publication, 'Power and Legitimacy in Contemporary Britain', in *The State and Society* (unit 23), Milton Keynes, 1984.

8 Accordingly, a high level of military spending has been maintained. 'The Government estimates that it will spend nearly £16 billion in the 1983-4 financial year – including £624 million on maintaining the Falklands garrison and repairing the losses of the South Atlantic war. . . . At this rate Britain is spending more than any of her major European allies, whether her military expenditure is considered in absolute terms, as a proportion of national income, or per head of population.' (*Guardian*, 7 July 1983).

9 It might be noted that item four of this programme is arguably inconsistent with items one and two. In fact, a tension exists in modern British Conservatism between those who assert individual freedom and the market as the ultimate concern, and those who believe in the primacy of tradition, order and authority, because they fear the social consequences of rampant *laissez-faire* policies. My account of the New Right concentrates on the former group, who have been most influential in current politics.

10 The institutions were the Church, the armed forces, the education system, the legal system, the press, trade unions, the police, parliament, the civil service and major companies. The monarchy was not included in the surveys, although 76 per cent of all respondents to a 1981 Marplan opinion poll thought the 'advantages of the Monarchy outweigh the costs'.

References

Abercrombie, N., Hill, S. and Turner, B. (1980) *The Dominant Ideology Thesis,* London: George Allen and Unwin.

Almond, A. and Verba, S. (1963) *The Civic Culture: Political Attitudes and Democracy in Five Nations,* Princeton, New Jersey: Princeton University Press.

Almond, A. and Verba, S. (eds) (1980) *The Civil Culture Revisited,* Boston: Little, Brown & Co.

Aronowitz, S. (1973) *False Promises,* New York: McGraw-Hill.

Beer, S. (1982) *Britain Against Itself,* London: Faber.

Benson, L. (1978) *Proletarians and Parties,* London: Methuen.

Bornstein, S. *et al.* (eds) (1984) *The State in Capitalist Europe,* London: George Allen and Unwin.

Bottomore, T. (1980) 'Foreword' in N. Abercrombie *et al., The Dominant Ideology Thesis.*

Braverman, H. (1974) *Labor and Monopoly Capitalism,* New York: Monthly Review Press.

Breugel, I. (1979) 'Women as a reserve army of Labour: a note on recent British experience', *Feminist Review,* Vol. 3.

Brittan, S. (1975) 'The economic contradictions of democracy', *British Journal of Political Science,* Vol. 5, No. 1.

Brittan, S. (1977) 'Can democracy manage an economy?' in R. Skidelsky (ed.) *The End of the Keynesian Era,* Oxford: Martin Robertson.

Butler, D. and Stokes, D. (1969 and 1974) *Political Change in Britain,* London: Macmillan.

Cambridge Political Economy Group (1974) 'Britain's economic crisis', Nottingham: *Spokesman Pamphlet, No. 44.*

Campbell, D. (1981) *Phonetappers and the security state,* London: *New Statesman.*

Chinoy, E. (1965) *Automobile Workers and the American Dream,* Boston: Beacon.
Coates, D. (1984) 'The character and origin of Britain's economic decline', in D. Coates and G. Johnston (eds), *Socialist Strategies.*
Coates, D. and Johnston, G. (eds) (1984) *Socialist Strategies,* Oxford: Martin Robertson.
Crouch, C. (ed.) (1979) *State and Economy in Contemporary Capitalism,* London: Croom Helm.
Dennis, S. (1983) 'Education and the European State: evolution, rationalization and crisis' in S. Bornstein *et al.* (eds), *The State in Capitalist Europe.*
Douglas, J. (1976) 'The overloaded crown', *British Journal of Political Science,* Vol. 6, No. 4.
Foucault, M. (1977) *Discipline and Punish,* London: Allen Lane.
Fox, A. (1974) *Beyond Contract: Work, Power and Trust Relations,* London: Faber.
Gamble, A. and Walton, P. (1976) *Capitalism in Crisis,* London: Macmillan.
Giddens, A. (1979) *Central Problems in Social Theory,* London: Macmillan.
Giddens, A. (1981) *A Contemporary Critique of Historical Materialism,* London: Macmillan.
Giddens, A. and Held, D. (eds) (1982) *Classes, Power and Conflict,* London: Macmillan.
Giddens, A. and Mackenzie, G. (eds) (1982) *Social Class and the Division of Labour,* Cambridge: Cambridge University Press.
Glyn, A. and Sutcliffe, B. (1972) *British Capitalism, Workers and Profit Squeeze,* Harmondsworth: Penguin.
Gough, I. (1975) 'State expenditure in advanced capitalism', *New Left Review,* Vol. 92.
Habermas, J. (1976) *Legitimation Crisis,* London: Heinemann.
Hall, P. (1984) 'Patterns of economic policy' in D. Held *et al.* (eds), *States and Societies.*
Hall, S. *et al.* (1978) *Policing the Crisis,* London: Macmillan.
Hall, S. (1979) 'Drifting into a law-and-order society', *The Cobden Lecture* (1979), The Cobden Trust, London.
Hall, S. and Jacques, M. (eds) (1983) *The Politics of Thatcherism,* London: Lawrence and Wishart.
Halsey, A. H. (1981) *Change in British Society,* Oxford: Oxford University Press.
Hartmann, H. (1976) 'Capitalism, patriarchy and job segregation by sex', *Signs,* Vol. 1, No. 3. Also in A. Giddens and D. Held (eds), *Classes, Power and Conflict.*
Held, D. *et al.* (eds) (1983) *States and Societies,* Oxford: Martin Robertson.
Held, D. and Keane, J. (1984) 'In a fit state', *New Socialist,* March/April.
Held, D. and Krieger, J. (1983) 'Accumulation, legitimation and the state' in D. Held *et al.* (eds), *States and Societies.*

Hibbs, D. (1976) 'Industrial conflict in advanced industrial societies', *American Political Science Review,* Vol. LXX, No. 4.
Hibbs, D. (1978) 'On the political economy of long-run trends in strike activity', *British Journal of Political Science,* Vol. 8.
Hobsbawm, E. (1952) 'Economic fluctuations and some social movements since 1800', *Economic History Review,* second series, Vol. 5.
Huntingdon, S. (1975) 'Post-industrial politics: how benign will it be?' *Comparative Politics,* Vol. 6.
Hyman, R. (1972) *Strikes,* London: Fontana.
Ingham, G. (1982) 'Divisions within the dominant class and British "exceptionalism" ' in A. Giddens and G. Mackenzie (eds), *Social Class and the Division of Labour.*
Jessop, B. (1974) *Traditionalism, Conservatism and British Political Culture,* London: George Allen and Unwin.
Jessop, B. (1980) 'The transformation of the state in post-war Britain' in R. Scase, *The State in Western Europe.*
Kavanagh, D. (1980) 'Political culture in Great Britain' in A. Almond and S. Verba (eds), *The Civic Culture Revisited.*
King, A. (1976) *Why is Britain becoming harder to govern?* London: BBC.
Lane, T. (1974) *The Union Makes Us Strong,* London: Arrow.
Lewis, J. (1984) 'Regional policy and planning' in S. Bornstein *et al.* (eds), *The State in Capitalist Europe.*
Lindblom, C. E. (1977) *Politics and Markets,* New York: Basic Books.
Lipset, S. M. (1963) *Political Man,* New York: Doubleday.
Lockwood, D. (1964) 'Social integration and system integration' in G. K. Zouschan and W. Hirsch (eds), *Explorations in Social Change,* London: Routledge and Kegan Paul.
Mann, M. (1970) 'The social cohesion of liberal democracy', *American Sociological Review,* Vol. 35. Also in A. Giddens and D. Held (eds), *Classes, Power and Conflict.*
Mann, M. (1973) *Consciousness and Action among the Western Working Class,* London: Macmillan.
Marcuse, H. (1941) 'Some social implications of modern technology' in A. Arato and E. Gebhardt (eds) (1978) *The Essential Frankfurt School Reader,* Oxford: Basil Blackwell.
Marcuse, H. (1964) *One Dimensional Man,* Boston: Beacon.
Marglin, S. (1974) 'What do the bosses do?', *Review of Radical Political Economics,* Vol. 6, No. 2. Also in A. Giddens and D. Held, (eds), *Classes, Power and Conflict.*
Marsh, A. (1978) *Protest and Political Consciousness,* London: Sage.
Marwick, A. (1982) *British Society since 1945,* Harmondsworth: Penguin.
May, A. and Rowan, K. (eds) (1982) *Inside Information: British Government and the Media,* London: Constable.
Middlemas, K. (1979) *Politics in Industrial Society: The Experience of the British System since 1911,* London: André Deutsch.

Morgan, H. O. (1984) *Labour in Power 1945-51,* Oxford: Oxford University Press.
Moss, L. (1982) 'People and government in 1978', prepared for a joint meeting of Applied Statistics and Social Statistics Committees of the Royal Statistical Society, April 1982.
Nairn, T. (1977 and 1981 2nd Edn) *The Break-up of Britain,* London: NLB and Verso Editions.
Nichols, T. and Armstrong, P. (1976) *Workers Divided,* London: Fontana.
Nichols, T. and Benyon, H. (1977) *Living with Capitalism,* London: Routledge and Kegan Paul.
Nordhaus, W. D. (1975) 'The political business cycle', *Review of Economic Studies,* Vol. 42.
O'Connor, J. (1973) *The Fiscal Crisis of the State,* New York: St Martin's Press.
Offe, C. (1980) 'The separation of form and content in liberal democratic politics', *Studies in Political Economy,* Vo. 3.
Offe, C. (1984) *Contradictions of the Welfare State,* London: Hutchinson.
Panitch, L. (1976) *Social Democracy and Industrial Militancy,* Cambridge: Cambridge University Press.
Pateman, C. (1973) 'Political culture, political structure and political change', *British Journal of Political Science,* Vol. 1.
Pateman, C. (1980) 'The civic culture: a philosophical critique' in G. Almond and S. Verba (eds), *The Civic Culture Revisited.*
Poulantzas, N. (1978) *State, Power, Socialism,* London: Verso.
Rose, R. (1974) 'The United Kingdom as a multi-national state' in R. Rose (ed.) (1974) *Studies in British Politics,* 3rd Edn, London: Macmillan.
Rose, R. and Peters, G. (1977) 'The political consequences of economic overload', University of Strathclyde Centre for the Study of Public Policy.
Ryder, J. and Silver, H. (1977) *Modern English Society,* London.
Rubinstein, W. D. (1976) 'Wealth, elites and the class structure of modern Britain', *Past and Present,* Vol. 70.
Scase, R. (ed.) (1980) *The State in Western Europe,* London: Croom Helm.
Smith, D. (1984) 'Education and the European State: evolution, rationalization and crisis' in S. Bornstein *et al.* (eds), *The State in Capitalist Europe.*
Stanworth, P. (1980) 'Trade, gentility and upper-class education in Victorian Britain', *International Studies of Management and Organization,* Vol. X, pp. 1-2.
Stanworth, P. and Giddens, A. (eds) (1974) *Elites and Power in British Society,* Cambridge: Cambridge University Press.
State Research (1982) 'Computers and the British police' in *State Research,* Vol. 29, London: State Research.
Stephens, J. D. (1979) *The Transition from Capitalism to Socialism,* London: Macmillan.

Thompson, E. P. (1968) *The Making of the English Working Class,* Harmondsworth: Penguin. First published by Victor Gollancz.
Thompson, E. P. (1978) 'The secret state' in D. Held *et al.* (eds), *States and Societies.*
Thompson, E. P. (1980) *Writing by Candlelight,* London: Merlin.
Thompson, E. P. (1984) 'Mr Attlee and the Gadarene swine', *Guardian,* 3 March 1984.
Townsend, P. (1979) *Poverty,* Harmondsworth: Penguin.
Wallerstein, I. (1974) *The Modern World-System*, New York: Academic Press.
Weber, M. (1972) *From Max Weber,* Oxford: Oxford University Press.
Young, H. and Sloman, A. (1982) *No, Minister,* London: BBC.
Zaretsky, E. (1976) *Capitalism, the Family and Personal Life,* London: Pluto.

Index

In this index, WW1 = World War 1 and WW2 = World War 2